For Alan

PENGUIN BOOKS

TALKING BACK

Andrea Mitchell has been chief foreign correspondent for NBC since 1994, reporting for *NBC Nightly News, Today, Meet the Press,* and *Hardball*. Before that she was the network's White House correspondent and chief congressional correspondent. She lives in Washington, D.C., with her husband, Alan Greenspan.

Andrea Mitchell

Talking Back

. . . to Presidents, Dictators, and

Assorted Scoundrels

PENGUIN BOOKS

PENGUIN BOOKS

Published by the Penguin Group

Penguin Group (USA) Inc., 375 Hudson Street, New York, New York 10014, U.S.A.

Penguin Group (Canada), 90 Eglinton Avenue East, Suite 700, Toronto,

Ontario, Canada M4P 2Y3 (a division of Pearson Penguin Canada Inc.)

Penguin Books Ltd, 80 Strand, London WC2R 0RL, England

Penguin Ireland, 25 St Stephen's Green, Dublin 2, Ireland (a division of Penguin Books Ltd)

Penguin Group (Australia), 250 Camberwell Road, Camberwell,

Victoria 3124, Australia (a division of Pearson Australia Group Pty Ltd)

Penguin Books India Pvt Ltd, 11 Community Centre,

Panchsheel Park, New Delhi – 110 017, India

Penguin Group (NZ), cnr Airborne and Rosedale Roads, Albany,

Auckland 1310, New Zealand (a division of Pearson New Zealand Ltd)

Penguin Books (South Africa) (Pty) Ltd, 24 Sturdee Avenue,

Rosebank, Johannesburg 2196, South Africa

Penguin Books Ltd, Registered Offices:
80 Strand, London WC2R 0RL, England

First published in the United States of America by Viking Penguin,
a member of Penguin Group (USA) Inc. 2005
Published in Penguin Books 2007

10 9 8 7 6 5 4 3

THE LIBRARY OF CONGRESS HAS CATALOGED THE HARDCOVER EDITION AS FOLLOWS:
Mitchell, Andrea.
  Talking Back . . . to presidents, dictators, and assorted scoundrels / Andrea Mitchell.
    p.   cm.
  Includes index.
  ISBN 0-670-03403-7 (hc.)
  ISBN 978-0-14-303873-3 (pbk.)
  1. Mitchell, Andrea.   2. Television journalists—United States—Biography.   I. Title.
  PN4874.M538A3 2005
  070'.92—dc22   2005042279

Printed in the United States of America
Set in Bembo   Designed by Carla Bolte

ACKNOWLEDGMENTS

When Viking Penguin president, Clare Ferraro, and vice president Pam Dorman, my editor, first suggested that I write a book about my experiences, I didn't realize how challenging it would be. For one thing, reporters don't know how to use the first-person singular. Being personal is not what we do. I am indebted to them and to Penguin Group (USA) president, Susan Petersen Kennedy, for believing in me from beginning to end, and for their patience as the story evolved through two wars, one election, and an abundance of breaking news. I could never have found my "voice" without Pam, a deft editor and kindred spirit. I am grateful to her for coaxing and prodding me out of my reluctance to dig deeper and be more reflective. I owe a great deal to Patricia Mulcahy, whose editorial expertise was invaluable in helping me organize and shape four decades of experiences into a narrative. Bob Barnett has been a counselor in every sense of the word and friend throughout my professional life, for which I am grateful. Chris Donovan turned research into an art form, finding anecdotes and facts that had long slipped my memory. His tireless work, through times of great personal travail, is a tribute to his skill and dedication. I am also forever grateful to him for being a painstaking and indefatigable fact-checker, with an able assist from Andrew Horesh. At every step, the first-class team at Viking Penguin has been generous with time and advice in all ways imaginable: Carolyn Coleburn, Judi Powers, Nancy Sheppard, Paul Buckley, Herbert Thornby, Carla Bolte, Julie Shiroishi, Leigh Butler, Sabila Khan, Tricia Conley, Victoria Klose, and Erica Rose, and of course Dick Heffernan and his outstanding sales group. I am grateful to Lucia Watson and Rakia Clark for always being so responsive to my many queries.

None of this could have been written without the support and encouragement of my colleagues at NBC News. I am thankful for Neal Shapiro, Bill Wheatley, David McCormick, Steve Capus, John Reiss, ML Flynn, Bob Windrem, and Albert Oetgen, among many others, for giving me the opportunity to do what I love. Tim Russert has been a mentor, advocate, and cheerleader all in one. Tom Brokaw and Brian Williams have shared their wisdom and always made me sound smarter than I am. In the Washington bureau, I have been blessed with the very best researchers and producers over the years including Gena Fitzgerald, Susan Lasalla, John Holland, Tammy Kupperman Thorpe, and Alicia Jennings. Marcie Rickun was a fount of knowledge on every aspect of presidential history. Libby Leist has shared in every adventure and been the best of partners and friends throughout these years, in addition to providing incomparable support as researcher and associate producer. Sarah Greenberg is an ally in everything I do, able to anticipate problems and solve them all at the same time. Tammy Haddad has given me opportunities to expand the reach of daily reporting into other broadcasts. Mary Murray helped me navigate the terrain of Fidel Castro's Cuba.

I am blessed in my friends, including many accomplished authors who encouraged me to think that I could join their ranks. Early and often, Kate and Jim Lehrer warned that this wouldn't get done unless I placed "bottom in chair" and wrote something, no matter how little, every day. Victoria Pope read an early draft of the opening chapters and offered valuable advice. Elaine and Jim Wolfensohn gave me safe haven and much love in Wyoming when I needed to escape Washington. Marylouise Oates and Bob Shrum didn't let me give up. Bob Woodward's groundbreaking reporting on the Bush administration's councils of war deepened my understanding of those years, and is separately acknowledged at appropriate places in the text. In particular, Michael Beschloss and Jon Meacham exceeded the normal bounds of friendship by reading and commenting on the manuscript at several key stages, as did Susan Greenstein, my sister, whose involvement in this book was an unparalleled act of love. Each was kind enough not to discourage me, despite some rough passages. I owe them a debt of gratitude for their expert advice that is not easily repaid. Sharing this adventure with my sister was joyful, deepening the companionship that has enriched both our lives.

I thank my brother-in-law Lewis Greenstein for his patience and many kindnesses throughout this project. To my parents, Cecile and Sydney Mitchell, and brother, Arthur, I am grateful for their tireless support, and for their forgiveness if I have miscast our shared history in any way.

Finally, there is Alan, whose love and indulgence gave me the confidence to continue long past the point where I was prepared to give up. He endured countless missed dinners, canceled vacations, forgotten holidays, and lonely evenings while I struggled to find the right words for this personal history. His enthusiasm for this venture never flagged. His patience seemed infinite, no matter how sorely he was provoked. I rely on his judgment on all things. He is my partner in life. Without his love, I could not have prevailed.

Andrea Mitchell
Washington, D.C.
April 2005

ACKNOWLEDGMENTS TO THE PAPERBACK EDITION

Writing a new chapter for this expanded paperback edition of *Talking Back* was a challenge: the past year has hardly been uneventful. How to find a focus that would encompass the tumultuous foreign policy of George W. Bush's second term in office? And, as I followed Condoleezza Rice around the world, when would I get off her airplane long enough to sit down and write? Wendy Wolf, executive editor at Viking Penguin, gave me the idea of how to narrow the field, and dig deeper, and so I did. I'm grateful to Wendy for her extraordinary patience, enthusiasm, and amazing good humor through-out this adventure. In addition to all of the wonderful NBC colleagues mentioned above, the paperback edition would also not have been possible without the terrific research of Michelle Perry, a great addition to the team.

CONTENTS

INTRODUCTION TO THE
PAPERBACK EDITION

As I write this, I am flying with the secretary of state as she wades into the Lebanon conflict. It is the last week of July 2006, but there is no summer respite from war or other crises. Critics say the administration has already waited too long to become engaged: for almost two weeks, Condoleezza Rice has resisted pressure to leap into shuttle diplomacy. Will it end as she hopes, in a grand reshaping of ancient rivalries? Or will this be another pragmatic retreat to what she derisively, and repeatedly, calls the "status quo ante"?

I have come to this point after forty years as a journalist, from the days when young women with my ambitions were literally barred from politics and newsrooms to an era in which women anchor network news and cover female secretaries of state. This book is the story of all of us, as seen through a kaleidoscope of adventures in local and state politics, presidential campaigns, the energy beat, Congress, the White House, and now, foreign policy.

It is also a behind-the-scenes tale of politicians and policy makers, from city ward heelers to presidents and kings. My profession has permitted me to follow the sweep of history from the Vietnam War protests to 9/11. Nothing has been more challenging than my current assignment, covering national security and foreign policy, in these stormy times. Reporting on a secretary of state as uniquely positioned to change policy as this one has opened yet another chapter.

An academic by training, Dr. Rice fashions herself a historian first—in other words, a deeper thinker than most professional diplomats. She does not want to settle for short-range solutions. Rather than urging an immediate cease-fire for Lebanon, she counsels a longer view, saying this is nothing less than the "birth pangs of a new Middle East," paraphrasing former Israeli prime minister Ariel Sharon. To many Arabs, Rice sounds at best naïve, at worst arrogant—especially after the administration's miscalculations in Iraq.

We lift off from Andrews Air Force Base late on a Sunday afternoon. I have no idea where we will land. The official schedule says Tel Aviv, but the plane is buzzing with rumors of a detour to Cyprus, where thousands of Americans have been evacuated from the war zone. The Israelis began bombing twelve days earlier, and the State Department has been widely criticized for not extracting Americans more quickly once the war started. Are Rice's image makers planning a surprise photo opportunity with grateful evacuees as they transit back to the United States—timed fourteen hours from now, just in time for the morning television shows? This would be a dramatic way to counteract criticism that she had waited too long to get involved.

Or perhaps she would go to Beirut? Stopping first in Lebanon would reinforce her strategic goal of propping up that country's beleaguered government. Rice's aides won't confirm anything. The element of surprise is crucial to her security.

I wonder, am I being too cynical? That is always the risk we journalists take, of crossing the line from appropriately skeptical to suspicious or just plain jaded. In this case, the world has been screaming for American intervention. But unlike many diplomatic missions, nothing has been precooked. I've been on many high-stakes trips in forty years of reporting, accompanying five presidents and nine secretaries of state. Few were as perilous diplomatically as this one. And the risks for Rice are enormous. Her professional reputation is on the line. By far the most popular figure in the Bush cabinet, she has largely escaped criticism for the Iraq war—even though she was national security advisor when the decision to invade was made.

But now critics are questioning policies that are squarely in her domain. Hezbollah did rise in the vacuum created when Syria was forced out of Lebanon by a popular uprising in 2005; America refused to deal with Iran and Syria, Hezbollah's chief sponsors, and the Arab world and Europe had begun to sense that the administration was treating the Middle East with benign neglect and was now giving Israel a green light to fight the terror group.

Rice comes back to brief us shortly after liftoff. She is perfectly coifed and stylishly dressed, but there are dark circles under her eyes. She has just come from a meeting at the White House with the Saudi foreign minister Prince Saud al-Faisal, accompanied by Prince Bandar bin Sultan, the legendary former Saudi ambassador to the United States. They want an immediate cease-fire. Rice tells them what will become a familiar, and seemingly contradictory, refrain on this trip: getting a cease-fire is urgent, but it is even more important to get one that lasts.

When the war began, Sunni Arab leaders in Egypt, Saudi Arabia, and Jordan criticized Hezbollah and resisted denouncing Israel, reflecting their own worries about Hezbollah's Shiite patrons in Iran. But now, as Israel continues to deliver punishing blows to Lebanon's infrastructure and people, moderate Arabs are distancing themselves from Israel, and from Rice's strategy. In fact, Rice was forced to move this week's crisis summit from Egypt to Rome: Egypt's president, Hosni Mubarak, no longer wanted to play host, and knowing his views, the United States didn't want to give him the international platform to shape the agenda.

Flying across the Atlantic, shortly after what had clearly been a tense send-off from the Saudis, I ask Rice about the widening gulf between the administration and its Arab allies. Her response is uncharacteristically edgy, even snappish: "Gee, Andrea, I thought it was more important what came out of a meeting than where you had it." She does not like us pointing out how isolated the administration is from its Arab allies.

In this crisis, and for months before, the administration's strategy has been to separate Syria's interests from Iran's by getting the Saudis and Egyptians to pressure Syria to control Hezbollah. But so far, Syria's president Bashar al Assad has not listened to appeals from his own Arab brothers. A veteran ambassador tells me Assad hasn't even answered phone messages from Egypt's Mubarak. And, although the Saudis share the administration's concerns about the growing power of both Hezbollah and the Shiite regime in Iran, politically, the level of destruction in Lebanon has become intolerable. Rice plans to warn Israel that it risks alienating the moderate Arab world, and the American public. She needs to learn more about their military endgame. The administration likely encouraged Israel to engage Hezbollah, but Israel's offensive is meeting unexpectedly tough resistance. Clearly, the United States is not comfortable with a bombing campaign that may continue indefinitely.

The administration's unequivocal support for Israel has other unintended consequences: most obviously, it has exacerbated existing anger toward the United States in the Arab and Muslim world. And the U.S. strategy of trying to isolate Syria and Iran could backfire, giving them more leverage over the eventual outcome. In particular Iran, a charter member of George Bush's "axis of evil," is increasingly defiant under its new president, Mahmoud Ahmadinejad. United States troops are overextended and vulnerable on both of Iran's borders, in Iraq and Afghanistan. Instead of Hezbollah, Iran's client, being blamed for the devastation of Lebanon, the radical world—and some not so radical—are pillorying Israel and the United States.

I wonder whether this was the inevitable result of the administration's decision to focus more on regime change in Iraq than resolving the main conflict between Israel and the Palestinians. Bush had pulled back from mediating a peace plan when he decided he didn't trust Yasser Arafat, the late Palestinian leader. Talks never got back on track. Some of his father's friends and advisors told me the son relied more on gut instinct than reasoned judgment. He didn't self correct. "I'm a decider," the president liked to say, even if his policies weren't working. And Condoleezza Rice had long since decided to support the president's instincts, rather than challenge them. It is no accident that even America's Arab allies thought Rice had come reluctantly to this conflict.

We refuel in Shannon, Ireland, and settle down to try to sleep, our only opportunity before we are expecting to land in Israel, when we will have to get right to work reporting. Suddenly, Rice's top Middle East advisors come back to our crowded press area in the back of the plane. We are not going to Jerusalem, at least not right away. Instead, the first stop will be Beirut. The secretary of state will chopper into the heart of the conflict, right as the *Today* show goes on the air— and I have no way to alert my producers where she is going.

This is no mere photo-op.

Silently, I give Rice credit. It is a gutsy play, designed to boost the political standing of Lebanon's prime minister, Fouad Siniora, who is hanging onto power by his fingernails. And she is foregoing a dramatic tour of the American rescue operation.

Although her plane must first land in Cyprus, where the evacuation is in high gear, Rice will not detour to the evacuation headquarters. Aides say it would be too distracting for already overburdened relief workers. Perhaps she also cannot be confident of how she would be received.

We touch down at the American embassy in Beirut minutes before seven in the morning, East Coast time—after an hour-long helicopter ride with the tail-gunner hanging out the rear as we try to survey devastated neighborhoods below. Across from the landing zone is the windowless shell of the old embassy building that was bombed in April 1983. Marines brought in to beef up security in the current crisis are now bivouacking there—camping out in the suffocating heat in the skeletal structure that stands as an unintentional memorial to one of Hezbollah's inaugural acts of terror.

As we hurtle down the switchbacks of the steep hill from the embassy in armored vehicles, I call in to the *Today* show for a live report by phone with Campbell Brown, anchoring in New York. "Right now we're on this hair-raising motorcade. You mention the security risks. They say that they manage the risk. They knew that by the element of surprise this would at least get them ahead of the game. . . . She's hoping to come home with some kind of solution where the Lebanese government, Lebanese army, supported eventually by multinational troops, will begin to create a buffer zone in the south. And while they say they don't want an immediate cease-fire, there's a lot of pressure from Egypt, Jordan, and Saudi Arabia to do exactly that. So within a week or so, I think you will see efforts toward a cease-fire. Of course the position is that that is basically doing Israel's bidding by letting Israel have another week to continue its ground and air assaults."

In fact, that perception, and the fallout from Iraq, had already circumscribed Rice's ability to mediate a solution. How many American diplomats had tried and failed—even died—over the decades trying to navigate the shoals of Lebanese factional politics? By the time we climb back on our choppers to leave Beirut, Rice had been going for more than thirty-six hours. When we arrive in Israel, our clothes, and the secretary's pale green suit, are stained with hydraulic fluid, residue of the helicopter flight. A perfect metaphor for America's muddied diplomatic strategy?

It is a harbinger of the negotiations to come. Throughout this mission, Rice finds her game plan undercut by the Israelis, all the while denying any rift to us. At her first meeting—after hurriedly changing from her soiled suit—she watches stonily as Israel's foreign minister makes a statement to the local press in Hebrew, despite having assured the State Department there was no need to bring a translator. Only later do we learn that instead of the expected pleasantries, it was a blatant political defense of Israel's position.

Still, Rice believed she could hammer out an agreement. After giving Israel more time to reach its military goals, Rice returned to Jerusalem five days later, sounding even more hopeful that her peace plan might work. Israel was prepared to give up territory it had held since the 1967 war. Rice would carry that concession to Beirut the next day and close the deal.

That's as close as she got. During dinner that night, as Prime Minister Ehud Olmert hospitably filled her wineglass to mark the ceremonial end of the Sabbath, he told Rice he still needed two more weeks to complete the job. But contrary to their agreement that the dinner be private, he brought government television cameras in to record the moment.

Preparing for *Nightly News*, I made a few last-minute calls to find out how their conversation had gone. I'd written a relatively optimistic story, reflecting Rice's view that they might be close to an agreement. But after dinner with Olmert, it was clear to me that the mood had shifted dramatically. Rushing to rewrite and get to the Jerusalem rooftop where we were to broadcast live at 1:30 in the morning—because of the time difference with the United States—I toned down my lead. As it turned out, my report was still too upbeat. None of us knew that a tragic accident of war was about to further complicate Rice's mission: At that very hour Israeli bombs were falling on the town of Qana in southern Lebanon. Israel said it thought it was targeting a Hezbollah stronghold. Instead, it killed twenty-eight civilians, many of them children.

The secretary of state didn't learn about the devastating attack until the following morning, during a meeting with Israel's defense minister. Further angering Rice, he didn't alert her to the unfolding tragedy—she learned about it from one of her own aides, who abruptly interrupted the meeting with a text message from the U.S. ambassador in Beirut. By then, jovial images from her dinner with the prime minister the night before were being broadcast around the world by Arab satellite networks. It was a completely false impression, but the propaganda value was inescapable; contrary to the actual facts, Condoleezza Rice and Israel's leader appeared to be celebrating an Israeli air strike that massacred Lebanese women and children.

Rice was clearly shaken by the awful events. In a call from Lebanon, Prime Minister Siniora told her she was no longer welcome in Beirut later that day. Rice had already decided she wouldn't be able to accomplish anything. It was a turning point for her and American diplomacy. There would be no peacemaking for her, no grand gesture that would immediately reshape the politics of the region. She would have to settle for a negotiated and limited cease-fire resolution. Scrambling to salvage something from what looked like a foreign policy debacle, U.S. officials persuaded Israel to agree to a forty-eight-hour bombing pause to help facilitate relief efforts. They announced it at midnight, just in time to reshape the next day's newspaper stories and our Sunday night newscast back home.

The bombing pause didn't last long. During a refueling stop on the way home, Rice's deputies learned that Israel had already launched new air strikes. On the plane, after so many setbacks, Rice faced more personal questioning than she'd ever had to encounter—and she was clearly uncomfortable. One reporter asked: "This seems like it's been your most difficult week as secretary of state. . . . Some of the columns back in Washington have been withering. Can you sort of talk about that? Has it been a roller coaster? Or do you just charge on ahead?"

Visibly recoiling, she replied: "Well, I hate to disappoint you. I haven't had much time to read the columns back home. So you can read them to me later."

Even more awkwardly, another reporter took another stab at the "feelings" question, unwittingly insulting the secretary of state. "I think a lot of us were seeing that you looked, you'll excuse me, you looked really bad at several times during this trip. I mean, you always look fabulous, but you looked tense. I mean tell us what you were feeling . . . give us a sense personally."

Stung, Rice replied: "I don't know, maybe I'm just not as self-reflective as you think I am."

On the surface, she seemed surprised at the inquisition. No one expected this to be easy. It would not occur to her that she was, to a certain extent, suffering the consequences of her own policies. Still, I had a nagging thought. Was she being held to a different standard than her male predecessors? I turned to one of the other women in the press corps and quietly asked, would they be asking Henry Kissinger or Jim Baker how he felt after a difficult week of shuttle diplomacy? Or would they simply focus on the likely next steps?

In assessing the damage, the administration was already being criticized for relying so heavily on Israel's military strategy. In this case, a novice prime minister, depending at first solely on air power, had seriously underestimated a resilient guerrilla force. His defense minister also had no relevant military experience. His top uniformed advisor was from the air force, not the army. No one involved knew how to plan a ground campaign. There's no evidence that the president or Rice asked the Pentagon's Joint Staff to analyze whether Israel could accomplish its military goals before the United States endorsed them.

It remains to be seen whether the Bush administration's ambitious—and controversial—diplomacy had also been rooted in a naïve conception of what is even possible politically in the Middle East, and whether any of the players can really control Hezbollah. In the short term, the unintended result of this great adventure in creating a "new Middle East," in the phrase Rice so awkwardly adopted, could be a stronger Iran—perhaps even, a stronger Hezbollah. Two weeks after our trip, Hezbollah's leader, Sheik Hassan Nasrallah, declared that his Shiite organization, not the government, would rebuild much of southern Lebanon. A prominent Lebanese reform leader called it a "watershed," in effect, a coup d'état. Iran's president declared victory. The influential *Economist* captioned its cover "Nasrallah wins the war."

It is not the first, or last, time this secretary of state will have to tangle with Iran.

———

Since 9/11, the war on terror has been the central metaphor for the president's foreign policy. But in his second term, he has seemed to find a different inspiration from the attack on America. It is an almost religious zeal to democratize the world. People differ about his motivation, and in fact, the president's second inaugural address remains a political Rorschach test. Conservative critics still complain that it was too Wilsonian, appealing to the aspirations of fledgling democracies and emphasizing human rights above security. Many liberals, and foreign policy pragmatists, found it too interventionist, worrying about his promise to stand with the oppressed against their oppressors. Would Iraq be followed by regime change in Iran?

In the first months of his second term, the president pointed to promising signs for his vision that democracy was on the march— the first elections in Iraq, Afghanistan, and the Palestinian territories, pro-democracy demonstrations that forced Syria out of Lebanon. On January 30, ten days after Bush's inauguration, Iraq confounded most skeptics by electing a national assembly—undeniably, an important milestone. But was it a turning point? The vice president and secretary of defense believed it was, and were ebullient at a small birthday celebration for Dick Cheney that night. Three days later, I was on the road again, this time, with a new secretary of state, as she tested that proposition.

As national security advisor, Condoleezza Rice had helped execute the president's tough foreign policy during his first term. According to former administration officials, she opposed every attempt they made to open conversations with Iran. And in January 2002, she signed off on language declaring Iran, Iraq, and North Korea the "axis of evil" in the State of the Union address, never questioning a hot-button phrase crafted by speechwriters for maximum political effect. Admittedly, not even seasoned diplomats anticipated its swift impact. Colin Powell, then secretary of state, first read advance copies of the text the day before the president was to deliver it. "Axis of evil" didn't jump out at him or his top deputies as anything more than the usual Bush rhetoric.

Rice now tells me she was equally surprised by the immediate response, but disagrees about its importance. She says it was more rhetorical than diplomatic. While others believe that the phrase helped shut down any promise of a dialogue with Iran's previous government, nominally led by Mohammad Khatami, Rice insists that reports of such openings were widely exaggerated.

In an interview for this book, Rice said, "I never really thought that the Khatami government was that fundamentally different in terms of its foreign policy except it had a better face to the world than the current government. But, just to be very clear, all of this talk about, you know, huge approaches toward us in 2003 and so forth, I do not remember any such thing."

Rice now tells me she'd thought the foreign policy headline out of that speech would be the president's call for the democratization of the Middle East. According to Rice, "the next day when I got up and there were huge headlines about the "axis of evil," I thought—because it wasn't intended to read into it that there was, you know, a group working together and so forth. It was people reading more meaning into it (than was intended). As it turns out, the substance of it was exactly right. You did have these three states that now, when people talk about the proliferation problem, who do they talk about? Iran and North Korea, Iraq having been settled."

Critics would find her conclusion that anything about Iraq is *settled* quite breathtaking, entirely aside from the failure to find any unconventional weapons newer than a decade old. But her comments offer an important insight into the thinking of someone who both shaped and reflects the president's views. And, despite frequent denials, may still evolve into a major political player within the Republican Party, if not a national candidate.

Understanding Bush's foreign policy—a central focus of my current assignment—requires exploring how his thinking has evolved over the years, and his relationship with his closest advisors. And no one is closer to the president than Condoleezza Rice. She may have acted in loyal lockstep with her colleagues as national security advisor, but she was no caretaker of history, and as soon as she took over as the president's top diplomat, Rice set out to change some of the policies she'd helped implement during the first term—often, over the objections of Colin Powell. And among these, none was more obvious—or potentially significant—than her role in the administration's evolving approach to Iran.

On her first trip to Europe as America's top diplomat in early February 2005, only five days after taking office, she clearly anticipated a storm of criticism over Iraq. Instead, to her surprise, France's Jacques Chirac and Germany's Gerhard Schroeder were literally kissing her hand. It was the beginning of a ten-country charm offensive, a march through Europe's capitals planned like Napoleon's—all laid out in a 180-page battle plan designed to soften up some of the administration's harshest critics. Usually blasé, veteran European commentators were smitten, praising her elegance, her polish, and, despite her Ph.D. in international studies, described her exchange with the German chancellor as "coquettish." She was a diplomatic rock star in both Paris and Berlin.

Did she find that patronizing or chauvinist? She shrugged off the question, telling us: "I don't think much about it. I will do what I do. I'm a package, you know? I'm who I am, and that includes being female."

After four years of being ignored by Washington, European leaders were delighted to be getting so much attention from someone who could speak so authoritatively for the president. They had admired Colin Powell, but he'd been closer to Bush's father than the current president. Powell kept losing crucial policy battles on Iran, Iraq, and North Korea. In contrast, Rice's unique power stems from being almost a member of the Bush family. During the first term, she had spent most weekends and vacations with the Bushes. At her swearing-in ceremony, the president said of Condi: "We love her. I don't know if you're supposed to say that." But he did. No one could remember him ever expressing his love for Colin Powell.

But for all her style and access, Rice was still confronting attitudes toward George Bush that had hardened over four years. "Old Europe" had failed to stop America from invading Iraq. Now the Europeans were determined to preserve their economic investments by avoiding American military action against Iran. Rice came back from Europe thinking that the president would eventually have to play the diplomatic card of offering to join the negotiations with Iran, but not yet. It was enough to signal during a stop in Brussels that the United States would let Europe be its proxy with Tehran.

Over the next twelve months, the situation deteriorated rapidly, especially after Iran elected Tehran's untested mayor Mahmoud Ahmadinejad as its new president. Two months later, he took office— an engineer with rough manners, unknown governance skills, and few relationships with the country's political elites. Even one of his own career diplomats confessed to me that he was a complete unknown. No one could penetrate his complex relationship with the clerics who actually ran the country. Nor could his own aides predict his foreign policy. CIA officials admitted they were again taken by surprise.

Once elected, Ahmadinejad scared his natural allies in Europe by denying the Holocaust and calling for Israel to be "wiped off the map." Even in Iran, many feared that he was stirring up too much international hostility toward Tehran. But Iran's large population of educated young people also yearned to prove their status to the rest of the world through technological advances. He appealed to those ambitions with a powerful symbol—Iran's nuclear research program.

The new leader immediately created a nuclear crisis. He rejected Russia's offer to enrich Iran's uranium on Russian soil, a compromise that theoretically would have provided him with energy sources but not weapons-grade fuel. He cut off negotiations with the Europeans. And he alienated the inspectors who would be the arbiters of whether or not Iran's nuclear research was civilian or military. In a fateful step, Iran broke the seals the International Atomic Energy Agency had placed on its nuclear equipment. Iran declared it was accelerating construction of centrifuges that could be used to create weapon fuel.

In the spring of 2006, Rice went to Berlin for emergency meetings. On March 30, both Russia and China said they would not consider sanctions against Iran. Russian foreign minister Sergei Lavrov said, "In principle, Russia doesn't believe that sanctions could achieve the purposes of settlement of various issues." China's vice foreign minister Dai Bingguo said, "There has already been enough turmoil in the Middle East." They did not trust American intentions after what had happened in Iraq. Whatever their motives, the way America went to war with Iraq was limiting Rice's diplomatic options toward Iran.

Rice realized she would not be able to forge a unified position with Europe as long as the United States refused all contact with Iran. She knew she needed to orchestrate a diplomatic way out of the crisis. At a lunch with the president in the small dining room behind the Oval Office five days later, she reported that the Berlin meetings had been a disaster. The coalition against Iran was on the verge of falling apart. Despite past opposition from Vice President Cheney and Defense Secretary Rumsfeld, George Bush signaled that he was ready to listen to new ideas. Rice had the green light to start devising a strategy of carefully calibrated inducements to get Tehran to suspend its nuclear enrichment, backed up by punishments if it didn't.

But how to unite Europe and Russia behind the idea of sticks—sanctions—if Iran refused the carrots? On Easter weekend, using pencils in three different colors, Rice sat in her Watergate apartment constructing an elaborate series of steps along three parallel tracks, leading to a new Iran policy. Before flying to New York on May 8 for one last round with the Russian and Chinese foreign ministers at the United Nations, she showed the color-coded calendar to Nicholas Burns, her point person on Iran. It was the kind of complex, phased diplomacy usually constructed by her staff. This time, the secretary of state was so engaged she did it herself.

Unfortunately, Rice didn't count on Iran stealing her diplomatic spotlight. On May 8, knowing the United States would be challenging his proxies on the Security Council, President Ahmadinejad released a letter he'd written to President Bush. It was eighteen pages, largely consisting of insulting accusations cloaked in religious rhetoric. At one point, Ahmadinejad wrote Bush, "Can one be a follower of Jesus Christ, the great Messenger of God . . . but at the same time, have countries attacked?"

That day, Rice came to NBC's New York headquarters for lunch with our top executives and anchors. I asked for her analysis of the letter. She said they still didn't have an official translation, but her initial reading from public reports suggested that it failed to address the major issue between the United States and Iran—Iran's nuclear ambitions. Hours later, the White House dismissed the letter as a rambling tirade designed to disrupt efforts to constrain Iran's nuclear research. Still, there was no denying that for the first time since Iranian students seized American diplomats as hostages in 1979, Iran was proposing direct talks with the United States.

Rice was ready to take on the hardliners in the administration who opposed any diplomatic contact with Iran. She had an influential ally—Henry Kissinger, who believed that the president could be missing an opportunity. Why not lay out America's conditions for engagement with Iran? After clearing his ideas with Rice, Kissinger wrote an op-ed in *The Washington Post* saying, "If America is prepared to negotiate with North Korea over proliferation in the six-party forum, and with Iran in Baghdad over Iraqi security, it must be possible to devise a multilateral venue for nuclear talks with Tehran that would permit the United States to participate—especially in light of what is at stake."

But no one in the Bush administration was willing to acknowledge the Iranian letter directly. They viewed it as insulting and not a legitimate opening worth exploring. Bush had authorized a diplomatic overture, but only on his terms. Was he making an offer he expected Iran would refuse? I wondered whether neoconservatives at the National Security Council and the Pentagon really thought they had military options against Tehran, as they and their allies claimed. Despite their misjudgments about Iraq, did they plan to target Iran's suspected nuclear sites, if they could find them? Or was all their rhetoric just more saber rattling to keep Iran on edge?

The night of Iran's missive, we were summoned to the lobby of the Waldorf Astoria where Rice and the other foreign ministers were meeting on the twenty-third floor to discuss the issue. We were told we'd be briefed shortly, as soon as they finished their dinner. For hours, we sat on the tufted velvet loveseats in the hotel lobby, watching the New York nightlife swirling around us. We had no way of knowing that tempers were erupting upstairs.

Russia's foreign minister LaVrov was furious about comments Nick Burns had made to the press in Moscow about Russia's arms sales to Iran. And he was angry that the week before, Dick Cheney had accused Russia of using its oil and gas riches to blackmail its neighbors. Standing up to what she took to be Russia's bullying tactics, the newest member of the club, Britain's inexperienced foreign secretary Margaret Beckett, rose to Burns's defense, sternly admonishing Lavrov "not to attack a colleague." For the novice diplomat, from which little was expected, it was a moment surprisingly resonant of the "Iron Lady" herself, Margaret Thatcher. But for the time being, there was no hope of reaching agreement within the United Nations.

Over the next few weeks, in secret meetings with Burns and a handful of other trusted aides, Rice constructed her own Iran initiative. If it worked, it could become her foreign policy legacy. It might even help overcome criticism over her support for the war in Iraq. It was a policy the president would never have permitted Colin Powell, Rice's predecessor, to pursue. During the first term, the president rarely sided with Powell when the secretary of state came in conflict with Dick Cheney and Donald Rumsfeld. The two camps fought constantly. Instead of brokering compromises, Rice—as national security advisor—usually sided with the vice president and the defense secretary. She either agreed with them or, critics say, she was not inclined to challenge the president's comfort zone. Iran was a frequent battleground.

The Clinton administration had opened secret talks with Iran. Both the United States and Iran wanted to control the Taliban regime on Iran's border in neighboring Afghanistan. Perhaps that mutual concern could lead to agreements on other issues, including terrorism. When the Bush administration took office, Powell had tried to keep the back channel conversation going. But Rice—perhaps reflecting the Cheney/Rumsfeld view—shut it down. The secretary of state tried again after a giant earthquake hit Bam, in southeastern Iran, the day after Christmas 2003. Powell saw it as a chance to use the offer to provide emergency supplies as a wedge for a limited diplomatic opening, and the president agreed. But this time Iran wasn't ready for a broader conversation. The Iranian ambassador said "not now" and the American initiative was stillborn.

Two months before Powell left office, there was one final opportunity, but it was too late. On one of Powell's last trips as secretary of state, he found himself seated next to the Iranian foreign minister at a conference in Egypt. It was obvious to both sides that the Egyptians had purposefully, even mischievously, placed them together to foster a dialogue. But neither man had enough leeway from his country's political leader to engage in meaningful diplomacy. Constrained by both politics and history, they had a cordial conversation, but both diplomats knew they couldn't go any further.

Where was Condi Rice during all this? One former official told me, with some bitterness, "She was with the rest of them on this. People forget her first four years as though she came in from nowhere." For four years, as national security advisor, she had readily endorsed the president's decision to isolate Iran. But by the spring of 2006, as secretary of state, she was able to persuade Bush to reverse course. For the first time, the United States, Europe, Russia, and China would approach Tehran together with a common negotiating strategy.

Administration hawks were holding their fire for the moment, perhaps betting that Iran would never comply. But there were other sources of pressure to take a hard line. In late May 2006, in the middle of the administration's internal debate over Iran policy, Israel's new prime minister, Ehud Olmert arrived in Washington for his first visit since replacing Ariel Sharon.

An implacable opponent of Iran, Olmert shared alarming Israeli intelligence with the president and vice president: Tehran was only twelve months from crossing a dangerous red line—a critical breakthrough in centrifuge technology that would bring Iran alarmingly close to building a nuclear weapon. United States intelligence officials believed it would take Iran more than five years to reach that level of technical expertise. The Israelis thought the Americans were naïve. After all, they could afford to be complacent; Tehran's missiles couldn't reach Washington. But after his second day of meetings, Olmert came away from a long session with the vice president convinced that the administration would never let Iran get to the point of producing a bomb. He signaled privately that the Bush administration knew its obligations and would not expose Israel to the threat of an Iranian bomb. Despite its misjudgments in Iraq and Afghanistan, the Bush team appeared to be ready, if necessary, to take out Iran's nuclear facilities in a preemptive strike.

It was a fundamental misunderstanding of the president's thinking, at least at the time. What Olmert, representing one of America's closest allies, didn't know was that at that very moment, two weeks after receiving Iran's letter, the president, at Rice's urging, was preparing to offer Tehran a deal full of carrots—rich economic benefits, including the light water nuclear reactors the administration had long opposed, if Iran suspended its nuclear weapons program. The United States would join the European negotiations. And the secretary of state was even prepared to dangle the prospect of sitting down with her Iranian counterpart one-on-one—a precursor to eventually restoring diplomatic relations.

A week after Olmert had been holding forth across Pennsylvania Avenue from the White House at Blair House, the elegant guest residence for visiting leaders, the secret new Iran policy was ready to be launched. The night before the announcement, Rice called the president one last time. Was he sure?

"Go do it," he replied.

That night, key allies—including Israel—were briefed for the first time. At the UN, U.S. ambassador John Bolton, a hardliner who had been frozen out of the secret planning, was brought up to speed so he could try to win over fellow conservatives. At eleven o'clock the next morning, Rice unveiled the dramatically new U.S. policy toward Iran—conceived in total secrecy.

Trying to reach over the heads of Iran's leaders, she said, "President Bush wants a new and positive relationship between the American people and the people of Iran—a beneficial relationship of increased contacts in education, cultural exchange, sports, travel, trade, and investment."

Then, she boarded her 757 to fly to Vienna, where she and the other foreign ministers would try to agree on exactly what it was they were offering Iran. As she greeted us in the back of the plane, it was obvious that she knew the hard part was still to come.

Having announced an agreement, the ministers now had to make sure they really agreed. That night, they gathered at the stately residence of the British ambassador to Austria. It would be critical to at least appear unified, even if it meant obscuring stubborn differences over how hard to press if Iran's leaders said "no." For some reason, the British, who were hosting the meetings, seemed to think it would be easy.

After flying overnight from Washington and working all day, we waited in the hotel pressroom, planning to order dinner while the diplomats talked. Suddenly, we were summoned to the British ambassador's residence. There was an agreement; a statement was imminent.

In the garden behind the embassy residence, there was an air of anticipation. It was a useful distraction from the miserable cold. We'd been told to expect spring weather. Instead, it was damp and windy. None of us had packed coats. Mercifully, Krzysztof Galica, my ever-resourceful cameraman, loaned me one of his jackets.

For hours, Rice and her counterparts struggled to gloss over their fundamental disagreements. At the suggestion of the Russians, they decided to remove all references to "sanctions"—a red flag to the Iranians. Instead, they played word games—call it diplomatic Scrabble—searching for euphemisms to take the sting out of potential punishments. What's a five-letter word for "sanctions" that won't alienate Iran? How about "steps?" Remarkably, Rice willingly accepted these linguistic subterfuges to soften the impact of whatever pressure would be brought to bear against Iran.

As important as the substance of any agreement is how it is presented. Rice and her colleagues knew that even if they didn't agree on everything, they had to project unity by choreographing a joint appearance for the cameras, a money shot, to symbolize accord.

In the days leading up to the announcement, the president had won approval for the broad outlines of a deal with his two most critical counterparts in the negotiations, Russia's Vladimir Putin and France's Jacques Chirac. Their negotiators had been given drafts of options. But how should they describe this balance of rewards and sanctions? If the package appeared to be too concessionary, it would inflame conservatives; if too punitive, the Iranians would reject it out of hand.

As an important signal that their offer was serious—not just an American publicity stunt—the foreign ministers agreed on an unusual pledge of secrecy. They would not reveal any specifics until they presented the package to Tehran. For politicians and professional diplomats, taking an oath of silence is like asking an addict to go cold turkey. Their work done, they ordered in dinner.

Shivering in the garden outside, we knew nothing of their progress, only that the talks were dragging on hours longer than anticipated. Unlike the newspaper reporters who were able to go to their rooms and sleep after our plane had landed that morning, the television correspondents had to start preparing right away for our morning news broadcasts. After appearing on the *Today* show I switched gears to start gathering material for *Nightly News*. None of us expected the meetings to go on into the night.

For hours, British security aides still kept us locked outside in the garden, save for occasional trips to the bathroom inside. I found myself repeatedly visiting the restroom just to get warm.

By ten p.m., the winds had picked up and the temperature had dropped to forty degrees. Our camera crews were standing in position, frozen on their feet. The press corps was increasingly restless. Was this turning into a debacle for American and British diplomacy? The only logical explanation was that the Russians had once again balked.

Soon the British realized they had a problem: an international mob of hungry, cold reporters and no outcome in sight. Suddenly, with the diplomatic touch for which Her Majesty's foreign service is justly known, someone ordered white-jacketed waiters to appear with silver trays of beer and wine. Instantly, the surly press corps became more reasonable. The scene even began to resemble a cocktail party, even if it were one where the guests were both captive and frostbitten. Rice's aides rushed upstairs to warn the ministers that they should stop eating dinner and issue some kind of statement, no matter how brief, to feed the hungry media beast outside.

When they finally emerged, the single speaker was the rather starchy British foreign secretary. The carefully calibrated joint statement contained precisely 140 words (138, if you didn't count "thank you"). Despite the long wait, they refused to take a single question.

It was getting late. My broadcast deadline of twelve-thirty a.m. no longer seemed very far off. We were brought back to the hotel to await a briefing. Usually, that means a senior official will anonymously give us unverifiable details of the negotiations, invariably self-serving.

This time, the official arrived at exactly midnight. He somewhat breathlessly declared themselves "very, very satisfied" with the commitments they had received. It was immediately clear that the word "sanctions" had been erased. The briefer said there would be "negative" repercussions if Iran did not accept, but he wouldn't specify what they were.

Since the live camera position was a fifteen-minute taxi ride away, I was calculating how much longer I could listen to his diplomatic dodges without missing the deadline for our broadcast. It was time to go.

The taxi driver got lost, and spoke no English. My producer, who knew far more German than I, translated frantically. We got there just in time. But because of a heavy load of domestic news, including the official start of the first hurricane season since Katrina, the *Nightly News* broadcast didn't have time for a detailed, scripted report. My story had to be boiled down to a live crosstalk of less than one minute.

Standing alone with my crew in the middle of the night outside the British residence, I explained how the Russians had finally agreed on a common approach toward Iran. Summarizing the briefing for Brian Williams, anchoring from New Orleans, I concluded: "This will be presented to Iranian diplomats by Europeans this weekend. And they're trying to avoid the use of the word 'sanctions,' hoping to make it sound as benign as possible to make it easier for Iran to say yes." It was fifty seconds, and not a second over.

When I finally got to my room at two in the morning, I slept fitfully, worried that I wouldn't hear the alarm clock. We were leaving the next morning, but first would each get five minutes to interview the secretary for our morning shows. I was told I'd go first, at nine a.m. in Vienna—three a.m. Washington time. One of Rice's aides, Josie Duckett, would serve as timekeeper to make sure none of us exceeded the allotted time. What could I possibly ask in such a brief interview that would be at all surprising? Or elicit an unscripted response?

I wanted to explore the limits of what she would say about the agreement. How far had she brought the Russians? What concessions had the United States been forced to make? But I also couldn't escape the conviction that all of this could have been negotiated more favorably four years earlier, at the beginning of 2002, when oil was nineteen dollars a barrel, and Iran had a fledgling reform movement, more moderate political leaders, and was years from building its first nuclear centrifuge.

Rice was adept at circumventing questions she didn't want to answer. Perhaps it was her training as a professor, but she always stuck to her lesson plan, no matter how unruly the student—or reporter. It was no different on this occasion, despite her fatigue after negotiating well into the night. When she strode into the room for the interview, Condoleezza Rice sat down across from me and sighed. Visibly exhausted, she said, "I'm a morning person." Apparently, her diplomatic colleagues are not.

The State Department's time clock was already running. I hurriedly asked whether Iran's instant rejection of the proposal that morning was definitive?

Rice answered, "We certainly hope that Iran will take a few days to think over a very serious proposal." And, she emphasized, this was not an American proposal but an offer from the entire international community.

Why should the administration now trust Iran? How would anyone verify compliance? In stark contrast to the administration's disparagement of international inspections before the war with Iraq, she said they would rely on the "competent" verification of the International Atomic Energy Agency.

Couldn't the United States have had the same deal a couple of years earlier, before the president called Iran a member of the "axis of evil" and before secret back-channel conversations were cut off? Couldn't they have had this deal with a more moderate Iranian government?

Rice said: "We had to take the time to build an international climate of opinion that Iran had certain steps that it had to take," adding, "This had to be built as a coalition, as a consensus among the international community."

In my report for the *Today* show that morning, I concluded that the administration now had no choice but to change its strategy. The president was under enormous pressure from his closest allies to resolve the Iran crisis. And, no matter what Israel claimed, most experts believed a military attack—even an air strike—on Iran's nuclear facilities would be difficult, especially with the U.S. military already overcommitted in Iraq and Afghanistan.

With only moments to catch the motorcade for the airport and the trip home, we shot my on-camera standup for the *Today* show in front of the Vienna Opera. My first visit to the Austrian capital—the subject of so many of my musical studies as a child—and that's the closest I got to a concert hall. During a brief refueling stop in Shannon, Ireland, I dashed off a blog for The Daily Nightly on MSNBC's Web site about the frustrations of seeing the world on a State Department press pass.

"For the first time in twenty-five years of covering presidents and secretaries of state, I had been to Vienna. I'd spent twenty-four hours across the street from the famed Opera House, with signs everywhere celebrating the 250th anniversary of Mozart's birth, and I hadn't heard a musical note. Sadly for Condoleezza Rice—a passionate fan of Mozart and Brahms—she had spent the last day in this fabled musical city the same way. But at least her talks were more harmonious than usual."

I was wrong. Months later, Rice confided that she had in fact enjoyed a secret musical interlude in the city of Mozart, Schumann, and Brahms. During a break in the diplomacy, she had sneaked off to a nearby museum at the invitation of the Austrian government to play a historic piano that had been given to Robert and Clara Schumann as a wedding present and was then inherited by Johannes Brahms. For Rice, an accomplished pianist, it was a thrill to play a piano that had once been owned by the master himself.

Such a private, unrecorded musical moment was unusual—in sharp contrast to public performances her public relations team has organized on most of her trips. These were photo opportunities designed to raise her profile internationally, and ultimately, increase her popularity at home. In China she reviewed young Olympic ice skating performances. In Paris, it was a children's music school. In Australia, she awarded medals to women swimmers during the Commonwealth Games. And, contrary to her predecessors, she is now greeted by popular sports and music stars when she arrives overseas—a touch of show business never before associated with stodgy diplomacy. All of this is carefully choreographed by the State Department—and it works. Despite Rice's deep involvement in many of the controversial decisions that preceded the invasion of Iraq, she alone among the Bush foreign policy team remains blameless to most of the public. Her political strengths are obvious—and many Republicans see her as a future vice presidential candidate, if not a candidate for the nation's top office.

But despite all the swimming medals and music lessons, her political prospects, and her legacy, will now rest largely on her Middle East diplomacy. Having ducked most of the anger over Iraq—a policy more associated with Donald Rumsfeld and Dick Cheney—Rice will be tagged with responsibility for Bush policies toward Israel, the Palestinians, and Lebanon. And, as she struggled to contain the war between Israel and Hezbollah in the summer of 2006, the media inevitably drew comparisons between Rice and her Republican predecessors, most notably Colin Powell, Henry Kissinger, George Shultz, and James Baker.

In some ways, the comparisons are not apt. No secretary of state, with the possible exception of James Baker, has ever equaled Henry Kissinger's sway over policy and president. At this moment, Rice was ascendant, but with power came responsibility. She was now the steward of a foreign policy plagued by multiple disasters: from what was arguably civil war in Iraq to the unconstrained nuclear ambitions of North Korea and Iran and unprecedented hatred of the United States in the Arab and Muslim world. Much of this resulted from policies Rice had either helped conceive, or at least blessed.

As I trace the frantic pace of American diplomacy and politics in this book, it will become clear that both the politicians and the reporters who trail them suffer from short attention spans. We seem to be able to focus on only one issue at a time. Today it is war in Lebanon; tomorrow, a terror plot against British and American airlines. Nothing illustrates this better than the way we ignored the genocide in Rwanda in the 1990s, or in Darfur, Sudan since 2003. After a brief peace accord in early 2005, the situation in Sudan deteriorated dramatically. During that time, the administration had focused on Sudan only episodically, except for efforts by the former deputy secretary of state, Robert Zoellick, and a tumultuous trip by Condoleezza Rice.

I'd wanted to go to Darfur and had talked to returning envoys overwhelmed by the human catastrophe. Until the summer of 2005, there had never been a way to persuade the network it was either safe or feasible. After her initial travels that spring and summer, Rice was more influential than ever before. Now she was willing to take on Sudan. Traveling with the secretary of state was a way to open a brief window on the population's suffering to the outside world. It didn't turn out that way.

When I titled this book *Talking Back . . . to Presidents, Dictators, and Assorted Scoundrels*, I was thinking about politicians I'd covered in forty years of journalism, from ward heelers to presidents, and dictators from North Korea to Cuba. I had not yet met Omar Hassan al Bashir of Sudan. But as I was to discover in the summer of 2005, he was all three—president, dictator, and worse than a mere scoundrel. It was Bashir who hosted Osama bin Laden as a guest of Sudan's government in the 1990s, before bin Laden returned to Afghanistan. I'm not sure why I was destined to tangle with the Sudanese dictator that July, but it turned into an international incident, prompting Condoleezza Rice to demand a diplomatic apology. In response, the government of Sudan issued a statement accusing me of being "in an abnormal state—maybe even drunk" at a morning photo opportunity that dissolved into a brawl. I'd better explain.

We arrived in Khartoum at one a.m., July 21, after a stopover at an African trade conference in Senegal. It was a moment of great potential for Sudan; two weeks earlier, under pressure from the United States, the country's southern rebels had joined a unity government. After years of civil war, costing as many as 400 thousand lives and displacing two million refugees, there was a small hope for a settlement. Rice was there to lend support to the fragile peace.

That morning, after only a few hours of sleep, she'd met with

John Garang, the charismatic rebel leader with a Ph.D. in agricultural economics who had just become first vice president, in his new government office. Seeing him in his fancy office, replete with chandeliers and enormous chairs, Rice said she was struck by how startling a transformation it was from his years as a guerrilla leader in the bush. Garang, whom Rice knew from visits in Washington, now had a title and some leverage within the government. She was counting on the former rebel leader to play a major role in the new government. But first, she had to persuade Sudan's dictator to stop arming the Arab militias known as Janjaweed who were still raping African Muslim women, murdering their men, and pillaging villages in the vast western territory of Darfur. Colin Powell, before stepping down as secretary of state, had raised the stakes by calling it what it was—genocide.

While Rice visited with Garang, we assembled for the bus ride to the presidential palace for her meeting with Bashir. From the outset, there was confusion and misdirection. Security officials turned us away, only to have U.S. embassy aides send us back. Then, we were told to wait in a separate building in the complex, at least seventy-five yards from the president's office. Realizing it might be a deliberate attempt to keep us from covering Rice and the Sudanese leader, our small press group marched down the drive to await Rice's motorcade.

What happened next was mayhem. The secretary of state arrived, but Sudanese security men separated her from the rest of her delegation, including her translator and top aides. One assistant, Jim Wilkinson, was blocked from entering and shoved against a wall. A laconic Texan, Wilkinson responded drily, "Diplomacy 101 says you don't rough up your guests." Especially since they were trying to persuade Rice to lift economic sanctions imposed on Sudan for sponsoring terrorism. With her translator detained outside along with the rest of us, Rice and her host sat awkwardly facing each other for at least ten minutes, neither able to converse in the other's language.

In the confusion, we thought we were lining up for a photo opportunity, only to discover that we, too, were blocked. Half the press corps was outside. The rest of us were inside, but in an anteroom, arguing that we had been promised we could cover the first few minutes of the official meeting. Wilkinson and Sean McCormack, Rice's other close aide, both tried to run interference for us. McCormack told the Sudanese information minister, "This is a free press, sir."

The spokesman for the Khartoum government replied, "No, no, it's not a free press" in Sudan. On that, he was correct.

With the help of McCormack and Wilkinson, we were finally permitted in. Rice and Bashir were facing each other in armchairs, in obvious discomfort, trying to make small talk with the help of the beleaguered translator, who had also finally persuaded the Sudanese he belonged. Following State Department ground rules for photo opportunities both at home and abroad, I asked Bashir, "Can you tell us why the violence is continuing, Mr. President? Can you tell us why the government is still supporting the militias?"

It was a case where talking back got me in trouble. On a gesture from Bashir, his security men grabbed me from behind. One yanked my left arm, pinning it behind my back. The other grabbed my microphone cord. I could feel my shoulder snap—what turned out to be a rotator cuff injury—and yelled in pain and embarrassment. Wilkinson tried to block them, saying: "Don't ever touch that journalist again." While the cameraman tried to keep his balance and stay focused on Rice, I was dragged from the room, shouting one more question: "Why should Americans believe your promises?" I'm told Bashir never answered my question.

Rice was furious. She boarded her plane for the ninety-minute flight to Darfur and came back to see if I were all right. Stone-faced, she told us, "I am about the only person they did not rough up. I expect an apology before we land." She waited on the plane until Foreign Minister Mustafa Osman Ismail called to express regrets for "the mistreatment" of the delegation.

We were later told that although her meeting with Bashir had been truncated by all the difficulties her aides had experienced getting there, Rice had managed to make her main argument; that the government needed to stop arming the militias responsible for most of the violence. Bashir replied, "If you disarm only one side in this conflict, the result is going to be genocide." They never bridged the gap.

———

When we arrived an hour and a half later at Al-Fasher in Darfur to tour one of the largest of the refugee camps, hundreds of children greeted us singing in Arabic, "Welcome, welcome oh Condoleezza." On the tarmac, a small contingent of Rwandan soldiers stood at attention in the blazing sun. They had only just arrived, having been flown in on a U.S. C-130 transport plane by NATO to lend some muscle to Rice's visit. The Rwandan soldiers were the first wave of an anticipated 7,500 African Union troops commissioned to help protect refugees and surviving villagers from the marauding Janjaweed. But the raw recruits were unarmed and barely trained. They did not inspire a great deal of confidence.

After a brief ride from the landing strip, we found ourselves surrounded by thousands of residents of the camp—all women and children. Encircled by a chain-link fence, Abu Shouk was a tent city, semipermanent home to more than eighty thousand people. Except when an American secretary of state was visiting with her armed security guards the fence didn't strike me as a great deal of protection from external threats to the women and children inside. Here, rape was not a random crime, but used by the militias as a weapon of war. But, at least for this day, there would be no danger of attacks on these women.

Rice heard about the dangers from aid workers and from listening intently to the accounts of women who had been raped or otherwise abused. She was told that they were being raped both inside and outside the camps, not only by the dreaded militias, but also by the rebels, and even by government soldiers supposedly protecting them.

I talked to some of the women through a UN translator. Not surprisingly, they were shy and intimidated, especially by the camera.

But with encouragement from the relief workers, a few opened up. One woman told me she had tried to leave the camp and return to her village with her sister, but was forced to return after other relatives were murdered.

"The government says it is going to protect you. Do you believe the government?" I asked. "No, we don't believe the government," she replied, her eyes betraying nothing but weary resignation. Abu Shouk had been created as a temporary way station for displaced persons. But like refugee camps from Lebanon to Peshawar, it was turning into a permanent city. I was drenched in sweat, and bombarded by flies and mosquitoes. I wanted to reach for a bottle of water in my bag but was self-conscious about drinking from it—I didn't have enough to pass around to these women for whom clean water was a prized commodity.

In the shade of a tent, Rice paused briefly for interviews. I asked her what the women had told her about how rape was being used as a weapon of war.

She said, "It is a difficult thing for these women to come forward and say this. They have to live here. But what I can go back and do is look at what the Sudanese government has said, they are prepared to do to deal with violence against women, to raise this issue more in the international consciousness, that this is a serious issue. We know of the humanitarian efforts that are being made here to feed people, to give them better clothing, to give them shelter. But we also need an international effort on violence against women and I'll take that message home."

Following up, I said, "Taking a message home is important. But with all due respect, there have been leaders here, your predecessor Colin Powell, Tony Blair, Kofi Annan, your deputy (Bob Zoellick). The Sudanese government keeps promising that they are going to stop the killings. And we have evidence that they are supporting the militias that are doing the killings. What good are their promises?"

"I said this morning that they have a problem with credibility, and I said it directly to them—that people need to see action, not just your words. And it is a new Sudanese government that is coming into being. It is a government that includes people from the south who were once in terrible humanitarian conditions and were brutalized by the central government."

I pointed out that the government had the same players, including Bashir. The cast of characters was the same, but she said there was a new "flavor" to the government and that the peace agreement gave them a new chance for a fresh start.

Rice was straddling competing interests with Sudan. Her own experts had said Khartoum had progressed from a failing grade on cooperating against terrorism before 9/11 to straight A's for helping the United States track al-Qaeda funds. The administration did not want to lose this new tool in the war on terror because of what officials considered a "soft" issue like violence against women. But on that day, in the suffocating heat of that refugee camp, after listening to first-person accounts of torture, I didn't doubt that Rice was responding as a woman, as well as America's top diplomat, to the horror of what she'd heard. Other priorities would have to wait.

When I asked her about the incident with me in Khartoum, she said: "Obviously, there was a problem. They have said they will deal with the problem. But we have a serious issue with the Sudanese government." Still, she noted, there were "new actors" like Garang in the government, whom she hoped would create "a new day."

My cell phone started ringing. It hadn't occurred to me that the wire services would have filed reports about the dust-up in Khartoum hours earlier. Now it was almost seven in the morning back home on the East Coast. First, Don Imus and now the *Today* show wanted me to do live reports by phone. On the air, Katie Couric, then anchoring *Today,* asked what happened.

Broadcasting live on my cell phone, I explained that the State Department had told the Sudanese we have freedom of the press in America, and they couldn't restrict questions. But when I kept asking questions, "they kept dragging me out and they had guns. So I got the questions but I didn't get any answers."

Katie then asked me about the refugee camp. By then, we were racing back to the military airstrip, rocking back and forth in an open truck. I could barely hear the question. Somehow I replied: "The goal is to push the government here to stop the killing and to improve conditions so that people can go back (to their villages). But I have to tell you, even though the violence has been reduced somewhat, according to everyone's count, people disagree about the number of deaths. Most people agree that the violence has diminished, but that's because the villages have all been destroyed. These people have been displaced, two million people displaced. . . . This is becoming a permanent settlement. It is a human catastrophe."

Four and a half hours later, we landed in Israel. Someone handed me a press release from Khartoum. The Sudanese information ministry had denied that any incident had taken place or any apology requested by the United States. Instead, the official newspaper reported:

The head of the presidential press office, Mr. Mahjoub Fadul, explained today the incident that took place at the presidential residence by saying that the U.S. reporter—who was posing a question at President al-Bashir, was crying and in an abnormal state, maybe even drunk. He further added that reporter was objecting to the fact that no questions were allowed to either al-Bashir or Rice, and that she was escorted outside of the room by U.S. security. Fadul further added that all reporters were allowed to take photos of Rice and al-Bashir before the meeting, even though they have arrived late.

Late, after arguing to get in for an hour.

At one-thirty a.m., standing on a Jerusalem hillside in front of the Western Wall, I appeared on *Nightly News* to report on what had happened when our day began so many hours earlier in Sudan. On the air, Brian Williams said he knew I was a reluctant participant in this story, but wondered how it left me physically and mentally?

Of course, he had captured the problem perfectly. The story was the plight of the women of Darfur. I was an incidental player, but that's what made the wire reports.

On the show that night, I told Brian: "I was outraged. I was really angry. Angry at becoming part of a story that I wanted to cover, not be a principal player in, and angry because it did take away, at least temporarily, from the focus of the trip. But in fact, I can leave Sudan to come here to Israel. The people in Darfur have no choice. They are stuck there, and they are under the control of this government, which is making some progress politically, but as Secretary Rice said tonight, they've got a long way to go."

One week later, John Garang, the former rebel leader whose participation in the new unity government had given Rice so much confidence, died in a helicopter crash. His widow vouched for it having been an accident. In the months afterward, the peace agreement quickly unraveled. Rice recently told me Garang's death was a "huge loss" because the former rebel leader had such "authority and presence" as well as "a real sense of purpose in building a more unified and a more humane and a more democratic Sudan." Despite his background as a guerrilla warrior or perhaps because of it, she felt he could have infused the Khartoum government with a different set of values and attitudes. With his death died all hope for an easy resolution of the civil war.

Once again, our focus on Darfur was short-lived. As often happened on these trips, competing crises erupted in each country we visited. That night was no exception. We didn't get to the hotel in Jerusalem until nearly three in the morning, after finishing our broadcast for *Nightly News*. At that moment, sleep was less important than soaking in the tub. A few hours later, at six-thirty, a phone call rousted us to a secret briefing downstairs. After a scheduled morning visit to Ariel Sharon's sheep farm in the Negev—where the prime minister pointedly showed Rice where a Palestinian Qassam rocket had landed near his gate—the secretary was going to make a secret trip to Lebanon.

Only days earlier, that country had formed its first government since protestors forced Syrian forces to withdraw in April. Would this fledgling regime someday validate the president's assertion that democracy was on the march? Once again, Rice wanted to help midwife a new government. But for security reasons, anyone who breathed a word to their news bureaus would be expelled from the press corps. We were in radio silence all the way to the airport.

I took this order seriously. I remembered the Beirut of the 1980s, when Americans were being taken hostage and terrorists were blowing up the Marine barracks and the U.S. embassy. Now, there was a new wave of political assassinations, as rival factions competed to fill the political vacuum created by the withdrawal of Syrian troops four months earlier, following outrage over Syria's presumed involvement in assassinating Lebanon's popular former prime minister, Rafik Hariri. I hadn't been to Lebanon in a while, but the Beirut of my memory was not for sissies.

Less than an hour later, Rice's Air Force jet rolled to a stop at the Beirut airport. Obediently, none of us had filed stories or alerted our networks. When we stepped off the plane, we were greeted by a mob of camera crews and reporters, told about the surprise trip by officials in all factions of Lebanon's government. So much for maintaining security—and keeping secrets—in the Middle East!

Rice's motorcade crisscrossed Beirut at breakneck speed, trying to navigate the rough political terrain and the security risks. She paid tribute to the slain former prime minister, a symbol of resistance to Syria, by paying a condolence call at his family's palatial residence. To drive the point home, she had her motorcade slow to a crawl as it passed the cratered site where Hariri died and paused to lay a wreath at his grave. Then, during a crowded news conference with the new prime minister, she warned Syria against choking off Lebanon's borders. And she snubbed Syria's remaining proxy, the holdover president, by seeing him only briefly. The choreography was hurried, but still masterful.

By nightfall, Rice was back in Israel, hoping to breathe life into the new Palestinian government by visiting Ramallah the following day. With Israel's withdrawal from Gaza scheduled in three weeks, Prime Minister Mahmoud Abbas was caught in a political cross fire between radical Palestinians and angry Israeli settlers.

I hadn't visited the territories since Yasser Arafat's death eight months earlier. In Ramallah, people we spoke with were bitter, but resigned. They viewed the Gaza withdrawal as a defeat, a sign of their government's weakness. They feared it would condemn Palestinians to economic imprisonment within the narrow confines of that strip of land. Israel was dictating the terms. The best Palestinians could hope for was that Rice would press Israel to at least guarantee border crossings with the West Bank and with Egypt for the flow of people and goods. But they had no answers from Israel or the United States about real gateways—the long-promised Gaza airport and seaport.

Rice told us that Palestinian leaders had shown a new determination to crack down on violence in the territories in the past week. But Ariel Sharon, in one of his last visits with her before his stroke, insisted the crackdown was only sporadic. On her last day in the region before returning to Washington, she went to Ramallah to reassure the Palestinians, just as word came from Egypt that terrorists had bombed a resort area in the Sinai Peninsula. One of our top executives called from New York to ask me if I could stay behind to cover it. Was there any choice? As I rushed back to Jerusalem to finish writing a script on Rice's Middle East diplomacy for that evening's broadcast, the Tel Aviv bureau frantically arranged a midnight charter flight to the site of the bombings in Sharm el-Sheikh, Egypt.

I delayed leaving Israel for an hour to see if I could first learn anything about the Sinai attack during a final meeting between Rice and Israel's Shimon Peres at our hotel. It was after sundown on Saturday. With the end of the Sabbath, young children were racing through the corridors after festive family dinners. The contrast between normal Israeli life and the ever-present threat of violence could not have been more vivid. Peres told Rice that after the Gaza withdrawal, security had to come first before they would open any borders.

Did the United States know if this attack—three simultaneous bombings—was the work of al-Qaeda or local imitators? Buffeted by competing demands from Israelis and Palestinians all day, not surprisingly, the secretary had no new information. I left for Tel Aviv and the airport with my producer, Lawahez Jabari, who is Palestinian. Neither of us anticipated what we were about to experience at the airport.

Israel's airport security is justifiably celebrated for its efficiency and painstaking attention to detail. Less well known is that they use the pretext of airport security as a cover for an extraordinarily intrusive intelligence operation. It seems I fit their profile of a terror suspect. Even though we were well credentialed, were traveling with a veteran Israeli camera crew, and had a private plane waiting for us on the tarmac, we were interrogated for more than an hour. What triggered their suspicions? My passport carried stamps from places like Afghanistan, Pakistan, and most recently, Sudan. Although I was still wearing press passes proving I'd just left Shimon Peres and Condoleezza Rice in Jerusalem, the intelligence agents wanted to know how well I knew Lawahez, and why I had spent part of the day at Palestinian headquarters in Ramallah. Before it was over, I had to show scripts of my *Nightly News* stories and transcripts of my interviews. They were doing everything but editing my reports—and who knows where the transcripts ended up.

As we waited on the tarmac impatiently, the runway was suddenly ablaze with the headlights of an approaching motorcade. It was Condoleezza Rice. Barely a hundred yards away, Rice and her entourage, along with all my colleagues, were boarding that iconic blue-and-white military plane with the stars and stripes on its tail. They'd be home in twelve hours. I was embarking on another adventure.

We landed in Sharm el-Sheikh at three in the morning. After failing to spot one thousand pounds of TNT buried under vegetables in Isuzu trucks being driven down the Peace Road, Egyptian police had finally figured out how to prevent another car bombing. They simply blocked all vehicles from approaching any of the hotels. Unfortunately, that meant we had to unload crates of television equipment and walk the last half mile to get to the front door and check in. Perhaps this explains why in the middle of the night, in a haze of sleep deprivation, I stumbled and broke a toe.

After three simultaneous bombings that killed as many as 88 people in separate locations, including a twenty-seven-year-old American woman, and wounded 150 more, hospitals were exercising triage. My toe was of little importance. So for the next few days, I hobbled around, struggling to interview Egyptian police and the provincial governor. Most devastating was a visit to an open-air market where charred wreckage from one of the three car bombs was still strewn about in the street.

Surveying the destruction, local officials told me the terrorist had likely been stopped at a checkpoint when he got to the square, so triggered his bomb before he'd planned. The clock tower had stopped at the moment of the blast: ten after one in the morning. Without intending to, the suicide bomber may have even survived, escaping on foot. Eventually, authorities determined that all the attackers were homegrown, perhaps inspired by Osama bin Laden but not taking orders directly from him.

—

The Sinai bombings illustrated a trend as local terrorists evolved in the years since 9/11, adopting the tactics of bin Laden and "al-Qaeda Central" without necessarily taking direction from them. Other attacks—such as the London bombings in July 2005 and the attacks in Madrid a year earlier—were more likely perpetrated by lineal offshoots of bin Laden's organization. Five years after 9/11, the terror organization was proliferating into dozens of local groups and imitators, harder to track, but perhaps not as well disciplined and therefore easier to penetrate.

But as we were to learn in the summer of 2006, al-Qaeda and its affiliates often returned to the scenes of crimes, both real and imagined. During a month when the world was already agonizing over the war in Lebanon and northern Israel, a foiled plot to blow up airplanes in flight reminded us again of the potential for unexpected and unimaginable horror. A few days later, I saw the president at the State Department. He had just met with Rice, Vice President Cheney, and the rest of the national security team to evaluate both Middle East diplomacy and counterterror efforts.

The White House had scheduled a series of events to highlight the war on terror and deemphasize Iraq—an obvious campaign strategy to reinforce an issue on which the president still enjoyed support. Only a week earlier, Connecticut senator Joe Lieberman had lost his primary election contest to Ned Lamont, an antiwar Democrat riding a wave of liberal blogs and groups like MoveOn.org. From his vacation home in Wyoming, the vice president called wire service reporters the next day to drive home the administration's new talking points about the national security implications of the win for an antiwar Democrat. He wasn't subtle: "The thing that's partly disturbing about it is the fact that, the standpoint of our adversaries, if you will, in this conflict, and the al-Qaeda types, they clearly are betting on the proposition that ultimately they can break the will of the American people in terms of our ability to stay in the fight and complete the task."

Now, the president had come to the State Department to herald Rice's hard-fought victory at the United Nations three days earlier. After failing to negotiate a halt in the violence while shuttling between Israel and Lebanon, she'd had to settle for a much weaker UN resolution than she'd been demanding. It did not establish who would disarm Hezbollah or give a multinational force real military power to intervene. Presidential visits to the Pentagon were routine. Stopping at Foggy Bottom was not. This was a calibrated effort to shift the focus from Rumsfeld to Rice, from the bloodshed in Iraq to a brand new cease-fire in Lebanon. Even though the war had ended badly for Israel, and therefore, for the United States, a newly emboldened Iran was defying demands that it give up its nuclear research. Israel no longer appeared invincible to its enemies. Hezbollah's leader had achieved heroic status throughout the Middle East.

The subtext of that day's presidential appearance was the unprecedented code red alert on flights from London five days earlier. But whatever White House political strategist Karl Rove's motive for capitalizing on the war on terror, there was no mistaking Bush's passion about the subject when he answered questions from a small group of us at the end of the day. To the president, combating the threat of global terrorism was a lot more than a political game plan or a campaign slogan.

As I had first learned as a cub reporter—even earlier, as a "copyboy"—there is no substitute for personally witnessing an event, or meeting a politician face-to-face. It is why I always wanted to travel with Ronald Reagan and Bill Clinton to major events when I covered their presidencies. Now, because of budget cuts and the constant deadlines of cable news, we often don't have the luxury of seeing things first hand. Given this opportunity to form my own impression, I was immediately struck by how Bush's eyes flashed with conviction, even zeal, when talking about terrorism, in a way that is difficult to fully understand from reading his comments, or watching him on television.

Chopping the air with his hands for greater emphasis, the president said: "The world got to see—got to see what it means to confront terrorism. I mean, it's the challenge of the twenty-first century. The fight against terror, a group of ideologues, by the way, who use terror to achieve an objective—this is the challenge. And that's why . . . I spoke about the need for those of us who understand the blessings of liberty to help liberty prevail in the Middle East. And the fundamental question is, can it? And my answer is, absolutely, it can. . . . And by that I mean people want to be free. One way to put it is I believe mothers around the world want to raise their children in a peaceful world. That's what I believe."

It was as clear a statement as I'd ever heard of the Bush doctrine—unambiguous and arguably simplistic, but the central thesis informing decisions that have dramatically changed our world since 9/11. Approaching the fifth anniversary of that attack, only days after the British had foiled another possible plot to blow up passenger planes, the president also blamed his predecessors—implicitly, including his father.

"For decades, American policy sought to achieve peace in the Middle East by promoting stability in the Middle East. Yet the lack of freedom in the region meant anger and resentment grew, radicalism thrived, and terrorists found willing recruits. We saw the consequences on September the eleventh, 2001."

Friends of Bush's father have told me how they cringe when the son criticizes "the old man." The contrast between the elder Bush's decision to stop at Iraq's border—to avoid what he feared would become civil war—and his son's invasion is one of the most bizarre, and painful, chapters in American history. That Condoleezza Rice—a protégé of the father's and his top advisor, Brent Scowcroft—is now reversing their policies (and some of her own) only adds to the human drama. George W. Bush's secretary of state has set out to shift the course of years of decision making. She sees this as an era of change in foreign policy—no less important than the one we entered at the end of the Second World War. For this, she and the president have been accused of everything from genocide to fuzzy thinking. Surely, even their harshest critics will acknowledge that it is more complicated than that.

In this book I try to portray the human beings behind the caricatures, sharing what I've learned about the ideologies and motivations of powerful men and women like George W. Bush and Condoleezza Rice. And I want to make journalism less mysterious, and I hope, less sinister. How do we reporters filter out our own opinions? Most people think we don't. In fact, deciding what is important—what constitutes news—is subjective. But most of us are agnostic about the issues we cover. Yes, we tend to be antiestablishmentarian, and that mindset can breed its own bias, especially when covering powerful industries, like energy. (It's been my experience that corporate leaders are often their worst enemies.) But outside of talk shows—a different genre—we reporters don't advocate. Many of us are driven by the desire to expose malfeasance and correct societal wrongs—as in the exposure of the government's failed response to Hurricane Katrina. My passion is not partisan advantage. It's storytelling about the colorful, inspiring, crooked, cantankerous, arrogant, self-serving, and self-sacrificing people I meet every day in politics and government.

The job can be maddening. I have to explain complex decisions under the pressure of deadlines and competition, in the increasingly combative atmosphere of a super-heated news media. The velocity of new information is at times overwhelming: new technologies have expanded our reach beyond anything I ever imagined when I first wrote stories for my hometown paper. Now, we blog, appear hourly on cable, record newscasts for cell phones, file columns for the Web. In this digital universe, the era of collecting string all day to weave into a textured report exclusively for the evening news is over. The personal stakes are getting higher, too; more journalists have died in Iraq than in any previous conflict. Sometimes, we fail, as we did before the start of the Iraq war—for reasons I detail in this book. I would like to believe we have learned to be less credulous, but inevitably, our collective failure on Iraq has contributed to the intense suspicion with which the mainstream media is often viewed to this day.

I've written this book for people who love politics and journalism, but occasionally hate politicians and journalists. I hope that by showing the human interactions that go into covering Congress or the White House or the State Department, people will better understand the successes and failures of both government and the news media. And why we reporters never stop chasing after that elusive next story—all the while, loving the chase.

PREFACE

Miss Virginia Clair could have been the character played by Rosalind Russell in *His Girl Friday*—the film remake of Ben Hecht and Charles MacArthur's newsroom classic, *The Front Page.* I idealized her as a tough, wisecracking newspaperwoman in a man's world. Appearing tall and imposing, at least to an eleven-year-old, she wore a hat and, improbably, gloves. As I remember her, she was never without a cigarette. The newsroom was a noisy, dark place in a sliver of a building on the corner of North Avenue and Main Street in my hometown of New Rochelle, New York. As the school editor of *The Standard Star,* Miss Clair was a pathbreaker. She had started, as women invariably did, writing "social" news, as part of the women's department, in 1947. Her salary was thirty-five dollars a week, her first byline a baby announcement. Four years later, she had worked her way up to assistant school editor, and by 1955, inhabited the top schools job herself.

I can't recall seeing another woman in the newsroom. Clearly, she had struggled to carve out a place for herself. Today, even she acknowledges that she was "tough" on us school reporters—one from each of the city's nine elementary schools, plus an alternate. Certainly, to this sixth grader, she was very intimidating.

I had won my "job" as school reporter for my elementary school in a writing competition. The assignment was simple: I'd go to all the other classrooms and collect stories about their latest projects. Mr. Paolicelli's class was doing a social studies report on New York State history; Mrs. Kinsler's class was having a mathematics contest. I was to choose the best examples and write about them.

On Tuesday afternoons after school, my mother would drive me downtown with my stories. New Rochelle in those days was a bedroom community of seventy-five thousand people, described by George M. Cohan in his 1906 musical as "Forty-Five Minutes From Broadway." We lived in the "north end," and I attended the Roosevelt School, named after Theodore, not Franklin. Unlike the rest of the town's population, the children in my elementary school were largely Jewish émigrés from Brooklyn or, in my case, the Bronx. For our family, having a split-level house in the suburbs with a backyard was a step up from the apartment building in the city where we'd lived until I turned six. New Rochelle had large Italian-American and African-American populations and a highly competitive school system, but until I went to junior and senior high school, I had little contact with children from different backgrounds. Our little neighborhood was an enclave on a dead end, ideal for riding bikes and playing softball. Always at the center of the action was my father, the pied piper of the block, organizing pickup softball games and eventually coaching Little League.

On those trips downtown to submit my news stories, I would sit in the passenger seat of the gray Olds with rear fins and a broad white stripe, hunched over as I balanced my lined notepad on my knees. In a pattern that has persisted over the decades, I was often late, scribbling my final version, or at least copying it over, in the car. Miss Clair was not happy about sloppy additions. She had a deep, throaty voice and edited with quick strokes of a soft pencil. I would stand nervously, watching her read the copy. Even if she liked it, which she rarely if ever telegraphed, that did not mean it would make it into print. There was a lot of competition from the other schools. I can still recall the stress of not knowing whether my work would make it into print until the schools column appeared every Friday afternoon.

Even at age eleven, there was a thrill when I saw my byline, and heard my voice on the air for the first time. My first broadcast? Making the morning announcements for my elementary school on the public address system. To this day, I remember feeling nervous in front of that microphone when I said, "Good morning, boys and girls. This is Andrea Mitchell reporting from the principal's office." From such moments ambitions are born. For as many years as I have been reporting, there is still a kick watching my stories on the news.

I've often thought about why I so love daily journalism. Fundamentally, it's the sheer joy of storytelling, the spinning of the narrative itself. It's like reading a good novel, or watching a movie. How will the story end? What will be the outcome of that close Senate vote? On the most exciting stories, honest reporters will tell you that we have no idea either.

Separately, there is the excitement of being an eyewitness to history. As journalists we are privileged because we gain entry to places where the average reader or viewer cannot go. Once we are there, it's our mission to relay the facts and more—context, background, the larger meaning of events. Often the challenge is to provide the right words to give focus to the lasting images that, stitched together, create our visual history. Even now, the moment that captures the beginning of the end of the Cold War for me is Ronald Reagan in Berlin on a June day in 1987 demanding that Mikhail Gorbachev tear down that wall. It is indelible, because I was there. Just as I will always recall the September morning in 1993 when Yitzhak Rabin and Yasser Arafat finally shook hands on the South Lawn of the White House, representing the first real hope that Israelis and Palestinians could someday live together in peace.

That day on the White House lawn, I stood on a box that raised me to eye level with the camera. As the two lifelong enemies reached toward each other, past Bill Clinton, to shake hands, the cheers were so loud from the invited guests that I could barely hear Tom Brokaw's questions through my earpiece. Only Clinton and his closest aides knew how tense that moment actually was for the participants. As former U.S. Middle East negotiator Dennis Ross later explained, Rabin had made Clinton promise to block Arafat if he tried to embrace the Israeli leader. Rabin was willing to shake hands as a step toward peace. Hugging the man he still thought of as a terrorist was going too far. It is a story that perfectly captures the ambivalence Israel felt about entering into a long-term relationship with the Palestinians.

On a much less elevated plane than becoming an eyewitness to history, being a journalist lets you satisfy the guilty pleasure of enjoying rumor, gossip, and special access to uncommon knowledge. Along with these impulses comes the nobler aspiration of educating and informing the public. We broadcasters also have that performer's gene, generating oversized egos that need constant nourishment.

Being a reporter has transported me from a row house in Philadelphia to a yurt on the steppes of Mongolia. I've tangled with politicians of all types and presidents of every political persuasion. I've been tossed out of bed by an earthquake and a NATO air strike on the same night in Belgrade, and had my job threatened by figures ranging from a big-city mayor to the chief of staff of the president of the United States. Along the way, from Kabul to Havana, I've seen courage and generosity that define the best of the human spirit. In the rain forests of Jonestown, Guyana, I've also witnessed how evil unchecked can twist the human heart and mind. From wartime to peace, through struggles over race, gender, and economic justice, I've been privileged to cover politics and foreign policy during the administrations of every president from Jimmy Carter to George W. Bush.

From the vantage point of a front-row seat, this is that story, and mine. It is the story of a woman who made her way in an old boys' world, ever Miss Clair's eager pupil, inspired not just by Miss Clair but also by amateur detective Nancy Drew and comic strip character Brenda Starr. In my dreams, I was that detective or that "Girl Reporter," eager to uncover plots and investigate mysteries—gutsy, glamorous, and ageless, an independent woman leading a fabulous life.

It hasn't always been a smooth ride, and I didn't often have a "roadster" or a plan of action as reliable as Nancy Drew's. But to this day I love digging for details, speed-dialing to find eyewitnesses, persuading insiders to talk. In a way I am still the police reporter I was trained to be as a young journalist in Philadelphia, puzzling things out, looking for the story behind the story, trailing a breaking lead the way I first responded to the bell when a fire alarm went off. It doesn't matter whether the final result will help one side or the other. The chase and the reporting are the reward.

Our job as journalists is to throw ourselves into this great game, celebrating moments of political courage while never hesitating to expose hypocrisy and corruption. Sometimes, that requires "talking back" to power, whether to presidents, dictators, or lesser scoundrels. That is still my mission today, as clearly as it was the first day I entered a newsroom, eager to share the latest news from the sixth grade.

CHAPTER 1

Copyboy

I'm not sure how I got to be so pushy. In the beginning, and even now, I wanted to emulate Miss Virginia Clair and be a lady and an ace reporter at the same time. It's a balancing act I'm still sorting out after nearly four decades in the business. Though I'm viewed by many of my colleagues (and my subjects) as aggressive, I see myself rather differently, as shy, trying to overcome a basic reserve and bookishness.

My mother, a first-generation American who lived through the Great Depression and World War II, used to worry that I was *too* tough when questioning political figures. As a younger woman she had a fear of authority, and she couldn't figure out where I'd developed such a "fresh mouth," as she put it. But I'd always been something of a rebel, getting into trouble talking back to teachers at school or cracking jokes in class. Maybe it has something to do with being the middle child of three, eager to carve out my niche and attract attention in my own way.

My parents provided an example of lives lived with a deep sense of purpose and a strong code of behavior. To them, and to most of their generation, nothing was as important as the work ethic. We were not just encouraged to perform; we were expected to outdistance all of our peers. If we came home with a score of ninety-five on a test, our father would ask, only half-jokingly, what happened to the other five points? Perfectionism was a family disease. I'm certain that my parents are responsible for the seriousness with which I tackled my new profession, even as a fledgling reporter. It was not a great leap from their lessons of social responsibility to my unquestioning belief as a young adult that journalism was a mission.

We were supposed to be adversaries of those in power, wardens against abuses and conflicts of interest. Both of my parents came from tightly knit Jewish families. A big part of their life was building and supporting community organizations, as well as sustaining the synagogue. In particular, my father came from a long line of scholarly, observant Jews, and took the traditions very seriously. From an early age, we were taught that we had a moral and religious obligation to give back to society.

My father built a business, manufacturing furniture and housewares, and ran it for forty years. After he finally sold it to new owners, they asked him to stay on, which he did; his attempts to leave always elicited eager offers of a more accomodating schedule, until he was past eighty. My mother worked just as hard, first as a homemaker and volunteer, then as a school administrator. She organized visits to nursing homes for our Girl Scout troop and spent years playing the piano at a school for children with developmental disabilities. Teaming up with a friend who was a former Rockette, my mother knew, intuitively, that music and dance would be good therapy. And although she began on the women's auxiliary of the local symphony orchestra, before long she was the president of the orchestra's board. When she had a goal in mind, nothing could stop her.

My family was always interested in politics. Even before we moved to the suburbs, my mother took my older sister and me to watch major events—like the first televised inaugural when Harry Truman was sworn in as president in 1949—on a television set in a store window near our apartment in the Bronx. Once we had our own television, I recall our parents watching the Army-McCarthy hearings, and being outraged by Joe McCarthy. As kids, we traded I LIKE IKE and ALL THE WAY WITH ADLAI buttons in elementary school. And by the time I was in high school, John F. Kennedy was debating Richard Nixon, Martin Luther King, Jr., was marching for civil rights, and the dinner-table conversations with my older sister and younger brother were dominated by arguments over the Vietnam War.

We all went to a public high school that was a hotbed of political activity. A stone building, it was beautifully situated on twin lakes that were perfect for ice-skating excursions with our father during the winter. But the bucolic atmosphere barely masked the temper of the times. The local NAACP organized groups to demonstrate at Woolworth's lunch counter, part of a national protest. A few more daring students became Freedom Riders down south. The entire school mourned the death of Mickey Schwerner, one of the three civil rights workers killed in Philadelphia, Mississippi, whose mother was our popular biology teacher. According to testimony in the 1967 trial of eighteen suspects, Mickey, twenty-four when he died, was known to the Klansmen as Goatee or Jew Boy. Four decades later, a seventy-nine-year-old preacher was finally indicted for the murders.

But even more than politics or public service, my adolescence was dominated by music. My mother, a fine pianist, gave boundless time and energy to foster our musical educations. Tirelessly, she juggled a complicated after-school schedule and ferried me to violin and piano lessons, choir practice, All-County Orchestra, and eventually, rehearsals for the Philharmonic Symphony of Westchester, a community symphony. My sister, Susan, played the piano, string bass, and bassoon; my brother, Arthur, played the cello. We had two pianos in our home, in order to play duets. Often, we fell asleep listening to our mother downstairs, playing Chopin nocturnes or Beethoven's Moonlight Sonata. The school system also made music education easily accessible. I was in first grade when a teacher first put a violin in my hands. Practicing was a joy, not a chore. I could close my bedroom door, shut out the rest of the family, and transport myself into a self-created world of beautiful sound. A junior high school teacher took us to the Metropolitan Opera, exposing me to rehearsals of *La Bohème* and *Lohengrin*. School choirs gave me my first chance to sing Christmas carols and, later, more advanced liturgical music.

I loved all types of music and listened to everything, even if it meant sneaking a radio under the bedcovers to hear jazz when my parents thought I was asleep. Because I lived so close to New York City, a favorite high school date was a trip to Greenwich Village to a jazz club. Being underage, I borrowed an ID from my older sister to get in. On Christmas Eve, her boyfriend Lewis Greenstein—later to become my brother-in-law—took us to Alexander Schneider's chamber music concerts at Carnegie Hall.

Having a sister so close in age—only two years older—was critical to shaping the person I have become. When we were four and six years old, she protected me from street bullies and taught me to read. As I became an awkward adolescent, she overlooked my sillier obsessions—like the fantasy that I could become a cheerleader—and concentrated on the serious stuff, like helping me prepare for college. This early love of teaching persisted, leading her to a career as a college professor in two widely different fields: British and African literature. Of course, being so close in age, we also fought as children, but our father's refrain—"You two will be each other's best friends when you are grown up"—has proven true. And I've often thought it was my special bond with my sister that helped me to develop strong friendships with other women, both in and out of work, for the rest of my life.

My siblings were less outgoing than I. In our family, I was the drama queen and classroom cutup. For two summers, my parents sent me to music school at the Aspen Music Festival, even though I was technically too young to qualify for the program. For a while, I thought I might even attend music school, like Juilliard or the Curtis Institute, rather than a liberal arts college. But soon I got beyond the stage where I could coast on whatever talent I had as something of a prodigy. In the world of professional music, I was not going to stand out.

So when I entered college, it was to study liberal arts. At the University of Pennsylvania, I studied English literature. My family and professors fully expected that I would go on to graduate school at Cambridge, England, where I had been accepted at one of the women's colleges, but I was determined to do something very different. It's difficult to recall what fueled my restlessness, but my parents had raised three very independent children. My sister and her husband went to Kenya as Peace Corps volunteers in 1966, when being in the Peace Corps was still considered very adventurous. My younger brother and his wife homesteaded in a remote section of northwest Canada, building a log house and running a general store in a small mining town.

My travel lust was satisfied more vicariously. I fell in love with broadcasting, with telling stories about other people's exploits. At first, I combined my love for English literature with educational radio by importing BBC programs on Chaucer and other writers for our campus radio station. When I proposed exploring further adaptations as part of graduate study in England, a faculty committee at Penn judging fellowship proposals dismissed the idea. Though I was groping toward the kind of programming produced successfully years later on *Masterpiece Theatre,* one of the committee members found the notion "vulgar." She and her husband, also a professor at Penn, were proud of not even owning a television. So instead of going to graduate school, I decided to take a stab at this vulgar profession.

———

Four years earlier, I had been introduced to broadcasting by accident. As a freshman at Penn, during a meeting on the top floor of Houston Hall, the student activity building, I heard music and wandered down the corridor to discover the studios of the university's fifty thousand-watt noncommercial radio station, WXPN. The format was almost entirely classical music, mixed with what we called folk music (some hillbilly, a lot of blues) on Saturday night, and jazz after midnight. They told me they could use help programming music, and before long I was hooked. I loved choosing the music, timing the cuts, balancing the selections. And more than anything, I loved performing on the air, introducing the pieces and reading notes about each composition. If I was in a hurry, I'd read the liner notes on the back of the albums. When I had more time, I dug deeper and researched the background of individual compositions.

Soon I had my own program, an hour of chamber music airing every Tuesday night at eight. Pretentiously, I called it "Musica da Camera." The theme was the third movement of Respighi's *Ancient Airs and Dances for the Lute.* I programmed my choices, back-timing each selection, and read introductions to fill the hour.

In those years, the station was entirely student operated, and we took ourselves very seriously. Nominally, we reported to the dean of students, but we were told the responsibility for protecting the FCC license that had been awarded to the university was entirely ours. The station had a four-person management team, by tradition and practice all male. Gradually I took on more and more responsibilities and by my second year became the first woman to break into their ranks by being selected to be program manager of the station. This could not have happened at the other Ivy League schools, even Cornell, which was coed; there was gender discrimination at Penn, but it was well known to have the fewest restrictions on women.

It was also a presidential election year, and as a member of a consortium of Ivy League radio stations, we participated in "network" coverage of election night. I had interviewed Barry Goldwater, the Republican nominee, when he came to campus to give a campaign speech. He was patient and responsive, much to my surprise, given my youth and inexperience. Heady stuff. As a result, I was a logical choice to go to Rockefeller Center in New York City and take part in election-night coverage for the Ivy stations and their radio audiences from Dartmouth to Columbia. The only problem was that when I checked in at the old Roosevelt Hotel near Grand Central Terminal, I was preregistered as "Andrew" Mitchell and assigned a roommate: a guy from Yale. It took me a while to get my own room.

Once again, no one in charge had given any thought to the possibility that a woman would be involved. I have no idea how we organized the coverage, except that I was assigned to broadcast results of the Senate races. All they expected me to do was rip and read the wire "leads," without doing any original reporting. It was pretty basic, but gave me a taste of how to combine my love of politics and broadcasting. By the summer of my senior year, I'd found a part-time job at KYW, one of Philadelphia's top radio stations and one of the first in the country to broadcast "all news, all the time." It wasn't to report the news. I only got in the door because my mother had forced her daughters to learn typing and shorthand as fallback insurance against life's surprises, and the station needed a summer-relief secretary.

Owned by Westinghouse Broadcasting, KYW Newsradio dominated the market and had a sister television station that was an NBC affiliate. As graduation neared, I decided to apply to the management-training program Westinghouse ran for young college graduates. Getting accepted was the easy part—the real challenge was persuading them to let me into the all-male newsroom. Instead, they tried to steer me toward jobs more traditionally held by women, in public relations or advertising, which didn't interest me at all. Finally, I told them I'd drop out of the management program if they'd give me an entry-level job in the newsroom for union wages, about fifty dollars a week.

With my Ivy League degree, I had talked my way into a job as a copyboy, which is what desk assistants were universally called in those days. I had to rip reams of wire reports spitting out from the old, clattering Teletype machines, then hang one copy on a nail in the wire room and distribute the others to the anchormen of each hour's newscast. It helped if you remembered which anchormen liked their coffee black and which took sugar and cream. Most of the men helped me learn the ropes. But some delighted in hazing me as the only woman in the newsroom. As best I could, I tried to deflect or ignore it.

To get interviews for their newscasts, I'd work the phones, calling locations to find someone I could interview when a story broke. In between, I'd edit and transcribe the "actualities"—that's what we called sound bites—from the interviews, and log incoming audio feeds from London and other Westinghouse bureaus.

They put me on the shift where they thought I could do the least harm, midnight to eight in the morning. Most of my friends were in graduate school, with more flexible hours. I felt isolated, especially because I had to try to sleep during the day. My social life was nonexistent. Working nights meant walking through the center of the city, crossing Philadelphia's Rittenhouse Square, to get to my graveyard shift. More than once the police stopped me, until I explained that I was a night worker, not a lady of the night. Although the hours were lousy, they were perfect for an apprentice reporter. The city reflected the national turmoil over race and the Vietnam War, often exploding on my watch.

———

Socially, Philadelphia was still a fairly provincial city, its business community governed by the mores of the Main Line. Politically, it was a cauldron of ethnic rivalries, dominated by competing Irish and Italian constituencies. When it came to political power, blacks need not apply. Add to this steaming stew the growing tensions over the Vietnam War and the movement for civil rights, and you had plenty of elements to fire the imagination of a novice journalist.

Sometimes, the opportunities were local crime stories, the bloodier the better for our audience. In 1967, the ambitious young district attorney, Republican Arlen Specter, who had developed the single-bullet theory of John F. Kennedy's assassination for the Warren Commission, was running for mayor. Specter was challenging the incumbent Democrat, James H. J. Tate. On the Saturday before the election, I was covering a Specter campaign rally on South Broad

Street when the head of the homicide division, an aggressive prose-cutor named Richard Sprague, wheeled up, jumped out of his car, and announced that a fugitive named Steven Weinstein had just been caught in Times Square.

Twenty-eight-year-old "Stevie" Weinstein, as the tabloid press called him, had run a tobacco shop near the Penn campus that had become a hangout for the college boys. The only problem was that one of the students had disappeared and later turned up in a trunk, floating in the Delaware River. A thirteen-state alarm was issued for the missing tobacconist. The lurid murder had become a campaign issue for the Democratic incumbent who accused his DA challenger of ignoring warnings about Weinstein's suspicious behavior. Now the murder suspect had been caught in Times Square, but much to the chagrin of the politically ambitious prosecutor, Weinstein was in the hands of the NYPD, beyond photo opportunity range for Specter until an extradition could be arranged from New York.

Without even finishing his speech, Specter jumped into a car with his aides and headed up the New Jersey Turnpike to handle the arraignment himself. I called my desk and was ordered to fol-low in hot pursuit. That's how I ended up in New York City, with barely a dime for a phone call, covering the booking of a murder suspect and trying to explain to nationally known correspondents like Homer Bigart of *The New York Times* why a simple arraignment was being argued by the district attorney of the City of Philadel-phia. Adding to the "color" of the story, Weinstein rode back to Philadelphia in Specter's car in handcuffs, with a pipe clenched be-tween his teeth.

For all of his grandstanding, Specter lost that election, although by only ten thousand votes. For me, it was a lively introduction to local politics. A year later, national politics were turned upside down by a dramatic announcement from the Oval Office. On Sunday evening, March 31, 1968, I was absentmindedly selecting tape cuts for upcom-ing newscasts as Lyndon Johnson addressed the nation in the after-math of North Vietnam's Tet Offensive. Suddenly, the president shocked the world by saying that with America's future challenged at home and abroad, "I will not seek nor will I accept" the party's nomination for a second term. It was an abdication of power that few people even in Washington had anticipated. Suddenly, adrenaline flowing, I was running tape and copy into the studio for the anchorman who, with no advance notice, had to deliver an entire newscast on the surprise development. It was only the beginning of what became a crash course in covering breaking news.

Later that same week, Martin Luther King, Jr., was assassinated. I'd kept a tape of his 1963 "I Have a Dream" speech on a shelf and scrambled to put together an obituary. Anticipating riots, Philadelphia's police commissioner, Frank Rizzo, declared a limited state of emergency and started shutting down the city's bars. The news director needed someone to cover what was happening in the streets, and I quickly volunteered. Grabbing a tape recorder, which in those days was an Ampex machine that weighed at least fifty pounds, I jumped into one of our "news wagons." It was painted red, white, and blue, with the logo ALL NEWS, ALL THE TIME bannered on both sides.

Feeling a little bit nervous, but not really scared, I drove to North Philadelphia, parked, and got out to interview people congregating on stoops and street corners. For the most part, they had poured from their walk-up apartments and the housing projects to share feelings of grief and outrage. Perhaps it was because of the partial curfew or the heavy police presence, but aside from some shattered storefronts, Philadelphia escaped the widespread violence that erupted in other American cities that night. Another factor that may have helped was the city's strong network of African-American civic leaders and ministers who worked hard to preserve the peace. Still, KYW repainted its mobile units soon afterward so that we could move around the neighborhoods more unobtrusively.

Only two months later, on June 5, I was home watching the returns from the Democratic primary election in California when Bobby Kennedy was shot. In what seemed like an instant replay of the shock and horror of the King assassination, America had witnessed another political murder and lost another leader. Without wasting time to call in, I ran through Rittenhouse Square to the newsroom, trying to absorb the impact of this shattering murder. The country seemed to be spinning out of control, and I was torn between my own reactions of grief and what seemed an inappropriately ghoulish desire to be part of the action, looking for a local angle to add to the national story. Finding none, I repressed my personal feelings of horror and pitched in as the newsroom scrambled to cover the story. I was learning a basic lesson of journalism: how to keep my own emotions in check when reporting on a tragic event. That year, we had too much practice.

———

For comic relief, there was plenty of colorful local politics to keep us busy in those years. Even before Watergate made investigative reporting fashionable, a young journalist could make her name covering corruption in Philadelphia. There was certainly enough of it. District Attorney Specter, today the state's senior senator but at the time the city's only Republican-elected office holder, was always investigating somebody. There were special grand juries, lots of indictments, and enough delays so that no one noticed the lack of convictions. Most of the Democratic politicians could have stepped out of the pages of a Damon Runyon story. There were men like the rotund leader of the city's congressional delegation, William Barrett, who wore spats, had a Tang-colored toupee, and returned from Washington each night to hold court in his row house neighborhood, passing out patronage.

When Barrett died only two weeks before the April primary in 1976, party bosses dictated that he be renominated from the grave. Scrambling to explain why on our morning newscast, I reached the local political boss, state senator Buddy Cianfrani. Cianfrani, who was later convicted of bribery and jailed at the federal penitentiary in Allenwood, Pennsylvania, explained the scheme: they were telling people to vote for the dead congressman so the party could handpick his successor. Their choice to replace him would be a little-known state legislator named Ozzie Myers. Later, as a member of Congress, Ozzie achieved notoriety on an FBI video for intoning, to explain his demand of a bribe during the FBI's undercover Abscam sting, the immortal words: "Money talks in this business and bullshit walks." The investigation led to the conviction of six House members and one senator, Harrison Williams of New Jersey.

By then an NBC correspondent, I got the network to chopper me to the parking lot of Philadelphia's sports stadium, knowing it was only blocks from Ozzie's home in South Philadelphia. We got there so fast I was able to talk him and his wife into an exclusive interview before he lawyered up. In October 1980, Myers became the first House member to be expelled from Congress since 1861, when three representatives were ousted for supporting the Confederacy during the Civil War.

But of all these colorful characters, none dominated the city's politics like the police commissioner and future mayor, Frank Rizzo. Larger than life, he was known to his fans and foes alike as the Big Bambino. Alternately, some people called him the Cisco Kid, because he wore pearl-handled revolvers, one on each hip. The barrel-chested police chief was the former head of the vice squad, notorious in those days for his celebrated busts and his busty girlfriend, stripper Blaze Starr. (She had earlier had a featured role in the private lives of Louisiana governor Earl Long and President Kennedy.) Loyal to his friends, Rizzo ran roughshod over his enemies. As police commissioner, he had become famous for outrages like ordering a group of Black Panthers to line up, face a wall, and drop their pants so he could bring in the news photographers to shoot their humiliation.

For stunts like that, he was idolized in many of the city's white wards and feared by minorities. The city was divided along a simple fault line: either you loved Frank Rizzo, or you hated him. In a city of neighborhoods segregated by race, his combustible personality only deepened the divide.

Rizzo had always enjoyed a fawning press corps, which made me very uncomfortable. As captain and then commissioner, he had fed the newspapers his version of reality, and the leaks greased his climb to the top. His notion of how to handle the few women reporters he encountered was fairly primitive. At first, he tried to charm us. If that didn't work, he tried intimidation. My verbal duels with him were legendary. At one point, during an antiwar rally, he even had one of his top lieutenants warn me that the civil disobedience unit was doing surveillance on one of my relatives, then a student on the Penn campus. The not-very-subtle message was that I should back off in my coverage of the police. It was frightening, but probably also stiffened my resolve.

By the time Rizzo ran for mayor in 1971, I was covering politics for KYW, having graduated from the police and schools beats. Rizzo's Republican opponent was Thacher Longstreth, the tall, courtly head of the chamber of commerce and former city council member. A Princeton graduate who favored bow ties, Longstreth was a perfect foil for Rizzo—the antithesis of the tough cop and urban legend he was opposing. The Republican civic leader might have carried the Main Line in suburban Philadelphia, but in a racially divided city, Rizzo embodied working class voters' resentments and aspirations. Although black Democratic voters defected, correctly reading Rizzo's law-and-order appeal as a coded racial message, the tough cop won with more than 53 percent of the vote.

The morning after he was elected, I interviewed the mayor-elect about his transition and, among other questions, asked whom he'd appoint to be his fire commissioner. To the shock of everyone listening, he laughed and said, "How about my brother?" He was serious, ignoring rules against nepotism to jump his kid brother several ranks and put him in the newly formed cabinet. It was a good hint of the way he planned to govern: headstrong, oblivious to ethical norms, and in a style entirely his own.

As a woman reporter among men, I knew that figuring out how to cover Rizzo as mayor was a special challenge. He was always ready with a cutting comment putting down women, but, paradoxically, that may have helped me to be a better journalist. His barbs only inspired me to ask tougher questions. Not that Rizzo was unique in his patronizing attitude toward women.

James Tate, the man Rizzo was succeeding, was just as bad. At a farewell news conference with Tate, I asked about a major controversy, the city's failure to win international approval for an international bicentennial exposition. Tate said, "The one thing about not being mayor is I don't have to answer your questions any longer, *little girl.*" He might as well have slapped my face. I was the top broadcast political reporter in town, and in an instant I felt like a ten-year-old who had just been dressed down by the teacher.

Rizzo took office and started remaking city government in his own image. KYW carried his news conferences live, and they soon became celebrated confrontations between the bullying mayor and the handful of reporters willing to take him on. On one occasion, *The Philadelphia Inquirer* reported that the police had shot an unarmed teenager in the back in West Philadelphia. The community was outraged. I called the mayor to see if he would agree to investigate the police. No, he said. "My men are right when they're right, and they're right when they're wrong and they're trying to be right."

The mayor called back a few minutes later to complain that his previous comments were off the record. No deals, I said, not after the fact. He was furious, and I was in trouble. After that, he was determined to make my life miserable.

Only years later did I learn from one of my early mentors, KYW's news director Fred Walters, that Rizzo had called at least once a week to try to get me fired. The complaints even went all the way up to the chairman of Westinghouse Broadcasting, Donald H. Mc-Gannon. Fred would tell the mayor to prove that I had been either inaccurate or unfair, and he would take action. Rizzo never produced the evidence and Fred never told me, he said, to avoid any "chilling effect" on my reporting.

I often wonder why I was either naïve or gutsy enough to confront Rizzo as I did. Six feet two inches tall and 250 pounds, he was tough, profane, powerful, and very intimidating. I found myself standing up to him almost as a matter of instinct, only afterward realizing that I was courting danger. At the same time, he charmed a lot of reporters, hiring some of the city's most experienced newsmen to become members of his cabinet. At one point he even suggested that I could be deputy managing director for housing. At fifty thousand dollars a year, it was a fortune compared to my starting salary of fifty dollars a week. But I knew my job was to be his adversary. It never occurred to me to accept.

The reporters who covered Rizzo worked in room 212, directly across from the mayor's office in City Hall, a baroque building that fills a large square around a central courtyard at the conjunction of Broad and Market streets, only blocks from the modest brick buildings where the Continental Congress wrote the Constitution. What would the Founders have thought of the way Frank Rizzo ran Philadelphia!

Our press room was filled with old desks and filing cabinets and reeked of cigar smoke, wafting from a side room that featured a nonstop pinochle game. Sometimes, they let me sit in and play a hand. I shared a corner of the room with a radio reporter from a competing station who kept a gun in his top drawer and occasionally brandished it to make a point. In this mix of men, some of whom actually wore porkpie hats, I was treated like a kid sister. It was an extended family, of sorts—except when I politely declined the case of booze delivered to each reporter from the city council president on Christmas Eve. Journalistic ethics, I murmured self-consciously, trying not to be so much of a bluestocking that I would stand out among my more easygoing colleagues.

In addition to the mayor's offices and city council chambers, City Hall housed the court of common pleas, the local criminal court. The corridors were lined with defendants awaiting trial, bail bondsmen, witnesses, lawyers, and other hustlers. The building was a quadrangle, with four wings each extending a city block long, the central core topped by the totemic statue of William Penn. The walls were a grimy tan. Restrooms could be found in each corner.

Ratio of men's rooms to women's facilities: three to one. When Rizzo, known for his well-creased pants and spit-polished shoes, took over, walls were soon repainted white, with blue and gold trim. The woodwork in his formal reception room was oiled and buffed. Carpets were replaced. He even consulted me about the color scheme, perhaps the best indication of what he thought was the appropriate role for a woman reporter.

But clearly, the take-charge new mayor meant business. Unfortunately for the city's taxpayers, that often meant business for his cronies. Reporters started investigating juicy contracts, like the ones awarded for airport construction and the new sports stadium to companies with suspicious City Hall connections. The state launched an inquiry into police corruption. And the head of the Democratic Party, Peter J. Camiel, accused Rizzo of offering him a political bribe, a trade of city contracts for the right to name the next candidate for district attorney—in the bathroom of the Bellevue Stratford Hotel, the same hotel where I later covered the first outbreak of Legionnaires' disease.

At the suggestion of an enterprising reporter, Zachary Stalberg of the *Philadelphia Daily News,* an afternoon tabloid, the two men agreed to take lie detector tests. As the city's former top law enforcement official was being strapped in, in full view of the press, he said, "I have great confidence in the polygraph. If this machine says a man lied, he lied."

The next day, the *Daily News* gleefully bannered the test results across its front page: RIZZO LIED, TESTS SHOW. In fact, he had lied on six out of ten questions. The story was colorful enough to get picked up by *The New York Times.*

Rizzo was already known nationally as the hard-line former cop who was the only big-city Democratic mayor to support Richard Nixon for reelection. Locally, he was the politician who would tell a news conference, without blushing, "Andy Mitchell, I'm so tough I'm gonna make Attila the Hun look like a faggot." Calling me by my nickname was a liberty he took deliberately. Being familiar was a way of belittling and co-opting us at the same time. Rizzo's heroes were Nixon, Moshe Dayan, Frank Sinatra, and J. Edgar Hoover—all tough guys. He held court at night in Palumbo's, a South Philadelphia Italian restaurant, but as soon as he was in office, he started building a stone family mansion in the tony WASP neighborhood of Chestnut Hill. Since there was no way that Rizzo could have afforded it on his public salary, the *Daily News* investigated and discovered that the mayor had accepted favors from contractors. Somehow, he got away with it.

On Wednesday, March 13, 1974, three years into his first term, what was left of his relationship with the press blew up when the mayor stormed out of a news conference that was being carried live on television and radio. According to an editorial in the *Daily News,* that day "Andrea Mitchell, KYW's soft-voiced but hard-nosed City Hall reporter, one of the best in the business, leads off the questioning. She asks the mayor about the issue that has the whole city talking, the police corruption report. Frank Rizzo, the man who pledged to run his administration in a fishbowl, passes. He'll only answer questions on parking at the airport, he tells reporters." It had been Rizzo's first news conference in four months, and it lasted all of five minutes.

There was another side of Rizzo, the one that made him such a successful politician. He had flair, an unstoppable ego, and a ribald sense of humor. When he rushed to the scene of a crime from a black-tie dinner one night, news photographers captured him in evening clothes, a nightstick stuck in his cummerbund. He had a police chief's desire to always be in the middle of the action, even if it meant tripping over a fire hose at a refinery fire and breaking his hip. This was the Rizzo who leveraged his endorsement of President Nixon's reelection into unusual access, for a Democrat, to Washington's Republican corridors of power. He was a huge political asset, the archetype of the "hard hat" Democrats Nixon hoped to convert into permanent Republicans. Rizzo was popular, even with the reporters who were most skeptical about his behavior. And he went to extraordinary lengths to try to co-opt his adversaries, especially in the press corps.

On January 24, 1972, Rizzo brought us along as he headed to Washington to see Richard Nixon. He bragged that he had so much clout he could get all of us into the Oval Office with him. When we arrived at the White House, we were ushered into the press briefing room, in those days crowded with cuspidors and overstuffed brown leather armchairs. While the mayor met with the president, we waited, clearly sticking out as a collection of local yokels in that assemblage of older, national correspondents. That is, until White House deputy press secretary Gerald Warren appeared in the doorway to the lower press office to ask if the Philadelphia press corps would come forward to be escorted to the Oval Office.

In a White House photo of that day, I'm the one hanging back, watching Rizzo introduce my newspaper colleagues to the president. All I remember is being so overwhelmed at finding myself in the Oval Office that I forgot to take notes. But Nixon's secret Oval Office taping system captured the moment: there, you can hear Rizzo introduce me to the president saying, "Oh, and Andrea Mitchell there is the political lady for KYW."

The tapes also reveal that during their private talks before we were brought in, Rizzo tried to ingratiate himself with Nixon, telling the president he didn't support Democratic leaders like Hubert Humphrey or Edmund Muskie. "Their philosophy is completely, it's not my thinking. I guess I must say I'm for President Nixon."

The two men also discussed what they called "the extreme left" and confided their sensitivities about race relations. Nixon said to Rizzo: "I know they say that we're a bunch of racists."

Rizzo replied reassuringly, "Let me tell you this, Mr. President, in my opinion, you have the blacks like I have the blacks."

The official tape log reveals that Nixon aide John Ehrlichman also attended the meeting, and that the men discussed whether Rizzo, as a Democrat, would campaign for Nixon. Later, we all had lunch with the mayor at Paul Young's, a lobbyists' hangout and the mayor's favorite Washington restaurant. He bragged: "I told you I'd get you in to see the president. I told you he was a good friend of mine." He was so proud of his accomplishment that I bet him fifty bucks he couldn't get us into his next meeting, with FBI director J. Edgar Hoover.

When we arrived at FBI headquarters after lunch, the same scenario unfolded. The grizzled veterans of the press room scoffed at our expectation that we would see Hoover, who had not been seen by any press in months. Before long, we were again ushered in for handshakes. Hoover's desk was on an elevated platform, and I was so nervous about meeting him, I tripped as we arrayed ourselves around him for a photo session. I recall Hoover's face appearing ashen and waxy: was this the real FBI director, or had we wandered into Washington's version of Madame Tussaud's? Rizzo had once again demonstrated his clout, and I was out fifty dollars.

This was my first taste of Washington, but my appetite had already been whetted for national politics. In 1968, I'd aggressively driven my KYW Newsradio mobile unit right into Hubert Humphrey's motorcade along Chestnut Street, wedging my way into line in front of the press bus while I broadcast on the two-way radio. A not-very-friendly Secret Service agent yanked open the car door as I drove, ordering me out of the motorcade and abruptly interrupting my report.

By 1972, I was assigned to cover both parties' national conventions in Miami Beach. On the floor of the Democratic convention, Pennsylvania governor Milton Shapp called me over to meet one of his colleagues. "Andrea," he said, "this is the governor of Georgia, Jimmy Carter. He's going to be our party's next candidate for president."

I remember sizing up Carter—an obscure politician of average appearance and no national reputation—and thinking that Shapp had lost his mind. Few people had ever heard of the Georgia governor, and at the time the party was about to nominate a far more liberal standard-bearer, George McGovern. The moment stuck in my mind. He was the first of many little-known political figures whom I would meet at political conventions, long before they became major players.

The Democratic convention was tame, despite the brouhaha over McGovern's initial choice for running mate, Senator Thomas Eagleton, because of the Missouri senator's past electric shock therapy treatments. It was a different story a month later at the Republican convention, held in the middle of violent antiwar protests. I was assigned to "dress down" and cover the students rioting outside. My bureau chief apparently thought that I looked young enough to fit right in. As a result, the night Richard Nixon was renominated, I was trapped outside with a crowd of demonstrators being peppergassed in Flamingo Park. Temporarily blinded, I ran into an apartment building on Collins Avenue and banged on the nearest door. A kindly elderly couple cracked the door, listened to my pleas for help, and helped wash my burning eyes.

Four years later, I'd gone a long way toward establishing my reputation as an experienced political reporter, at least at the local level. I'd covered Minnesota senator Walter Mondale's abortive run for president in 1974 and Washington senator Henry "Scoop" Jackson's defeat in the 1976 Pennsylvania primary. Once again, in 1976 KYW radio sent me to cover both national conventions—the Republicans in Kansas City and the Democrats at Madison Square Garden in New York City.

It was a great introduction to national politics. In those years, I worked alongside my television colleague from KYW, Jessica Savitch. Jessica, who later came to NBC, died in 1983 in a car accident when she was only thirty-five. I tracked the critical role Pennsylvania's delegation played in the hard-fought battle for the nomination between Ronald Reagan and Gerald Ford. When Ford debated Carter at the Walnut Street Theatre in the fall campaign, I helped anchor Westinghouse's radio coverage. Chasing the candidates and their strategists was the culmination of all the political conversations I'd loved since childhood, at our family dinner table. I knew I'd chosen the right career.

———

The morning after that debate, the president campaigned in South Philadelphia's Italian Market for a young congressman running for the Senate, John Heinz. I had covered Heinz's congressional campaigns, but had never before met his wife, Teresa, a doctor's daughter from Mozambique. On that day, completely overlooked in the crowd around the president and her husband, she seemed overwhelmed by the crush of people. I suggested we duck into a greengrocer on the corner, assuring her she'd never be missed. It was the start of a relationship that continued through the election and Senate service of her husband, who distinguished himself working on environmental issues and helping to preserve the fiscal solvency of Social Security.

Jack Heinz could have stepped out of a Fitzgerald novel, except that, unlike Gatsby, Heinz's air of quiet confidence was not faked. His wife, Teresa, was a reluctant recruit into the world of politics, although already passionate about her causes. But, the young Teresa was primarily a mother and homemaker who tended to defer to her husband on most subjects. She and Jack were a couple so blessed with brains, good looks, and great fortune that his death in a freak plane accident seemed all the more shocking.

On April 4, 1991, Jack Heinz was flying to a district committee hearing in Pennsylvania for his subcommittee on aging, part of his ongoing investigation into Medicare fraud. Instruments on his private plane indicated that the landing gear had jammed. A passing helicopter volunteered to fly by and do a visual check to see if the gear had descended. It flew too close and its rotor blade sliced the senator's plane, which exploded. Both aircraft landed in a suburban schoolyard, killing seven people, including the senator and two children on the ground.

By then a national correspondent in Washington for NBC, I was driving back from an assignment when we got the first word. The office asked me to confirm the loss. It was one of many times in my career when I found myself torn between personal emotion and professional obligation. I drove to Teresa's home in Georgetown, expressed my sorrow, and, despite feelings of conflict over my dual role, returned to the bureau to write Jack's obituary for *Nightly News.*

That night, a visibly shaken Tom Brokaw, who had been friends with Jack, said the senator was "a man who had it all, but he never took it for granted." Struggling for the right words to convey Jack's special qualities, now forever lost, I described a man who could have lived a life of great leisure, but instead gave himself to public service, a man who still had much to give, and died too young.

Teresa was shattered. Encircled by family and friends, she retreated into her grief, briefly considering, and refusing, the ritual party offer to accept appointment to her husband's Senate seat and later run to fill out his term. Instead, she answered a different call, taking over the family's immensely complex charities. Gradually, she transformed herself into an effective CEO, without losing the values or the soft, even quirky, qualities that made her uniquely "Teresa." A year after Jack's death, she had so much emotional clout in Pennsylvania politics that a single campaign advertisement endorsing his Republican colleague, Pennsylvania senator Arlen Specter, was enough to reelect him in a close race. It was not surprising that this woman who disdained politics might learn to love it, and eventually find a new life with another tall, athletic senator educated at Yale, a man Jack Heinz had first introduced her to on Earth Day in 1990—John Kerry of Massachusetts.

As much as I loved my life in Philadelphia, if you want to cover national politics, there is only one place to go—Washington. Even though I was at home with the rhythms and neighborhoods of Philadelphia, and knew the city's deepest political secrets, it was in some ways too comfortable. I knew it was time to move on.

———

The CBS affiliate in Washington, WTOP, needed someone to cover the corruption trial of the governor of Maryland, Marvin Mandel, who had been indicted on more than twenty separate counts of fraud and racketeering. It seemed tailor-made for someone who had cut her teeth covering Frank Rizzo. The news director at the Washington station was a broadcast legend, James Snyder, a CBS veteran who had already trained a long list of future star correspondents. And the owner, Katharine Graham of *The Washington Post,* was known to run one of the best broadcasting companies in the business. To my surprise, the mayor gave me a farewell dinner and presented me with a gold-rimmed City of Philadelphia "Liberty" bowl.

The station lived up to Mrs. Graham's high journalistic standards, in contrast to the "if it bleeds, it leads" motto of many local stations. Snyder had figured out that the Washington audience of federal workers and political junkies wanted to see news of their government. As a result, unlike at most local stations, we were often assigned to what were actually national news stories. I covered congressional hearings, Carter White House stories, and several Supreme Court arguments, including the landmark Bakke reverse discrimination case. At a time when the Equal Rights Amendment was big news, Jim sent me to Houston to cover the first National Women's Conference.

For all our focus on national news, one of my most memorable stories involved me facing down a redneck tow truck operator in rural Maryland suspected of running a stolen-car ring. It became known as "Andrea versus the junkyard dog." I'd gotten a tip that the ring was cannibalizing stolen cars that were too hot to fence and selling off their spare parts. My cameraman, Kline Mengle, and I drove out to the junkyard to interview the guy. Furious, the man charged into poor Kline. The resulting videotaped confrontation was such an uneven matchup that it's hilarious. All of five feet three inches, I jumped in between the two men, trying to protect my cameraman.

The suspect then shouted that he was going to get his shotgun. On the tape, you can see me following the guy into his run-down trailer, pleading, "Please, sir, we just want to talk to you." Sir, no less! When he came out waving his gun, we finally retreated. I did return a few more times, but with the police—who arrested the ring on charges of auto theft.

But most notably, I specialized in covering a different kind of scoundrel, the political variety. My news director felt all those years tracking Philadelphia's Democratic political machine qualified me to tackle the colorful characters of Maryland's crony politics, made nationally famous during the bribery investigation of the state's former governor, then–vice president Spiro Agnew.

There was Irv Kovens, the godfather of Mandel's crowd, who financed all his campaigns, and Bootsie, the governor's estranged wife, who locked him out of the Governor's Mansion in Annapolis when she discovered he was having an affair with a beautiful blonde whom he later married. In the course of the bribery trial, the governor broke down while discussing his divorce settlement, for which he had borrowed forty-two thousand dollars from an order of Roman Catholic missionaries for back alimony payments. Who could make this up?

The federal trial was in Baltimore, forty-five miles from my home in Washington. I'd speed up I-95 to get to court in time each morning. During a rare July 4 court session in 1977, I got *two* speeding tickets, five miles apart. Meeting me in Baltimore each day was a courtroom artist, Roxie Munro, a freelancer who later left Washington to become a highly successful graphic artist, with many *New Yorker* covers to her credit. During the course of the lengthy trial, in the late seventies, profound technological changes were transforming our business, the first of many tectonic shifts that expanded our reach as broadcasters. When the trial began, we were commuting to and from Baltimore. By the time it was over, we were reporting live, by satellite, a new technology that revolutionized our profession.

At first, I could cover only the morning and early afternoon testimony, ordering artwork to illustrate key witnesses, before having to race back to Washington in time to go live on the six o'clock news. Roxie would finish painting the illustrations in the backseat of my mustard brown Toyota, waving the poster-sized sketches out the car window to dry them in the breeze. I would drive down I-95 and outline my script at the same time, but without the benefit of a cell phone or any other means to communicate my progress to the editors. We'd run into the newsroom and give the sequence of sketches to the director. Then, at the very last minute, I'd put the illustrations, some barely dry, on easels in the studio. The control room would switch back and forth among the illustrations, as the stage manager flipped the cards by hand and I narrated my text, sitting next to Gordon Peterson, the anchorman.

Rarely did we have time to tape anything in advance. Gordon, a veteran newsman who has anchored local news in Washington for decades, has the rare gift of making people who appear with him sound smarter than they usually are. Mentoring us all was Jim Snyder, who built a news organization that dominated the Washington market for years. He was demanding, somewhat taciturn, and alternately fatherly and tough. Above all else, he loved the Mandel saga and wanted to give it as much play on the air as possible. Between Jim and Gordon, I had a road map to the rich political history of Maryland politics. Now I needed to immerse myself in the gritty details of the political drama unfolding in Baltimore.

In today's age of computer graphics, our techniques for covering the trial seem primitive. But by the time the jury was considering its verdict, we had our first satellite truck and were able to feed the artwork back to our studios in Washington as I stood in front of the federal courthouse in Baltimore and narrated my script. It wasn't a live feed from Kabul, but it seemed very cutting-edge at the time. Fighting off feelings of inadequacy after being on top in Philadelphia, I plunged in and tackled what was, for me, alien terrain. At the time, I had no idea my enthusiasm for the story would lead to another turning point in my career—the job at NBC.

———

The Mandel trial story was so compelling, and the demands of the daily narrative so relentless, that it became a crash course in the basics of television reporting. In addition, the technology was changing rapidly; we were all but inventing it as we went along. NBC executives were watching. Often in my career, big changes took place more by accident than design. I would have stayed at the CBS affiliate in Washington happily, surrounded by as talented a group of local reporters as was ever assembled on one team. But in 1978, Mrs. Graham, advised that the U.S. Supreme Court would likely decide against cross-ownership that permitted newspapers to own television stations in the same market, sold the *Post's* D.C. station. We were being traded to new owners, *The Detroit News,* because of a rule—since rescinded—that greatly hurt the quality of local television news by divorcing stations from their newspaper owners. When a call came from NBC, some good-hearted executives at Post-Newsweek persuaded the new station owners to let me out of my contract. On August 1, 1978, I started work less than a mile away, at the NBC News Washington bureau on Nebraska Avenue, where I have worked ever since.

I lived only a mile from the office. For a city girl, I had, with the help of my indefatigable mother, found a very different kind of nest: a Victorian cottage facing a national park on a winding country road, only five miles from downtown. It was just four rooms, too small for my furniture, but a perfect retreat from the craziness of the news business.

I had come a long way from Philadelphia, but I had not yet closed the book on my coverage of Frank Rizzo. Only a few short years later I went back, but this time as a network correspondent to cover one of the mayor's patented power grabs. He was trying to change the city's charter so that he could run for a third consecutive term. Not surprisingly, he had become a national story with his outrageous suggestion that supporters "vote white." At the same time, he blithely called suggestions that he was racist "hogwash."

After he lost his attempt to change the charter, I returned to do a story for NBC on what everyone thought would be the end of the Rizzo era. He wouldn't grant an interview, so I went to his house, hoping I could talk him into it. On the day his successor was being sworn in, Rizzo came out of his house to joust with me, wearing a tan lumber jacket, feisty as ever. I saw him once more, in 1991, when he tried for a third time to recapture his old job. He had a new career as a radio talk show host, and had not mellowed a bit. During a televised confrontation, the seventy-year-old politician practically decked a local reporter, shouting, "I want to fight you," and even called the newsman a "crumb, creep, lush coward." Vintage Rizzo.

He was also still a dirty campaigner. In that final election, having by then become a Republican, Rizzo accused his opponent, the city's district attorney, of being drunk because he staggered—even though the man walked with a limp because he'd lost a leg in Vietnam and used crutches. When reporters pressed Rizzo on how he knew his opponent was drunk, the former mayor answered, "You can be on crutches and still be under the influence."

At our final meeting, Rizzo, a little grayer and some pounds heavier, welcomed me into his office and reminisced about his earlier days in politics. Why did he give up a big-bucks radio show to go back into politics? "I love the challenge," he said, adding, "You know the best part? Dealing with the press. I love to go head-to-head with some of them suckers. I really do." We made our peace.

Only a few months later, I was watching a budget debate from NBC's Senate broadcast booth when the phone rang. It was a Philadelphia reporter asking me to comment on the death of Frank Rizzo. He had died of a massive heart attack in the middle of his comeback campaign. Once asked what he wanted on his gravestone, Rizzo had joked, "He's really dead."

When it was finally true, I cried.

CHAPTER 2

Understudy

I was thirty-two years old when on Thanksgiving Day 1978, I went to Georgetown, Guyana's colonial capital, 140 miles away from Jonestown through dense virgin rain forest. One of the most significant experiences in my life as a journalist began with a routine phone call from the NBC assignment desk. At the time, I was a general-assignment correspondent, which meant covering everything and nothing. Having made the uncertain leap to the network, once again I had to prove myself. The only way I knew how was to answer any call, at any hour of the day or night.

A California congressman, Leo Ryan, had been assassinated on a jungle landing strip near a place few Americans had ever heard of, Jonestown, Guyana. Guyana, in South America, is a country no larger than Idaho, situated north of Brazil and west of Suriname. Settled by the Dutch in the seventeenth century, then colonized by the British two hundred years later, it stood apart from most other countries in the region because, even before independence in 1966, Guyana had a Marxist government.

Congressman Ryan had been investigating reports that some of his constituents were being held against their will by a charismatic but dictatorial preacher, a San Francisco demagogue named Jim

Jones, who had transported his mystic theology combining Christianity and communism to the rain forests of Guyana. Ryan had brought with him a group of newsmen, including a correspondent, producer, and camera crew from NBC. Attempting to leave the next day with cult members who wanted to defect and were willing to provide evidence of widespread abuses, the group was gunned down by hit men working for Jones. Before escaping into the bewildering tangle of rain forests laced with streams, creeks, and marshes, the gunmen ran over to the wounded congressman and three newsmen and shot each of them in the head.

Two of the murdered journalists were NBC correspondent Don Harris and cameraman Bob Brown. Incredibly, Brown recorded the incident as he was dying, camera rolling until the final shot was fired, and he fell to his knees. His partner, soundman Steve Sung, badly wounded, along with Ryan's aide, Jackie Speier, lay on the airstrip's tarmac for twenty-two hours before being rescued.

By then, Guyanese soldiers had moved toward the commune and discovered the full horror of Jonestown: 913 people, including at least 276 children and a 108-year-old man identified as Pops Jackson. Their swollen bodies were decomposing in the tropical sun after a ritual orgy of mass murder and suicide as they followed the paranoid dictates of Jim Jones in a well-rehearsed plan. They had all drunk Flavor Aid, similar to Kool-Aid, laced with cyanide, some willingly, others, including the children, because they had no choice.

A colleague who had previously covered the war in Nicaragua, Fred Francis, had flown in and helped rescue Bob Flick, the NBC producer, who had not been wounded. Fred then finagled his way into Jonestown to get the first pictures of the disaster. Now the editor in New York needed more help covering the story. The Jonestown assignment would have been a challenge even if the tragedy had not involved fallen colleagues. With no preparation, I was flying to a Third World country to cover a massacre and mass suicide, on my own, without a clue as to what to do. I didn't even know how to book a flight to go overseas for NBC.

There was no way to escape the emotional horror of what had happened. But for NBC, coming to grips with it was infinitely more complicated because this was a death in the family. As a reporter, my normal reaction, drilled into me over the past decade, was to remain loftily above the stories I covered. Jonestown blew that certainty apart.

It is easy to forget this now, but at the time Jim Jones was fairly well known and very well connected, having become something of a celebrity for having carved Jonestown out of the rain forest. He had endorsements from Rosalynn Carter and Vice President Mondale, largely because of his political clout in the minority and fundamentalist community on the West Coast. Jones's flock were mostly of the same race (African-American), religion (Protestant), and economic status (poor) as many of the people of Guyana. The massacre and its aftermath was a potentially embarrassing story for the Carter White House.

From a practical standpoint, there was another problem: the two NBC producers assigned to take over were expected to switch instantly into combat mode and also deal with me, a newcomer at the network with no experience working overseas. They'd arrived in the country shortly after the murders, and, like many in Guyana, were fearful of retaliation. Perhaps to mask their fear, they were also angry with me and the desk editors who'd sent a novice, and a woman to boot, to cover such a difficult story. In the aftermath of the massacre, everyone who remained was psychologically damaged: the cult members most of all, but also the surviving journalists.

The capital was alive with rumors that roving hit squads from Jonestown had fled into the rain forest and would target any survivors, especially anyone from NBC. I was told by the NBC producers not to travel unaccompanied, but I had to get the story. Adding to the chaos and suspicion was the ham-handed behavior of the local police, Third World bureaucrats suddenly overwhelmed by an international media storm. They decided to hold possible material witnesses, including surviving cult members and several of

Jones's lieutenants, in the same hotel. Once grand, the Park Hotel was now a seedy colonial relic distinguished by a spacious veranda with a tall cupola. Waiters took soft drinks and meals to the rooms of the survivors, and the lobby swirled with conspiracy theories.

Falling back on my experience as a police reporter, I knew I had to find consular officials from the embassy, the local police, and the military—anyone who could provide real facts about the murderers of Don, Bob, and Congressman Ryan. Georgetown, with its palm tree–lined streets, was the sort of place where you'd expect to see vacationing tourists sitting in a hotel lobby drinking rum punches with little umbrellas. Instead, it now felt as though I'd stepped into a Graham Greene novel.

I walked the streets, knocking on doors, trying to get in to see American diplomats. I knew agents from the CIA were there, as well as people from the Justice Department, but it was all so hard to penetrate. You knew there were layers of the story to be told, but you just couldn't get below the surface of things. Following the investigation was complicated enough. More difficult was trying to explain the unfathomable: why hundreds of people had submitted to the mind control of a madman and murdered their own children before killing themselves.

Then there were the technical challenges of filing whatever you did manage to uncover. This was years before video phones, satellite uplinks, and other ways to broadcast instantly from remote locations. Laptop computers? A future fantasy. The only way to file my story was to fly by chartered jet four hundred miles to the nearest broadcast satellite in Trinidad and Tobago. That meant getting the videotape out past Guyanese customs officials, who were becoming increasingly defensive about charges that they had ignored clear signs of Jim Jones's madness because he was bringing desperately needed dollars to their impoverished country.

As I drove to the airport with my footage each night, my stomach knotted from fear that they would confiscate the film. I felt lost, not knowing what I didn't know, but aware that I was out of my league. Fear of failure overwhelmed what would have otherwise been a more rational fear of retaliation from Jim Jones's men. What I managed to repress, temporarily, was the emotional weight of the human tragedy we were sent to cover, partly because it was still theoretical to me. It wasn't until I got my first glimpse of Jonestown itself, hundreds of miles away, in a remote clearing in the rain forest, that the full scale of the event hit me.

For days, we had been pressing the Guyanese for access to the site of the mass deaths. Finally, the government loaded a pool of reporters and cameramen onto vintage Guyanese Defense Force helicopters to fly to the airstrip near Jonestown where the murders had taken place the week before. For the first time, I was scared, haunted by memories of a helicopter crash during floods from Hurricane Agnes in 1972 that had killed a good friend, local CBS newsman Sid Brenner, near Harrisburg, Pennsylvania. When we got to Jonestown, it was clear that the government had tried to sanitize any sign of the murderous ritual that had unfolded barely days earlier. The area was cleared of bodies, but they couldn't erase all of the evidence. It was eerily ghoulish, made more terrifying because what remained was so ordinary: a single child's shoe, a playground with swings and other play equipment, a baby's bottle encrusted in dirt. It looked like a summer camp that had been evacuated. Jonestown ranged over three hundred acres and included rows of cottages, dormitories, and workshops all lined up in tidy rows.

Time was limited, and the search for visual evidence became a clinical scavenger hunt. We pointed out solar equipment and the pavilion from which Jones had exhorted his followers. Our shoes sank into the mud, which I kept trying to avoid because the bodies had decomposed in the summer heat, and I had a terror of sinking into what might have been graves. There was a terrible smell. With growing horror, I realized that the quagmire could not have been completely cleansed of dead bodies.

Unlike the other network correspondents, I was on my own. My producers, emotionally drained from having lost two colleagues, were hundreds of miles away, back in the capital. As the military started herding us toward the helicopters to leave the carefully staged press tour, a veteran CBS producer, taking pity on me, helpfully reminded me that there was very little time to shoot an on-camera stand-up showing me on location.

It seems so cold-blooded, but one of the notable things about a situation like this is that being part of the press pool helps create an artificial barrier, enabling you to distance yourself from your emotions at what you're witnessing. Rather than being solely a death scene, the setting is now the backdrop for a television story. You can concentrate in a kind of robotic, instinctively journalistic fashion, and worry about being scooped by the other networks or not getting your camera in place in time.

This happens at crime scenes of every size and dimension. The reality of your job becomes the scrim that shields you from the emotion of the moment. At its worst, it explains how reporters can ask family members how they feel at the scene of a tragedy. People ask me, "How can you be objective as a reporter?" I answer that it becomes an automatic reflex. You have to filter out your personal point of view. Your role as a neutral-as-possible witness imposes its own set of rules.

A journalist can be viewed as unfeeling, yet in times of war or other crises, this neutrality provides an essential separation from the events swirling around us. It is how a broadcast pioneer like John Chancellor of NBC was able to stand up to local abuses and tell the world what was happening when those young students first crossed the color line and entered Central High School in Little Rock, Arkansas. It's how many sons and daughters of the Deep South were able to cover the civil rights struggle so brilliantly, ignoring cultural taboos from their own childhoods. The reporter becomes cloaked in an invisible shield that makes it possible to report the story without becoming emotionally engaged. At the same time, inevitably, reality does penetrate that shield. But we try to deny it.

My report on the massacre was, if not a disaster, completely undistinguished. I was so new to the network that Gilbert Millstein, an

NBC script editor known for his sardonic wisecracks, looked up at the screen and asked the newsroom: "So who's the Peruvian hand-maiden?" (At the time, I was a brunette.)

It didn't take long for the network to send in the cavalry. Veteran correspondents Bob Hager and George Lewis took over. Both would later become good friends and colleagues, but we never discussed Guyana. I flew home, embarrassed and defeated, still not fully absorbing what I'd experienced in that muddy field. The dynamic behind the carnage was hard to fathom. This was before the disaster at Waco, before we understood cults and deprogramming and all the psychological dimensions of mass deaths. It wasn't until the cab dropped me off at my cottage in Washington and I climbed the steps to the front porch that the accumulated fear and revulsion of the past weeks flooded over me.

I felt nauseated, sweaty and cold at the same time. Crying hysterically, I tore off my shoes and clothes, right on my own front porch, desperate to discard anything that could remind me of the stench of death. Perhaps I was trying to get rid of an emotional burden I didn't want to acknowledge. Whatever the reason, I threw out every vestige of clothing from the trip. To me, it smelled and always would.

More than a decade later I ran into James Reston, Jr., for the first time since we were both in Guyana. He had written the definitive history of Jonestown, *Our Father Who Art in Hell: The Life and Death of Jim Jones,* based on more than eight hundred hours of tapes Jones had made to record the events leading up to the "white night" of the mass suicides. I hadn't thought about Jonestown for years, at least not consciously. But talking with Reston's wife, I admitted for the first time that Jonestown still haunted me. I was shocked when she told me that none of the newsmen who'd been there had shaken it off, either, and most had sought help. It had never occurred to me that my reactions weren't unique.

As a woman, I'd been so eager to cover up any sign of weakness that I'd never considered the most logical response—seeking professional help to recover from the aftereffects of covering a tragedy of such dimensions. Until then, most of what I covered, especially in local and national politics, could be reduced on some level to farce. Usually, we focused on some new evidence of hypocrisy and incompetence by government bureaucrats. Occasionally, misbehavior rose to the level of mendacity and criminal malfeasance. It was relatively easy to separate myself from the unfolding dramas we reported. All of that changed with Jonestown. I didn't experience the same depth of despair again for another twenty-three years, until September 11, 2001.

————

Before being sent to Guyana, the most exotic trips I'd taken for NBC were from our Washington bureau to Capitol Hill. When I arrived at the network, I was assigned to everything that came along, even though I had no knowledge of any beat in particular. Once again, I was learning from the bottom up. If the assignment desk needed someone to take notes at a congressional hearing, I was it. When President Carter went on vacation in Plains, Georgia, I went along.

After Jonestown, this type of assignment was comic relief. It meant sitting outside the pond house of Jimmy Carter's mother, Miss Lillian, at five-thirty a.m. Christmas morning while the Carter family opened gifts inside, and then following the president as he performed the same holiday ritual at the home of his mother-in-law, Miss Allie. If you weren't accustomed to juggling a tape recorder, reporter's notebook, and microphone while jumping out of a Secret Service van in time to catch a glimpse of the chief executive before he went inside, it could be humiliating.

Running to the front of the motorcade on Christmas morning, 1978, I tripped over a microphone cord and fell, badly cutting my leg, outside the small ranch house of Rosalynn Carter's mother. The White House doctor had to be called to patch me up. His main job that Christmas was to take care of a presidential ailment so embarrassing that the president wouldn't disclose it. That is, until poor

Carter learned over Christmas that his good friend, Egypt's president Anwar Sadat, had appealed to his fellow Egyptians—Muslim and Christian—to pray for a cure for Jimmy Carter's hemorrhoids.

My job that day was to watch as Secret Service men assumed their posts on Miss Allie's front lawn, facing outward toward the street. On the lawn behind them, eleven-year-old Amy Carter and her young cousins set off caps that sounded like gunfire, delighted when they managed to startle the long-suffering agents.

That first Christmas in Plains at times had the surreal feeling of a Fellini movie. To attract attention from the assembled national news media accompanying the president, Native Americans gathered to protest against his policies toward their tribes. The protestors danced and chanted and banged ritual drums. At the same time, farmers rode their tractors into Plains to underscore their demands for higher price supports. On another corner, Taiwanese protested Carter's decision to normalize diplomatic relations with mainland China, while a group of Klansmen marched against the president's human rights policies.

Our only diversion was to spend silly amounts of money on souvenirs in the one or two shops catering to tourists attracted by Plains's newfound celebrity. A favorite was the rubberized Jimmy Carter bottle opener. We ate endless bags of peanuts. I went to the supermarket so that I could cook holiday meals for the camera crews in the microwave of the Winnebago that served as our office and editing room. Homesick, we organized Christmas Eve caroling.

At the time, none of us realized how much the kitsch of the surroundings would end up trivializing the chief executive himself. What could have been charming local color soon became tiresome, and eventually fodder for late-night comedians, as the president shook up his cabinet and commentators diagnosed his political malady as a case of midterm malaise. A good runner, Carter couldn't even get a break during a charity run at Camp David. Dehydrated, he stumbled, creating a picture that seemed to symbolize and reinforce his political frailty.

Jimmy Carter was an outsider, not comfortable with Washington's power brokers. His inexperience, and that of his top aides, often made them the subject of ridicule, especially on Capitol Hill. But from the moment he took office, Carter focused with a single-minded determination rarely seen in Washington on achieving peace in the Middle East.

Barely two months after becoming president, Carter launched negotiations to get Israel to trade land for peace. The outline of the basic deal hasn't changed in the decades since: Israel would withdraw from territory it occupied in 1967 in exchange for open borders and Arab recognition. It took more than a year of persuasion, but in September of 1978, Carter brought Israel's prime minister Menachem Begin and Egypt's Anwar Sadat together for their historic summit at Camp David.

When the summit began just after Labor Day in 1978, I had been at NBC for barely a month. Carter cleared his schedule, canceling a political trip to San Antonio, so that he could try to broker peace between Begin and Sadat. Rosalynn Carter was sent to Texas in his place, and I was assigned to accompany her on Air Force Two. While the senior correspondents were dealing with issues of world peace, I would be covering the first lady. It was hardly a plum assignment, but it would be the first of countless trips I would take over the succeeding years on one of the iconic blue-and-white aircraft in the presidential fleet stationed at Andrews Air Force Base in the Maryland suburbs. I was thrilled.

Instead of covering high-powered summitry, I went shopping for what I imagined were the appropriate clothes to cover a first lady: a long-sleeved silk shirtwaist and high heels. Perhaps it was suitable for church, but it was hardly the right garb for riding on a flatbed truck in a Labor Day parade in Garland, Texas, on an afternoon when the temperature reached ninety-eight degrees.

The trip didn't start well, either. I was to interview the first lady when we arrived in Texas Sunday night and put together a story for Monday morning's *Today* show. With delicate negotiations about to get under way at Camp David, the first lady was understandably silent on the only subject everyone cared about, Middle East peace.

And, at the last minute, Mrs. Carter's staff decided that the color of the sofa in the interview room at our hotel clashed with what she was wearing. It was either get her to change clothes, or find a new couch. We changed the couch. That delayed the interview so long, we had to race to the Alamo shortly before midnight to shoot my on-camera stand-up in front of the only recognizable building that would be well lit against the night sky. Just as I was getting ready, the lights at the Alamo were shut off for the night, leaving me standing in front of a black hole.

The next day, drenched from the stifling humidity and almost suffocating in my silk dress, I gamely tried to keep my balance, teetering in high heels on the flatbed truck that followed Mrs. Carter in the parade. Our first-generation videotape recorder broke down in the high humidity, but it hardly mattered. Clearly, there was no news in this spousal campaign appearance, especially in contrast with the Middle East negotiations the president was organizing.

But at the end of the parade, NBC's Texas bureau chief Art Lord suddenly appeared to whisk me onto a helicopter to get to our Dallas affiliate. *Nightly News* wanted a report on Labor Day events around the country. Art had made his reputation during the Vietnam War as our Saigon bureau chief, and he still wore the khaki jacket of a war correspondent. How could I tell him about my fear of helicopters? Making it worse, Art put me in the copilot's seat so that I could have an even better view through the 360-degree Plexiglas bubble. I was terrified, afraid to admit it, and had to write a script in less than a half hour. Fortunately, considering the state of the long-sleeved silk dress, there was no need to go on camera. Nonetheless, I had completed my first White House trip, survived, and somehow gotten on the *Nightly News.*

While I was covering the East Wing, Jimmy Carter was making history. The talks almost failed several times. Sadat later acknowledged he had come close to walking out. But finally, on September 18, after thirteen days in the Western Maryland retreat, the president presented the results to a joint session of Congress. Despite all of the bloodshed since, the essential terms haven't changed over the intervening decades. Palestinians would decide on a form of local government. New Israeli settlements on the West Bank would be frozen during the negotiations. There was no mention of the most difficult issues, like what to do with East Jerusalem, claimed by both sides. Not surprisingly, two days later, Begin told *The Wall Street Journal* that Israel and the U.S. had differing interpretations of how long he had promised to freeze the West Bank settlements.

Presidents usually insist on guaranteed outcomes before they agree to spend political capital on high-risk diplomacy. Not so Jimmy Carter, and his gamble paid off. Prior to Camp David, only 39 percent of the people interviewed by the Gallup poll approved of his performance in office. Barely two weeks later, the president's approval rating had jumped to 56 percent, the sharpest gain for a chief executive in four decades of Gallup surveys, at least until George W. Bush's leap from 51 to 86 percent in the wake of the September 11, 2001 attacks. Unfortunately for Carter, that high did not last. His popularity dropped precipitously from March to June of 1979, reaching a new low in June of only 29 percent. Carter was in particular trouble with fellow Democrats, who told pollsters they did not like his domestic policies.

The Camp David agreement was one of his widely applauded accomplishments, in contrast to the rest of Carter's record in the spring of 1979. When it came time to sign the accords on the North Lawn of the White House, I was given a choice assignment, broadcasting alongside our anchorman and commentator John Chancellor. From our position on the roof of the Hay-Adams hotel across Lafayette Square, we had a panoramic view of the ceremony. Jimmy Carter read from the Bible and the Koran; Anwar Sadat proclaimed it one of the happiest moments of his life; Menachem Begin recalled the atrocities inflicted upon Jews during World War II. In the audience sat eighteen hundred invited dignitaries, while millions of viewers watched on live television.

I provided "color," or background, for John's play-by-play analysis, adding details such as the curious fact that the document was signed on an oak table that had served the cabinet of Ulysses S. Grant in the 1870s. It was the first time I'd been included in the network's coverage of an historic event, and on that sunlit day when the world imagined the creation of a lasting Middle East peace, anything seemed possible.

———

I hungered for my own beat, but, as a new correspondent, for the most part, my job was to cover presidential movements to and from Camp David or church. At first, I spent every weekend taking notes on the president's Sunday school lessons, often as a "pool" reporter sharing Carter's biblical prescriptions with the other networks. It wasn't great journalism, but for a Jewish kid from New York, it sure was an education in the New Testament.

As a general-assignment correspondent, I spent a lot of time covering congressional hearings, cornering members of Congress when they took breaks, asking witnesses or their aides for more details as they arrived or left the room. Long before C-SPAN covered the Senate, we did our own legwork, watching the chambers from the press galleries and using courtroom artists to depict major debates. Not yet tethered to computers so that we could be in constant communication with our producers, we wandered the corridors, corralling sources.

If you wanted to know what was happening with a piece of legislation, you'd go over and ask the sponsors, or the opponents. My favorite hangout was the Speaker's Lobby. You could mill around among the House members and send in requests to call someone off the House floor to answer a question. It was a taste of what I'd experience a decade later, covering Congress full-time.

In those early days, many of the hearings I went to were investigative inquiries by the House Commerce Committee or its subcommittees, whose members included John Dingell, later to become chairman, and Young Turks such as Democrats Al Gore and Ed Markey. Often the focus was energy policy, as America faced a growing oil crisis with OPEC. Unlike CBS, then our chief competitor, NBC did not have an energy correspondent. Spotting a vacuum, and a big story, I volunteered for the job.

———

America's struggle to wean itself from overdependence on foreign oil became the defining economic story of the Carter years. Carter was the nation's "energy warden," adopting the tone of a World War II neighborhood scold as he addressed the nation, affecting informality in his sweater, to tell us to turn down our thermostats.

Television had a hard time telling the energy story. Looking for easy explanations, the networks found a convenient target in the oil industry. Carter's Energy Department obliged, with a patchwork quilt of new regulations that almost guaranteed Big Oil would violate one rule or another. *Nightly News* had an insatiable appetite for stories about fines against anyone in the oil industry. Conspiracy theories abounded about offshore tankers secreting supplies to maintain the shortages and keep prices high. It was difficult to explain the complex oil refining and distribution system in terms accessible for *Nightly News*.

Then, and now, we have only a half hour—approximately twenty-two minutes when commercials are subtracted—to cover all the news of the day. It requires making difficult choices, and sometimes losing texture or minimizing complexity. All *Nightly News* anchors, correspondents, and producers hunger for a full hour's newscast. During times of great moment or crisis, like 9/11 or Inauguration Day, the network has given us the extra time. But that does not happen often.

My new energy beat put me up against an experienced CBS competitor, the late Nelson Benton. The secretary for the newly created Energy Department was James Schlesinger, who had previously served as defense secretary under Presidents Nixon and Ford, until Ford fired him for insubordination. Schlesinger didn't suffer fools gladly, especially a novice to the beat.

Dealing with Schlesinger was a challenge, but fun, intellectually. (Last year, I ran into him and mentioned that I would be going on a tour of the Energy Department's weapons facility at Oak Ridge, Tennessee, to see centrifuges for nuclear fuel production given up by Libya. As irascible as ever, Schlesinger snapped, "I hope you do your usual tough job and don't let them get away with pretending this is a big deal, because it's not." He hasn't changed a bit.)

Back in 1978, U.S. energy policy was more focused on fossil fuel supplies than nonproliferation. My bureau chief, Sid Davis, wanted me to go to the Energy Department and treat it the way I used to work a police beat, developing sources and looking for leaks. I wasn't quite sure how to go about it. Part of Sid's prescription was to take people to lunch. With the U.S. desperate to find alternative energy sources, I started calling energy officials, congressional aides on the energy committees, and executives in the oil shale business. It began to pay off. We did stories on wind farms and natural gas, nuclear power and new oil drilling techniques. I had to learn everything from scratch. It was great fun, but I was not at all sure I could keep up. And while the beat was exciting, as well as productive, most of the stories were painfully boring visually. So one unforgettable night, I tried to bring some extra creativity to what should have been a simple report. We'd been assigned to do a story on gas lines, and I had the notion to make the segment as cinematic as possible. I asked the camera crews to capture the frustration of drivers waiting on long lines for gas, complete with natural sound of car horns and people complaining.

Unfortunately, I wasn't the only relative beginner on our team that day. To transform my overambitious script into a taped package for the broadcast, I was working with one of our less-experienced tape editors and a producer who had never before "cut" a spot for *Nightly News*. To make sure that everyone meets the evening news deadline, there is always another producer supervising all of the editing rooms. As luck would have it, on that night we had a rookie in that slot, too.

I started writing the script as the tape came in, but the video arrived late and the segment started falling further and further behind. Looking at the video before I wrote, I realized that there were too many interviews, and too much sound. We weren't timing each segment properly, and as the pressure mounted, the editor and producer became even more flustered. My attempt to play Hollywood director was only contributing to the overall panic.

In television terms, we "missed air." David Brinkley, then at NBC, read the lead-in, saying something along the lines of, "Andrea Mitchell has more on that." But nothing happened. The tape was not ready to roll.

My team and I had committed just about every sin in the broadcast playbook. We didn't time things properly and, even worse, we didn't give the producers in charge a heads-up that we were going to miss the deadline. The senior person downstairs in EJ ("electronic journalism") came into the edit room and said, "Okay, we've got to face the music," and together we all walked to the control room, where Bob McFarland, then the senior producer for *Nightly News,* was screaming, "Is it ready? Is it ready?"

When he was told that the segment was finally ready, he discovered that it was forty-five seconds long. Not only had we missed our place in the rundown; in a business where being five seconds long is a lot, and ten seconds is unforgivable, being forty-five seconds long with an overdue piece that now had to be run further down in the show was practically a firing offense. McFarland began to shout, "What is this? Amateur night?"

I thought my career was over. It was a Friday, and I had a friend arriving for the weekend from Philadelphia. Instead of going out, I went home, crawled into bed, and pulled the covers over my head; I hoped somehow that by retreating I could make the specter of the missed spot disappear.

On Monday morning, *Nightly News* had its usual morning call at nine-thirty a.m. to plan that evening's broadcast. At the end of the call, three days after my embarrassing failure, Paul Greenberg, then executive producer of *Nightly News* in New York, joked, "Oh, by the way, you can roll the Mitchell spot whenever it's ready." Apparently I was being given a second chance.

The whole incident was a searing experience, not because I'd gotten any facts wrong or had a technological breakdown, but because of a domino effect of human error. It was an early, if painful, lesson in the nature of teamwork in television. When it clicks, it can be brilliant. We make our little videos, trying to re-create reality for our viewers in a telescoped form—that's the medium. But when it fails, the humiliation is very public. Fortunately, except for the evidence on videotape, we do rush on to our next challenges. To paraphrase Scarlett O'Hara, tomorrow is another deadline.

———

I was still on the energy beat at 9:06 a.m. on March 28, 1979, when the Associated Press ran a brief bulletin that said, "Officials at the Three Mile Island nuclear plant have declared a 'general emergency,' a state police spokesman said today." It was a place none of us had ever heard of. Suddenly it thrust the country into a situation for which no one was prepared. The actual incident had been triggered five hours earlier, when the main-feed water pumps at the nuclear reactor in the Pennsylvania farm community of Middletown, near Harrisburg, somehow failed, preventing the steam generators from removing heat. Control room operators didn't spot the danger as first the turbine and then the reactor automatically shut down.

A relief valve, designed to prevent the pressure from becoming excessive, opened. Once the pressure decreased, the valve should have closed automatically, but it didn't. Failing to see signals that the valve was still open, the control room was oblivious to a developing calamity: water was pouring out of the open valve, causing the reactor to overheat and approach meltdown. Rapidly, the situation spun out of control. Operators misread their instruments, and the instruments provided conflicting information. It was later determined that about half of the reactor core melted during those early stages of the accident. It was eerily similar to the plot of a film that had been released a month earlier, *The China Syndrome,* starring Jane Fonda, Michael Douglas, and Jack Lemmon, about a faulty water pump that causes a nuclear plant to melt down.

Federal and state officials were caught flat-footed. Shortly after nine a.m., the call came to the White House. Jessica Tuchman Mathews, the National Security Council's point person for nuclear energy, sent a short memo to her boss, National Security Advisor Zbigniew Brzezinski. By ten a.m., he was briefing the president in the Oval Office. At the Nuclear Regulatory Commission's headquarters in Bethesda, Maryland, twelve miles from the White House, Harold Denton, chief of reactor operations, recalled being confused by the conflicting information coming in from the field. Quickly, NRC officials headed north toward their regional office in King of Prussia, Pennsylvania. No one knew how close the reactor was getting to meltdown. By that evening, the teams on the site thought the damage was slight, perhaps affecting 1 percent of the reactor core.

Three Mile Island was run by a local utility, Metropolitan Edison, for its parent company, General Public Utilities. The twin cooling towers dominated the rural landscape along the Susquehanna River. Until the accident, residents of this farm community only ten miles from the state's capital in Harrisburg liked their relatively cheap energy and viewed the reactor as a benign presence. But on Friday, March 30, a larger amount of radiation was released from the plant's auxiliary building to relieve pressure on the primary system.

The public began to panic. An even more alarming danger had emerged: a hydrogen bubble developed in the container that held the reactor core. No one knew whether the bubble would burn, or explode, possibly rupturing the concrete containment vessel that by then was the only barrier between the countryside and nuclear disaster. How close was the reactor to a nuclear meltdown? How much radiation had already escaped into the atmosphere? Pennsylvania's governor, Richard Thornburgh, consulted federal officials about evacuating the area. Pregnant women and preschool children within a five-mile radius of the plant were told to leave.

When we first got word of the accident, I was immediately sent to the NRC's suburban Maryland headquarters. Once it was clear that a meltdown of the reactor core had been averted—although it would be years before we knew how close they had come to a catastrophic event—the main concern was that dangerous levels of radiation had been released into the atmosphere. The bureau assigned a rotating group of correspondents to go in and out of Middletown, none spending more than twenty-four hours so as to avoid excessive exposure to radiation. By the end of the first week, I realized that the correspondents being sent to the scene had two things in common: none was NBC's energy correspondent, and they were all men.

On Friday night, the evening of greatest fear about the hydrogen bubble, I marched with the only other woman in the bureau, Carole Simpson, into Sid Davis's office to ask why we had not been sent to Three Mile Island. He said he wanted to protect women of childbearing age from the potential damage of radiation.

In many ways, Sid was a father figure for me, having recruited me to the network and guided my career since. We had also covered national campaigns together years earlier for Westinghouse Broadcasting. But even now, I can feel the sting of his paternalism, however kindly his intention. How could he unilaterally decide to keep me off the most sensational story my beat had ever produced? Without hesitating, I shot back that men's testicles were as vulnerable to radiation as women's ovaries. I was on a plane to Three Mile Island the next day.

Middletown, Pennsylvania, was as Middle American a place as you could find. It was a small town along the banks of the Susquehanna where people were accustomed to feeling safe. The nuclear power plant was the largest local industry and a steady source of jobs. Residents didn't question the safety of the twin nuclear cooling towers. Now, suddenly, people were terrified, and the source of the danger was invisible. How do you know if radiation is harming you? How do you protect yourself against it? You can't.

When I first arrived, the officials at the local utility company were completely unprepared to handle the emergency, or the media invasion that accompanied it. Governor Thornburgh was doing his best to get information out to the public, but this close-to-the-ground farm community was understandably suspicious. A frenzy of reporters at the scene fed the growing panic.

There was no evacuation plan. Later, it became a requirement that any region with a nuclear power station, like Indian Point, north of New York City, had to have a specific way of moving large populations away from reactors in an emergency. Because the highway systems in most communities are already overburdened, few areas are able to comply.

Once I finally got to the scene, I was given a dosimeter to wear, to make sure the cumulative radiation I was absorbing from the atmosphere hadn't reached dangerous levels. Since no one had tested the air immediately after the accident, no one would ever know how much radiation had escaped. When we weren't waiting for briefings at the plant, we covered town meetings or drove the narrow country roads looking for people willing to talk about their reactions to the near-meltdown.

We returned to Pennsylvania a year later and reinterviewed the residents. Studies backed up our observation that there had not been long-term physical effects on the local population. Even years later, there was no noticeable increase in the incidence of diseases like thyroid cancer. But all this was unknown at the time of the incident.

Before Three Mile Island, America was oblivious to the dangers or benefits of nuclear energy. It just existed, with very little government oversight. The Nuclear Regulatory Commission had grown out of the old Atomic Energy Commission, which had been created to promote the viability of atomic or nuclear energy. Rather than regulating the industry, the commission was its advocate. All that changed with the meltdown. In the aftermath of the incident, President Carter appointed an independent commission, headed by a prominent mathematician, Dartmouth College president John Kemeny, to investigate what had gone wrong. It was the biggest story of the day, inspiring intense media scrutiny and heavy pressure to scoop the competition with the commission's findings. More than anything, Sid Davis wanted me to beat CBS and its correspondent, Diane Sawyer.

An old-school Washington newsman, Sid ordered me to take the commission chairman to lunch. Following his instructions, I invited Dr. Kemeny, a gracious Hungarian immigrant, to Le Pavilion, then the most expensive French restaurant in Washington, and put it on my expense account. These days, we consider ourselves lucky to find time for a yogurt or salad at our desks in between cable news appearances and reporting for *Nightly News*. But in the years before cable and more complex preparations for the evening news, we often spent hours wooing sources over expense account meals.

But my culinary assault on the Three Mile Island investigator was for naught. We discussed everything from his start as a mathematician to his time at Dartmouth and our fathers' adjacent childhood neighborhoods in the Washington Heights section of Manhattan. By the end of lunch, Dr. Kemeny had revealed nothing about the cause of the reactor meltdown, only that he knew I would understand that he could not discuss anything about the secret findings of his commission.

Abandoning the French-cuisine approach, I tried old-fashioned shoe leather. Having cultivated another source connected to the commission, I waited in the stairwell of the office building where the panel was meeting, got a purloined copy of the report, and raced down several flights of steps to deliver the scoop Sid wanted. NBC was first to report that the commission had concluded that to avoid future accidents, fundamental changes needed to be made in the way nuclear reactors were built, run, and regulated. The panel recommended that the president abolish the Nuclear Regulatory Commission and establish a new agency to police the industry.

A year after Three Mile Island, I went to Rancho Seco, California, to visit a reactor of the same type and model as Three Mile Island in order to assess the mood of that community toward atomic power. It was a rural area of farms and cattle ranches. Instead of finding suspicion and fear because of the nuclear accident back east, I learned that most of the local residents were completely comfortable with their nuclear neighbor. As far as they were concerned, the reactor was providing cheap energy to power their ranches and farms, and they were perfectly happy living with the giant cooling towers.

In retrospect, what is most striking about America's worst nuclear accident is how badly managed the facility at Three Mile Island was. Kemeny's presidential fact-finding group found that the plant's procedures were "inadequate" and "confusing." This has since changed, under new ownership. But to make nuclear power viable and safe, utility companies have to be good corporate citizens and not cut corners on safety even during periods of lax regulation. The payoff, as France and other countries have learned, is less dependence on imported oil.

Although investigators did not recommend a moratorium on new nuclear power construction, after the accident, the marketplace dictated a freeze on any new plants. Insurance was now simply too expensive, and the licensing requirements too burdensome, to make nuclear energy economically viable during the years of relatively cheap oil. But with the rising cost of oil, that may now change. In 2003, I returned to Three Mile Island to find out what had happened in the twenty-five years since the accident. I concluded that the risk premium on oil as a reliable source of energy in this age of terror might lead us to better research, not only on hybrid cars, but also on safer ways to produce nuclear energy. But first Americans have to reexamine their fears about nuclear power. The legacy of Three Mile Island is still with us.

———

The oil shocks that had so paralyzed the Carter presidency were only a prelude to an even greater crisis—the taking of American hostages in Iran. We were all slow to recognize the seismic effect of the Iranian Revolution when it began in February of 1979. America's ailing ally, the Shah of Iran, had left the country in January, claiming he was only taking a vacation abroad. In reality, he was getting out while he could. Within a month, an uprising of rebellious government troops and armed civilian followers of the radical cleric Ayatollah Khomeini seized power. Their spiritual and de facto political leader, Khomeini returned from exile in France as the CIA frantically began dismantling its listening posts along the Soviet-Iranian border. After nine months of near anarchy, five hundred Iranian students stormed the American embassy, taking ninety hostages, including sixty-six Americans, most of them diplomats working at the U.S. embassy.

What became the hostage crisis marked a new role for American television. Before the advent of cable news, our responsibilities were generally limited to scheduled newscasts in the morning and at the dinner hour. With the exception of our coverage of the assassinations during the sixties and Watergate in the seventies, there were few occasions requiring nonstop broadcasting. Suddenly, the Iranian hostage crisis changed what was expected of us. Instead of preparing scripted newscasts, we were now self-appointed monitors of national emergencies, on duty twenty-four hours a day. As one of the more junior correspondents, I worked the night shift, helping the Washington bureau maintain its vigil. My assignment was to be on call through the night, occasionally sleeping on a well-worn newsroom couch, so that we could go on with a bulletin at any moment.

Over the succeeding months, a team of reporters and producers assigned full-time to the story prepared detailed histories of each of the hostages. As they dug into the background of each captive, they discovered one of the great media conspiracies of the time: there were six more American diplomats still in Tehran who had not been taken captive when the embassy was overrun, and several media organizations knew it. The Americans were hiding in the Canadian embassy in Tehran—something no one ever reported until they escaped three months later. They flew out of Tehran posing as Canadian diplomats and holding false Iranian visas.

The continuing crisis for those who remained quickly overwhelmed Carter's presidency. Americans were not used to being held hostage. It created a feeling of vulnerability and impotence, undercutting expectations that an American president be strong and effective. Pictures of the angry mobs in Tehran dominated the evening news. Ted Koppel's nightly reports on the hostages became a fixture of American television, eventually becoming the long-running program, *Nightline*.

After Ted Kennedy defeated Carter in the New York primary in March, political pressure intensified for the president to take military action and end the standoff. When we criticize the friction among George W. Bush's first-term foreign policy advisors, it's useful to remember the brutal policy disagreements between Carter's national security advisor, Zbigniew Brzezinski, and his secretary of state, Cyrus Vance. In 1979, when I was covering a commencement speech the president gave at the Naval Academy in Annapolis, I was able to easily spot which paragraphs had been written by Brzezinski, and which by the secretary of state. The two men held diametrically opposing views on most issues, and the president often couldn't decide between them—so he chose something from each, like a Chinese menu of foreign policy.

Vance strongly opposed a military mission to rescue the hostages, arguing it was better to rely on diplomacy, so Brzezinski waited until the secretary of state was in Florida for the weekend before taking final military plans to the president. Vance learned about it in time and protested, but Carter rejected his arguments. The secretary of state handed the president his letter of resignation, the only contemporary example of a cabinet secretary resigning on principle.

The night of the rescue mission, code-named Eagle Claw, our White House correspondent John Palmer got a tip that the lights were on unusually late at the White House. He rushed downtown and pieced together enough information to determine that a military operation was in play. Calling Jody Powell, Carter's press secretary, John talked him into promising an exclusive account of the operation from the president himself once the rescue mission was out of Iranian airspace, as long as NBC reported nothing that night. It was in fact a bluff: John did not have enough information to report the story, and never would have done so in the middle of a rescue attempt.

Nonetheless, after midnight on April 25, John was called into the Oval Office. Jimmy Carter told him that the mission to rescue the hostages had not succeeded because of what he called "equipment failure." It turned out to have been a series of calamitous events. First, three of eight helicopters on the mission developed a hydraulic problem, forcing Carter to call off the operation. During the withdrawal, a sandstorm caused one of the helicopters to crash into a refueling plane at a spot in the Iranian desert called Desert One. Eight crew members were killed and five others injured. Palmer broke the story minutes before one a.m. on the East Coast, just before the end of network programming for the night. On the West Coast, it was still prime time, and a huge exclusive story.

The collapse of the rescue mission doomed Carter's reelection chances, although he still held out hope for a breakthrough. Warren Christopher, then deputy secretary of state, had been dispatched to try to negotiate the release of the hostages. Two days before the election, Christopher awakened the president at three forty-five on a Sunday morning with word that the mullahs might be ready to make a deal. Carter, in Chicago for a campaign stop, rushed back to Washington so quickly he left most of the press corps behind. Judy Woodruff was one of the few who made the motorcade's departure, but only because she ran for the cars without pausing even to take out her hair curlers. Some reporters never were able to retrieve the underwear they'd left behind with the hotel laundry. I was called to race to the White House in time for the president's return.

Vice President Mondale took over the rest of Carter's campaign schedule, and the first lady filled in for Mondale.

It turned out to be false hope, based on an overly optimistic reading of the signals from Tehran. Carter wrote later that during the last thirty-six hours of the campaign, the news media were "saturated" with vivid reports about the hostages, making it impossible for the voters to hear anything else. Carter had won renomination, despite a stiff challenge from Ted Kennedy, on a wave of anger and national pride after the hostages were seized. Now he faced defeat because the country had lost patience with his failure to bring the hostages home. Reagan took 51 percent of the vote and forty-four states, while helping his party to win twelve new Senate seats and control of the Senate for the first time in twenty-six years. Once defeated by Ronald Reagan, Carter spent his last days before the inaugural clinging to the chance that he still might be able to make a transatlantic dash to escort the hostages personally from an American military base in Germany, which would be their first stop on the way home. But in a poignant footnote to Carter's presidency, the complex deal was finally struck with Tehran only twenty-four hours before the defeated president was to leave office. Weary and emotionally drained, Carter came into the White House press room at 4:55 a.m. on January 19 to announce the agreement. The Iranians still dragged out the handover, denying Carter even the consolation of making the trip before he left office.

In fact, Iran didn't release the captive Americans until noon on January 20, just as the new president was being sworn in. They had been held 444 days. The timing of their release was not an accident. The Iranians wanted to further humiliate Carter by holding the fifty-two remaining Americans just long enough so that he would no longer be president to welcome them home. For Carter, it was a final blow.

That only increased the drama, adding a bittersweet note to the transition when Ronald Reagan took office. The ceremonies heralded the return of pomp and circumstance to the capital after four Spartan years in the "plain" style of Plains. But for me, it was a marathon day, and hardly glamorous. At dawn, I was on Pennsylvania Avenue covering the inaugural for the *Today* program. Heavily bundled in gear designed for snowmobile drivers because of predictions of freezing weather, we were pleasantly surprised by warm, bright sunshine for Reagan's first inaugural. Later, I covered the parade, alongside our irrepressible weatherman, Willard Scott. Then, still dressed in my outdoor garb, I spent the evening in the NBC bureau, voicing over pictures being fed in from the inaugural balls in reports for our local stations around the country. It never occurred to me that viewers might think I was actually attending the galas, rather than watching a video monitor, a practice that has since become commonplace on all manner of stories as networks trim their staffs.

Later, just before midnight that same day, I was sent to Andrews Air Force Base to watch Carter administration officials leave to join now former President Jimmy Carter in Plains, from where they would depart for Germany to pick up the newly released hostages. Carter would be bringing them home on the same 707 aircraft he used to fly as Air Force One. Now the plane was on loan. And without a president on board, it was known simply by the military designation on its tail, 27000. I spent the night stretched out on a table in a corner of the press center at the air force base, catching a brief nap in case I needed to file an update on the hostage release for the next morning's *Today* show.

The hostages returned to Washington a week later, after a few days in seclusion at West Point. They traveled with their families in sixteen buses as a quarter of a million people, waving flags and yellow ribbons, cheered their progress through the streets of the capital, taking the same route as that of the inaugural to a triumphant and emotional reception at the White House. In a speech on the South Lawn, Ronald Reagan swore "swift and effective retribution" to terrorists. It was a muscular new policy designed to help restore American stature. The combination of those two events, the inauguration of a new president and the release of the hostages, seemed to rekindle a sense of national pride and hope.

———

The way Ronald Reagan took office—riding a wave of patriotism that crested with the return of the hostages—was, I think, ultimately damaging to the new administration. Reagan had watched Jimmy Carter become increasingly paralyzed by the crisis that eventually defeated him. The experience helped shape the new president's overemotional response to his own hostage crisis when Americans were taken captive in Lebanon four years later. We didn't realize it at the time, but the modern Age of Terror, with its origins in the sacking of the American embassy in Tehran, would within a few short years explode again with the 1983 attacks on our embassy and marine barracks in Beirut.

Reagan's hostage crisis, involving seventeen Americans held in Lebanon, became the driving force behind the greatest scandal of his presidency: Iran-Contra. After forcefully declaring that the U.S. would never negotiate with terrorists, once the crisis became personalized, Reagan couldn't resist. At the start of every day, he would ask his national security advisors about any news of the hostages. Inevitably, his obsession with their welfare created an expectation for action, and an opening for a brash colonel in the National Security Council, Oliver North. In ways that would recur through successive administrations of both parties, presidents or cabinet secretaries fail to realize the power of their own suggestions, even of their offhand remarks. I observed many times while covering the White House that overeager aides will do whatever it takes "to make the old man happy." In administrations that lack discipline, or are led by chiefs of staff short on character or judgment—as with Bob Haldeman in the Nixon White House, and Don Regan under Ronald Reagan—underlings desperate to please the boss start breaking rules.

But none of this occurred to me as I witnessed that most noble of American rituals, the peaceful transfer of political power. My first two years at the network had been more searing than anything I could have imagined. From the rain forests of Guyana to the looming twin cooling towers that shadowed the grassy riverbanks at Three Mile Island, I'd experienced things that changed my life, in ways both subtle and dramatic. Covering politics was often high comedy, even farce. Now, without even realizing it, I had developed a new specialty—disasters.

CHAPTER 3

Designated Shouter

I learned everything I ever needed to know about questioning artful dodgers by covering the most artful of them all, Ronald Reagan. For Reagan, performance was as much a part of governing as understanding the details of the federal budget. He was an actor who had become a politician; by combining his skills, he became a better politician than he'd been an actor. I came to the White House not knowing much about the man behind the public face. Eight years later, I could anticipate his decisions, second-guess his reactions, mimic his gestures, and recite his speeches by heart. But the essential Reagan was more elusive. He so inhabited his role that to almost everyone but his wife the man himself was still a mystery.

If Jimmy Carter was ridiculed for focusing too much on details, Ronald Reagan was thought to have the opposite problem: he was adept at the quick aside and the instant quip, often to avoid having to give a substantial, thoughtful answer. Once, during his 1984 campaign against Walter Mondale, the president was beating a hasty retreat from a Rose Garden ceremony to avoid any contact with the press. I shouted, "What about Mondale's charges?"

Without missing a beat, Reagan responded, "I think he ought to pay them."

While Ronald Reagan was clever at parrying impromptu questions with a quip, he wasn't at his best in formal news conferences. He was clearly far more effective performing as part of a set piece: a stage, a speech, a TelePrompTer; and at campaign events with plenty of balloons and a cheering audience—nothing unexpected, like a gotcha question from a journalist.

I had not covered Reagan's campaign, or the White House for the first few months of his presidency. When Reagan replaced Jimmy Carter, I was still covering energy. Then, in March 1981, our entire Washington bureau mobilized in response to John Hinckley's attempt to assassinate the president. When the nation's leader is struggling for his life, reporters are no different from other citizens; they feel shock and worry, but know they cannot give in to these emotions, because they have a story to cover. I was sent to the traffic island outside George Washington University Hospital, where the injured president had been taken. It was a twenty-four-hour vigil.

No one had seen John Hinckley, who had been tackled and arrested immediately at the scene of the shooting. So it was a big deal when we learned that he would be transferred one morning by helicopter, landing across from the Tidal Basin so that he could be driven to the courthouse for his preliminary hearing. With military precision, the assignment editors plotted how to get a picture of the suspect, live, during the *Today* show. The camera crew would set up across the water from the landing pad at Hains Point for just a picture; but at the last moment, the bureau chief sent me along. When I arrived it was clear that there was no way to see Hinckley getting off the helicopter other than through a telescopic lens. The cameraman could see Hinckley, but I couldn't. I was hooked up so that I could hear the *Today* show, but was told once again that since I couldn't add anything to the coverage, they wanted only the picture—no correspondent required.

Yet as Hinckley emerged from the chopper, one of the producers must have told the anchors, Tom Brokaw and Jane Pauley, that I was at the scene, because they asked me on the air to describe what I could see. In fact I couldn't see a thing—only the cameraman could.

Completely unprepared, and not having the wit to ad-lib, I froze, saying nothing! Finally I stammered, "Hinckley, I hope you can see, is the man between two security men being brought in to the limousine," except that I had no idea what I was describing. Mercifully, they cut it short.

Bill Small, then president of NBC News and previously a veteran newsman at CBS, said it was the worst performance he'd ever seen. He and Steve Friedman, the executive producer of the *Today* show, banished me from television—unbeknownst to me. Bad as my performance had been, even I did not realize how poorly it had been received in the front office. The first hint that I was in big trouble came a week or so later, when I noticed that my name did not appear on the Washington bureau's daily assignment sheet. Brady Daniels, the business manager, said, "Didn't anyone tell you? They've switched your contract from TV to radio." It was an execution, apparently without a trial. My career seemed to be over, yet again.

I turned to Chris Wallace, with whom I shared an office at our bureau. Chris was a second-generation broadcaster, having been raised in the business by his stepfather, CBS News president Bill Leonard, and his father, Mike Wallace, of *60 Minutes* fame. He consoled me, counseling that, "If there's anything my father has told me, it's that this is a profession for long-distance runners. This is not the end of you. Just pick yourself up." Good advice. The bureau found a place to hide me, far from live television, until my contract ran out: NBC Radio at the White House.

Fortunately for me, John Palmer and Judy Woodruff, the White House correspondents, were taking turns doing weekend duty and wanted more time off. So the bosses figured out that I could go to the White House to file for NBC Radio during the week, and give John and Judy a break by doing television on weekends. I was in effect being banished from weekday *Nightly News,* the flagship broadcast. Wasn't it a big step backward?

Nightly News anchorman Roger Mudd advised me, "Get your foot in the door there. You'll make something of it."

So that's how I got to the White House—in disgrace, after I'd almost lost my job for blowing the Hinckley coverage, and through the back door of NBC Radio. After having been one of the most visible correspondents a year earlier, covering Three Mile Island and my energy beat, I was starting over. And not having covered Ronald Reagan's rise to power, I didn't have any sources inside the White House. Once again, I had to work my way up.

Luckily, I had landed in the right place, working under two senior correspondents who, to this day, defy every stereotype about our cutthroat business. Judy Woodruff and John Palmer were two of a kind. Perhaps their characters were shaped by their similar backgrounds, both having come from small Southern towns. Judy grew up on army bases and in Augusta, Georgia; John in Kingsport, Tennessee. They were smart, successful, and famous. But they were also unspoiled by their status and willing to share the beat with a newcomer. They both became mentors and willing guides to the arcane practices of the White House beat. I was rescued, and my badly shattered confidence was gradually restored.

In the fall of 1981, Judy Woodruff achieved a journalistic and personal milestone. On September 16, she worked a full day, filing a report for *Nightly News*. At 2:57 the next morning, she delivered Jeffrey Woodruff Hunt, the first child for her and her husband, then *Wall Street Journal* Washington bureau chief Al Hunt. Chris Wallace announced Jeffrey's birthday a few hours later on the *Today* program, and John Chancellor showed video of the happy mother and child on that evening's *Nightly News*. Judy had appeared on both broadcasts and given birth, all in fewer than twenty-four hours. Born with a spinal cord defect known as spina bifida, Jeffrey quickly became very important to me, as have his parents. Five years later, Jeffrey was joined by Benjamin, and then by the "baby" of the family, Lauren, my godchild, who came from Korea. In many ways, they and my nieces and nephew have become surrogates for the children I never had.

At Lauren's christening, her father joked that every baby should have a Jewish godmother. I had no idea what my responsibilities were in terms of religious instruction, but somehow I felt I'd figure them out. The Woodruff-Hunt family welcomed me and my husband, Alan Greenspan, to celebrate with them every Christmas morning, creating new traditions that bind our families together through both wonderful times and tragedies. I've learned a lot about love and determination from all the Hunts as they've rallied around Jeffrey, who is in many ways the most courageous person I've ever known. At sixteen, a bright and physically active teenager, he suffered a terrible medical accident during what should have been routine surgery. With remarkable persistence and determination, he has struggled to rebuild his life.

Judy and Al, and John Palmer's wife, Nancy, along with their three girls, made covering Ronald Reagan a family affair. On extended presidential vacations, married correspondents often brought along the kids, and saved on hotel bills by renting houses in Santa Barbara (Jeffrey's debut on the White House beat was a trip to Barbados in 1982, where he distinguished himself as a teething seven-month-old by eating his press pass).

But the other effect of Jeffrey's birth, and Judy's maternity leave, was that I got to go to my first presidential news conference. Early in his administration, Ronald Reagan held his news conferences in the afternoon, when his staff thought he could do the least harm because television audiences were small. But the strategy backfired. When he made mistakes, there was no time to correct them: the reports on the network evening newscasts, which in the days before cable dominated the political agenda, could be devastating.

There were numerous instances where his staff felt he had stumbled in the give-and-take with reporters. The anchors would go on the air at six-thirty with headlines that for all intents and purposes said, "The president held a news conference today. Here are three reports on his six most alarming mistakes." The Associated Press started running fact checks on his errors. He found the fuss extremely annoying, occasionally calling reporters himself to defend his accuracy. Once, he called Betty Cuniberti of the *Los Angeles*

Times to complain about reports that he had made six errors in a news conference in January of 1982, on topics ranging from the "marriage penalty" in the tax code to a social program in Arizona.

"The truth was, I was right on five of six," Reagan told Cuniberti on the phone. "And the one was a technicality."

He wasn't right, but had persuaded himself he was.

That fall, there was a long list of questions to ask the president, and few opportunities to ask them. Since his news conferences were rare, my job as the junior varsity NBC person assigned to cover the White House was to yell above the sound of the helicopter as the president arrived and departed. I was the "designated shouter." That's how Ronald Reagan had come to know me. Since he rarely met reporters in formal sessions, I had to entice him into responding to questions on the run.

The day before the news conference, Sid Davis told me that there was an additional NBC seat, but it was in the rear row, wedged up against the camera tripods. It would be impossible to establish eye contact with the president, so to have any chance of being called on I'd have to do something to get his attention. Sid's advice was to wear red; in a sea of gray-flannel-suited men, I'd stand out. I dressed in a blazing red jacket, and studied hard.

Under the bright lights of the East Room, I watched from the cheap seats in the rear and sat as tall as I could so as to be visible to Reagan as he followed the time-honored protocol of calling first on Helen Thomas of UPI, followed by her counterpart from the Associated Press. Then, before singling out any of the television or print superstars in the front-row seats, he tilted his head to the side in his trademark fashion and said, "Now, Andrea, what is it you've been trying so hard to ask me?"

Had I been jumping up and down or shouting from the rear of the room? my mother asked later. What could the president possibly have meant? The explanation says a lot about Reagan's basic kindness. He was, above all else, a gentleman, and as he got on or off his helicopter heading to or returning from Camp David, he'd been walking by me as I shouted questions. He knew his handlers didn't want him to stop, but at his core, ignoring me conflicted with his code of behavior. It was bad manners. Even though all of us were shouting, he felt *he* was being rude. So two days before the news conference, when the staff began drilling him with test questions and answers, he had told them he wanted to call on "that nice woman who kept trying to ask a question."

Reagan used to practice in the White House amphitheater for these sessions, rare as they were. Aides would sit in, sometimes with name tags identifying them as Sam Donaldson, Judy Woodruff, John Palmer, or Lesley Stahl, the lead network correspondents of the day. He was told that the tougher questioners would be on one side, the easier on another. If he got into trouble, he was to call on one of the more oddball members of the press corps, such as Sarah Mc-Clendon, a colorful former member of the Women's Army Corps during World War II, who represented her own news service and berated successive presidents for being unfair to the farmers of her native west Texas and to veterans in general. Or Lester Kinsolving, an ordained minister and iconoclastic radio personality who could be counted on to ask something so outrageous it would embarrass the members of the press corps more than the president. In any case, the harassing questions would make viewers feel sympathetic to the chief executive and he'd be off the hook. The news conferences were in fact highly choreographed. The press secretary and his staff assigned seats by rank and, sometimes, by whether or not a correspondent was in good standing with the West Wing.

On this occasion, in the pre–news conference drill, the staff showed him a picture book with a lot of "nice women" correspondents: Ann Compton of ABC; Ann Devroy, then of Gannett and later a star at *The Washington Post* until her death from cancer in 1997. No, he kept saying, until he spotted my press pass photo and said, "That's the one I want to call on."

"No, you don't," Mike Deaver, White House chief of staff, responded, according to another Reagan aide. Even at that early stage, my reputation as an aggressive questioner was well established with the staff.

Fortunately, at that first news conference, I was prepared to ask the president about a new missile system under study at the Pentagon. He deferred to his defense secretary. It was an important lesson: White House correspondents always had to be ready. If I'd thought about it, questioning the president of the United States might have been intimidating. But I had developed a healthy skepticism about what any politician claimed to be the truth. Was that the result of going to school in the sixties, being an outsider in a man's profession, or just being feisty by nature? Or did it grow out of a sense of mission, sincere if sometimes misplaced, that made me one of the more annoying characters to those in charge of the unruly White House press room?

Looking back, I see that my pushiness may also have been tied to the fact that after being ousted from *Nightly News,* I was fighting my way back to network respectability. Ever the best of colleagues, Judy Woodruff and John Palmer conspired to find opportunities for me to show my stuff. Most memorably, they came up with the idea of shooting a story on how White House advance men and the Secret Service would all but invade a small Caribbean island—Barbados— to prepare for a presidential vacation trip.

———

It was Easter 1982, and the Reagans had decided to visit one of their glamorous Hollywood friends, Claudette Colbert, at her Barbados retreat. Judy or John suggested that I go several days earlier with one of the network's best cameramen, to portray the backstory behind the visit. To the surprise of all of us, the New York producers bought the proposal. From a creative perspective, nothing could have been further from the simple one-minute radio spots I was cranking out each day than producing three and a half minutes on how a sleepy island reacts when suddenly subjected to all the security requirements of the modern presidency. The story had to be very visual, and somewhat humorous. My cameraman and I started looking for telling moments as soon as we arrived.

On the second day, good fortune struck. We heard that the giant military cargo jets were about to arrive at the airport, ferrying in equipment for the visit. Scrambling to find a vantage point, we positioned ourselves on a hillside with a wide-eyed group of local children sitting on overturned buckets in the foreground, looking down on the runway—just as two enormous cargo jets thundered to a stop and lowered their ramplike doors, disgorging the president's armored limousine, gold seal glittering in the tropical sun, accompanied on either side by a phalanx of dark-suited Secret Service agents marching down the ramp. We had our opening scene.

What followed was even better: a trial run of the motorcade through the town's fishing village, with people wildly cheering the limo and its follow cars, not realizing it was a rehearsal rather than the real thing. Those wonderful pictures helped tell a story: streets being washed, traffic lines being painted, all in preparation for a head of state who would then spend the rest of the holiday weekend in complete seclusion at Claudette Colbert's seaside retreat—and all at considerable local expense.

Barbados was dressing up because company was coming. We spent days editing the piece, marrying the cameraman's beautifully evocative pictures to my narrative. With the luxury of time, and more than a little rum, we turned out a piece with just the right slightly ironic tone to close the broadcast the night Reagan finally arrived.

What made the Barbados trip unusual for a White House correspondent was that it was a rare opportunity to get into the field and shoot a "picture" story, independent of the team of producers—from both the network and the White House—who accompany every trip. Usually every backdrop, every movement, was carefully controlled, stage-managed like a Hollywood movie set. As Reagan, just before leaving office, told David Brinkley, when David asked if anything he'd learned as an actor had been of use to him in the presidency, "There have been times in this office when I've wondered how you could do the job if you hadn't been an actor."

———

For a time, the skill of the Reagan team at producing his events helped limit the political damage of the age factor. What those of us covering Reagan often couldn't determine was whether the White House put so much effort into orchestrating his events in order to mask the fact that he was losing his grasp. He had never been a detail man, but occasionally, he seemed to be utterly disengaged, at times not even recognizing his own aides.

Questions about his age and mental ability continued to dog Ronald Regan. Was it an early stage of Alzheimer's? His doctors insist not. I've talked to former aides, friends, and family, and no one believes he had a medical problem in his first term. A few aides do acknowledge that they had suspicions about his alertness toward the end of his presidency. In any case, the staff knew better than to suggest an age problem. The first lady would have pounced on any hint that her husband was frail or deteriorating.

The staff's nervousness about any mention of Reagan's age in news stories only increased after a disastrous 1982 trip to Europe, where the president fell asleep during an audience with the Pope. Nancy had warned about overscheduling her husband, and she'd been right. During that first European trip, he went from Versailles to Rome to Windsor Castle in one frantic day. Is it any wonder he was photographed dozing off with the Holy Father?

So I was treading on very dangerous turf when, less than a month later, I tackled the age question head-on. On the Fourth of July in 1982, we were in California for the landing of one of the space shuttle missions. The White House had planned a grand, red-white-and-blue patriotic arrival ceremony at Edwards Air Force Base to give Republicans a boost in the hard-fought midterm elections. But a NASA whistle-blower told me that the shuttle was going to orbit the earth one additional time just so that the president could get an extra hour's sleep. Given the fact that this was early in the space shuttle missions, when safe landings were not routine and at a time when the president was being scrutinized to determine whether he was really up to the job, it was clearly an explosive detail.

The shuttle was to land on a Sunday during the holiday weekend. The entire press corps was moved from Santa Barbara to Edwards Air Force Base, accompanying the president. Bands played, balloons went up, and the space-craft glided to a perfect three-point landing. It was, for all intents and purposes, a campaign rally celebrating American technology, with five hundred thousand people watching the reentry. The last thing the White House wanted to see on that evening's news was any reminder of the president's age or, worse, any suggestion that they were putting the astronauts at risk to give Reagan extra nap time.

I reported it on *Nightly News*. The White House never challenged the accuracy of the report, and it added to the lore about his age being a problem.

Most important, from my perspective, Mike Deaver was furious with me because of the shuttle story. I was told that I was persona non grata at the White House. I had touched on one of the most sensitive issues for the president's aides. It was a recurring question, one that became more exacerbated over time. Two years later, in his reelection bid, Reagan's rambling and confused responses during the first televised encounter with Walter Mondale occasioned a great deal of commentary. *The Wall Street Journal*'s lead story the next day had the headline: Fitness Issue: Is Oldest U.S. President Now Showing His Age? Reagan Debate Performance Invites Open Speculation on His Ability to Serve. Later, after the second debate, the press corps jokingly referred to it as the president's "going down the Pacific Coast Highway." He had clearly lost his train of thought, although he scored points by quipping that he was not going to exploit his opponent's "youth and inexperience."

At the time, Nancy blamed Deaver for failing to prepare the president properly for the debate. In truth, it probably was a combination of age and hearing loss, but since he was a relatively old candidate for reelection, the president's every word and gesture were scrutinized intensely. Reagan's staff spent a great deal of time trying to "manage" stories about the age issue by having the president appear only in the most controlled settings—hence Mike Deaver's sensitivity to what I had reported about the shuttle rescheduling.

At a recent gathering of former Reagan aides, I was reminiscing with one of his top White House advisors. Without prompting, he said, "Don't forget how much trouble you got into for that story about the shuttle landing." Twenty-two years later, I learned that it was even worse than I'd known at the time: the staff had been ordered not to give me access. No wonder my calls went unreturned, at least for a while. It just made me work even harder, trying to cultivate new sources to get around the problem.

———

In the fall of 1982, decisions far beyond our NBC White House booth changed my world. We were on a campaign trip to New Jersey, where Reagan spoke at a rally for Congresswoman Millicent Fenwick (an elegant, outspoken septuagenarian and the role model for Lacey in "Doonesbury"). Halfway through the event, Judy Woodruff got a message to call the bureau chief right away. She was going to become a national correspondent for the *Today* program, and John would be the *Today* show's news anchor in New York. Chris Wallace, my office mate at the bureau and a rising star at the network, would be replacing them as NBC's new chief White House correspondent immediately. I would be his backup, doing the morning show and late-night duty.

That night, we rode back to Washington on the press charter, trying to figure out how our lives would change. I struggled not to cry, realizing that I was losing my two closest NBC colleagues to other assignments. They had befriended me, mentored me, and protected me when I was at my lowest point at the network. And I didn't know what to expect from Chris Wallace.

Chris was charming and, at first, eager to let me help him figure out the rhythms of the place. The journalism he got right away: he was very smart and experienced at covering politics. What I failed to realize was my "proper" place as his subordinate. At times our personalities clashed, and neither of us knew how to smooth over the rough spots as we traveled around the world, often jet-lagged and for long stretches spending more time with each other than with our own families back home. On one particularly silly occasion, we got into a fierce argument over who would use the one NBC telephone in Guam to check in with the desk, much to the amusement of the rest of the press corps. Even thinking about it today embarrasses me. Eventually, we developed a healthy respect for each other's talents, and I think Chris knew that I would never fail to help outrun or outgun the competition on his behalf. But by then, he was ready to move on to a bigger job at ABC, and ultimately to his own Sunday morning show on Fox News. I'm sorry we wasted a few years tripping over each other before we figured out that we could be friends.

—

In the Reagan White House almost nothing was left to chance. A routine campaign event was artfully constructed to project a comforting image of an America that existed only in a Norman Rockwell painting. It *was* morning again in America, as the Reagan reelection slogan claimed, or at least it would be made to look that way. The deficit could be skyrocketing, the Cold War threatening, but Father Reagan was in the White House and all was right with the world. The stage-management of presidential events was most elaborate on trips abroad. The scenes come to mind as brightly imagined as a recolorized film: Reagan at the Great Wall of China; Reagan in Ballyporeen, Ireland, his family's ancestral home, in early summer 1984; perhaps, most emblematically, Reagan—the last American leader of the Cold War—at the demilitarized zone separating North and South Korea.

I was the pool reporter representing the networks that day in November 1983. The White House was embroiled in a fight over the defense budget. Even Republicans like Senators Bob Dole and Pete

Domenici, both deficit hawks, thought Reagan was spending too much. What better way to convey the need for a stronger defense against Communism than to stage an elaborate photo opportunity in Communism's front yard, at the DMZ? We were brought to Guard Post Collier, a watch station overlooking the vast expanse of no-man's-land that separates North from South. The only interruption on the horizon was a small enclave the U.S. called Propaganda Village, a completely fake town with giant loudspeakers blaring nonstop messages to harangue our soldiers.

Since I was the only network correspondent, my crew and I were brought in to the watch station before the president in order to shoot his arrival. The advance men had thought of everything; unable to wire the remote location for camera lights, they had measured the angle of the sun the day before so as to mark the exact spot where the president's face would best be illuminated in natural light. Reagan arrived dressed for the part in an olive green army jacket, the better to convey military strength. He climbed onto the parapet, pausing to look out at the frontier of North Korea, one of the last bastions of Communism, a country still technically at war with the United States despite an armistice. The only problem was that the president didn't stand on his mark.

Considering his previous profession, that was surprising. To save the moment from missing pure White House perfection, Dave Fischer, Reagan's "body" man, or personal assistant and closest aide (the part of Charlie Young on *The West Wing*), crawled on his hands and knees, below the angle of the cameras, tugged on the president's jacket, and stage-whispered, "Sir, you're not on your mark." Without missing a beat, Reagan moved over, raised his field glasses, and looked out at Propaganda Village.

Someone in the press corps gathered below, probably Sam Donaldson, shouted, "Mr. President, what do you see?"

Reagan replied, "It looks like a Hollywood back lot, only less important." As he addressed the troops, a choir of Korean orphans sang "Jesus Loves Me" to complete the tableau.

Sometimes the carefully produced White House mini-movies didn't come off exactly as staged, such as the midterm election trip to a hog farm in Iowa on a sweltering August day, designed to distract angry farmers at the nadir of the 1982 recession. Waiting for the president, we watched his stage managers try to pre-position an 800-pound hog, attempting to drag the poor animal out of its shed into the midday sun as Marine One approached overhead. The pig knew better, and stayed inside. (Have you ever stood in the mud and muck of a pig farm as a helicopter blew in for a landing? I don't recommend it.)

Or the visit to a bird sanctuary on the Eastern Shore of the Chesapeake Bay, in July 1984, when Reagan was being excoriated for his controversial environmental policies. When asked questions about the appointment of Anne McGill Burford to an advisory panel about oceans and the atmosphere after she'd been forced to resign for mismanaging the Environmental Protection Agency the year before, and the president did one of his famous duck-and-cover numbers as White House press secretary Larry Speakes literally stepped in front of him to block our questions.

Standing behind Speakes, Reagan said, "My guardian says I can't talk," as the White House turned off the camera lights, leaving our photographers shooting in the dark.

Their efforts to block our lens only made the moment more memorable, overshadowing their carefully planned "environmental" event—this, after the president had spent most of the day watching bald eagles from a fifty-foot observation tower at the sanctuary and lunching with local crab fishermen to show his interest in the harvest.

On one highly choreographed White House trip overseas, one of the most important of Reagan's presidency, I almost upset months of planning and superpower diplomacy. We were traveling on a Pan Am press charter, accompanying Ronald Reagan on his first trip to Communist China. Reagan was taking what we referred to as the slow boat to China: Nancy was not going to let him be jet-lagged when he landed in Beijing, so we had spent a weekend in California, followed by two days in Hawaii and a stopover in Guam.

Finally, once the president's body clock was considered sufficiently adjusted, our entire entourage left for China.

I had prepared endlessly for this part of the trip. The idea of Reagan, a fervent anti-Communist, negotiating with the leaders he still called the Red Chinese, fascinated me. I read books by all the old China hands and talked to State Department experts and intelligence officials. Reagan might not know what he was about to encounter, but I sure was ready. The flight would last about eight hours. Shortly after arriving, I was assigned a live *Today* show report, featuring an interview we would tape in Beijing with National Security Advisor Robert "Bud" McFarlane.

That morning, as we left Guam on our Pan Am 747, the flight attendants handed us orange juice and began serving breakfast right after liftoff. It was a routine they had perfected: the same crew flew with us on all our trips, and had become pals and traveling companions. Suddenly, I became flushed, weak-kneed and light-headed, and began itching uncontrollably. I was also having trouble breathing. A navy nurse on board quickly diagnosed it as anaphylaxis, a severe allergy to something I'd had to eat or drink. Nothing like this had ever happened to me; I was losing control of my body. The flight crew stretched me out on a plastic trash bag on the floor in the rear of the plane, where the camera crews and extra Secret Service agents usually sat, and radioed the president's doctor on Air Force One, flying just ahead of us, for instructions.

Cockpit to cockpit came the medical advice: epinephrine, which is basically adrenaline, and an antihistamine, Benadryl. My dear friend Steve Weisman of *The New York Times* put cold compresses on my head and kept telling me I'd be all right. At one point, I drifted off; later, the nurse monitoring my vital signs told me she thought my heart had, for a brief moment, stopped. Gradually, I came to, but on Air Force One the president's foreign policy advisors were debating whether after months of delicate diplomatic negotiations to resolve every last detail of the president's arrival in Beijing, they could risk offending the Chinese by taking a detour to drop me at a U.S. military hospital in Okinawa. After a huddle the White House correspondents voted to fly to Okinawa, letting the small group of reporters on Air Force One proceed and cover the president's historic arrival in Beijing.

I was embarrassed and desperate to stay with the trip. Minute by minute, the nurse on the press charter was passing my blood pressure numbers to the pilot so he could radio them to the doctor on Air Force One. They decided that if I stabilized by the halfway point, they'd let me continue. Only years later did one of Reagan's cabinet officers confide that at their rump National Security Council meeting on that flight, one of the president's top advisors had suggested I'd gotten sick on purpose, just to ruin their beautifully planned arrival ceremony.

When we finally did get to Beijing, they carried me off the plane to an ambulance waiting on the tarmac. The ambulance reeked of diesel fumes and was so old it could have been used on Mao's Long March. Determined to stay out of a Chinese hospital, I told them to take me to the press hotel. Three hours later, eyes still puffy from my allergic reaction, hair matted down from the cold, wet compresses, I somehow got through my *Today* show report and went to bed.

As I recovered, I found China fascinating. Beijing was in the early stages of its fitful opening to the West. The streets were still jammed with bicycles, not automobiles. There were open sewage ditches along the sides of the roads, and toddlers wearing split pants squatted at will in the streets. We were a motley crew after all our travels. Much to our amazement, the Chinese were so egalitarian that they invited the entire press corps to the state dinner they hosted for the president in the Great Hall of the People. They treated us like members of the official delegation, seating us in the enormous hall alongside the president's official party, and feting us with multiple courses of Chinese delicacies. Of course, we still had to leave early to go file our stories.

Outside the capital, we went to Xian to see the ancient life-sized terra-cotta horses and soldiers. Embedded in the press corps was an elderly, white-haired widow, Naomi Nover, who had inherited a news service from her late husband and insisted on keeping his White House press pass entitling her to travel on foreign trips. While we covered the president, she shopped. Occasionally, the fruits of her excursions created obstacles for the rest of us. We'd be lining up to race to an event. Her shopping bags would block us from making a quick exit from a bus or plane. Naomi cut quite a figure for foreigners not acquainted with her history, especially the Chinese soldiers guarding the terra-cotta warriors. She wanted to get closer to the statues. They tried to hold her back. Finally, Gary Schuster, the correspondent for *The Detroit News,* had an inspiration that quickly resolved the standoff. He pulled a dollar bill out of his wallet and showed the picture of George Washington to the Chinese guard. Washington's portrait did, in fact, bear an uncanny resemblance to Naomi. Figuring that she must be very important indeed if her face was on America's currency, the guards quickly cleared the way.

China was also a revelation to Ronald Reagan. A lifetime anti-Communist, he was greatly charmed by the warmth of his welcome and the ingenuity of the Chinese. In the mainland's very Westernized city, Shanghai, the president was so intrigued by the lively students at Fudan University, he began moderating his rigid views of the world's most populous country.

By the time we had stopped overnight in Alaska, he was calling the Chinese the "so-called Communists," and marveling at their incipient capitalism. As he had famously said when breaking a no-tax pledge as governor of California: "The sound you hear is the concrete cracking around my feet." At age seventy-three, Ronald Reagan was once again confounding his critics by showing that he could adjust to change.

But while traveling the globe conducting this very public diplomacy, Reagan was concealing the darker side of his foreign policy, the secret operations being run out of the National Security Council.

Already, Oliver North was organizing CIA missions in Central America against the Nicaraguan government, in violation of congressional prohibitions. There were tentative overtures to Iran, in the hopes of getting the Iranians to influence the release of American hostages being held in Beirut, Lebanon. Only a few years later, the two operations would come together with tragic consequences for the president's second term.

———

The summer of 1984 marked the fortieth anniversary of the Normandy invasion and my first trip to cover the commemoration of D-day. With American and Allied veterans gathered on a promontory over Omaha Beach, Ronald Reagan delivered one of the most poetic and powerful speeches of his presidency, written by his elegiac speechwriter, Peggy Noonan. As Reagan described the daunting feat of the Army Rangers who had climbed the cliffs in a hail of gunfire, he gazed at the aging veterans assembled in front of him and said, "These are the boys of Pointe du Hoc." The words were largely Peggy's, but in Reagan's unique way, he gave them life. In that one speech, the president re-created the past, celebrated the present, and memorialized the achievements of the D-day veterans for all future time.

Occasionally, if rarely, there are moments to pause and reflect on the experience during a White House trip. Later that day, walking in the American Cemetery at Colleville-sur-Mer, I thought about Reagan's unforgettable speech, in that historic setting, and the response of the D-day survivors. I realized anew that journalism was for me more than a business or a profession. It was a way of living, of experiencing the world even as I instantly distanced myself from it, in order to re-create what I'd witnessed for the public. Often, it required making a conscious effort to stand back a step or two for better perspective. To a degree, everything I experienced immediately became vicarious. But there were risks. After spending so many years standing apart from events, sometimes I found myself seeing real life as though through a camera lens. I would instinctively visualize how something would appear on television, rather than feeling it as it happened. By creating an emotional barrier, you are able to cover horrific stories like 9/11, or the earthquake and tsunami that devastated so much of South Asia on the day after Christmas 2004. But it eventually robs you of the ability to respond as a human being. Or delays the reaction, as I had learned after my experiences in Jonestown, Guyana.

Normandy was different. There we were memorializing events that were uniquely courageous and inspiring. I permitted myself to respond more personally. Nothing our generation had done could match the heroics of those who landed on that beach and scaled those cliffs while under fire. Ten years later, when we returned to Normandy with a new president, Bill Clinton, for the fiftieth anniversary of the invasion, Tom Brokaw found the central metaphor for this experience and for what made the men of Pointe du Hoc and their brethren "the Greatest Generation."

If Normandy in 1984 reaffirmed my love for the business, what happened next was like a cold shower. From France, we went to London to cover Reagan at the economic summit. I'd planned to stay on in England and drive to the Lake District with my sister, but as was so often the case, a family outing was interrupted by the requirements of my job.

The front office in New York called. The entertainment division of NBC was giving the separate news division airtime to run a prime-time show for thirteen weeks. The only problem: the hole in the programming schedule that needed to be filled was on Sunday night, opposite the ratings monster *60 Minutes*. All of the male anchors at NBC had turned down the opportunity, thank you very much. So our bosses came up with a novel alternative format that they boiled down to "live television, with two chicks and a truck." They wanted me to coanchor with Linda Ellerbee, crisscrossing the country on a new satellite truck. In fact, the truck was the real star. As my witty colleague Linda later put it: "We were supposed to do 'Gidget Goes Network.'"

If that sounds sketchy, it was. The idea was to try out the news division's latest toy, a satellite truck that enabled us to broadcast live from remote locations. They wanted to test its training wheels on the road, live from a different city each week. The rationale for the program? We'd make it up as we went along. The producers? NBC all-stars, but borrowed while still carrying out full-time duties on other, ongoing shows. The cast? That's where it got *really* creative. Take the best writer in television news, Linda Ellerbee, a somewhat bawdy Texan more at home in an Austin bar than the U.S. Capitol (think Debra Winger in *Urban Cowboy*), and add a hyperactive White House correspondent who, when asked by a reporter, "What do you do to get rid of stress?" replied, "Have another cup of coffee!" And we had only two weeks to get ready for our first show, which NBC called *Summer Sunday, U.S.A.*

To paraphrase Dr. Johnson, like the dog that walks on its hind legs, the wonder of the thing was just proving that we could do it at all. Linda would spend the week lining up the show with the producers (her extraordinary talent later led her to create her own company, Lucky Duck Productions, which has won numerous Emmy Awards for, among other programs, breakthrough children's television). My job was to cover the president of the United States five days a week, fly to meet Linda and the crew on Friday night, write the script Saturday, rehearse Sunday, do the broadcast, and take the red-eye back to Washington to start the whole sequence all over again.

For our first broadcast, we went live on the Mall in Washington during the July Fourth holiday weekend, thinking it would be safer to kick off the show close to home base. The theme was the nation's independence and the challenge of immigration policy. For one segment, the idea was to contrast the easy entry to America for celebrities with the hard choices facing undocumented workers. I was supposed to interview two immigrants: a celebrity teenage Chinese tennis player and an undocumented worker from Mexico. Hu Na, the tennis player, was on location, on tour in Detroit. The Mexican woman, whom we called Rosa Maria to protect her identity, was sitting next to me.

When I started asking Hu Na questions about her passage to America, she could only answer, "Please." Thinking she had trouble hearing, I raised my voice and repeated myself—still nothing. Finally, I was practically screaming at the poor kid, who still responded with a blank stare. As it turned out, no one had checked to see if she spoke English. In desperation, I turned to the Mexican woman to my left, only to discover that she had gotten cold feet during my misadventure with Hu Na and, fearing exposure, had covered her face with a giant straw hat. As Ellerbee described the moment in her memoir *And So It Goes,* "Andrea went ahead with the interview, never mentioning the hat, never seeming to notice she was interviewing a hubcap." The show was crashing around me, but I was trapped in my preparation, unable to acknowledge the absurdity of the moment. As one of the kinder producers said, "At least it's only television."

There were twelve more shows. We broadcast from Max Yasgur's farm in Bethel, New York, to commemorate the fifteenth anniversary of Woodstock (in a downpour, which was fitting, considering the weather at the original rain-soaked event). One memorable Sunday I was told to interview United Nations ambassador Jeane Kirkpatrick about our military conflicts in Central America. First we played a report from Fred Francis, in Nicaragua, about the CIA's illegal mining of the harbors to covertly undermine the communist Sandinista government. I asked Kirkpatrick to comment, but in what was becoming a bad habit for my guests, she said nothing. The only way I knew she hadn't had a stroke was that she swiveled in her chair, occasionally staring at her nails.

Finally, I said, "Madame Ambassador, can you respond?"

Kirkpatrick answered tersely, "I never respond to lies."

I never regained control of the interview. Somehow, I had managed to appear both mean and ineffectual at the same time. Even worse, I never got the answers I was seeking, and Kirkpatrick felt sandbagged. Afterward, even my parents told me that it looked as though I'd set her up. The president of NBC News "suggested" I write to Kirkpatrick and apologize.

And how did the truck do? For thirteen weeks of live programming, we had audio and video, but rarely both at the same time. Nor did we ever recover from our first, truly dreadful, review, unfortunately written by the dean of television critics, Tom Shales of *The Washington Post*. After that first show with Hu Na, Shales wrote, "This colossally pointless NBC show comes equipped with its own truck for fast getaways. . . . On the premiere Mitchell was cold and wooden; Jack Webb as 'The D.I.' was a veritable Smurf by comparison."

I learned important lessons that summer: If you think you can do two full-time jobs, people will expect you to do three. Don't get wedded to scripts and TelePrompTers. Instead, make sure you listen to what your guests are saying, and improvise. And when disaster strikes, when traveling with an entourage that occasionally resembles a rock group on tour, it isn't a good idea to be the only sober person in the room.

Being on the road all that summer was exciting, but also very, very tough. Increasingly, NBC was dominating my life, personally and professionally. How much was choice, how much necessity? After almost a decade in the nation's capital, I still didn't have an answer to that question.

———

When I first moved to Washington from Philadelphia, I was a bit lost. I'd left behind rich associations built in college and afterward during my apprenticeship as a journalist during the difficult Rizzo years. Then came my move to the network, with the deeply disturbing first posting abroad to Jonestown, followed by other professional setbacks on the *Nightly News*. I had survived it all, and grown, yet I was still unsure that I was indeed a long-distance runner capable of sustaining this career. I'm not sure I could have stuck it out without the friendship and support of people who showed me that

Washington was not just a city of marble buildings and smoke-filled rooms and power brokers, but also a town full of people who do care about each other, in good times and bad.

Soon after arriving in Washington, I'd begun to meet people outside politics. A Philadelphia friend introduced me to a Washington writer named Judith Huxley, whose living room was often the setting for an informal literary salon. Judy collected people the way other people enjoy good bottles of wine. She drank us all in, and loved nothing more than introducing her special friends to one another. An extraordinary cook, she also wrote a food column for *The Washington Post,* a biweekly essay with superb recipes that even I could follow as a guidebook for creating a perfect meal for friends. I spent so many evenings and holidays with her and her husband, Matthew, that Judy became my Washington family. It was through her that I met a whole group of other writers and artists, Washington intellectuals and public servants who crossed several generations.

Judy once wrote a column for the *Post* called "The Blow-Dried Duck Technique," about an indulgent birthday dinner she cooked for me, which started with fish pâté and included roast duck with ginger-lemon sauce. The highlight was supposed to be a fabulous birthday cake, a meringue torte. To her horror, a greedy raccoon came in through an open window and ate the cake she'd set out to cool the night before. Making a virtue of necessity, Judy created an instant dessert out of things she had in the freezer, whipping up an ice cream bombe in the shape of a cake in no time flat.

Judy never showed the world her private struggle: for thirteen years my friend valiantly fought breast cancer, but finally it spread to her spine and lungs. Doctors at the National Institutes of Health tried all kinds of new protocols, but when she finally succumbed, it was at home, surrounded by family and friends. She was only fifty-six years old. Again, I was torn in different directions. She died on the same day in 1983 that snipers attacked U.S. marines in Lebanon, and I had to go to work. (Only a week later, a suicide bomber blew up the marine barracks in Beirut, killing 241.) I think of Judy all the

time, even to this day. I wish she had lived long enough to see her
grandchildren and know the man I have married.

But she lives on through her legacy of friendship. Through Judy,
I met other women, including Elaine Kurtz, a painter whose husband had been the IRS commissioner under Jimmy Carter; Sheela
Lampietti, a landscape gardener; and Maria Schoolman, a sculptor.
We all came together around Judy's illness. For years afterward, we
celebrated holidays, cooked Judy's recipes, and heard her voice in
our ears.

Inevitably there were awkward moments when my private and
public life collided in almost comic ways. As a White House correspondent, I spent years covering presidents and their guests as they
partied and vacationed. Long before I met Katharine Graham, who
became a friend, I was assigned, along with Sam Donaldson, to stake
out her house on R Street in a snowstorm because Ronald Reagan
was having dinner there. My bureau chief, Sid Davis, said, "I don't
care if he's covered by the White House pool camera in the motorcade. I want a White House correspondent there in case he chokes
on a chicken bone."

So Sam and I stood outside, watching the limousines pull into the
driveway. Despite what many people may think, it's hardly a glamorous life. As coverage has become more relaxed, White House correspondents don't have to do this any longer, although producers
often do. But in those days, especially after the assassination attempt
in 1981, we covered Ronald Reagan around the clock. If he went to
his friend Charles Wick's on Christmas Eve to sing carols, we were
there, too, standing outside. In a strange way, it was a virtual life. We
experienced holidays as bystanders and observers, far from our own
families. Many of us tried to turn the press corps into our extended
families, creating a nest wherever we found ourselves. The holiday
rituals of White House press corps road warriors replaced those of
our childhoods.

In fact, the White House assignment had its own seasonal
rhythms. We had all been lulled into a comfortable routine. Summers

and most holidays we were in Santa Barbara, headquarters for the western White House, even though the president was safely ensconced at his mountaintop ranch, at least thirty miles away. The only glimpse we got of him was when he rode horseback, a figure dancing in and out of focus in the heat waves, seen only through enormously long camera lenses originally designed to track space launches. You could hardly tell it was Reagan, who, with his trademark puckishness, liked to tease that he could *really* get the press corps going if he clutched his chest on one of his morning rides, pretending to have a heart attack, just to watch us scramble.

On New Year's we were scarcely any closer—outside the walls of the hundred-acre Palm Springs estate of former ambassador to the Court of St. James's Walter Annenberg and his wife, Leonore, who was Reagan's chief of protocol. When the Reagans gathered at the Annenbergs' for a yearly reunion with their California friends, we would take turns standing outside at the intersection of Frank Sinatra Drive and Bob Hope Boulevard. In between, there were trips to Europe and Japan for summits with the allies—foreign capitals experienced almost entirely from inside a hotel ballroom, where the White House would brief the press.

Though most of our contact with Ronald Reagan was at carefully staged photo opportunities, the subjects we covered—the arms race, budget debates, the midterm recession, and the president's campaign for reelection—were fascinating to me, and I worked hard to develop sources that would help inform my reporting. That meant staying late, working weekends, calling outside experts, and reading, reading, reading.

Even today, I get e-mails and calls from young women asking for advice about how to get into television. Almost always, their goal is to be a "television anchor." Rarely do they say they want to be journalists. Few understand that the best anchors, only the credible, successful ones, are, first, good reporters. Not many of these eager aspirants are prepared to be desk assistants, researchers, and associate producers, in small television markets if necessary, before getting that first job in front of the camera.

Years after those trips to Palm Springs, I went with my husband, Alan Greenspan, and former secretary of state George Shultz and his wife to visit Lee Annenberg, who had become a friend as a fellow trustee of the University of Pennsylvania. We were on our way to California, where Alan was to speak at Stanford. Lee said, "Come spend the weekend here." Walking into her house, I was immediately struck by the beauty of the setting, including a nine-hole golf course carved out of the desert. But perhaps because I had spent so many years outside, with my nose pressed against the window glass, watching the "grown-ups" go in to play, it still seemed a bit of a fantasy, not quite real. I tried to imagine what it must have been like when the Reagans were there, celebrating New Year's Eve.

———

The first time I actually attended a Washington official function as a guest, rather than a reporter, was with Alan. It was the winter of 1985, at a black-tie dinner in honor of the Reagans on Embassy Row, at what used to be the Fairfax Hotel—in fact, the same hotel where Al Gore, he of the rural Tennessee roots, had grown up as the son of a leading senator. Even in Washington, growing up in a hotel suite was unusual. Gore's parents never had a home in the capital.

At that first Reagan dinner, I was seated next to Bill Casey, Reagan's 1980 campaign manager and CIA director. Casey was one of the most secretive men in Washington. He couldn't have been thrilled to be seated next to a reporter, even an off-duty one. I wish I'd been able to take notes, especially after discovering a year later that at the time Casey was already running the illegal Iran-Contra operation.

I'd known of Alan Greenspan since 1983, when he was head of the President's National Commission on Social Security Reform. Among other assignments at the time, I was covering White House budgets, which included trying to fact-check the fiscal wizardry of Budget Director David Stockman and explain Reagan's trickle-down economics. On a regular basis I'd question David Gergen, then assistant to the president in the Office of Communications, about the latest budget numbers.

During 1983 and 1984, I hammered Gergen with questions about whether the White House budget assumptions were credible. Finally he said, "Why don't you ask an outside economist? Learn economics the way you learned about arms control—it's the next step for you."

It was smart advice. He suggested I consult Alan, who at the time ran an economic consulting firm in New York.

When I called Alan, with no introduction, he was very helpful. Soon, we were talking fairly regularly, and at some point I asked him to one of those correspondents' dinners to which reporters invite their sources. As it turned out, Barbara Walters had already invited him, but he said that if I ever got to New York, I should call him for lunch. There was something in the way he said it that prompted me to call Gergen and ask, "Is this guy single?"

To which he replied, "Don't you know? He's a really eligible bachelor," confirming my growing suspicion that Alan was interested in more than the budget.

Still we didn't get together. Both of us were busy, and we lived in different cities. Finally, in December of 1984, I was in New York to do a year-end report for the *Today* show, and Alan invited me to dinner. It was December 28, that lovely time between Christmas and New Year's when the tree is still up in Rockefeller Center, the holiday store windows are festive, and New Yorkers are no longer rushing past each other to finish their shopping. I envisioned doing the *Today* show live and then taking the rest of the day off to primp for dinner.

But a story broke that day in *The Washington Post* that *Nightly News* wanted me to cover. Instead of preparing for my date, I scrambled to pull together a segment for the evening news. Barely an hour before I was to meet Alan, I raced back to the hotel to change clothes and grab a cab to the restaurant. By then it was snowing. It was also rush hour at Christmastime, and there were no cabs to be had. So I trudged across town to the restaurant, tired, wet, and not very glamorous by the time I arrived at Alan's favorite restaurant, Le Périgord.

He was already waiting at the table, a pattern that has in fact been repeated in all the years since—Alan waiting patiently, while I finish reporting an unanticipated story. But the moment I sat down with him, the evening was transformed. We connected, talking about music and baseball and our childhoods. I found this shy man known for convoluted explanations on economic trends to be funny and sweet and very endearing. We had such a good time, he suggested extending the evening by going for a drive through Central Park in the snow. That was our first date.

We saw each other after that, but not seriously. I was always traveling with Reagan, and he was seeing other people in New York. Then, in February 1985, David Stockman and his wife, Jennifer, came to dinner at my house. On that day, I'd interviewed Margaret Thatcher for the *Today* program, always a challenge, and then reported a separate story for *Nightly News*. Now, feeling a little like Superwoman, I was giving a dinner. Fortunately, I had a lot of help from my longtime housekeeper Emilia Almeida, who for years has made sure I eat, can somehow find things in my overstuffed closets, and occasionally throws out the accumulating stacks of newspapers. Alan was coming down from New York to attend. Other guests included Judy Woodruff and her husband, Al Hunt, as well as Vice President George Bush's chief of staff, Craig Fuller, and White House assistant Karen Hart.

At the time, Stockman's wife was seven months' pregnant, and he himself was worn out, having spent the day testifying in front of a hostile congressional committee. During his first year on the job, in 1981, Stockman—who was the youngest budget director in history— barely survived several controversies, including proposing that ketchup be reclassified as a vegetable in order to save money on school lunches for poor kids. He was also taken to the White House "woodshed" for confiding doubts about the president's trickle-down economics to *The Atlantic* magazine. Now, four years later, David was close to quitting and had become even more outspoken about pork barrel spending. After hectoring from several congressional committee members, he'd even lost his temper and said that military pensions were too fat, and that many farmers had only themselves to blame for their economic problems and did not deserve government bailouts. His own mother, who raised corn and soybeans on the family's farm in Michigan, told an Iowa radio station her son's comments "don't set too well with me."

At dinner that night, David was so exhausted, he leaned back in his chair and passed out. The chair fell backward, and his head snapped back so hard, the impact punched a hole in the plaster of my dining room wall.

Chaos. Once I realized David was breathing, my first worry was Jennifer, almost at her due date and now terrified that her husband was having a heart attack. When the emergency rescue people came to take him to nearby Georgetown University Hospital, all of us, still worried, trooped off behind them. What we didn't know was that the Associated Press was monitoring police and fire department emergency radio communications. Word got out that it was Stockman in the emergency room, and a reporter showed up at the hospital. That's how my relationship with Alan Greenspan became public.

Early on, I decided to play by a very strict set of rules at social occasions: everything said was off the record. As I began to socialize more frequently with Alan among the people I covered in the administration, it was the only way anyone could feel comfortable being around me. If someone said something of particular interest, I would call the next day and ask whether we could revisit the subject, and discuss it on the record or, if not, at least "on background"— meaning it could be reported, but without attribution.

Alan took me to my first White House state dinner, for Jose Napoleon Duarte, president of El Salvador, in the fall of 1987. Having covered many such dinners as a reporter, I felt strange being inside, looking out. Although wearing an Oscar de la Renta gown that almost broke the bank, I went through the receiving line still feeling as though I didn't really belong. Nancy Reagan made it a practice to invite at least one press couple to each of these affairs, but I wasn't senior enough to get on that invitation list. In fact, Alan had been invited to come alone. Normally Mrs. Reagan, a stickler for etiquette, did not permit unmarried couples at White House social functions. But Alan made a special request to be able to bring me along as his date. By this time, he had moved to Washington to accept the job at the Federal Reserve. We were dating regularly, but still sorting through our feelings about each other. Neither of us was ready to make a commitment, and there wasn't much time for socializing. Alan was focusing most of his energy on learning the intricacies of his new job. (Which was a good thing: only five days later, the stock market crashed and Alan's efforts were critical in limiting the long-term damage.)

State dinners are carefully choreographed to create an atmosphere of elegance. They are as close as we come in this country to a kind of royal experience, stiff occasions that are hardly what you'd call kick-up-your-heels kind of fun. The table settings are exquisite, with beautifully arranged, abundant flowers. The menus, engraved by calligraphers at each place setting, are treasured mementos. And for each dinner, the White House pastry chef strains to surpass himself with an elaborate dessert confection. Into this mix add the power of the assembled guests, carefully chosen from the domains of politics, business, Hollywood, and the arts, and you have the ingredients for a sparkling evening—especially in Nancy Reagan's White House.

Mrs. Reagan brought a distinctive style to the White House. She set out to restore a sense of formality, even pomp and circumstance, in contrast to Jimmy Carter's more down-home administration. You didn't see Ronald Reagan carrying his suit bag off Air Force One, as Carter did to create the image of a common man. Certainly, you never saw an eleven-year-old child seated among the guests, reading her homework, as Amy Carter had at a state dinner. With Reagan, more likely, you'd hear a fanfare and "Ruffles and Flourishes." Those of us who wore blue jeans during the Carter years, largely because the president himself did, rarely dared even wear slacks when Reagan was president.

A certain dress code was understood. Those were the days of Adolfo designer suits and bouffant hairdos, what Alan teasingly called my "Republican" helmet hair. Looking back at pictures from the Reagan years, I'm sometimes amused, if not horrified, at my appearance, with big jewelry (in my case, fake) and big hair. It was a time of conspicuous excess, both on Wall Street and the Washington social circuit. But, early in the administration, all this extravagance struck a discordant note as the economy slumped and more and more people lost their jobs.

As the gap widened between rich and poor, Nancy Reagan was sharply criticized for acquiring new china, even though it was donated; for accepting designer gowns and not paying for them; for borrowing jewelry to wear to Princess Diana's wedding. She took an unholy beating in the press, including cruel articles caricaturing her appearance. Nonetheless, her power was near complete. It didn't matter whether you were the chief of staff or a member of the press corps. If you got on her bad side, you were in trouble.

But for all the caricatures, Nancy Reagan played a unique and critical role in the administration. She was always her husband's best political advisor, even helping engineer a crucial switch in campaign managers that helped him win in 1980. Once her husband was elected, Mrs. Reagan obsessed over every slight in the news columns. In the spring of 1982, she began reconstructing her own image with a brilliantly self-deprecating performance at the annual press Gridiron dinner. Dressing as a charwoman in the style of one of Carol Burnett's most memorable characters, the first lady sang a parody about "Second Hand Clothes," a takeoff on the Streisand song. Landon Parvin, a brilliant satirist who has crafted humorous after-dinner speeches for two generations of politicians, mostly Republicans, wrote the skit. Over the years, as Nancy grew more confident, she became more philosophical about criticism of herself; but she never let down her guard when it came to her husband's critics.

———

Perhaps Mrs. Reagan's most important contribution to her husband's presidency was getting him to rethink his attitude toward the "Evil Empire." In the fifth year of his administration, Ronald Reagan still had not met a Soviet leader. When pressed about why he hadn't negotiated with the Russians, Reagan would say, "Well, they keep dying on me." After Leonid Brezhnev died in 1982, there were two successors—Yuri Andropov and Konstantin Chernenko— in the course of just three years. Both died in office.

If these transitions were difficult for the head of state, they presented a different challenge to us broadcasters. If one of these leaders died in the middle of the night, we had to scramble to go live on the *Today* show. Unfortunately, we were in Santa Barbara when we got the word about Andropov. I'd been out to dinner, and had consumed more than my share of wine. When I got back to my room around midnight, there was a call from the news desk at *Today* about a rumor circulating that the Soviet leader had passed away, based on the observations of *Washington Post* Moscow bureau chief Dusko Doder that official Soviet radio had switched to funeral music. The people at the *Today* show wanted to know if I could confirm the rumor. Desperately I tried to locate Larry Speakes, who was AWOL.

When I finally got someone at the National Security Council, I was able to confirm the story. Incredibly, the American embassy in Moscow was caught completely unaware. I went on the *Today* show at 4 a.m. West Coast time, but not enough time had elapsed for me to be completely sober. John Palmer was anchoring in New York. I barely got through my report, and it taught me an important lesson about the risks of letting your hair down on the White House beat—something I never did again.

Chernenko died in March 1985—after serving for only one year— and was replaced by a young man by Soviet standards: fifty-four-year-old Mikhail Gorbachev. It's difficult to convey how electrifying the change was to the White House, and to all of us covering foreign policy. After years of Cold War threats from a series of colorless Kremlin apparatchiks, Gorbachev was an entirely new kind of Soviet leader: more open intellectually, and curious about the West. He was interested in ideas on economic reform that, once fully formulated, would become known as Perestroika. Margaret Thatcher was the first European leader to meet him, and validated him for the West. "I like Mr. Gorbachev. We can do business together," she said. By the time Gorbachev took over, Ronald Reagan was himself rethinking the possibility of arms control and détente. He was also almost religious in his fervor about eliminating the need for nuclear weapons by creating a perfect defense against them. As a result of the influence of scientist Edward Teller and others, he was convinced that missile defense, pejoratively referred to by critics as Star Wars, could somehow protect America from a Soviet first strike with an invisible shield.

It had never been tested. In fact, at that point, it hadn't even been invented. But the fact that Reagan was willing to invest in the systems scared the Soviets and helped get them to the bargaining table. One of the great, unintended consequences of Reagan's missile defense plan was that it made the Soviets feel more vulnerable and willing to negotiate. They also spent so much money trying to compete with the phantom American technology, it helped bankrupt their system, accelerating its collapse. The administration's foreign policy team was still bitterly divided over whether to negotiate with the Soviets, but George Shultz and the State Department diplomats eager for arms reductions had a secret weapon of their own: Nancy Reagan.

———

Long before her husband, the first lady believed that there had to be a way out of the arms race. Whether she accomplished it through pillow talk or not, she weighed in against Pentagon hard-liners like Defense Secretary Caspar Weinberger, and helped get Reagan to a summit with Gorbachev in 1985. Not that Weinberger was without resources. He leaked a hard-line memo to the press just as the president was heading to Geneva, a last attempt to subvert the negotiations. And now there was another player on the arms control front, one with no experience in either diplomacy or nuclear weapons—the new chief of staff, former treasury secretary Donald Regan.

Donald Regan was colorful and profane. He had a healthy ego, but as the former head of Merrill Lynch had more of a salesman's knowledge of Wall Street than a deep knowledge of economics. But typically, when Reagan was first forming his administration, he appointed Regan treasury secretary without having even met or interviewed him. It was enough that he was the choice of the kitchen cabinet of California advisors in charge of the presidential transition.

Realizing that James Baker was weary from the stress of four years running the White House, Don Regan had cleverly proposed a job swap at the beginning of the second term, and Baker became treasury secretary. Incredibly, the two officials presented it to the boss as a *fait accompli*. As long as "the boys" said it would work, the chief executive saw no reason to question their suitability for their new assignments. With perfect timing and an innate sense for avoiding political disaster, Baker left the White House and became an extraordinarily good treasury secretary. But his departure left the president with a chief of staff who had little experience in politics, and less in foreign policy.

Taking over the White House, Regan was more authoritarian than Baker had been. Baker came from an old and privileged Houston family, but never affected a sense of pride or entitlement. Regan was different. Unlike the rest of the senior White House staff, he had made a lot of money and felt that made him the president's equal rather than just a staff man, a subordinate. He tried to cement their relationship by sharing an endless collection of jokes, which he told with flair and great Irish wit. When he ventured into foreign policy, his wit ran out.

In the first Reagan term, more experienced cabinet officers like Secretary of State George Shultz had had to fix Regan's mistakes at

Treasury more than once. During the first economic summit Reagan hosted, held in Williamsburg, Virginia, in 1983, Shultz and Regan were constantly at odds, and at the end even held separate competing news conferences. Shultz had to reassert his ground over and over again, as the Treasury Department meddled in areas where foreign and economic policies overlapped.

Only a few months after Regan took over, he faced his first controversy—one that put him on the wrong side of the first lady. Mrs. Reagan was far more attuned to how events would play with the public than either her husband or his chief of staff. She was the first to realize that her husband's plan to visit a Nazi cemetery in Germany in the spring of 1985 was going to elicit a storm of criticism.

The White House advance team for the trip, including Mike Deaver, had visited the Bitburg cemetery during the winter, when the incriminating headstones were blanketed in snow. That was their explanation for not knowing that the elaborate ceremony they were arranging to honor victims of World War II was going instead to memorialize SS soldiers who had been part of the Gestapo.

After the controversy exploded, Reagan dug in his heels, refusing to cancel the event to prevent further embarrassment for his host, German chancellor Helmut Kohl. Making the situation worse was Reagan's earlier refusal to visit a concentration camp on the trip. Defending his plan, Reagan said, "I think that there's nothing wrong with visiting that cemetery where those young men are victims of Nazism also, even though they were fighting in the German uniform, drafted into service to carry out the hateful wishes of the Nazis . . . They were victims, just as surely as the victims in the concentration camps."

There was an outcry from Jewish leaders, who said the president's statement about the poor SS men was a perversion of history. A White House official told us that Reagan had read a sympathetic treatment of the SS men in a 1973 *Reader's Digest* magazine. Many of the stories that got him in trouble over the years came from popular magazines, not history. The issue came to a boil when, three weeks before his trip to

Germany, Reagan was to award Holocaust survivor Elie Wiesel the Congressional Gold Medal. After agonizing over whether even to accept the award, Wiesel decided to go ahead with it but use the White House event to make his own point.

Looking up at Reagan in the Roosevelt Room, Wiesel, with his painful history all but mapped on his deeply lined face, pleaded with the president to change his mind. "May I, Mr. President, if it is possible at all, implore you to do something else, to find a way, to find another way, another site. That place, Mr. President, is not your place. Your place is with the victims of the SS . . . the issue here is not politics, but good and evil. And we must never confuse them."

Reagan appeared stricken, momentarily silenced by the power of Wiesel's argument and the emotion of his expression. The White House had in fact dispatched aides to try to silence Wiesel, or get him to modulate his disagreement with Reagan. Instead, Wiesel became a symbol for all Holocaust survivors, standing up to power and speaking truth.

To try to quiet the critics, the White House added a stop at a concentration camp, Bergen-Belsen, and in the long run Reagan's visit may have had an unintended diplomatic payoff. It avoided a rupture with Kohl, a crucial ally. Four years later, when Germany was at the center of critical decisions surrounding the end of the Cold War, the close Reagan/Kohl friendship became a major factor.

But the decision to go to Bitburg was one of the early stumbles for the new chief of staff, Donald Regan. The first lady let it be known that had Jim Baker still been on the watch, the mistake would never have been made in the first place.

Almost immediately after moving across the street from Treasury, the new chief of staff tried to establish himself on the world stage. His most dramatic opportunity was the president's first summit with a Soviet leader, an event the foreign policy team had been working toward for years.

Arriving in Geneva that November of 1985, Regan immediately propelled himself into the limelight. While Secretary of State Shultz and National Security Advisor Robert McFarlane focused on the arms control agenda, and Mike Deaver choreographed the public encounters between the two Cold Warriors, all Regan seemed to care about was projecting his own importance at the summit. At his direction, the ceremonial group photo of the leaders' first meeting with their foreign policy teams showed only three people: the two leaders and Don Regan, with no other advisors in view. In almost Soviet fashion, on Regan's orders, all the others present, including the secretary of state and the national security advisor, had been cropped out of the picture, erased as nonpersons.

In fact, even before they arrived in Geneva, Regan had caused an international stir when he told a writer for *The Washington Post,* Donnie Radcliffe, that women didn't care about the nuclear arms race because "They're not . . . going to understand throw weights or what is happening in Afghanistan or what is happening in human rights." Technically, throw weight, an arms control term, is the amount of lift needed to propel a missile and its warhead. To Don Regan, these were clearly male concerns. The next day, a *Post* editorial suggested that Mr. Regan stop worrying.

"Women are clever," said the *Post* with the stiletto wit of its peerless editorial page editor, Meg Greenfield. "They've mastered vacuum cleaners and washing machines, and some can even figure out the family phone bills." Her editorial suggested that the former Wall Street salesman had had so much coaching in preparation for the summit that he was becoming known as "the Eliza Doolittle of arms control." No sooner had we arrived in Geneva than Sam Donaldson of ABC saw an opportunity to embarrass Regan at the first photo opportunity between the two Cold War leaders.

As Regan watched, his face becoming more and more flushed, Sam asked Gorbachev and Reagan whether they agreed with the chief of staff that nuclear arms treaties were not of concern to women. Clearly unaware of the original story, Reagan seemed mystified. Gorbachev, seeing an opening even if he didn't understand the context, jumped in: "Both men and women in the United States and the Soviet Union, all over the world, are interested in having peace for themselves and being sure that peace would be kept stable and lasting for the future. . . ." Much to the annoyance of the president's political and foreign policy advisors, round one went to the Soviet leader, thanks to Don Regan.

By the time Regan returned to Washington, he had already been widely criticized for his handling of the summit, but still agreed to do a live interview with me on the *Today* show. He wanted to talk about the details of the arms control negotiations that had taken place in Geneva. Having covered the issue intensively since Ronald Reagan had been in office, I knew that Regan had no idea what he was talking about. After giving him a chance to extol the summit's many accomplishments, at the end of the interview I leaned over and asked, "Mr. Regan, what is throw weight?"

For what appeared to be fifteen seconds, an eternity in television, he sat silently before he could fumble a response. "Well, uh," he said, "from the point of view it's—it's the amount of actual warheads that come from the, uh, curve of the missile from the time it leaves to the time it actually lands, and how much do you actually drop."

Clearly, Regan was out of his element. Even though it was a gotcha question, I wasn't the least bit sorry. But Regan would make me pay for it later.

Nancy Reagan clearly did not appreciate Regan's bumbling performance in Geneva, but she had her own problems with the summit's public relations. If there was a possibility of détente between the leaders of the two superpowers, the Cold War was becoming a deep freeze between their spouses. At their first meeting, Nancy took an instant dislike to Raisa Gorbachev; the two of them were oil and water. Nancy saw Raisa, who was more ideological than her husband, as hopelessly didactic and humorless. The two women spent more time jockeying for position than communicating. In her 1989 memoir, *My Turn,* Nancy Reagan said of Raisa Gorbachev, "We were thrust together although we had little in common and had completely different outlooks on the world." The two first ladies met initially when their husbands were holding their first substantive arms talks. The men were hitting it off. The women's encounter set a chilly tone for what was to come. The following October, Mrs. Gorbachev only irritated Nancy Reagan further by showing up at the Reykjavik summit in Iceland, after Mrs. Reagan had been told wives were not invited.

In December 1987, the Gorbachevs came to Washington, and there was even more awkwardness when Raisa appeared more interested in the reporters accompanying the official entourage on a tour of the White House than on her hostess's commentary. Nancy was smoldering. In his 1988 memoir, *For the Record,* Regan reported that after Mrs. Gorbachev lectured the president during a dinner given by the Reagans, Nancy exploded, "Who does that dame think she is?" In her own book Mrs. Reagan concluded, "During about a dozen encounters in three different countries, my fundamental impression of Raisa Gorbachev was that she never stopped talking. Or lecturing, to be more accurate." It was the kind of delicious catfight we in the press loved to cover.

Still, Nancy knew how to create social settings that would ease some of the tension. I was the broadcast pool reporter, representing the television networks at the state dinner for the Gorbachevs during their Washington visit. As a representative of the proletariat, Gorbachev would not wear black tie, so he came in a business suit, much to the annoyance of Nancy. The Reagans wore formal dress. But they somehow managed to break through the frostiness with the entertainment. Nancy had thoughtfully chosen Van Cliburn, still hugely popular in Moscow even though twenty-nine years had elapsed since his youthful triumph in the Tchaikovsky Piano Competition. And after playing the requisite classical pieces, Cliburn charmed the Gorbachevs by performing one of their favorite Russian folk songs, "Moscow Nights." Glowing, perhaps from the very good red wine, Gorbachev sang along, endearing him to the Reagans—and to many Americans watching on television—as he displayed a sentimental side of a Soviet leader rarely seen in public.

At their summits, Reagan and Gorbachev began to develop a relationship both personal and historic. Years later, I interviewed Gorbachev and asked him why he thought he could negotiate with Ronald Reagan, the Cold Warrior. Gorbachev said simply, "I liked him." Historic changes sometimes are the result of great men, sometimes of accidents of timing, sometimes a combination. After Reagan's death, analysts, and I include myself, were accused of giving him too much credit for ending the Cold War. So did this fervent anti-Communist end the Cold War, or only help hasten the collapse of the Soviet Union? The answer is complicated.

———

In his first term, Ronald Reagan had been confrontational, strident, siding more often with his defense secretary, Cap Weinberger, than his diplomats. In fact, at his first news conference as president, he said of the Soviets, "They reserve unto themselves the right to commit any crime, to lie, to cheat." On his first trip to Europe in the summer of 1982, he was widely criticized by the "elites" for a speech he gave at Westminster predicting the collapse of the Soviet empire and heralding "the march of freedom and democracy which will leave Marxism/Leninism on the ash heap of history." Condoleezza Rice, a young Soviet specialist at the time, recalled that many critics were horrified, commenting, "Oh, my God, how undiplomatic that is."

What the critics failed to take into account was the impact Ronald Reagan's stance was having on the Soviet intelligentsia. As much as they resented Reagan, he also provoked them into reexamining the structure of their society. Still, there were huge philosophical gaps to be overcome. Years later, when NBC interviewed Gorbachev after Reagan died in 2004, the former Soviet leader recalled that when the two men first met, they had to overcome years of mistrust: "After the meeting, I told my team, he's a real dinosaur, and he said I was a hardheaded Bolshevik."

But in Gorbachev Reagan found a pragmatic leader struggling with a collapsing economy and a rising number of dissidents, a man open to ideas on free markets and human rights. And Gorbachev now says that Reagan was a man with the popularity and vision to help open the door for Soviet reforms. During a visit to Moscow in 1988, Reagan addressed the Russian people on television and radio, an unprecedented act. His message was revolutionary: that the status quo was not acceptable, and not only on arms control. He saw the world as black and white, and insisted that human rights were a fundamental value, not a peripheral issue.

Gorbachev's final verdict: "Ronald Reagan wanted to finish his time in the presidency as a peacemaker, as a man who wanted to change the world for the better."

Many of the American and Russian analysts I've talked to over the years believe that while the political transformation in the Soviet Union was encouraged by the ideas of Ronald Reagan, the driving force was the dynamic of what was happening internally within the Soviet state. Former national security advisor and defense secretary Frank Carlucci disagrees, crediting Reagan's unwavering strength and consistency for propelling change in the Soviet system. After Reagan's death, Carlucci told me, "He saw it as a corrupt system, and he believed that if you just opened it up, it would fall of its own weight, and it did."

If Reagan had stuck to his big ideas—ending the Cold War and expanding the economy—he could have avoided the controversy that almost brought his presidency to its knees.

CHAPTER 4

Of Arms and Men

For me, the scandal that almost brought down the Reagan White House began as an innocuous inquiry from my desk editor on November 3, 1986. We were in California covering the president's final campaign push in the midterm elections before returning to Washington when an obscure Lebanese newspaper reported that the former national security advisor, Robert McFarlane, had secretly visited Iran, with whom the U.S. still had no diplomatic relations. His mission was to persuade Iran to help win the release of hostages being held in Lebanon, over which Iran had significant control. What was going on?

The decidedly unsavory cast of characters included a Middle Eastern arms merchant, Adnan Khashoggi, who claimed he hadn't been fully paid for an arms deal he'd helped broker as payment for the release of the hostages. I had been covering the White House for five years and knew nothing about any of this. In fact, none of the White House correspondents had any idea that in the basement offices of the National Security Council, Oliver North and CIA director Bill Casey were running their own completely secret and illegal shadow government.

How could something like this go undetected? It is difficult to describe just how isolated the White House press corps can be, traveling inside the "bubble" created by the Secret Service, the White House staff, and all the comforts and conveniences of network producers, official transcripts, and charter aircraft. A small pool flies on the president's airplane, but rarely sees the president. In fact, although we had a camera crew on Air Force One in case Reagan should appear, Larry Speakes wrote that he decided to close off the press cabin in the rear of Air Force One because of me. It seems, according to Larry, that I once tried to film the president in sweatpants, instead of a shirt and tie. Speakes wrote that he then assigned the president's military aide to close the door that separated the staff cabin from the press area. In his book, *Speaking Out,* the former press secretary writes, "I doubt if the aide considered that job quite as important as his usual task, which was to carry the codes that would be used to signal our nuclear forces to retaliate if the Russians attacked us." I can't imagine what the military aide must have been thinking about being on door patrol, instead of nuclear watch.

There are perks to traveling with the president. For security reasons, you deliver your bags to White House transportation office employees before departure from Andrews Air Force Base in suburban Maryland, and you next see them in your hotel room, wherever you are traveling in the world. Whether at the Great Wall of China or a campground in the Grand Tetons, the White House communications office installs telephones for the press, with the expense paid by the networks and newspapers in the traveling press corps.

The availability of advance texts and transcripts shortly after each event enables reporters who prefer dinner or souvenir shopping, especially in exotic locations, to skip a president's speech entirely. If that practice encourages laziness among reporters, it also carries risks for the chief executive. Living in the bubble can leave him isolated, too, and unchallenged. On one trip early in Reagan's presidency, flying back from South America, we had a rare session with the president on Air Force One. We asked Reagan for his reflections on his first visit to Latin America. He said, "You'd be surprised, yes, because, you know, they're all individual countries. I think one of the greatest mistakes in the world that we've made has been in thinking, lumping—thinking 'Latin America.'" He seemed to be just discovering that fact.

Comments like that contributed toward a tendency by reporters, and others, to underestimate Reagan at first. People didn't realize that he had an instinctive ability to assess allies and adversaries alike, and to see the big foreign policy landscape. But, at the same time, he relied far too heavily on his advisors, delegating decision making more than most presidents. That is partly how Iran-Contra evolved from a presidential wish to get some hostages home into an elaborate plot that threatened the very core of Reagan's presidency.

Still, it is remarkable that no one uncovered the plot before it began to unravel in the Middle East. Perhaps it is because even the most diligent correspondents covering Reagan, those who developed congressional and independent sources to maintain perspective and context, were often at the mercy of immediate deadlines or were separated by several time zones from those who really knew what was going on. In addition, it wasn't often that we got the opportunity to talk to the president, especially on foreign trips. Journalism's dirty little secret is that if an administration wants to keep something under wraps, it often can. White House correspondents can be kept completely out of the loop, even on routine stories. When it came to the illegal Iran-Contra scheme, clearly the National Security Council and the Central Intelligence Agency were not going to volunteer that they were conducting a top secret arms-for-hostages operation in defiance of Congress.

So when our editors first called us in Santa Barbara that November day in 1986, we were dismissive. The charge was that Ronald Reagan was selling missiles to Iran—a country with which we had no relations—in violation of his own arms embargo. It was tantalizingly easy to accept the president's denial. When we asked about it on November 6 at a bill signing ceremony in the Roosevelt Room, the president tried to deflect the question, replying: "Could I suggest an appeal to all of you with regard to this, that the speculation, the commenting and all, on a story that came out of the Middle East, and that to us has no foundation, . . . that all of that is making it more difficult for us in our effort to get the other hostages free."

Still hoping to salvage a deal for the hostages, the National Security Council approved a carefully crafted White House denial: "We don't negotiate with terrorists." That should have set off alarm bells for those of us covering the story. The word "negotiate" left a lot of room for maneuvering. So did the definition of "terrorist."

Behind the scenes, the White House was in turmoil. Those in the small circle who knew about the secret operation had to figure out what to say to their colleagues. Then they had to assess the political damage, and the impact on U.S. foreign policy. All this while attorney general Ed Meese was investigating whether any laws had been broken. As a result, it was four days before the White House even confirmed that McFarlane had been to Iran. With the media now in a full uproar, a week later the president addressed the nation from the Oval Office. He acknowledged selling "small amounts of defensive weapons and spare parts" to improve relations with Iran— not as ransom for hostages. In Watergate terms, that kind of limited admission was known as a "limited hangout." The cover-up was on.

How did an administration rooted in Reagan's strong principles get involved in this mess? You had to know Reagan to realize how important releasing the hostages was to him, and how easily he could deceive himself and be deceived by his staff. Although he had pledged, immediately after taking office, that he would never make concessions to terrorists, his response was completely human, if not presidential. He reacted to the plight of the American hostages viscerally, riding to the rescue as though he were playing the hero in one of his Westerns. This was a man who had so fully absorbed his Hollywood roles that he once claimed to have filmed newly liberated Nazi concentration camps, though he had only "experienced" those events from the safe remove of a military film unit in Hollywood.

———

Selling arms to Iran raised a complex set of political and foreign policy issues for Ronald Reagan, who thought of himself as the chief defender of Western values and certainly of the lives of Americans at risk abroad. To him, Iran held a special place in the pantheon of suspect states. Given that Reagan had been the unintended political beneficiary of Carter's hostage crisis, he knew the ayatollahs were open to deals. As a result of the Carter experience, Reagan was predisposed to be wary of the potential political damage of a protracted hostage crisis on his watch. In addition, he was angry about the murder of CIA Beirut station chief William Buckley, who had been captured, tortured, and executed in 1985 by the Lebanese Shiite Muslim group Islamic Jihad, or "Holy War," an organization backed by Iran. Reagan took personally what had happened to Buckley, repeatedly asking his national security team for details about his capture and death.

Buckley's death followed a tumultuous period in the early 1980s. In retrospect, it was the beginning of the anti-American terrorism we've had to endure for the last quarter century. In the aftermath of Israel's invasion of Lebanon in 1982 and the resulting violence against Palestinian refugees by Lebanese Christian militias supported by Israel, the Reagan administration got trapped into guaranteeing the safe exit of Yasser Arafat and his followers from that country. Suddenly, the United States was the unlikely protector of the Palestine Liberation Front and its leaders, injecting us into the middle of a war for which we were not equipped. It wasn't long before we ourselves became the target of the terror movement, first with a bombing outside the U.S. embassy in Beirut in April 1983, and then the massive attack on the marine barracks in the Lebanese capital six months later. Two hundred forty-one U.S. troops were killed, the worst military losses in a single incident since the Vietnam War. The Islamic Jihad claimed responsibility.

In that climate, it isn't difficult to understand the origins of the Iran-Contra scheme. Reagan had described the contras fighting the communist regime in Nicaragua as the moral equivalent of the Founding Fathers. The CIA, under the direction of Bill Casey in Langley and Oliver North and National Security Advisor John Poindexter in the White House, was circumventing congressional prohibitions to direct the covert operations. Already involved in "cowboy" operations, it was not a big leap for the administration to combine that initiative with another presidential imperative, freeing the hostages being held in Lebanon. And given that the president was wired emotionally to identify strongly with the captives, it did not take a presidential order for his aides to know that gaining their release was his top priority.

When a major story begins unfolding, there is almost a tangible smell in the air as well, a physical manifestation of crisis. The briefing room becomes a chaotic jumble of camera crews and correspondents doing round-the-clock updates. Newspaper and magazine reporters more accustomed to cozy "background" sessions over lunch with "senior officials" suddenly show up and wait, joining broadcast correspondents who can never leave the White House for fear of missing a new development. And the press area becomes a sea of half-eaten takeout containers delivered by the networks to their captive employees. It's a mess.

The White House staff was scrambling, and so were we. The attorney general was conducting his—somewhat limited—inquiry to uncover the scope of the National Security Council operation. I rightly suspected that there was a parallel effort by some of the participants to cover their tracks. But nothing prepared me for the shock of learning the full dimension of the scam being run out of the White House basement.

With Jim Baker no longer in the White House, the president was left without anyone close by with political antennae to sound the alarm when policies veered off course. Baker's move to Treasury, across East Executive Avenue, was only yards from the White House. But it was far enough that Don Regan, a man with little judgment and even less political skill, could take firm charge of the most critical operations of Ronald Reagan's presidency.

Regan and I had clashed at the Geneva summit. Now, a little over a year later, we would go up against each other again, during a night of high drama in the East Room of the White House where the president was finally holding a prime-time news conference to explain the exploding Iran-Contra scandal. The room was bathed in light from the elaborate crystal chandeliers and the television klieg lights mounted on tall poles. As NBC's second correspondent, I was seated midway toward the rear of the room: there was no guarantee I'd even manage to catch Reagan's eye and be called upon. As the president faced the press, my colleague Chris Wallace asked about something Regan had told us, that the U.S. condoned Israel's shipment of arms to Iran. Wasn't that in effect sending the message to terrorists or states like Iran who sponsor them that they could gain from holding hostages?

Still in full denial, the president replied no, because he didn't see where the hostage takers had gained anything. He was still unable to accept the linkage between Iran's ability to purchase the weapons and the Iranian-supported terrorists holding Americans in Lebanon. A few minutes later, Reagan called on me and I followed up on Chris's question, pointing out that his chief of staff had confirmed that the U.S. condoned an Israeli shipment of missiles to Iran shortly before an American hostage was released in September of 1985. The timing was critical because it was four months before the president had issued a legal directive giving authority to make such arms shipments without notifying Congress.

Standing in the glare of the floodlights, I asked the president, "Can you clear that up, why this government was not in violation of its arms embargo and of the notification to Congress for having condoned American-made weapons shipped to Iran in September of 1985?"

Ronald Reagan said, "No, I never heard Mr. Regan say that, and I'll ask him about that, because we believe in the embargo." Caught up in the moment, I asked if he would now assure the American people that he would not "again, without notification, and in complete secrecy, and perhaps with the objection of some of your cabinet members, continue to ship weapons," if he decided it was necessary. It was the kind of direct, challenging question you might not ask if you had time to rehearse it. Reagan's answer indicated he had still not accepted the reality of what his rogue national security team had done.

He replied, "No, I have no intention of doing that, but at the same time, we are hopeful that we are going to be able to continue our meetings with these people, these individuals." Despite everything, he still held on to the fiction that his envoys were negotiating with independent Iranian "moderates" and not the leadership of Iran. I could see panic on the faces of the president's aides standing in the front of the room. The president had been working off a chronology initially prepared by the CIA, but as it worked its way through the NSC, it had been altered to protect top White House officials, like John Poindexter.

This left Ronald Reagan exposed and vulnerable at the most important press conference of his presidency, briefed with a misleading chronology. It was a particularly explosive combination given Reagan's penchant for misstating facts even when his staff wasn't misleading him. As a result, at a moment when he needed to correct the record and show that he was cleaning up the scandal, the president instead repeatedly denied a central element in the case—that Israel had secretly shipped the weapons to Iran for the U.S. The press conference ended at 8:35 p.m. Chris Wallace rushed out to the North Lawn camera position to go live, as I returned to our small cubicle in the White House to start writing a story for the *Today* show the next morning.

Fifteen minutes later, an announcement over the press room loudspeaker stated that the president was going to issue a written statement clarifying something he had just said. It was unprecedented for this or any White House—a correction, within minutes of a presidential news conference. The mea culpa stated, "There may be some misunderstanding of one of my answers tonight.

There was a third country involved in our secret project with Iran." Reagan was acknowledging Israel's involvement, mere minutes after his vigorous denials.

Looking at the clock, I realized I had only minutes to get the correction to Chris on the North Lawn before our expanded post–news conference coverage concluded and the network resumed entertainment programming. I'm a good runner, but I broke all personal records getting to the camera position before we went off the air. On my knees so that viewers couldn't see me, I handed Reagan's statement to Chris. Without missing a beat, he read it live, adding it was "something that I have never seen before in my years at the White House."

Tom Brokaw responded, "That doesn't say much about the president's hands on the reins of foreign policy, does it?"

The next morning, *Washington Post* TV critic Tom Shales, who felt the president had at least won the viewers' sympathy after the grilling he'd endured, reflected on the high stakes intensity of the moment: "At times, the president behaved like a student trying to remember details on which he had been drilled, as undoubtedly he had."

But the drama of the night didn't end with my sprint to the North Lawn. Out of breath from running, I returned to the NBC White House booth to grab a ringing phone. It was Don Regan, yelling and cursing, threatening to ruin my career and have me fired. How dare I embarrass him with the president in front of the entire world? I have never been so frightened, before or since: I could feel my stomach cramp, and stammered that I was only asking obvious questions about points that were in the public record.

The call did not end well. I've "talked back" to a lot of powerful men over the years, from Frank Rizzo to the men around Reagan, Clinton, and both Presidents Bush. Until recently, men running for president did not even include any women among their top advisors. It was rare to find women of any real power in the West Wing. Unused to dealing with women as professionals, men in the

White House often bullied the women correspondents. But even in that kind of men's club atmosphere, Don Regan was in a class by himself. He wielded power roughly, and ruthlessly.

In the White House briefing room on November 25, 1986, the president introduced Ed Meese to tell the world that the secret arms sales to Iran had an even more secret component—a slush fund for the CIA-backed contras in Central America. It was perfect in its simplicity: to pay for counterinsurgency operations in Nicaragua and other Central American countries banned by Congress, the NSC used funds made on illegal arms sales to Iran. Essentially, it was a contra tax on the unsuspecting mullahs. Ollie North and his operatives delighted in the irony of the situation: why shouldn't the Ayatollah unwittingly pay for the illegal war in Central America? Through a series of complex transactions known as cutouts, international versions of three-card monte, the Iranians paid $30 million for the American missiles. But according to subsequent investigations, the weapons cost less than half that amount. As much as $20 million was diverted, some to the contras, the rest to shadowy middlemen.

To maintain secrecy, the operation was laundered through a convenient third country. What could add more irony onto the overall scheme than using Israel—Iran's avowed enemy—as the middleman for the secret arms transfer between the United States and the Ayatollah's regime?

I sat in the briefing room that day stunned as the president rushed out to avoid answering questions, leaving his attorney general on the firing line. Helen Thomas asked whether the president knew or had known about the diversion. I followed and asked whether Meese was still saying the policy of trading arms was "not a mistake," since at that point he was still claiming that they were investigating only an "aberration" from the policy.

Quickly, the barrage of questions focused on what the president knew, and when he knew it. Did he approve the diversion? If not, what was his exact role in the arms sale? Who else knew? What about John Poindexter and CIA director William Casey? Meese stated, "The president was informed generally that there had been an Israeli shipment of weapons to Iran sometime during the late summer, early fall, of 1985, and then he later learned in February of 1986 details about another shipment that had taken place in November of 1985."

If the president hadn't known, I asked, "Why did he call the Israeli prime minister to thank him for his real help in sending that shipment of arms?"

Meese responded, "I don't know, because that is something I have not discussed with the president."

The press corps smelled blood. Sam Donaldson, Bill Plante, and Chris Wallace—the leading network correspondents—bombarded Meese with questions he couldn't or didn't want to answer.

"Will there be more resignations?" I asked.

Press Secretary Larry Speakes interrupted. "Andrea has had a few questions already."

True, but Speakes wouldn't have intervened to silence one of the men. As Lesley Stahl of CBS and other women who covered the Reagan White House have written, Speakes used a heavy hand when it came to punishing female reporters. As I was about to learn when the White House became besieged by the Iran-Contra crisis, threatening the tenure of Speakes's boss, Chief of Staff Donald Regan, it was a dangerous time to be a woman correspondent.

In the following months, Regan retaliated. Two colleagues told me he had been slandering me in public settings. I was scared, and unable to strike back. It was the low point of my White House career.

As he was to find out, Regan himself was vulnerable. In addition to his tone-deaf comments about women not understanding throw weight and other foreign policy issues during the first Reagan-Gorbachev summit, six months later he suggested that the United States could not impose economic sanctions on South Africa for apartheid because of the potential impact on the world diamond trade.

Asked Regan, "Are the women of America prepared to give up all their jewelry?"

Nancy Reagan, among others, was not amused. Aside from his stupidity, Regan had forgotten the first rule of a staff person in the West Wing: Never forget that you are only staff, unelected and most definitely subordinate to the first family. Instead, Regan began to see himself as the president's "prime minister." He even tried to use the president's helicopter to shorten his trips to Bethesda Naval Hospital in suburban Maryland when the chief executive was recuperating from surgery for colon cancer. Not even Nancy Reagan used the helicopter, instead commuting to the hospital by car.

When Iran-Contra embarrassed the president on Regan's watch, he and Mrs. Reagan began fighting openly. As both have recounted in their memoirs, he even hung up on her during a heated argument over whether the president should risk having a press conference shortly after recovering from prostate surgery. By December 1986, the first lady's confidant Michael Deaver had secretly recruited Bob Strauss, a Democratic "wise man" astute in the ways of Washington, to help persuade the president that Regan was protecting himself at the expense of the Reagans. Characteristically, the president found it difficult to confront Regan himself. He gave the job to Vice President Bush, who called Regan in to suggest that it was time to go.

By his own account, Regan exploded. He was damned if he'd leave under fire, and cared more about how his departure would affect his reputation than the political damage he was causing the president. A blue-ribbon commission led by Senator John Tower, appointed by the White House to investigate the charges, was about to report its findings on Iran-Contra. Regan did not want his departure to be linked to the Tower Board's conclusions about the scandal. But the president's political advisors, desperate to stop the political hemorrhaging, leaked Regan's firing to CNN. The proud former Wall Streeter learned of his replacement by former Senator Howard Baker, a courtly and experienced Southerner highly regarded in Washington, only after the news appeared on cable.

It was a humiliating and angry departure. The depth of Don Regan's resentment only became apparent when he struck back at the first lady in his book by revealing one of the White House's darkest, and most bizarre, secrets: Mrs. Reagan had occasionally relied on an astrologer to determine the president's travel schedule, perhaps in reaction to the assassination attempt, trying to figure out how to avoid "dangerous days." Only later, reading how furiously Regan fought to save his job, did I realize how abusive he had been to everyone, even powerful figures like Nancy Reagan and George Bush. It gave me some context for his explosion at me.

———

On March 19, 1987, four months after the president's last, highly damaging news conference, he met us again in the East Room. By then, Howard Baker had replaced Don Regan as chief of staff and persuaded the president to acknowledge his mistakes over Iran-Contra to the American people in an Oval Office address. An investigation conducted by John Tower, Brent Scowcroft, former secretary of state Edmund Muskie, and other foreign policy experts had concluded that the president was at fault for permitting the illegal diversion of funds and for putting the personal welfare of the hostages above broader foreign policy principles. It had been a long time since the press corps had had a chance to question the president, and a lot had happened. The star reporters—Helen Thomas, Sam Donaldson, and Chris Wallace—hammered away at the inconsistencies of the Iran-Contra operation and cover-up. I was seated toward the rear of the room, straining in my seat in order to catch Reagan's eye. Finally, just as the allotted time for the session was expiring, he called on me. But before I could rise, the *New York Times* correspondent sitting in front of me jumped up and took my turn.

I was crushed, realizing I wouldn't get to ask a question at one of the most important news conferences of Reagan's presidency. But I hadn't counted on the kindness of Ronald Reagan. Showing the same unfailing courtesy he always did, even when taking a beating from the press, instead of walking out, Reagan turned back toward me and said, "I remembered, I promised you I'd call on you."

I asked about the Tower Board's finding that there had been extensive U.S. military support for the contras for two years, involving airstrips, phony corporations, and tax-exempt foundations. How could all this take place without his knowing it? And, if he had been truly unaware of Oliver North and John Poindexter directing millions of dollars to the contras, and couldn't remember approving the Iranian arms sale, what did that say about his management style?

Ronald Reagan's answer was a primer to understanding his presidency. He said, "Andrea, I've been reading a great deal about my management style. I think that most people in business will agree that it is a proper management style. You get the best people you can to do a job; then you don't hang over their shoulder criticizing everything they do or picking at them on how they're doing it."

The president had outlined broad policies and let his national security officials carry them out. The result was Iran-Contra, a scandal that clouded his tenure and cast a long shadow over his successors. It created a sharp divide between Shultz and Jim Baker over the role of Baker's patron, the vice president.

Shultz had fiercely opposed the arms deal and testified that he thought the proposal had been nipped in the bud. Instead, Shultz said, it had become "a hostage bazaar." Each time arms were swapped for hostages, a hostage was released—but another was taken. Testifying to the joint House-Senate Iran-Contra investigating committee, Shultz was blunt in his outrage: "You cannot spend funds that the Congress doesn't either authorize you to obtain or appropriate. That is what the Constitution says, and we have to stick to it."

Shultz's candor, after the appearance of so many administration witnesses who seemed to be suffering from amnesia, was refreshing. John Poindexter did offer a conflicting account. He claimed Shultz had deliberately closed his eyes to the illegal operation once the secretary of state realized the president was going to proceed anyway, against his advice. But Shultz emerged from the scandal with the reputation of being the last honest broker on the foreign policy team. He called Washington policy making a "seething debating society."

Shultz was the most senior person in the cabinet, and enormously popular with career foreign service officers at the State Department. A stolid ex-marine, he had served previous presidents in three other cabinet posts. Usually phlegmatic, he had a flair for occasional flamboyance. At state dinners, Shultz always managed to get himself seated next to stars like Sophia Loren. And although he dressed as nattily as an advertisement for *GQ*, he was ahead of his time in one fashion: a proud Princetonian, he reportedly had a tattoo of a tiger strategically placed to advertise his alma mater to anyone following him to the shower.

Interestingly, in light of the 9/11 Commission's recommendation seventeen years later for the establishment of a single intelligence czar, Shultz suggested a different remedy to the Iran-Contra investigators: separate intelligence analysis from policy making and covert action. He wanted to set up barriers to prevent a future Bill Casey from circumventing the State Department to pervert policy.

Shultz's testimony cast suspicion for the first time on Vice President Bush, threatening to put Bush in the middle of the exploding scandal. That could potentially harm Bush's hopes of becoming president. After Bush was elected, and Jim Baker succeeded Shultz as secretary of state, Baker made his displeasure clear. He never called Shultz for advice, not even about Middle East diplomacy, one of his areas of expertise. There was never a special envoy's assignment, or special ambassadorship. In fact, once Bush became president, Shultz and Weinberger, who had both served with him under Reagan, were not invited back to the White House until March of 1991, and then only at the request of Margaret Thatcher.

President Bush was awarding Thatcher, no longer prime minister, the highest civilian award given by the United States, the Presidential Medal of Freedom. A dinner was arranged, upstairs in the White House residence more private and special than even a state dinner in the downstairs official rooms. I was invited as the guest of Alan Greenspan, with whom Thatcher had had a long and admiring professional relationship. It was my first time upstairs in the Yellow Oval Room, for what appeared to be a reunion of the Reagan White House. Thatcher had wanted all the foreign policy officials with whom she had worked under "Ronnie" to attend, so the White House was obliged to invite the former Reagan cabinet, despite their strained relations with Bush over the residue of Iran-Contra.

On that evening, Bush's popularity was at its peak because of the first Gulf War. Thatcher had been his first, and most stalwart, ally. "Remember, George, this is no time to go wobbly," she'd chided him when Saddam Hussein invaded Kuwait the previous August. With everyone now in a celebratory mood, there were effusive toasts from Bush, Thatcher, and her husband, Sir Denis. (His uninhibited whoops of delight at his wife's success were among the high points of the evening.)

Alan was seated at the president's table, as was Barbara Walters, whom he had dated during the Ford, Carter, and early Reagan years. I was at another table next to her escort, Virginia senator John Warner, a former secretary of the navy and member of the Armed Services Committee. After many testy interviews with the formidable prime minister, often live on the *Today* program, I didn't know what she would be like at a private dinner. On morning television, she would challenge the assumption behind every question, getting into a spirited debate. On an occasion such as this, would she behave very differently?

Not a bit. Instead of responding informally to the president's toast, the Iron Lady delivered a rousing, but lengthy, speech about her view of American "exceptionalism" that could have been delivered at Westminster. Sir Denis even punctuated it with shouts of "Hear, hear."

I enjoyed being a fly on the wall at a private dinner in the White House; at the same time, I felt that the "designated shouter" from the press corps was a little out-of-place upstairs, sitting with officials whom I covered. I knew I could neither ask questions, nor quote anything that was said to me. It gave me an uncomfortable feeling that I might be gaining unusual access, but losing some independence.

———

My life had indeed become complicated. In June 1987, I was giving a birthday party for my friend, Reagan biographer Lou Cannon, who at the time was covering the White House for *The Washington Post*. Almost all of the other guests were reporters, except for Alan and our mutual friend Margaret Tutwiler, then assistant secretary of the treasury, working for Jim Baker. I sat Margaret next to Alan at the foot of the table, and noticed that the two of them were especially jolly, laughing and talking with great animation.

It was only after everyone else had left that I found out why. Alan took me aside and said, "Today, the president called and asked if I wanted to be chairman of the Federal Reserve." He had, in fact, learned of his nomination in an unlikely setting. His back was bothering him, and he'd been on the examining table at the doctor's when the presidential call came through. Of course, he'd accepted. Margaret, as an assistant to Baker, had been in on all the details.

We sat up late that night, trying to sort out how this would change our lives. Somehow, our commuting relationship had given each of us a way out of making a full emotional commitment. Now Alan would be moving from New York to Washington, and we would have to think about what we meant to each other, as well as how to handle the possible conflicts of interest.

Our first test came the very next morning, because I now had inside information that had to be kept secret until the president's announcement. I had to prove I could be trusted, and Alan had to show he was not a risk, despite his ongoing personal relationship with a member of the fourth estate. That day, I sat with Chris Wal-

lace in the Old Executive Office Building, the site of many White
House briefings. At the end of a press conference by the secretaries
of state and treasury in advance of an upcoming economic summit
in Venice, Italy, Press Secretary Marlin Fitzwater stood up and said,
"The president will be in the briefing room for an announcement at
ten o'clock."

We didn't see Ronald Reagan very often in the briefing room,
so everyone jumped up to rush back to the White House. We
needed to notify our networks quickly, so our bosses could determine whether the announcement was important enough to warrant
interrupting the soap operas that generate a great deal of advertising
revenue. This was all pre-cable at NBC, before we had a twenty-
four-hour news operation.

As Chris and I, by then working well together, sprinted across the
street toward the White House, he wondered aloud, "What personnel announcement could this be? Perhaps, a new FBI director?"
Then he said, "What about Volcker?" because Fed Chairman Paul
Volcker's term was about to expire. I was very quiet.

All of a sudden Chris looked at my silent self and said, "Oh, my
God, it's Alan, isn't it?"

I couldn't lie to my colleague, but I said, "If you tell them, Alan's
credibility is in tatters with Jim Baker. He'll never trust him, or me,
for that matter."

We raced to our little cubicle, where Chris informed our boss
that it was indeed important to carry this briefing live, but preserved
my secret as to the identity of the new appointee about to be announced. For that, I will always be grateful to him.

When Alan walked in at the stroke of ten that Tuesday morning
alongside the president and Paul Volcker, a gasp went up from the
briefing room; I wasn't sure whether to beam with pride or slump
in my seat to avoid notice. Years later, Jim Baker told me he and his
aides had all been backstage, watching the TV monitors before they
walked out, waiting to see if NBC broke the news first. An important test, the first of many more to come.

After that, I sat down with my bureau chief to work out the rules of the road. I removed myself from any economic coverage that would conflict with what Alan does. In fact, even if I weren't a reporter, he wouldn't be able to talk shop with me. His work is highly classified, market sensitive, and very complex. I am no economist, and his decision making covers an array of monetary and regulatory issues. I enjoy talking to him about broad philosophical issues, but when it comes to policy, we draw the line.

Certainly, we never would have gotten together if we weren't already involved in a relationship at the time he was appointed. But neither of us had any idea Alan would ever return to government.

As chairman of the Federal Reserve, Alan was invited to many official events, but our status as an unmarried couple created a few awkward moments. One magazine writer described me dropping him off at work in the morning when he was waiting to be confirmed. What was our relationship? Everyone wondered. At times, so did we.

As he prepared to move from New York to Washington, I helped him furnish an apartment at the Watergate. To no one's surprise, domesticity was not Alan's strength. How much would I participate in his public life? We decided that for the time being we would try to find a comfortable balance enjoying our life while taking care to be reasonably discreet.

Doors did begin to open for Alan, in the way Washington embraces people who hold powerful jobs. There were official invitations, more than someone with Alan's work schedule could ever accept. When Mikhail Gorbachev came in May 1990 for a summit with President Bush, we were invited to the state dinner. It was what Washington considered a "hot ticket," with 127 invitations highly sought by business leaders, politicians, and socialites.

A private person not eager to make small talk, Alan tried to rush past the reporters waiting to cover the arrival of guests. As *The Washington Post* described us the following morning, "When photographers tried to cajole a smile from Mitchell's escort Alan Greenspan, she quickly set them straight: 'For a Federal Reserve chairman, that *was* a smile.'" Having covered all the Reagan-Gorbachev summits, I was fascinated to watch another chapter in the U.S.-Soviet relationship, this time as a guest at the party.

The warmth of the toasts between the two presidents marked the close of the Cold War era. Gorbachev said, "The Soviet Union does not regard the United States as its enemy. We have firmly adopted the policy of moving from mutual understanding through cooperation to joint action. I think the work we have been doing together with President Bush during these days can be considered as another step toward a more humane and just world."

For his part, Bush said, "You deserve great credit for the course that you have chosen, for the political and economic reforms that you have introduced, and for creating within the Soviet Union this commitment to change. . . . We want to see Perestroika succeed. We want to see this transition now under way in the Soviet Union maintain its momentum."

I was struck by how much had happened in the decade since I'd first come to the White House, when the Soviet Union was an "evil empire" and our two nations were threatening each other with nuclear annihilation. Now, Bush and Gorbachev were trying to define a new kind of relationship, something between former enemies and future allies. And Don Regan, who had tried so hard to dominate that first Geneva summit, was long gone.

Three years later, my husband and I hosted a retirement dinner for the head of the Bank of England. When Alan first became Fed chairman, Sir Robin Leigh-Pemberton and his wife, Rose, were among the first in the very traditional world of central banking to welcome us to their country home, even though we were not married. So I was eager to reciprocate and arranged a dinner in their honor at the Chevy Chase Club, just outside of Washington. It was a lovely evening, but our British friends had of course asked that we invite all of the officials with whom they'd interacted in Washington. That meant including the former secretary of the treasury, Don Regan.

The only correct response was to put on a "social" face and get through it. In fact, there was a touching quality to Regan once he was out of office. He had moved to Florida, and was painting landscapes as well as doing occasional television commentary for CNBC, our business cable network. He was still charming, a wonderful raconteur. You could see the sparks of what Ronald Reagan had liked so much in him. But now the former chief of staff was much more vulnerable, softer than when he reigned supreme in the White House.

I saw him once more, at a dinner hosted by George Shultz and his wife, Charlotte. The Shultzes were participating in one of those little-known, but charming, Washington traditions: when a new treasury secretary is appointed, his predecessors, from both political parties, welcome him with a dinner. This particular occasion was in honor of Paul O'Neill, George W. Bush's first treasury appointee. (Two years later, O'Neill was fired, and became the first Bush cabinet member to criticize the president in a confessional book—rare for an administration that prides itself on absolute loyalty.) But at that time, O'Neill was flush with his new appointment.

The dinner was held two blocks from the White House at the Metropolitan Club, a somewhat stuffy gathering place that for years has helped Washington men make connections and preserve the old-boy network.

In fact, one of my NBC White House colleagues once told me I'd never make it as a correspondent because I couldn't join a club. Shortly afterward, his own contract at the network was dropped. But the Metropolitan, and all it stands for, still dominates a certain sector of Washington life. Nonetheless, in 1988, one tradition changed: its members bowed to pressure and began accepting women.

On this occasion, all the former secretaries of both political parties were invited. With at least forty people in the room, what were the odds of my being seated next to Don Regan? Yet there we were, side by side. Again, he was friendly and well mannered, with none of the rough edges that had abruptly ended the public service of an otherwise bright and engaging personality.

In fact, I still have sympathy for some of the people who've fallen from grace in Washington. The feeding frenzy can be so unforgiving, especially in this day of nonstop cable news. How do you explain to your kids the invasion of privacy and humiliation when network cameras arrive on your front lawn before dawn? I was embarrassed when camera crews didn't clean up after themselves while hounding the Clintons' Arkansas pal Webster Hubbell, the Justice Department official who pleaded guilty to cheating his former law firm. And sometimes, the Washington hunt for scandal traps the innocent. As Ray Donovan, Reagan's labor secretary, put it after he'd been falsely accused: "Which office do I go to, to get my reputation back?"

As tough as I can be in reporting a story, I don't enjoy going in for the kill. Despite the abuse I had suffered at Don Regan's hands, I couldn't help feeling kindly toward him.

The Don Regan debacle explains a great deal about Ronald Reagan and his presidency. As politician and president, Reagan could persuade himself of almost anything. He did not trade arms for hostages. He could not confront unpleasantness, and was reluctant to think ill of those around him. He had accepted Don Regan as treasury secretary, and then as chief of staff, passively, on the recommendation of others. Incapable of being cruel himself, he could not recognize cruelty in others. And for all the criticism of his wife's involvement in West Wing dramas, he badly needed her protection. The rest of the world finally understood that during the last decade of Ronald Reagan's life.

———

Nancy Reagan was an inseparable part of her husband's life, but for many in the press, she was unapproachable. For an interviewer, Nancy Reagan was not an easy subject. Smart and well rehearsed, she was rarely spontaneous. And she was the kind of woman who responded more charmingly to male interviewers, especially personal favorites like Tom Brokaw or Mike Wallace, two old friends. With them she was not only more comfortable; she could even be a little flirtatious.

It made for very good television. In addition, she had a special con-nection, through Mike, with his son, my colleague Chris Wallace.

With me, Nancy was wary. We did several interviews, one for the *Today* show in New York, another in the White House on her "Just Say No to Drugs" campaign. Each time, she was determined to keep the focus safely on her antidrug agenda, which did a great deal to fo-cus national attention on drug abuse among children and teenagers. I asked Mrs. Reagan how she could raise those issues while the White House was cutting funds for drug prevention and cures. She gave me a steely gaze and stuck to her scripted answers.

But for all the cynicism with which some reporters greeted the "Just Say No" campaign, it was important work. With Mike Deaver's help, Nancy Reagan found a real cause. People made fun of the campaign, but Nancy Reagan greatly expanded the job of a modern first lady, going even beyond the substantive role Rosalynn Carter had played in the White House.

Mrs. Carter had been criticized for sitting in on cabinet meetings, but behind the scenes, Nancy Reagan played an even more impor-tant policy role in her husband's administration, as a powerful advi-sor without portfolio. It was Nancy who, relying heavily on her brother, a medical doctor in Philadelphia, persuaded her Ronnie to be more open-minded about the scourge of AIDS. He resisted mightily, until it got personal—when their good friend Rock Hud-son was afflicted and died on October 2, 1985. Still, Reagan did not give a major speech on AIDS until 1987.

I really admired Nancy and Ronald Reagan's marriage. It didn't work for the children, at least when they were younger, but that is their own story; the bond between the two parents in a way ex-cluded everyone else. But I can't imagine a closer couple. Reagan's handwritten letters, published recently, show that he had a natural gift of expression that not even Peggy Noonan, his talented speech-writer, could have supplied. And many of his most beautiful letters are odes to his Nancy. Every woman secretly longs to receive letters like the ones Reagan wrote his wife.

By the time they left Washington, Nancy had already overcome the negative impression she'd made in the first years, the years of "Queen Nancy" and all the criticism of her clothes, borrowed jewels, and White House china. Her campaign against drugs had given her a platform from which to lead a national cause. She had suffered and survived breast cancer, following Betty Ford's groundbreaking example in speaking out as a role model for other women who might not otherwise have sought medical help.

As I stood on the east front of the Capitol and watched the Reagans lift off in their white-topped helicopter, I could not have imagined the sadness that would shade their retirement. For *Nightly News* that evening, I reflected only on what the Reagan revolution had wrought, and how on their way out of town they had circled the White House for a last, nostalgic farewell.

Reagan's death after a ten-year retreat into the silent world of Alzheimer's disease was a great sadness for the nation. For Nancy Reagan, the preceding decade had been a long, mournful time of almost unbearable, unending loss. Though she had to have help to relieve her of some of the duty, she was constantly at his side. As the former president retreated into the darkness of the disease, his wife refused even to consider a nursing home or other kind of facility.

When Ronald Reagan finally died, the outpouring of affection, even nostalgia, for his presidency surprised many of us who had covered his White House. Some felt it was a political decision by the networks to celebrate a Republican life. In fact, the coverage did not go beyond the amount of airtime the networks devoted to the state funeral services for Lyndon Johnson, long before extended live coverage was the norm.

By the time of Reagan's death, his son Ronald Prescott Reagan and daughter Patti Davis were finally reconciled with their mother, and gave eloquent tributes to their father. Reagan's devoted daughter Maureen had already died from cancer, far too young. In their complicated family, a role at the services was also carved out for his son Michael, often estranged from his father. And Reagan's beloved Nancy, a lightning rod for criticism during much of his presidency, had in the years since stirred the nation with her example of steadfast, and selfless, devotion. Her strength and serenity on his final trip to Washington only completed the circle of the Reagans' extraordinary journey in life and death.

On the day Reagan was buried, I again found myself in a dual role—appearing on the *Today* program with Katie Couric outside the National Cathedral before the service, then going inside with Alan to attend the memorial as a guest. Afterward, I rushed back outside to rejoin Tom Brokaw and Tim Russert, who had also been at the service. All of us were moved by what Reagan had represented.

During Ronald Reagan's presidency, the world had gone through momentous change. The Soviet Union had declined and was on the edge of collapse; AIDS had become the scourge of entire populations; taxes had been slashed; defense spending had ballooned; the Supreme Court had been altered for a generation to come; conservatives had taken ownership of the Republican Party.

The outpouring of affection for Reagan during that week telegraphed something more important about his presidency. He was criticized at times for delegating too much, for being late to understand the significance of AIDS, and for being stuck in a 1950s attitude toward minorities. He was praised, perhaps too extravagantly, for ending the Cold War and downsizing government. But his true legacy may have been to give Americans a feeling of hope and optimism that they hadn't had since the days of John F. Kennedy and Franklin Roosevelt. Reagan, like those predecessors, had a rare ability to convey the inherent goodness of America. It meant overlooking some of the nation's flaws, but it marked a man who was a true leader, and a great politician.

Reagan's presidency was also the period during which I came of age, as a reporter and as a woman. I had become more skilled as an interviewer, and more humble, discovering how little was really transparent at the highest levels of government. I'd made extraordinary friends, and been an eyewitness to a transforming era in our nation's foreign policy. But most important, I had met the person with whom I wanted to spend the rest of my life.

CHAPTER 5

Scandal on the Hill

Would I ever again be with my family to eat a Thanksgiving turkey, instead of waiting outside while the president of the United States ate his? I was beginning to doubt it. Once again canceling a holiday trip home, I found myself in Kennebunkport, Maine, over Thanksgiving weekend in 1988, watching George Bush buy an extension cord at the local hardware store and rent the video *Broadcast News*. At least there would be a payoff: I expected to become chief White House correspondent for NBC, the job of my dreams. The campaign was over, and I was covering the transition to the new White House. Chris Wallace had decided to leave NBC for ABC, and I was moving on from my role as "second banana" at last.

Bush's election seems now to have been preordained, given the collapse of Michael Dukakis. But it wasn't always that obvious. In fact, as Bush headed toward his nominating convention in New Orleans in 1988, Dukakis was seventeen points ahead in the polls. For the media, there was only one story: Whom was George Bush going to choose to run as his vice president? There was talk of both Bob and Elizabeth Dole, Jack Kemp, John Danforth, Alan Simpson of Wyoming, a close friend of the Bush family, and Dick Lugar from

Indiana, a solid senator with seniority on both the Foreign Relations and Agriculture committees. He'd been mayor of Indianapolis and head of the National League of Cities, and, while not charismatic, came from a swing state. But I was also hearing that Lugar's very junior Indiana colleague Senator Dan Quayle was on the list. Then, days before the convention opened, a story appeared in *The New York Times*—planted, many suspected, by the Baker forces—that Dan Quayle was under serious consideration. It was a trial balloon, an attempt by the Baker faction to get Quayle eliminated, in favor of Bob Dole or one of the other, more senior, senators. But as it turned out, Quayle had a lot more support with the vice president's inner circle than even Baker had reckoned. Bush's campaign manager, Robert Teeter, and political consultant Roger Ailes had both worked for Quayle. They and Lee Atwater were all arguing that Quayle would bring a needed injection of youth to the ticket. And Bush friend Nicholas Brady, a former senator, was promoting Quayle as well.

Everyone was trying to find out what Bush was about to decide, but we were told he hadn't yet made up his mind. Then, on Tuesday, August 16, my colleague Tom Pettit, who was traveling with Bush, and I both got word that Bush had finally chosen his running mate. As we later learned, the first person Bush confided in was Reagan, whispering in the president's ear when Reagan arrived in New Orleans. Bush then told his wife, Barbara.

His staff did not learn his surprising choice until they had all gathered at the home of the base commander where their plane had landed in New Orleans. As I learned later from several of those present, the vice president was stretched out on a bed, resting and talking to his aides. Margaret Tutwiler and Lee Atwater were sitting on the floor of the bedroom; Baker, Ailes, Teeter, and Craig Fuller, among others, were arrayed around the room. All were eagerly waiting to hear whom Bush had anointed. When Bush told them it was Quayle, there was dead silence. No congratulations, no pro forma nods of approval, just—silence. Even Teeter and Ailes, both Quayle supporters, were reluctant to laud the decision. Finally, to break the ice, Baker spoke up and said, "Mr. Vice President, now we have to start notifying people."

When we got word that Bush had chosen someone, we jumped on the phones to try to find out whom he'd picked. There is a hierarchy on each network team at the conventions, which have long been proving grounds for reporters. With the nominations now sewn up months in advance because of changes in the primary system, the conventions serve no meaningful purpose except as advertisements for each party and reunions for political reporters. But in 1988, the pending announcement of Bush's running mate was real news. Breaking that story would be the only shot at network glory. The real contenders to get it were the floor correspondents, the stars of each network's reporting team. They were the ones, four per network in those days, who wore funny headsets and roamed the floor of the convention snagging interviews.

At NBC, the floor correspondents continued a long tradition of celebrated broadcasters from the 1960s and 1970s, most notably John Chancellor, who was carried out of the Republican convention in San Francisco in 1964 by party goons trying to restrict the movement of reporters. Chancellor's memorable sign-off was "This is John Chancellor, somewhere in custody." In Chicago, at the Democratic convention in 1968, Dan Rather of CBS was knocked down while covering the ejection of a Georgia delegate. Anchorman Walter Cronkite announced angrily, "I think we've got a bunch of thugs down there." Careers were made—and broken—on convention performances. At the podium, positioned to grab the best "gets"—the big speakers—was a single "super" correspondent from each network, usually an anchor of a Sunday talk show or prime-time magazine. For us that year it was Connie Chung, glamorous and outgoing, the only woman known to wear stiletto heels on the convention floor, putting the rest of us, dressed for comfort in sneakers, to shame. In the booths, converted sky-boxes high above the mayhem on the floor, sat the ultimate network stars: the anchors themselves.

I was the most junior of the lot, still not a full-fledged floor reporter, assigned to the perimeter of the convention to float and "run and gun" wherever I was needed. But I was determined to crack this thing, and started dialing everyone I knew—repeatedly. I'd been calling people on the list of possible candidates, to see if they had received the call from Vice President Bush. Once we knew that Bush had notified the winner, and that the designated person was en route to New Orleans to be unveiled, I could eliminate those who hadn't heard from him.

One by one, I called those who hadn't made the cut. By process of elimination, I was closing the circle when I finally reached someone who told me that the nominee was Quayle—the least likely, all of us had assumed, of any of the potential choices. I called the control room and got Tom Brokaw on the phone.

I said, "It's Quayle; it's Quayle."

He replied, "Are you sure?"

Because Tom would be putting his credibility on the line, and I had only a single source, rather than two, I offered to confide the identity of my source. The minute he heard who it was, Brokaw knew my information was gold-plated. He went on the air and announced that I had learned that George Bush had selected Dan Quayle to be his running mate.

Quayle was little known to most of the country, and his introduction a few hours later was a disaster. On live television, the Republican ticket appeared at a riverside dock, before thousands of people. As Bob Woodward and David Broder of *The Washington Post* have reported, Quayle had been campaigning secretly for six months to be chosen. But when it happened, he was completely unprepared. Grabbing Bush, Quayle flapped his arms and shouted to the crowd, "Let's go get 'em. All right? You got it?"

The impression he created was of someone both overeager and not prepared for the national spotlight.

Quayle's lack of experience, and the controversy over how his family had helped him get into the National Guard, became the dominant story of the convention and the following weeks. During live interviews with each of the network anchormen the night after he was introduced, Quayle stumbled so badly about how he'd gotten into the National Guard during Vietnam that Baker woke him up at three a.m. to be grilled by Dick Darman and other White House aides. We all stayed up all night, calling Baker's aides, trying to find out if Quayle was going to be yanked off the ticket. He toughed it out, but Baker assigned his most trusted political advisor, Stu Spencer, and other campaign veterans, to take charge of every move Quayle made for the duration of the campaign.

Although Quayle had only himself to blame, he and his wife, Marilyn, never forgave Baker for the damaging way Quayle was introduced to the nation. It is true that Baker could barely conceal his lack of enthusiasm for Bush's choice of running mate. At one point, he told reporters, "The issue is not who might have been the very best qualified to be president. The issue is getting someone who is extremely well qualified to be president and who might have some other attributes as well." But the Quayles could hardly blame Baker for the young senator's series of malaprops, or for walking into his opponent Lloyd Bentsen's trap ("I knew Jack Kennedy. Jack Kennedy was a friend of mine. Senator, you're no Jack Kennedy.") during their debate.

My role in breaking the Quayle story helped people within the network realize I could be a player. The lesson was that, in a world where glamour counted for a lot, shoe leather and good reporting skills still mattered, too. Tom was very generous about making sure people knew that I should get the credit for the scoop. NBC even took out a print advertisement that mentioned me, headlined, NBC NEWS CLOBBERED ITS COMPETITORS, a quote lifted from a story written by Tom Shales of *The Washington Post.* Suddenly I was better known in campaign circles and was chosen to participate in the second, and what was to be the last, of the Bush-Dukakis debates.

The debates did not lend themselves to intensive questioning. Over the years, they'd devolved into set pieces, formatted by negotiators for the candidates, especially in the case of an incumbent president. Jim Baker had played this role so successfully that although Michael Dukakis wanted four debates, the Republicans would only agree to two, and only accepted the second debate a few days before it was to take place. Because of Baker's delaying tactics, the second, and final Bush-Dukakis debate was held only 26 days before the election, on October 13. Neither the members of the press nor the Democratic challenger had much time to prepare, which is exactly what the White House strategists wanted.

We flew to California the day before the debate, which was to take place on the UCLA campus. The panel consisted of Ann Compton of ABC, Margaret Warner, then of *Newsweek,* and me, with CNN's Bernard Shaw as moderator. Once in L.A., I huddled with Bill Wheatley, then the executive producer of *Nightly News,* and Tim Russert to brainstorm about possible questions. Tim had not yet moved to Washington to take over the NBC bureau or his position as moderator of *Meet the Press,* but was an NBC executive, and from his years working for Mario Cuomo and Pat Moynihan, had a keen sense of how to frame questions that left politicians no wiggle room.

We knew that under the limited format negotiated by Jim Baker, each panelist would get only six questions and a few follow-ups. I wanted to probe their knowledge of the budget deficit and explore their priorities for strategic defenses: very high-minded, but, Tim warned, not at all sexy. I should have listened to Tim.

The morning of the debate, we panelists met at the hotel for breakfast. The rules were so restrictive that, as moderator, Bernie Shaw was only going to be able to ask one question of each candidate. He was determined to have an impact. To avoid duplication under pressure, we compared notes. Ann wanted to ask Bush about White House ethics scandals and Dukakis about entitlement cuts. Margaret wanted to question Bush about abortion. I was still focused on war and peace, and deficits.

What was Bernie, the sole man in the group, planning? He had decided to ask Michael Dukakis whether, if Kitty Dukakis were raped and murdered, he would favor an irrevocable death penalty for the killer, changing his long-held opposition to capital punishment. Ann, Margaret, and I were horrified. Politely we tried to suggest that such an emotionally laden question was a bit too tabloid, or un-fair, or worse. But Bernie was adamant.

That night, in the glare of the Hollywood lights, the candidates arrived on the red-carpeted stage. Sitting in a row behind a desk, the rest of us watched tensely as Bernie opened the debate by dropping his bomb of a question on Dukakis. In the control room, the director and producers looked for a flash of spontaneity in the candidate's eyes, but found none. Without flinching, the Demo-cratic candidate for president repeated his stock answer on the death penalty, that "there are better and more effective ways to deal with violent crime," expressing no emotion or outrage at the suggestion of his own wife as victim in Bernie's hypothetical scenario.

The election was over. Perhaps imitating the preternaturally calm behavior of the candidate, those of us on the stage behaved as though nothing had happened, and continued with our prepared questions. Ann Compton tried to shake the candidates out of their memorized answers by asking whether, in the midst of this brutally negative campaign, there was anything nice they could say about each other. She got an anodyne response about how they each came from good families. I asked the vice president to name three new weapons systems that he would cut from the budget. He said, "If I knew of three new weapons systems that I thought were purely waste, and weren't protected by the Congress, they wouldn't be in the budget." But he did suggest one—an $850 million heavy truck. Then, turning to Dukakis, I asked him to assume, for the sake of argument, that the economists who criticized his deficit reduction plan were correct. If so, and he had to increase taxes, which would be the least onerous?

Dukakis asked, "May I disagree with the premise of your question?"

Without flinching, I said, "For the sake of argument, no."

My friend Connie Chung later sent me a framed picture of myself asking the question with that caption. Afterward, in the spin room, I looked for anyone who could give me an objective assessment of what had transpired. No one was talking about anything except Bernie's question and Dukakis's answer. The next day, I flew home and was listening to David Letterman while getting ready for bed. In what can only be described as an out-of-body experience, I heard him ask the audience whether anyone had noticed that in the presidential debate, Andrea Mitchell had become a blond. (A visual illusion because of very bright lights hitting me from directly overhead, but a precursor of hair color changes to come.) Such was the impression I had created—instead of becoming known as a fearless interrogator of presidential candidates, I was a throwaway line on late-night TV.

David Letterman and my debate performance notwithstanding, the campaign had given me more national visibility. I gained valuable experience on the road with Dukakis, as part of the entourage on the plane we nicknamed Sky Pig because of its miserable accommodations and messy network camera crews. The Quayle scoop didn't hurt, and during other long stretches, while Chris Wallace was off on campaign duty, I was the lead White House correspondent covering Reagan. With Chris about to leave the network, I assumed I'd be promoted to the number one White House correspondent's job for the incoming administration. The strongest signal was that the network had me covering the transition, trying to ferret out who would serve in the new cabinet. But for the first time in years, I planned to spend Thanksgiving with my own family rather than in a Santa Barbara hotel room monitoring Ronald Reagan's celebration from afar.

That was my expectation, until I was assigned to follow the president-elect to Kennebunkport for the Thanksgiving weekend. I complained that I'd more than earned a holiday of my own, but to no avail. The bureau chief at the time told me it was expected of me since I would soon be covering George Bush full-time. In other words, there was no choice in the matter.

We arrived in Maine on a Wednesday afternoon, barely in time to file for *Nightly News*. We did a "soft" feature on how Kennebunkport was about to suffer what Plains, Georgia, and Santa Barbara, California, had experienced: the invasion of the White House press corps. The seaside Maine community was hardly prepared for the onslaught. Harbormaster Ross Anderson suggested that the Secret Service would soon prevent fishermen from working near the Bush home. The lobstermen were up in arms, ready to form a naval protest. The president-elect addressed a hastily convened town gathering, trying to reassure people that the life of their small village would not change.

Neither the Bush team nor the reporters knew what to expect of each other in the early days of the new administration. The Bushes thought they could retain their privacy. The news media were determined to get advance notice of any presidential movement, as we had for decades. The first excursion was a disaster. The president-elect, doing his best imitation of "Harry Homemaker," decided to go to the hardware store, unencumbered by anyone except the normal complement of Secret Service agents. Having been rebuffed when we tried to negotiate a pool arrangement whereby a small group of reporters would accompany Mr. Bush at all times, we *all* jumped into our cars in hot pursuit.

The only problem was that Kennebunkport has one main road and many tourists; because we hadn't had any warning of the hardware store excursion, we had to scramble to catch up. Inevitably, the town's lone sheriff was going to find a miscreant breaking the speed limit and pulled me over for a full license check—only to discover that I was one of those dreaded reporters, speeding to catch up with the town's most famous citizen.

Clearly Barbara Bush was not happy about our invasion of her family's idyllic vacation retreat along the Maine coast. But with typical graciousness, she opened the Bush home to the newly arrived press tribe for wine and cheese (purchased by the president-elect earlier that day at the Tipsy Mouse wine and cheese shop) and a tour of the house. At the president-elect's insistence, the itinerary included a must-see stop in a restroom upstairs, from which we could view the ocean from the window above the "throne." Still smarting from the reporters who had turned a simple trip to the hardware store into a New York–style traffic jam, George Bush nonetheless surrendered to the inevitable loss of privacy that comes with high office. Grudgingly, he accepted a designated pool arrangement and promised not to sneak out without us.

The day after Thanksgiving, the incoming president faced a different kind of initiation: the quadrennial firestorm over Medicare cuts. Every chief executive confronts the same issue, and inevitably backs down. Once again, a leak about possible budget cuts in the sacrosanct entitlement program for the elderly forced a new White House into denial and full retreat. It was our lead story on *Nightly News*. As I went over my script, Bill Wheatley sent a computer message from headquarters in New York to call after I'd finished writing and recording my report for that evening's broadcast. He wanted to discuss my new assignment. New assignment?

I called immediately, of course, to ask what he meant. There was a long pause. Hadn't anyone told me I was being sent to Capitol Hill? Once again, I'd been passed over for the top White House job. I was devastated, trembling with a mixture of disappointment and anger. I'd gone to Kennebunkport on false hopes, and now would be humiliated in front of my colleagues and the new administration. Why had I invested so much time getting to know the new players?

Wheatley suggested I try to reach NBC News president Michael Gartner at his home in Iowa, where he had been a celebrated newspaper editor and still maintained his chief residence, for an official explanation.

Somehow, I got through *Nightly News* before calling my good friend Al Hunt, who had covered the Senate before becoming Washington bureau chief for *The Wall Street Journal*. Sobbing on the phone, I told Al and his wife, Judy Woodruff, that I was being transferred to the Hill. Al tried to sound sympathetic, but couldn't help laughing at my naïveté. Congress, he said, would turn out to be the best place I'd ever work as a journalist. Patiently, he pointed out how isolated and controlled the White House environment had become for a serious reporter. Later, Tom Pettit, the wry, veteran NBC correspondent, also shared his advice after years of covering the Senate.

"Sis," he said, "you've died and gone to reporters' heaven."

In Congress, he explained, I would find 535 politicians and countless aides, all eager to get on television. In those days, reporters had the freedom to roam the corridors, with few if any security restrictions. And we could cover anything we wanted: foreign policy debates, budget hearings, disputes over energy policy—the kind of substantive reporting I loved. All this without being interrupted by all those silly photo opportunities that made White House reporting so dependent on imagery and public relations. Still, that holiday weekend in Kennebunkport, I was miserable. A friend from *The Washington Post* coaxed me out to a lobster dinner. Tourists at the restaurant stopped at the table to ask for autographs. I kept bursting into tears.

Why didn't I get the job? At the time, it didn't strike me that gender was an issue, because Lesley Stahl had covered the White House during the Reagan years. But in fact, except for Judy Woodruff's tenure during Jimmy Carter's term, NBC had never had a successful run with a woman as a chief White House correspondent. And Judy had shared the beat with John Palmer. I'm not sure that the men running the networks thought that a woman could do the job by herself.

It was considered the most authoritative beat among the correspondent jobs, and there was still a reluctance to assume that women could handle it. Frankly, I don't think anyone questioned my reporting skills, but I think there could have been concerns about the image of a woman standing on the White House lawn, giving the nation the view from the Oval Office. And the beat was often used as a testing ground for future anchors, a different career track from mine. Except for a few women far more glamorous than I, the big anchor jobs have always been reserved for men. In any case, the assignment went instead to one of my pals, John Cochran, who had come back from being a foreign correspondent for NBC to cover the State Department. He was moved over to the White House beat and distinguished himself there over the next four years. We worked as a team on a wide range of stories, cementing our friendship. But that doesn't mean I wasn't miserable during that Thanksgiving weekend in Kennebunkport—on my way to what I thought was a dead end on the Hill.

———

It turned out to be the best decision that anyone had ever made for me. The years I spent on Capitol Hill were some of the most interesting and fulfilling of my career. Congress was a political circus, reality television with drama, scandal, and political reshuffling and realignment, much of which reverberates to this day. The savings and loan debacle, the Thomas-Hill hearings, the fall of Jim Wright and John Tower, the pillorying of Judge Robert Bork—all led directly to the rise of figures such as Newt Gingrich and Dick Cheney, and the Republican Revolution.

The first controversy erupted when the newly elected president nominated John Tower, the former chairman of the Senate Armed Services Committee, to be secretary of defense. With his network of connections in the Senate, Tower seemed to me like a shoo-in for the post. I thought even the Democrats among his former colleagues would be compliant. After all, he had ruled his committee with an iron fist, instilling fear of God and pork, alternately, in all of them.

By 1989, the Democrats were in control of the Senate, and Sam Nunn, the highly respected senator from Georgia, was in charge of Tower's confirmation. I had just arrived on the Hill and started to pick up signals that there was going to be a problem. I was developing sources among the senators, many of whom I'd known because they had been frequent visitors to the White House over the years. There were reports of heavy drinking and infidelity. All of a sudden, what should have been an easy confirmation was becoming a major crisis for the new administration; the story accelerated so quickly that *Nightly News* wanted to have it on the air competitively every night.

As the newest of the Senate correspondents working against senior players from the other networks, including Bob Schieffer from CBS and Jim Wooten from ABC, my skills were quickly tested. It was a very fast lesson in how different this beat would be from the White House. I found myself following senators underground on the Senate's internal subway to catch them in an off moment, and wandering through the hallways to grab people after hearings and caucuses—most often without a camera, because these were places camera crews could not go.

Luckily my training as a police reporter in Philadelphia kicked in once again. In addition to getting to know secretaries, who, as at the White House, zealously guarded their bosses, on the Hill there were hundreds of knowledgeable legislative aides who were often willing to talk. And you could literally trail the main players themselves, the primary sources. I loved every minute of it. It *was* a reporter's dream, exactly as Tom Pettit had forecast.

I quickly learned that, contrary to what the president and his aides thought, the opposition to John Tower was not driven entirely by politics. In the case of Sam Nunn, it came instead from a deeply felt, ingrained sense of duty. Nunn, a dedicated military expert, had very strongly held views about what was deemed appropriate and inappropriate behavior. His nightmare was that some figurative red phone would ring in the middle of the night to inform John Tower that a nuclear warhead was flying toward Washington, and Tower might be in a compromising position—or too drunk to respond properly.

Part of my job was also to separate the wheat from the chaff and make sure that everything we reported was accurate and fully sourced. For instance, there was one story circulating about Tower and a ballerina who danced on a piano; it had all sorts of permutations, and it was probably wrong—certainly it had not been corroborated. So as we covered Tower's nomination in that overheated environment, I often found myself calling Bill Wheatley and saying, "We don't want to report this; it's not true." Before the advent of multiple cable networks, you could easily kill a bad story with one call. This was long before the Internet facilitated a constant flow of rumor and gossip. In the 1980s it was a lot easier to filter out inaccurate information. These days, with twenty-four-hour cable news and talk, it is more complicated. In fact, there is a rarely acknowledged but implicitly different standard for what we can say on cable talk shows, as compared to *Nightly News* or the *Today* program.

Tower's nomination set the tone for my years on the Hill. Despite my years covering controversial figures like Mayor Frank Rizzo in Philadelphia and Governor Marvin Mandel in Maryland, and the Carter and Reagan administrations, the Tower debate was the first time I'd encountered scandal of such a highly personal nature. The Iran-Contra scandal had involved the nation's policy on terrorism, and the appropriate roles for the National Security Council and the CIA—big issues, like whether a rogue group inside the White House could circumvent congressional authority. But the Tower scandal raised different questions. Instead of affairs of state, these were alleged affairs of the heart. Personal reputations were at risk; and by their very private nature, the charges were almost impossible to verify.

There was a signal moment when John Tower went on the David Brinkley program on ABC one Sunday morning. Sam Donaldson, one of the panelists, raised the issue of Tower's alleged womanizing.

The twice-married Tower bristled and turned the question around, asking Cokie Roberts, also on the panel, to define "womanizing." Paraphrasing the Supreme Court decision on the definition of obscenity, she replied, "I think most women know it when they see it."

The exchange turned the debate. It quickly became clear that Sam Nunn was not going to let Tower be confirmed, despite the beleaguered nominee's extraordinary public pledge, on that same program, to abstain henceforth from what he quaintly called "beverage alcohol." Tower's nomination was defeated along party lines, 53 to 47. John Tower was only the ninth cabinet appointee in U.S. history to be rejected by the Senate.

The Bush team was badly shaken, because this was the first defeat for a new presidency, and it signaled to the Hill that the new administration could blink first in a showdown. In a big game of poker, the president had lost the first hand. Fortunately for him, he had a highly credible and politically popular person ready to substitute for Tower—Dick Cheney, then a member of Congress from Wyoming. Cheney had experience on the House Intelligence Committee, and had been chief of staff to President Ford. I had covered him as a member of Congress for several years, and then gotten to know him because he was a friend and former colleague of Alan's from the Ford years. His nomination zipped through.

At the time, Cheney, the number two man in the House Republican leadership, was thought of as fiscally conservative but otherwise middle-of-the-road. Even though he was more of a social conservative than many people probably realized, his association with Gerald Ford had given him the stamp of moderation. Unlike some of the more partisan members of the House, he had Democratic friends, including Tom Foley, majority leader and later speaker of the House. Cheney's elevation to the cabinet had the unintended consequence of changing the history of Congress. As the Republican whip, his nomination as defense secretary sparked a battle among House Republicans hoping to replace him. Among those eager to move up was a backbencher named Newt Gingrich.

Gingrich and a few of his more rebellious colleagues were smart, impatient, and bold. They seized the opportunity of Cheney's departure to challenge the more moderate approach of Republican leader Bob Michel. Gingrich and his cronies were chafing at what they considered decades of Republican passivity in the face of Democratic hegemony on the Hill. They felt that Michel had not been ideological enough, and that Cheney's designated successor would not challenge the House leadership forcefully enough. The Democrats had been dismissive and abusive to the Republican minority for years, and now the Republicans saw their chance to get even.

Gingrich used his new power to do something that had been previously unthinkable—he brought down the speaker of the House, a Democrat. Gingrich had been orchestrating an ethics complaint against Jim Wright, the speaker, for accepting gifts and outside income, including book royalties. One of Wright's top aides was also revealed to be a convicted felon who had once assaulted a young woman. After a yearlong ordeal, Jim Wright resigned dramatically in the "well" of the House, asking in a fiery speech that "this period of mindless cannibalism in the House" cease. Wright was the first speaker in history to be forced out because of scandal.

Suddenly, Newt Gingrich was a powerful force—the guy who had taken down the speaker of the House. Although lacking in seniority, he had growing support among the Republican rank and file to make a run at the leadership post himself.

We could barely keep up with all the political drama. In the Speaker's Lobby you could mingle with members and send a message onto the floor to ask someone to come out and talk. Again, the only frustration was that all this wasn't visible to the cameras, so I had to find ways to convey the atmosphere without pictures. The mission was to tell a story, and illustrate it by creating a mini-video, trying to capture the excitement of a lengthy House debate within the time constraints of a network TV news story. The challenge was to do it without losing context or distorting the substance of the story.

Critical to making this work was my bureau chief, Tim Russert, who had worked for New York's legendary Senator Pat Moynihan and loved the Hill the way I was learning to. He was deeply involved in shaping the coverage on *Nightly News,* briefing the New York producers each morning about which of the day's developments would likely prove to be the most important.

There were fights over gun control, access to public and private buildings for the disabled, extending civil rights protection to women, affirmative action, tax increases, tax cuts, the savings and loans scandals, and public housing rip-offs. There were investigations into sexual improprieties and financial skullduggery. When it came to judicial confirmations, Republicans were still seething over what had happened during the Reagan years, when Judge Robert Bork had been nominated and rejected for the Supreme Court. Reagan, ever the pragmatist, got over it immediately. The Senate judiciary chairman at the time, Joe Biden, has since recounted a remarkable one-on-one meeting he had with Reagan shortly after Bork was defeated. Biden says he walked into the Oval Office and Reagan congratulated him on having defeated his nominee. Biden demurred, saying he was sorry to see anyone suffer defeat this way, but that the Democrats just felt Bork wasn't the right person.

Reagan said, "Well, let's move on. Who would you like to see?' "

Biden replied that as the head of the Judiciary Committee, it wasn't his role to decide, but the president's. "Whomever you select, we're going to take a close look at," he told Ronald Reagan.

To which the president responded, "Well, let's go through the list."

What happened next completely contradicts conventional wisdom about Reagan being disengaged or unwilling to compromise. Biden reports that he and the president then sat together and went through a list of possible nominees, jointly vetting them. Finally, Reagan suggested Judge Anthony Kennedy, a moderate who was on the Court of Appeals for the Ninth Circuit in California. Biden said,

"That's a good name; assuming that we go through his writings and he's okay, that can fly." That's how Justice Kennedy, who has since become a crucial swing vote with another Reagan appointee, Sandra Day O'Connor, got to the Supreme Court.

Ronald Reagan had been able to move on after Bork was rejected, but rank-and-file Hill Republicans could not. They wanted to pay back their perceived enemies on the Senate Judiciary Committee and the liberal interest groups who worked closely with the committee's Democratic staff. The atmosphere in both the House and Senate during the early years of the Bush administration had become poisonous.

I can trace it to the winter of 1989, shortly after I arrived in Congress, when members tried to award themselves a pay raise: 7.9 percent more for that year, plus an additional 25 percent increase in 1991. The raise was coupled with new ethics reforms, eliminating speaking fees paid to legislators by special interest groups, and limiting gifts and free travel. The idea was that if the senators and representatives were paid better, there would be fewer inducements to accept income or gifts from special interest groups on the side. The increases may well have been justified, but they quickly became a cause célèbre on talk radio. This marked one of the first instances where powerful talk radio hosts, particularly conservatives, campaigned against the Washington bureaucrats and members of Congress. Even traditional liberal allies were divided on the issue: Common Cause, the government watchdog group, supported the initiative because it was linked with ethics reforms, while consumer activist Ralph Nader objected, claiming that it amounted to a bribe to get legislators to do the right thing.

These episodes sparked a revolution in the relationship between politics and television. The popularity of talk radio quickly gave birth to television talk shows, as well. Cable news had begun in 1980 on CNN, but as other cable networks began to proliferate, and as they saw the commercial success of talk radio, they initiated their own shows built around angry debate and commentary. Neutral observers did not get invited back. The most heavily courted guests were the people who would be the most provocative. There was a premium placed on bullying government figures; being well informed was secondary.

It became an escalating war of words: politicians and pundits competed to be as outrageous as possible in order to get invited back on the air, so that they could increase their lecture fees, or sell a book, or make money in some other fashion. They could even become paid consultants to one of these networks, or parlay their exposure into jobs as campaign aides in a national race. Better yet, from their perspective, some of the "talking heads" became candidates, before returning to their roles as television commentators—a revolving door of political insiders.

Soon, legislating became almost impossible. Special interest groups could kidnap an issue by exploiting the talk show phenomenon. One celebrated example was what happened when Congress passed catastrophic health insurance in 1988. It would have provided coverage for long-term disability and major medical problems, but seniors would have had to pay higher premiums. It passed with 80 percent public support. But within weeks, lobbying groups, including the American Association of Retired Persons and the Committee to Save Social Security and Medicare, started campaigning against it. As opposition mounted, the bill's chief supporter, Ways and Means chairman Dan Rostenkowski, went back to his district and was ambushed.

Outside a hearing in his Chicago district, sixty-one-year-old "Rosty," one of the most powerful Democrats in Congress after thirty years, was forced to flee like a fugitive, as dozens of elderly people shouted "Liar!" and "Chicken!" and banged on his car windows with canes, walkers, and picket signs. All this was captured on television nationwide. Pressure mounted so quickly that within months Congress reversed itself, repealing the hard-fought catastrophic-insurance legislation.

It was an important signal that voting to change the guaranteed benefit programs was political suicide. In a memorable phrase coined by Tip O'Neill's counsel Kirk O'Donnell, Social Security became known as the third rail of politics, and it's been nearly impossible to reform it ever since. The Republican White House and the Democratic majorities in Congress learned that dealing with the long-term fiscal solvency of these enormous programs was risky business.

The incident also helped make Rostenkowski vulnerable. In him, Newt Gingrich and the Republicans saw another chance to challenge the Democratic leadership. Before long, Rostenkowski was the target of a federal investigation into his personal finances. He ended up being indicted on seventeen counts of embezzlement, corruption, and fraud, and served time in jail. The Republicans also investigated one of Congress's little-known perks, the House bank, which was used as a private piggybank to give credit, basically interest-free loans, to House members, mainly Democrats. They were overdrawing their accounts—free of charge. That outraged a public already infuriated by the pillaging of the nation's savings and loans.

Quickly, the scandal spread. Congress began to look like the capital of perks. In addition to the House bank, there was the barbershop, the postal services, gifts from the gift shop—all sorts of cut-rate services that had built up over years and years of unchallenged Democratic leadership. An underlying sense of entitlement had finally been challenged; once the Republicans started peeling back the layers, more and more was unearthed. None of this would foster comity, the tradition of genteel collegiality for which the Hill had long been known.

When I first started covering the Senate, a centrist group of moderates in both parties worked together trying to craft compromises. Gradually, the atmosphere so eroded that these senators began retiring—people like John Danforth of Missouri, who became special envoy to Sudan and, briefly, ambassador to the United Nations under the second President Bush. Danforth, thoughtful and avuncular, was in fact an ordained Episcopal priest. In that role, he had officiated at the funerals of Teresa Heinz Kerry's first husband, Senator John Heinz of Pennsylvania, Katharine Graham, and later at the state funeral of Ronald Reagan. During his years in the Senate, the only time Danforth was openly partisan was during the bitter fight over Clarence Thomas's nomination to the Supreme Court. But that was because Thomas had been a Danforth protégé. On most issues, Danforth got along well with Democrats, and wanted to get things done.

There were others, in both parties: Sam Nunn and John Chafee, David Boren and Pete Domenici, Pat Moynihan and Bob Dole. These were men who honored the constitutional mandate of advice and consent, of healthy debate, but always in the spirit of Senate collegiality.

The atmosphere began to change, though, particularly as some House Republicans ran for the Senate to fill the seats of those who had retired. The House had always been scrappier, full of people with sharper elbows. They had successfully dumped the speaker. They were taking on the leaders in the opposing party, challenging authority. They weren't raised with the same genteel rituals that had become embedded in the DNA of the Senate. Now the upper body changed as well, in ways that rewarded partisanship rather than co-operation.

One of the nastiest of these early investigations involved the Department of Housing and Urban Development, and HUD secretary Samuel Pierce, the only African-American in the Reagan cabinet. He had such a low profile, he was informally known as Silent Sam. There were reports that he left his underlings in charge, while he spent the day watching soap operas. As Mary McGrory wrote in *The Washington Post,* there was speculation that he'd only come to Washington on the hope that if Thurgood Marshall were "subpoe-naed by heaven," Pierce might be named to the Supreme Court. Reagan had once even referred to him as "Mr. Mayor." Seeing an African-American in the usually all-white Reagan White House, the president had assumed Pierce must be a big-city mayor!

After he left the cabinet, when called to testify before a House subcommittee about whether housing contracts had been awarded to political cronies, Pierce took the Fifth Amendment against self-incrimination. Even for ethically challenged Washington, having a former cabinet member refuse to testify on the grounds of self-incrimination was stunning.

Relying on a little-known McCarthy-era House rule that permitted subpoenaed witnesses to exclude camera crews, Pierce's attorneys made sure we were kicked out of the hearing room to miss the former HUD secretary's star turn. If it didn't happen on television, the theory went, it hadn't really happened. So when the embattled housing secretary finally emerged from the hearing room, there was blood in the water and we were the sharks. Flanked by aides and Capitol police, he raced down the hall looking for an escape. As he moved faster, so did we. Finally, trying to get him to comment, I chased him into the elevator; what viewers saw on *Nightly News* was the elevator door closing on my arm and the microphone and Sam Pierce all but pinned against the elevator wall trying to duck the camera's lens.

Inevitably, all this had a corrosive effect on attitudes toward Washington. There was so much rough-and-tumble that the public was getting the impression that the government was rife with corruption: so much was happening at once, and the scandals were unraveling equally in both parties.

———

The savings and loan mess was a classic example of the bipartisan malaise of the time. During the 1988 campaign, no one had questioned either candidate—Bush or Dukakis—about the insolvency of the nation's savings and loan system. Both political parties were so deeply dependent upon contributions from the S&Ls that nobody wanted to turn over that rock—neither Bush nor Dukakis nor any of their minions. But shortly after the election, it became clear to thrift regulators, who'd also been asleep at the switch, that something was dreadfully wrong.

The poster child for the scandal became an S&L operator named Charles Keating, who had a number of friends in Congress. The Senate began investigating whether several senators who were friends of Keating had taken favors from him in exchange for helping him with a business badly dependent upon federal subsidies and regulations. Savings and loans started collapsing; the depositors were generally older people on fixed incomes who were losing their retirements. It was a case made for national television.

The Senate opened hearings into what became known as the Keating Five—five senators who had different degrees of complicity. As the investigation began, it was generally believed that Senator Dennis DeConcini of Arizona, which was Keating's home state, was deeply involved. But also tarred by this broad brush were at least two other senators who really had no business being part of it. One of them was John Glenn, hero of World War II and Korea, as well as the space program, and a candidate for president during the primaries in 1984. No one could have been more of a straight arrow than this former marine pilot, but all of a sudden he was being swept up in a media feeding frenzy, because of a peripheral connection to Charles Keating.

The other person who was unfairly captured in this mess was Arizona Senator John McCain, because the Democrats did not want it to become an exclusively Democratic scandal. So the Democrats on the Ethics Committee insisted on including one Republican. McCain, who knew Charles Keating and whose family had taken airplane rides with him—a common practice by members of Congress—became an easy target. To this day, McCain is deeply resentful at having been included, with good reason. A decorated Vietnam prisoner of war, he had national ambitions; now he could see his whole career being wrecked.

As the investigation proceeded, it became clear to the Ethics Committee special counsel, Bob Bennett, that neither McCain nor Glenn had any business being in the dock. Bennett, in fact, had privately recommended to the committee that the ethics complaint be streamlined to become "the Keating Three," excluding McCain and Glenn. But the committee refused to go along, because to remove

Glenn and McCain would make it look bad for the remaining Democrats, Senate banking chairman Don Riegle and Alan Cranston of California, a prodigious fund-raiser for the Democratic party.

The hearings were turning into a full-scale Washington drama when the controversy hit home for me: it was revealed that four years earlier, before Keating's Lincoln Savings and Loan was in trouble, a prominent New York law firm representing Keating had hired a private economist with a big reputation to do a study on what kinds of investments savings and loans should safely make. Then running a Wall Street firm, Alan Greenspan had given his "Good Housekeeping" seal of approval to a Keating proposal that savings and loans be permitted to invest directly in real estate. Now these practices were being criticized for helping make the S&Ls excessively vulnerable to swings in the economy. Suddenly in the middle of my coverage of the biggest scandal in town, everyone was focusing on the fact that Greenspan, by then Fed chairman, had years earlier given Keating what was being interpreted as a clean bill of health.

For the first time since Alan's appointment, I had a real conflict, especially because John McCain was pointing to Alan's study to justify his own earlier conclusion that Keating was reliable. I had to take myself off the story, at least until Alan's role was cleared up. The criticism didn't bother him at all, but knowing his rock-hard integrity, it galled me to hear people taking his earlier work for Keating out of context and attempting to drag him into the current scandal. Finally, the facts caught up with the news coverage. Alan's limited role was resolved, and the investigation refocused on the senators.

A year later, I was able to cover the outcome of the hearings, as the Senate Ethics Committee meted out varying punishments to the five senators. But it was an important example of how suddenly issues could arise that required separating my professional life from Alan's, erecting a firewall between his work and mine. We also had to be careful to avoid even the appearance of a conflict of interest. As a result, I avoided showing up with him on some occasions usually attended by spouses. As much as I would have liked to attend one of his five confirmation hearings, for instance, I thought it better to avoid drawing attention to our relationship. And when I was covering Congress, I made sure I was nowhere nearby any time he came to the Hill.

The savings and loan scandals made average Americans feel vulnerable about the safety of their savings, perhaps for the first time since the Great Depression. They realized that some of the people they'd trusted to handle their money—often friends and neighbors, pillars of their small-town communities—had swindled them. It played to a recurring populist resentment of corporate America that dates back to Teddy Roosevelt's trust-busting and Lincoln Steffens's muckraking journalism in the first decade of the twentieth century. It is the same anger we now see, justifiably, in response to corporate scandals, and it feeds a more generalized outrage against big business that animates much of the rhetoric in contemporary politics.

The S&L scandal caused real damage to people's lives, and to the federal budget. The government had to spend more than $480 billion bailing out the thrifts, and many depositors lost their savings. In fact, an interagency group of regulators, including Alan, was appointed by the president to work nonstop on the bailout. A pattern of abuse in the private sector, followed by a government rescue, was established.

The other outcome was that the millions of dollars that the savings and loans institutions had poured into congressional campaigns—a million from Keating to the five senators alone—exposed Congress's ugliest secret, the campaign finance system. For John McCain, it was an epiphany. He knew he had to purge himself of supporters like Keating. To resurrect his career, he transformed himself into the nation's leading advocate of campaign finance reform.

It became his new persona: he helped sponsor every major campaign finance bill that followed. The issue distinguished him from his colleagues and positioned him to become a national force for independent-minded politics in succeeding years. As he himself would say, as a reformed sinner, someone previously dependent on contributions from men like Charles Keating, he could be even more zealous in trying to change the system.

———

Until then, my years in Congress had been consumed by scandal and corruption. As exciting, and productive, as it was, after so many years of covering foreign policy in the White House, I missed international news, presidential summits, even military conflicts. But soon enough, I'd have more foreign news than I'd want. On August 2, 1990, Saddam Hussein invaded Kuwait. America had been Iraq's unofficial ally during Saddam's eight-year conflict with Iran, a country the administration viewed as even more sinister than Iraq. But when Saddam's troops crossed the border into Kuwait, he threatened to seize an even greater prize, the oil fields of Saudi Arabia. America's showdown with Iraq was on. At the time, it felt like a final confrontation. We didn't realize it was only the first chapter in a much longer engagement.

The president and his defense secretary, Dick Cheney, knew they had to mobilize a military force to push Saddam back, but few of Iraq's neighbors in the Persian Gulf were willing to permit American forces on their territory. Even the Saudis, whose oil and territory were most at risk, resented having to request American help and wanted to limit their population's exposure to more Westernized countries. Cheney's secret mission was to persuade Gulf monarchs, who had previously insisted on only the most secret military arrangements with the United States, to permit U.S. forces to take up positions openly in their countries in preparation for an all-out assault against Iraq. That meant siding with the "infidel" against a fellow Arab, but one whose secularism and territorial ambitions were deeply threatening.

Because Congress was gone on summer vacation, euphemistically known as district work periods, I was available to go with Cheney as the network TV representative in a small group, or pool, of reporters from the major newspapers. We went to the relatively closed societies of Oman, Qatar, and Saudi Arabia, and to more Western countries like Bahrain. Routine photo opportunities became culture wars: our group included several women, and we found ourselves asking questions of Arab rulers who never expected to be questioned by a journalist, much less an American woman. Although we didn't wear chadors and veils, we tried to respect their religious imperatives by wearing long skirts and long sleeves. But even appropriately dressed, I startled the emir of Qatar when I presumed to ask a question at a photo opportunity. (It was actually pretty intimidating; I felt like Oliver Twist asking tremulously for another bowl of porridge.)

It was during that trip, on board the aircraft carrier USS *Eisenhower,* that I first realized war was inevitable, despite the feints toward diplomacy. We were in the Red Sea, accompanying Cheney, on August 18. Two days earlier, under new United Nations resolutions authorizing an embargo of all but medical and food supplies to Iraq and occupied Kuwait, ships from the U.S. and its allies had begun intercepting merchant vessels that challenged the blockade. According to the Pentagon's "after-action report," in the Gulf of Oman, the USS *Reid,* a guided-missile frigate, fired the first shots of Operation Desert Shield across the bow of an Iraqi tanker that refused to alter its course in the Persian Gulf. Another encounter with an Iraqi tanker followed, this time in the Persian Gulf itself. The USS *Bradley* fired three warning shots when the tanker wouldn't turn back. All ships in the region, including ours, were put on general quarters, with their crews sent to battle stations. Rather than feeling frightened, we were excited to be close to the action. Dick Cheney was briefed on the incidents while on board the USS *Scott,* a destroyer in the Eisenhower battle group. The *Scott* had peacefully turned back a Cypriot freighter loaded with chemicals only hours earlier at the opening of the Gulf of Aqaba. Cheney told the crew that they were doing tough, hard, dirty work, but that it was perhaps the most important moment for the nation for the rest of the century. There was no doubt about his mind-set; he was determined to take on Iraq.

The military consequences of these early encounters were negligible, but that wasn't the point. Through the cat and mouse game with Iraqi ships, the United States was seeking to project strength and determination to Iraq and the rest of the world. The sanctions would be enforced. It may have been a minor skirmish to the rest of the world, but to those of us on the flight deck of one of the two U.S. aircraft carriers in the region, it sounded like World War III. I scrambled to file live reports on the action for the pool, and for *Nightly News* from "Pri-Fli," or primary flight control.

Visually, nighttime flight operations are stunning. Acoustically, it is a complete assault on your senses: when flight operations are under way, the noise is thunderous. What is also striking to the uninitiated is how close the quarters are, even on a carrier. When these men are in their "racks," as the bunks are known, they are literally sandwiched one on top of another, with only a few inches on either side. It is claustrophobic, but somehow the crew manning this enormous ship, essentially a small town afloat, works together, in peace and wartime. The experience gave an outsider like me a new and healthy respect for the chain of command and the discipline that make such a highly choreographed operation possible.

It was my first visit to Saudi Arabia, and it was obvious that the royal family was deeply ambivalent about the trade-off between preserving its culture and accepting Western help to defend its borders against Saddam. Until we arrived in Jeddah, very late one night, I had no concept of how deep a chasm existed between American culture and the strict Wahabi form of Islam that governs Saudi Arabia, and that has, through its clerics, been responsible for radicalizing a generation of Saudi youth. By the time we had completed the formal arrival ceremony and traditional drinking of tea, it must have been two in the morning, but Cheney immediately went to see King Fahd, as was expected. We learned later that it was a critical meeting to obtain the king's consent for a massive, and unprecedented, U.S. troop deployment on Saudi soil.

Our small press group was taken to what appeared to be an Inter-Continental Hotel. Once inside, it was surreal, like something out of *Last Year at Marienbad.* There were no other guests, as far as we could ascertain. The only people in the hotel were the five or six of us from the press pool, vastly outnumbered by the staff. It turned out that instead of being at a commercial hotel, we were staying at an official guesthouse reserved for the royal family.

One of the most obvious differences about being in the kingdom was the lack of television news other than the officially sanctioned Middle East Broadcasting on every channel. The Saudis were not going to permit their people to see Western media. Not being in a real hotel, we also had all sorts of technical challenges in getting our stories out: we hadn't arranged for satellite feeds, because the networks had not anticipated that this would be a newsworthy trip—but it was quickly developing into one.

At that time the Saudis were not readily granting visas to American journalists to enter the kingdom. We got in only because we were accompanying the secretary of defense. Several newspaper reporters wanted to take advantage of this monthlong visa to stay in Saudi Arabia, rather than returning home directly with Dick Cheney. But when they tried to book flights from Jeddah to do more reporting at the American military base at Dhahran, they immediately ran into another Saudi rule: unmarried women could travel only if accompanied by a male relative.

So Dick Cheney cooperated by writing notes, as though he were writing a teacher's permission slip or a doctor's note, for Molly Moore of *The Washington Post* and some of the other women journalists, saying that they were the sisters of Michael Gordon of *The New York Times.* The secretary of defense was creating instant families by fiat.

After we returned home, a month later, I had a glimpse into the way diplomatic relationships are cemented behind the scenes. It is a secret world, parallel to official Washington, and perhaps more important. Prince Bandar bin Sultan, Saudi Arabia's legendary ambassador to the United States, and his wife, Princess Haifa, invited us to dinner on September 28, at their palatial home in McLean, Virginia, on the banks of the Potomac near the CIA. The only other guests were Dick Cheney and his wife, Lynne, and Ken Duberstein, Ronald Reagan's last chief of staff, and his wife, Sydney.

Alan and I accepted immediately, but then I got a call from Ken. "What are you going to do about the Bandar dinner?" he asked.

"Of course we're going," I replied, having not really focused on the calendar. But he pointed out that the dinner was scheduled for Yom Kippur. Not only wouldn't we be fasting, as required by Jewish religious law, we'd be eating at the home of the Saudi Ambassador. In the end, we both decided that the Lord, and our parents, would somehow understand, and we drove to the Saudi residence. On Kol Nidre, the holiest night of the Jewish calendar, we found ourselves being inspected by the well-armed and very tough-looking British security men who guard Bandar's estate.

Bandar is the son of Prince Sultan, the Saudi defense minister, and therefore a member of the royal family; although, because his mother was reportedly a Sudanese servant, he is not believed to be in the line of succession. Trained in British schools and by the British and U.S. military as a jet pilot, he is the dean of the diplomatic corps in Washington, having served as ambassador since 1983, longer than any of his colleagues. He is flashy, extravagant, witty, politically astute, and extraordinarily charming. On this evening, he displayed all those assets, and more. I confess that the meal, on this Jewish fast night, was superb, reflecting two cultures: first a Western dinner heavily influenced by French cuisine, followed by several beautifully seasoned courses of traditional Arabic food.

After dinner, in a throwback to an earlier Washington practice that Georgetown doyennes Kay Graham and Sally Quinn had helped eradicate, the men and women separated. The men remained with Bandar for cigars, brandy, and conversation, while we joined Bandar's wife, Princess Haifa, who was the late King Faisal's daughter. We marveled at how she managed to bridge two worlds, and how the cultural divide affected her teenage daughters. What did they do about wearing the veil?

She explained that the girls wore Western dress in the United States, but changed into traditional Saudi attire on the plane before they arrived home. Did she ever resent the way women were treated in her society? Not at all, she said. In fact, she viewed the veil as a way to protect her identity from the intrusion of men's scrutiny. It made her feel more, not less, independent. But how could she see, with her face fully covered? We were so curious, she suggested we try it ourselves.

Ringing a silver bell, she gave a servant some orders in Arabic, and promptly the woman returned with a silver tray carrying several black veils. Soon King Faisal's daughter was expertly draping veils over Lynne Cheney, Sydney Duberstein, and me. Much to our astonishment, you could actually see through the diaphanous layers. Whether that is the way we wanted to see the world was another issue.

———

As the months progressed, we learned that Cheney's mission had been very successful in persuading reluctant Gulf leaders, including the Saudis, to permit U.S. forces to pre-position troops in their countries. The United States began a massive expansion of air bases, some secret, into the region. It became very clear that the administration was going to war. But shockingly, after a decade of spending a trillion dollars on defense, the United States was not prepared. The military had been training to fight in the desert but was buying weapons to fight the Cold War. Instead of building fast ships to move troops and equipment to the Persian Gulf, the navy had spent billions on Trident submarines and warships. As a result, the U.S. deployment took months to accomplish, and had to be synchronized with painstaking diplomatic maneuvering. To antiwar critics, the diplomacy was all for show, a delaying tactic until the troops were positioned.

In what now sounds like a preview of more recent history, on December 3, 1990, Dick Cheney and Colin Powell, then chairman of the Joint Chiefs of Staff, told Congress that they disagreed with a parade of former officials who felt sanctions could work against Iraq if given more time. At a Senate Armed Services Committee hearing I covered for *Nightly News,* Cheney testified, "While we wait for sanctions to work, Saddam Hussein continues to obliterate any trace of Kuwait and her people."

Cheney added, perhaps prophetically, "It's far better for us to deal with him (Saddam) now, than it will be for us to deal with him five or ten years from now."

Sam Nunn, then the committee chairman, tried to make the case for sanctions: "If we have a war, we're never going to know whether they would have worked, are we?"

Cheney also upset some senators by suggesting that the president could commit combat troops without asking Congress to declare war, reviving a longstanding separation-of-powers dispute between the executive and legislative branches that recurs no matter which party controls the White House and which is running Congress. But Powell, now thought of as a dove in the war councils of the second President Bush, had the most hawkish line of the day. When the administration witnesses promised Congress that they were using diplomacy and the threat of force—both carrots and sticks—the senators asked, where is the carrot?

"The carrot," said General Powell, "is that we won't use the stick."

The argument over which branch of government could declare war moved swiftly over the next days and weeks to what threatened to be a constitutional showdown. In one hearing, Senator Pat Moynihan, the Senate's premier historian and scholar, asked Vietnam-era defense secretary Robert McNamara whether the administration was correct when it claimed that the president could send "young kids" into battle without Congress's approval.

Still debating his Vietnam record with himself, McNamara said, "I do not believe any single human being should take this nation to war by his own decision, and that includes the president."

At that point, America had gone into battle two hundred times, only five times with formal congressional declarations of war. But many in Congress were insisting on their constitutional prerogative. As the 102nd Congress convened in January, the president quickly announced what sounded like a peace initiative: Secretary of State James Baker would meet with Saddam's foreign minister, Tariq Aziz, in Geneva. Democratic leaders, Tom Foley in the House and George Mitchell in the Senate, delayed a war debate until Baker had time to complete his mission. Democratic doves turned on their leaders, demanding a more forceful challenge to the president.

As the administration expected, Baker's ultimatum to Tariq Aziz failed to win concessions from Iraq. I packed for the Gulf, with mixed emotions. We were told to prepare for chemical or biological attacks. Everyone assumed it would be a long, bloody engagement. By then, Alan and I were living together, quietly. I didn't want to be away from him for such a long time, but as always, my domestic instincts were fighting my hunger for adventure. It was also a career challenge: I wanted to be on the front lines of whatever was the most important breaking news of the day. But before I could leave, I had to cover the final chapter of Congress's challenge to the president's march toward war.

On January 12, a Saturday, the Senate held a rare weekend debate on war and peace, a debate that remains one of the most elevated in recent memory. All of us, reporters and senators alike, knew we were witnessing an historic battle of ideas. In fact, reputations are still being made and lost over how aspiring politicians performed on that day. Al Gore, for example, was alleged to have switched his vote in exchange for an offer from the Republicans of more speaking time in the floor debate. Senator Alan Simpson of Wyoming claimed that Gore arrived at the Senate that day with two speeches in hand, one for the Democrats, and one for the Republicans, and that he only voted for the resolution to use force in the Gulf because the Republicans were going to give him a prime slot for his speech. Gore has repeatedly denied the charge.

Senator Sam Nunn was once again the most compelling voice against George Bush on behalf of the Democrats, as he had been during the Tower nomination debate. Interestingly, John Kerry voted against the war, a vote that critics in the 2004 presidential campaign cited as evidence of his inconsistency. But he was not alone among senators deeply immersed in foreign policy: Robert Byrd, Sam Nunn, George Mitchell, and Joe Biden all took the same position. The final vote approving the war resolution was 250 to 183 in the House and 52 to 47 in the Senate.

I booked my flights for the following Friday, headed for the U.S. command post in Saudi Arabia. But then the French launched a last-minute peace initiative, hoping to win concessions from both sides before a UN deadline for negotiations expired later that week. NBC ordered me to stay in Washington long enough to cover the diplomatic maneuvering. It was a fateful decision. At seven p.m. eastern standard time, on January 16, the United States and its allies attacked Baghdad. Outside of the U.S. government, only CNN, with its intrepid correspondents in Baghdad, led by Bernard Shaw, knew it. We were all on standby, speed-dialing our sources, trying to confirm what we were watching on cable news. Knowing that the White House would have to notify congressional leaders, I called them all, repeatedly. Speaker of the House Tom Foley was out, I later learned, buying shirts at Brooks Brothers when he got the White House call. With a striking lack of creativity, the prearranged code Jim Baker used to alert Senator Jesse Helms and others not on secure telephones was, "The balloon is up."

Minutes later, we were able to confirm that the battle for Iraq had begun. But most phone lines in Baghdad, except for CNN's, went down, and most correspondents were out of communication anyway, in a basement bomb shelter. The night belonged to CNN. For seventeen hours, they reported by telephone, vividly describing the American bombardment of Baghdad from where they were holed up in the Rashid Hotel. In *The Washington Post* the next day, Tom Shales wrote that the ultimate compliment to CNN was Tom Brokaw interviewing Bernie Shaw live by phone and praising his team's enterprise and bravery. Brokaw told our viewers, "CNN used to be called the little network that could. It's no longer a little network."

Watching Shaw and the others, I wished I'd had the guts to force my way at least to the American theater of operations before the war started. I thought I'd still get there before the war was over. But fortunately for our forces, if not my war correspondent ambitions, it all ended quickly; Iraq surrendered in six weeks. People assumed that there would be enormous casualties. No one, not even the administration, anticipated how rapidly the war would progress. Most commentators and U.S. officials figured that Saddam would make greater use of his Scud missiles, especially against Israel. Few thought his air force wouldn't even get off the ground. Our expectations, as opposed to the reality, of Saddam's conduct of war became a dress rehearsal for what we experienced in later confrontations with him, under both Presidents Clinton and Bush.

In retrospect, our later misjudgments about Iraq's weapons of mass destruction were also rooted in what we learned from the first Gulf War and its aftermath. After the UN inspectors got into Iraq in 1991, we learned for the first time that Saddam had come dangerously close to developing an active nuclear weapons program and was surprisingly advanced in his manufacture of chemical and biological weapons. In fact, it took four more years, until his sons-in-law defected, for the UN inspectors to discover the full extent of his secret biological program. That critical lapse in the inspections program had a lasting impact on several of the key figures from the first Gulf War, notably Dick Cheney, who would be making crucial decisions a decade later.

It led to much of the faulty analysis that convinced the second Bush administration once again to invade Iraq. At the time, it could have seemed reasonable: if Saddam was so expert at evading international sanctions, and had not fully accounted for the weapons he'd stockpiled before the first Gulf War, what did he produce during the four and a half years when the inspectors were out of the country, from 1998 to 2002? How could anyone be sure he didn't still have an active weapons program? Their assumptions caused the Bush policy makers to discount warnings from UN weapons inspectors who were arguing for more time to assess the evidence of Saddam's weapons program.

At the end of the first Gulf War, however, few people questioned the decision to stop short of Baghdad. Dick Cheney and Colin Powell told us that occupying Iraq would saddle America with the burden of running it. National Security Advisor Brent Scowcroft cautioned that Iraq had been patched together by the British to start with and would likely spin apart into three ethnic divisions without Saddam Hussein. All of this sounded sensible. Why spoil a good military victory with the burdens of occupation?

Most of us predicted that George Bush, enjoying stratospheric postwar favorability ratings, would coast to reelection. But the glory faded quickly, and we were late to capture the brewing discontent across America, as more and more people felt alienated by the stagnant economy and loss of opportunities. As Americans turned inward, away from foreign policy and toward domestic concerns, there was also an awakening of anger about civil rights and women's issues. Bush administration policies on abortion, gun control, and race widened the growing gender gap between Democrat and Republican.

———

All of these forces came to a dramatic crescendo in the Clarence Thomas hearings, a historic confrontation that crossed the divide between the political and the personal in ways never before contemplated. For the first time, America was debating racial and sexual stereotypes rarely, if ever, acknowledged, even in private. It was a bizarre dramatization at the intersection of public policy and soap opera, with testimony so shocking we didn't know how to put it properly into any known context.

As people watched our live coverage, they separated along lines that superseded partisan loyalties: men and women, employer and employee, husband and wife. Individual reactions depended on whether a woman had ever experienced harassment herself—and how many hadn't?—and whether a man identified with Thomas's dilemma. Add to all that the powerful racial component, which in many people aroused additional feelings of guilt and shame.

This unusual national debate was triggered by what initially seemed a predictable, if not cynical, political decision. Seeking to improve his record with minorities, President Bush nominated an African-American to the Supreme Court to replace the legendary Thurgood Marshall, who was retiring. Bush's surprising choice was a federal appeals court judge little known outside judicial circles, and not distinguished for any scholarship, Clarence Thomas. Thomas was being promoted by a group of powerful conservatives active in Republican politics. As the director of the Equal Employment Opportunity Commission under Ronald Reagan, he had been one of the most prominent African-American opponents to affirmative action. Despite a relatively thin résumé, Thomas, at best a controversial choice, was described by the president as the best qualified man in the country for the high court.

At his initial confirmation hearing, Thomas did not impress most senators with the depth of his legal background or judicial wisdom. But politically, Democrats were reluctant to take him on, and the nomination moved forward toward a final Senate vote. Then suddenly everything was thrown into turmoil. An obscure law professor from Oklahoma came forward, reluctantly and belatedly, with startling accusations of sexual harassment. Anita Hill had confided in colleagues and the committee that she had serious concerns about Clarence Thomas's commitment to equal justice because of his aberrant behavior when she had worked for him from

1981 to 1983, first at the Department of Education, and later at the EEOC.

Her account was leaked to Nina Totenberg of National Public Radio, and Thomas saw support for his confirmation rapidly evaporate. But he had powerful backers shepherding his confirmation: John Danforth, who had mentored him in the Missouri attorney general's office; Ken Duberstein, from the Reagan White House, now a lobbyist; and Ricky Silberman, who had worked with Thomas at the EEOC and was the wife of Judge Laurence Silberman, a fellow judge of Thomas's on the U.S. Court of Appeals. In addition, Clarence Thomas had a great personal story, which Americans love. He had been raised poor in Georgia by his sharecropper grandfather, and had risen via Yale Law School to the highest levels of government.

But Hill's charges resonated with women in Congress, which had always been a bastion of male prerogatives. On the day a final vote was scheduled, a handful of completely outnumbered congresswomen, led by Representatives Pat Schroeder and Barbara Boxer, marched on the Senate, challenging the upper chamber to hold a more extensive debate on Clarence Thomas's nomination, instead of rubber-stamping it. With my camera crews in full chase, the women tried to storm the weekly lunchtime caucus of the Senate Democrats as they discussed whether to reopen hearings so Hill could air her charges. The Democratic senators, outraged at the presence of House members in their midst, blocked their entrance. (The Senate's only female Democrat at the time, Barbara Mikulski, was clearly outnumbered.) Now there are fourteen women in the Senate, including, notably, Hillary Rodham Clinton. I wonder if she could have turned that small rebellion into something bigger?

Separately, the women House members, despite having no constitutional role in the process, tied up unrelated legislation in the lower chamber as a further protest. It was mayhem, on both sides of the Capitol. The issue of sexual harassment had struck a nerve in the body politic. Finally, late in the day, the White House caved. Bowing to the inevitable, Thomas's supporters agreed to postpone a final vote until the charges could be heard and answered.

I knew and trusted people on both sides of the issue, including Thomas's principal sponsors, Duberstein and Danforth. Both swore that Thomas was incapable of behaving as Anita Hill described. Opposing them, a phalanx of Washington lawyers and Harvard scholars long active in civil rights law vouched for Anita Hill. Both Thomas and Hill had grown up poor, earned law degrees at Yale, and gone to Washington to make their way. Now their seemingly exemplary lives were going to be picked apart in what we all knew would be a brutal hearing.

We had no idea *how* brutal it would be. Anita Hill arrived in Washington under heavy police guard because of telephone threats. It was a mob scene. The stage was set for the hearings to open in the fabled Senate caucus room where the Watergate hearings had been held. Not since then, nearly two decades earlier, had there been such high drama in the Capitol. The high-ceilinged, columned neoclassical room, lit theatrically for television coverage, was jammed with spectators and reporters. We were covering it all live, all day, preempting the soap operas. The nation was transfixed. The Thomas-Hill hearings were better than the soaps; few people complained about missing *Days of Our Lives*.

Thomas appeared first, anguished, nervous, defiant, and categorically denying all charges of sexual harassment. Sitting behind him at the press table, I scribbled notes furiously as he intoned in a deep baritone, "I have been racking my brains and eating my insides out trying to think of what I could have said or done to Anita Hill to lead her to allege that I was interested in her in more than a professional way and that I talked with her about pornographic or X-rated films."

Even more forcefully, he added, "Enough is enough. I'm not going to allow myself to be further humiliated in order to be confirmed. . . . Confirm me if you want. Don't confirm me if you are so led, but let this process end."

I raced out to the Russell Building rotunda to go on the air, trying to summarize a denial almost stunning in its sheer emotional power. How could anyone who'd been so categorical be lying? Or had he so carefully separated his outer and inner selves that he no longer knew the truth? It was a classic case of he said, she said, and as a reporter, I had no way to discern who was telling the truth. My role was to present both sides, analyze the senators' responses, and put it all within the context of the political outcomes yet to come.

Anita Hill arrived next, looking young, somewhat fragile, but with a startlingly direct gaze. The contrast between the soft-spoken professor and the outrageous behavior she described was striking. At times, I felt like gasping at the horrific detail, but kept scribbling notes until my wrist was stiff and tired. For seven hours, Hill described how Thomas had allegedly trash-talked about all manner of pornography and bragged about his own sexual prowess. It was unlike anything ever heard in the Capitol or on the broadcast networks. Thomas's Republican supporters on the Judiciary Committee were initially chastened, but then started falling all over each other to impeach her credibility. During an extraordinary three days of hearings, Orrin Hatch even seized on an excerpt from *The Exorcist* that sounded similar to one of her charges, to suggest she had been inspired by the book to imagine the entire episode. Strom Thurmond, to the extent anyone could understand his thick drawl, belittled her.

To those of us on Capitol Hill who knew of the elderly senator's own legendary sexual exploits, it was almost comical. (Telling details of the exchange were satirized brilliantly the next night on *Saturday Night Live*.) Leading the charge against Hill was Arlen Specter, the most experienced former prosecutor on the committee. Having infuriated Republican leaders a few years earlier when he helped defeat Ronald Reagan's nomination of Judge Bork to the Supreme Court, Specter seemed to be going out of his way to be tough on Hill in order to reestablish his conservative credentials.

For whatever reason, Specter went after Hill with a vengeance, at one point even accusing her of perjury. Why hadn't she complained earlier? Why hadn't she given all the details to the FBI? And why had she followed Thomas to another job at the EEOC, after allegedly being harassed by him in the Department of Education? To Specter, the last question was the most perplexing, and the most damning to Anita Hill.

Still, even after Specter's cross-examination, Hill's account was devastating. It hung over the hearing room, a litany of smutty charges leveled and unanswered. Badly shaken by such shocking testimony, but affecting a steely calm, I went on the air to speculate on how Thomas would rebut her claims. After a dinner break, he arrived with his wife, Virginia, loyally at his side for an unprecedented weekend session, to face the scandalous charges involving a Coca-Cola can, pubic hair, and porno movies starring "Long Dong Silver."

For almost two hours Clarence Thomas faced down the all-white panel of senators. In a strategy that I learned was devised by the White House, he countered Hill's charges of sexism by playing the race card. Putting them on the defensive, he was a portrait of African-American outrage, expressing a cold fury at the committee and its process as he tried to discredit his accuser. When Thomas bitterly denounced what he called "a high-tech lynching," for all intents and purposes the political fight was won.

Under the force of his counterattack, Judiciary Committee chairman Joe Biden withered, telling Thomas that because they checked out what they thought were credible allegations from a credible woman, "doesn't mean we take the charges at face value." Alan Simpson, a rangy, acerbic Republican from Wyoming, said that if it was a tie between the two, and the senators didn't know whom to believe, Thomas didn't have to prove his innocence or be condemned just because these charges had been made. "If there is any doubt," said Simpson, "it goes to Clarence Thomas. It does not go to Professor Hill."

As I ran out to our live camera in the Rotunda to interview some of the Judiciary Committee members, it was clear to me that they didn't know what had hit them. Pat Leahy acknowledged that after hearing conflicting stories from two such compelling witnesses, the senators felt confused. Critics later questioned whether Senator Kennedy, the committee's highest-ranking Democrat outside of the chairman, was reluctant to go after Thomas on sexual harassment issues because of his own past reputation as a womanizer and, of course, because of Chappaquiddick. You could feel the momentum shifting back toward Thomas. Still, whatever happened in the Senate vote, I knew that this national debate over sexual harassment had changed workplaces around America forever.

Just before midnight, as we concluded our marathon live broadcasts for the day, Tom Brokaw asked me, "Andrea, you have prevailed as a woman correspondent in what has been traditionally a mostly male field. You work on Capitol Hill in Congress, which has always been described as one of the most sexual arenas. Do you think it will change?"

I answered, "I think it will change in a lot of workplaces. I'm not so sure it will ever change on Capitol Hill until more women are in powerful positions. Because this is the last plantation for men."

On Sunday morning the hearings recessed so that members could go to church. Several of them came to *Meet the Press,* Washington's version of Sunday worship. The emotions of the confirmation battle immediately spilled over into our television studio on Nebraska Avenue. Senator Alan Simpson claimed to have previously undisclosed information regarding Professor Hill that had come to him unsolicited from people in Oklahoma, her home state.

Regarding this highly nonspecific "information," I asked, "You've raised this now at the hearings, and you've raised it just now on national television. Isn't this McCarthyism of the worst order?"

To which he replied, "Not in my mind. McCarthyism of the worst order is to have someone gather up everything on a man for 105 days that has nothing to do with his ability to serve on the United States Supreme Court. Your people have done a magnificent job of that, going into his garbage to see what the titles of his books are."

I shot back, "Not my people, Senator Simpson."

Simpson then retorted, "I had one of your craft use the F-word on me about three times the other night in an abject—"

I jumped in. "We're not monolithic, either—we only speak for ourselves as individuals."

Such was the level of acrimony that gripped the Capitol as the vote on the nomination approached. That day, Anita Hill volunteered to take a polygraph test and passed. It didn't matter. The scientific models that drive most political decisions in Washington are polls. When the instant surveys came in, the public, including blacks and most women, had decided to believe Thomas over Hill, by a big margin. The senators had been waiting for guidance. Now they had their political cue. Faced with a no-win situation, the easiest way out was to follow public opinion, not try to lead it. Even though Hill's backers had come up with a surprise witness also alleging sexual harassment by the nominee, the senators refused to hear any more testimony. The case was closed.

The committee voted first, at two o'clock in the morning, agreeing to send the nomination to the Senate floor for a final vote. Anita Hill retreated to Oklahoma, as Thomas's supporters mobilized for a final onslaught. The eight-hour debate was as mean-spirited at the end as it had been at the beginning. One of the worst examples, during the final hours of debate, was an acrimonious exchange between Ted Kennedy and Arlen Specter. Kennedy argued that there was no proof that Hill had perjured herself, as Specter had claimed, and said, "Shame on anyone who suggests that she has."

To which Specter replied, "We do not need characterizations like 'shame' in this chamber from the senator from Massachusetts," in a broad reference to Chappaquiddick.

The floor debate escalated quickly until the senators sounded like schoolchildren.

"Let me finish."

"No, I will not."

"Yes, you will."

"Just let me make a point."

This was the world's greatest deliberative body?

We broadcast the roll call vote live, and as the ninety-eight men and only two women of the Senate cast their ayes and nays, it became obvious that Thomas would be confirmed. The final vote was fifty-two in favor, and forty-eight against, with only two Republicans, Bob Packwood and Jim Jeffords, voting against Thomas. Eleven Democrats voted yes to the appointment. At 11:35 that evening, we went back on the air, preempting *The Tonight Show.* The news division rarely, if ever, wins permission from network entertainment chiefs to preempt such a top-rated show. But this news story had the advantage of being more lurid than anything network programmers could have scripted.

As we concluded our coverage, Tom Brokaw said, "There are more than a few bodies scattered across the landscape here, Andrea."

I replied, "This was a sorry spectacle, an ugly fight that raises serious questions about our system of divided government. Even when the vote was certain, they kept slugging it out."

The ordeal was finally over, as Brokaw put it, not with a bang, but with a sense of exhaustion.

———

I don't think I've ever received so much mail about any subject that I've covered. Although a majority had indicated support for Thomas in polls, women around this country, from all backgrounds and income groups, felt disenfranchised by the system, and suddenly gained a focal point for their anger. Looking at their television screens, they concluded that the men of America were making decisions about them and their lives and their futures—and women had no say.

Some women wrote that watching the way Professor Hill was treated reminded them of the way rape victims are often interrogated about their sexual histories. To many women, the innuendo directed toward this woman was excruciating to watch. Similarly, Thomas and his supporters deeply felt the humiliation of a man nominated to the highest court in the land having to explain what videos he rented and whether he had ever made sexual overtures to his coworkers.

The hearings demonstrated the degree to which the country was polarized, both racially and sexually, and how disconnected Washington was from the rest of the nation. From the perspective of many women and African-Americans, there was no question that the white men on the Judiciary Committee just didn't get it. Even Kansas Republican senator Nancy Kassebaum, daughter of onetime vice presidential nominee Alf Landon, said as much during the final debate. Hardly a feminist, the experience had radicalized her.

We were all affected. When it was over, I still didn't know, with any degree of certainty, whom to believe, but people were passionate on one side or the other, and wanted conclusions. Advocates for Hill didn't want to hear about all the legal ambiguity surrounding what constitutes sexual harassment. Thomas supporters argued that if you couldn't easily define it, how could you legislate against it? Teachers around the country organized seminars analyzing "What Is Sexual Harassment?" Employers instituted programs to sensitize their workers, male and female.

It struck home. Even behavior we had tolerated in the past seemed more offensive when reexamined in the light of the Thomas-Hill debate. For instance, while we worked together in NBC's small White House cubicle during the Reagan years, some of my male colleagues often delighted in watching provocative programs they knew made me uncomfortable. It never occurred to me that I had grounds to object.

The debate surrounding Clarence Thomas's nomination expanded divisions over gender that until then had been fought primarily over abortion. Now the culture warriors were fighting over whether it was right to legislate against something as arguably subjective as sexual harassment. Can men's behavior be regulated? Did women have the right to object to offensive language or behavior in the workplace? What were the obligations of employers in these matters? The nation was gripped by an emotional and extensive debate on sexual mores.

In the Senate, men like Strom Thurmond still wielded consider-able power. Who could forget how he had demeaned Anita Hill? Years before Thurmond was exposed as the father of an unac-knowledged, interracial daughter, he was known as "the pincher" to women throughout the Senate. One of the first things young interns and new female correspondents were told was not to get on an ele-vator alone with Strom.

At one point, I had an intern, a law student, who would take notes for me at stakeouts when I was tied up on another side of the Hill. Once, she came back beet red, flushed, obviously embarrassed. When I asked what was wrong, she replied that she had just had an uncomfortable encounter with Senator Bob Packwood, but didn't know how to interpret it. All of us had to wear our ID passes around our necks. Packwood had come up very close to her, way too close, and had grabbed hold of her pass, which was hanging on her chest. Pretending to examine her picture, he said, "Oh, what is your name?"

Only later, during the Thomas-Hill hearings, did I realize that I should have warned the young woman about sexual predators on the Hill, and in fact about the senator's actions. But at the time, none of us focused on Packwood's behavior. Later, he faced accusations from more than a dozen women, and left the Senate after the Ethics Committee recommended he be expelled. He was only unusual in that he was caught, and punished.

Barely a month after the Thomas-Hill battle, another civil rights battle erupted, but this time John Danforth, the White House point man for the Thomas confirmation, led the opposition. Danforth strongly objected to a White House proposal that would have lim-ited affirmative action programs for women and minorities. Most of the president's cabinet, including the secretaries of labor, health and human services, and transportation, agreed with Danforth. In the end, the president was forced to retreat. But coming so soon after the Thomas fight, the attempt to circumvent the civil rights law fueled suspicion that the White House was pursuing a deliberate strategy of currying favor with the right wing.

———

There had been a long history of racial polarization on the Hill. A year earlier, I had covered a Senate race that raised questions about the racial strategy of at least one Republican. North Carolina's Jesse Helms, arguably the most conservative man in the Senate, was facing an African-American challenger, Charlotte mayor Harvey Gantt. Trying to follow Helms on the campaign trail became an exercise almost as comical as a Michael Moore chase film. You could call it "Jesse and Me." Helms was not to be found. The senator didn't have a schedule and he didn't think he had to. The last thing he wanted was for anyone to cover his speeches. Instead, his campaign consisted of running television ads with a significant, far from subliminal, appeal to white racism.

One TV ad, known as the White Hands ad, featured the hands of a white man crumbling a rejection letter from a potential employer, as the voiceover intoned, "You needed that job, and you were the best qualified—but they had to give it to a minority because of a racial quota—is that really fair?"

Many of his supporters didn't bother to hide their sympathies. In Smithfield, North Carolina, a town of eight thousand, many of the residents wanted to turn back the clock. One man told me, "I hope I never vote for a black man. They're taking over now. We'll all be ruled by them in a few more years because their population is growing faster than the white." And he didn't hesitate to say it on camera.

In the course of the campaign Helms also stirred local prejudices by telling supporters, "Mr. Gantt's got all of my enemies as his supporters, the lesbians, the homosexuals." Jesse Helms did almost no campaigning, but easily won 53 percent of the vote, to Harvey Gantt's 47 percent.

In person, Helms was unfailingly courtly and old-fashioned, even though he treated me like a nuisance to be avoided. That became a problem in 1995 when he became chairman of the Senate Foreign Relations Committee, and I needed access to him and his staff. I wasn't the only person he intimidated. As chairman, he controlled the State Department's budget and could decide the fate of policies ranging from superpower weapons treaties to contraceptive programs in developing nations. Helms so enjoyed his reputation as an obstructionist that he collected political cartoons caricaturing him as "Senator No." And he was so open about his opinions, that the new Foreign Relations chairman said half jokingly that if Bill Clinton—the sitting president of the United States—tried to cross the border into North Carolina, he'd need a bodyguard for protection.

As a result of Helms's power, people as important as Madeleine Albright, Richard Holbrooke, and Kofi Annan bowed to his authority. Albright went so far as to join Helms at a softball game between their staffs, and gave him a T-shirt that proclaimed, SOMEONE IN THE STATE DEPARTMENT LOVES ME. She also made a pilgrimage to his hometown in North Carolina to appear with him. And, in one of those peculiar Washington courtships, when Albright threw herself a sixtieth birthday party, Jesse Helms had the first dance.

I followed Helms home once more in 1996, to report on the senator's opposition to Clinton's efforts to expand diplomatic relations with Vietnam. Clinton, who was still trying to live down his antiwar past, had won the support of two heroes of that war, John McCain and John Kerry. Despite their many political differences on other issues, they came together behind Clinton because of a shared conviction that it was time to heal the wounds of Vietnam.

As head of the Foreign Relations Committee, Jesse Helms had a virtual veto over Vietnam policy. Yet, at the same time, he was trying to help his state's tobacco industry by selling cigarettes to the Vietnamese. I wanted to explore that paradox. Helms had invited ambassadors from every Asian country, including Vietnam, to his hometown to tour an R.J. Reynolds tobacco plant. Cigarette manufacturers were losing their American markets because of government health regulations. The companies—all headquartered in North Carolina—wanted to make up their lost domestic profits by selling more tobacco to Asia, where people were heavily addicted to tobacco. Critics said it amounted to exporting cancer to Southeast Asia.

I started shooting the story in Wingate, North Carolina, a picturesque town where Helms had located his foundation in a charming Victorian house. Much to my surprise, the senator showed up to escort me on a personal tour. As he showed me his mother's pictures and other family memorabilia, I was caught in one of those classic instances—as with Frank Rizzo or Don Regan—where a powerful adversary was suddenly displaying a softer side of his personality.

I felt somewhat conflicted, because I was warming up to him personally and didn't want to be inauthentic. It got even more difficult when he sought my advice on architectural drawings for the expansion of his foundation and museum. It reminded me of Frank Rizzo's asking me to choose the colors to redecorate City Hall in 1972.

Helms may have been offering genuine hospitality; perhaps, he was trying to co-opt me. But the senator was so obviously proud of his construction project that I could appreciate the moment—while still being a bit nervous about it. All I knew was that if I'd been a male correspondent, the conversation probably would not have taken place.

Suddenly, later that afternoon, the office paged me with awful news. There had been a plane crash in Croatia, killing an official delegation led by Commerce Secretary Ron Brown. I knew Ron well. He had previously been chairman of the Democratic National Committee, and earlier, in 1988, was the party's intermediary with Jesse Jackson, as Jackson bargained for a bigger role. Since I had been assigned to cover Jackson at the Democratic National Convention in Atlanta that year, I'd also gotten to know Ron, his son Michael, and his wife Alma.

Ron's assignment had been to handle Jackson's complaints and clear the way for the party's choice, Michael Dukakis. Jackson had taken a bus caravan to Atlanta, and was threatening to create a serious challenge to the party's attempt to unify behind Dukakis's candidacy. My job was to hang out just off the floor, next to the Jackson trailer where he had his war room operation, on the opposite side of the railroad tracks that ran around the stadium. It was a thankless task; most of the time, the trailer was empty because the action was on the floor. Except, one night, when Washington's mayor Marion Barry wandered by with a young companion. Perhaps he thought he could use Jesse's trailer for a secret rendezvous. Instead, he walked right into the blinding lights of our network cameras.

Ron had done a first-rate job of containing Jackson and, later, re-organizing the party for Clinton. Now the sudden death of this young, energetic man was a terrible shock. I went over to explain to the senator that I'd have to return immediately to Washington.

I said, "Senator, I am so sorry to tell you that there's been a plane crash, and Secretary Ron Brown has been killed."

Jesse Helms looked at me, smiled, and said, "That's good."

I was stricken. I didn't know—and don't know to this day—whether he really heard me. But I think he did. And I think that was his honest response, unfiltered by the conventions of Washington and the corridors of the Senate. This was Jesse Helms at home.

Democratic Washington mourned Ron officially for a full week, and then congregated at the National Cathedral to celebrate his life. His good friend President Bill Clinton told the gathering, "The Bible tells us, 'Though we weep through the night, joy will come in the morning.'"

Afterward, the procession wound past the palatial embassies, where Ron had dined often as an A-list guest, and then on to the city's poor neighborhoods, supposedly representing his modest roots. In fact, Brown had come from a relatively privileged family in New York City, but the symbolism of the route his cortege took was fit-ting. Despite his elegant clothes and powerful connections, Brown had never forgotten rank-and-file Democrats, especially those living in the inner cities.

The most striking thing about Ron's death, though, was how par-tisan the response was to his life. As commerce secretary, Ron interacted daily with the largely Republican business community, but none of them came to the cathedral to pay their respects. The absence of the Republican congressional leadership also caused a great deal of bitterness in the black community.

———

Many racial and sexual tensions came into sharper relief during those years. Looking back, I still regret that Alan missed the most transformative event of the period, the Thomas-Hill hearings in the fall of 1991, because of an economic meeting in Bangkok. It was difficult to explain to someone who had not experienced the showdown that weekend why it was so significant. But, unlike anything Washington, or the nation, had ever witnessed, the hearings exposed the differences between the way men and women interpreted the same set of facts.

Alan and I had grown up in different ages, but he is in many ways a very modern man. I often think of him as a feminist, because he is so blind to gender when it comes to judging people on their merits. When he ran his Wall Street economic consulting firm, he always had strong women around him. In fact, throughout his previous tenure in government, during the Ford administration, he turned his company over to several women employees to manage until he returned several years later.

With me, he has always been unfailingly supportive. He adjusts to schedule changes, no matter what the emergency or how short the notice. And he is my biggest fan. (I think everyone needs an unapologetic, nonobjective fan.) He has the endearing, if somewhat embarrassing, habit of tuning out everything, including important staff meetings, when I pop up on the evening news. He even calls my office to ask if I'm "in the show," so he knows to watch.

Contrary to what has often been written about him, Alan is not a social animal. Alan's idea of heaven is to stay home, have a simple supper, and watch baseball. It almost doesn't matter who's playing, as long as they use bats and balls and run four bases ninety feet apart.

But to please me, he goes to a certain number of special events in Washington. And nothing could have been more special than the visit of Queen Elizabeth II in the spring of 1991.

It was one of those times when Washington got so crazed that you would have thought the colonies had failed to win the Revolution. It was sheer monarch envy. We wanted to have some royals, and here they were. In his inimitable fashion, George Bush invited the queen to a baseball game in Baltimore, at Memorial Stadium, the run-down, old-fashioned stadium that preceded Camden Yards. In those days, Washington still had no major-league baseball franchise, and Baltimore was the next best thing.

The team's owner, Eli Jacobs, invited us to be part of the group that met the queen when she arrived at the ballpark. Losing sight of the fact that it was just a ball game, on one of the hottest days of the year, everyone got all dressed up, as though we were going to a garden party. I wore a silk dress with a jacket, one of those matronly floral prints that made me look at least twenty years older than I was. The dress had long sleeves—shades of that trip to Texas with Rosalynn Carter. At the stadium we were seated in the owners' box, on the other side of a glass partition from the queen and the president.

Unfortunately, because of security concerns, the Secret Service had ordered the front of the box enclosed and covered with a bullet-proof glass window. With the window in place, air couldn't circulate and everyone began to sweat—if queens sweat—through his or her clothes. The queen had never seen American baseball, and was clearly feigning interest as the president tried to explain balls, strikes, pop-ups, and double plays. During her half century as a monarch, I'm sure the queen has suffered worse—perhaps a visit to some tropical island—but I can't imagine anything hotter or more uncomfortable than that baseball game that day at Memorial Stadium.

Before the royal party retreated, in the third inning, there was an unintended breach of protocol. American royalty approached British royalty: Joe DiMaggio, one of the invited guests, passed a baseball to the queen's personal secretary so that Her Majesty could autograph it for him. Instead, the ball was politely handed back down the row. DiMaggio, an American icon, was told, "Her Majesty does not sign baseballs."

The next night, the British embassy hosted a dinner, to which Alan and I were invited. I splurged on a white gown and even called a store in New York to find a pair of white kid gloves that reached above the elbow. For someone who grew up in the sixties, and had never been anything close to a debutante, this was as dressed up as I'd ever get. As we moved up the receiving line toward the president and the queen, President Bush, who knew me well (he'd shown me his bathroom in Kennebunkport, if nothing else!), took my arm and said, "Your Majesty, this is one of our premier American journalists." Then he turned to me and said, "Hello, Barbara."

Since he was standing next to Barbara Bush, I assumed at first that it was a slip of the tongue. Only a few minutes later, when I was halfway down the receiving line, did I realize that he'd mistaken me for Barbara Walters, who had previously dated Alan.

The next day, there was a delivery to the house, a personal note from President Bush. Well known for his good manners, he'd sent a White House souvenir key chain to apologize for his mistake in confusing me with the other Greenspan television date.

He wrote, "It was the 'excitement' of the Queen's evening; it was my 'heart;' it was the 'medicine;' it was that I'm 'almost 67;' it was that you 'looked great;' alas it was that I screwed up. A thousand sorries. Here's a peace offering! Am I forgiven? Con Afecto, George Bush."

Bush was still popular, and the Democrats worried about finding anyone strong enough to challenge him. Covering Congress put me right in the middle of the campaign coverage, since most of the candidates came from the Senate. I did long interviews with all of the senators who were thinking about it: Tom Harkin of Iowa, Jay Rockefeller of West Virginia, Bob Kerrey of Nebraska, Al Gore of Tennessee, and former Massachusetts senator Paul Tsongas. Rockefeller and Gore later decided not to run, for family reasons. Gore explained that he wanted to sit out the election because his young son was still recuperating from being hit by a car after attending an Orioles game—in the same ballpark where the president had entertained the queen.

By early winter of '92, I had spent time with all of the likely contenders except one: the governor of Arkansas, Bill Clinton. So I decided to go to New Hampshire to meet him. At that early stage of the campaign, Clinton was traveling with two aides, Bruce Lindsey and George Stephanopoulos, on a tiny plane, courting New Hampshire voters almost one by one. My producer Carroll Ann Mears and I landed at Boston's Logan Airport and rented a car. Carroll Ann was driving, and I was navigating—supposedly. We were in a hurry to get to Keene because Clinton's people had promised an interview if I got there in time.

Typically, we didn't realize we were in trouble until we looked up and the sign read, WELCOME TO VERMONT. Somehow, we'd taken a wrong turn, and Carroll Ann and I had missed New Hampshire. Perhaps this was the best metaphor for what was to become my coverage of Bill Clinton's presidency.

CHAPTER 6

"White House Pit Bull" —The Clinton Years

One of the first times I ever saw Hillary Clinton, she looked like a trapped animal, fighting for her life. Still in her headband long hair mode, she had joined her husband to campaign in New Hampshire as he tried to cope with twin scandals: first, allegations that he had not been truthful about avoiding the draft during Vietnam; and second, that he'd had a longstanding affair with a lounge singer named Gennifer Flowers when he was governor.

Though Hillary was there to help save her husband's campaign, the presence of the "wronged woman" in the marital scandal only increased the media's appetite. As Bill Clinton tried to cross the street with his wife after delivering a speech to the New Hampshire legislature that winter day in 1992, a mob of reporters and camera crews wielding shotgun and boom microphones was in hot pursuit, trying to corner the couple, then backpedaling to get in front of them. Typically, like a hunting dog chasing a fox, I was leading the pack, running alongside to ask a question, then racing ahead to get another shot at the pair. The frenzied scene could have been an out-take from *Primary Colors,* but no film could capture the sheer terror, and anger, that Hillary must have been feeling.

Hillary Clinton was quarry we were chasing; but at the same time I felt such sympathy for her, not only as a woman, but also as another human being. I could separate myself from the situation and see that there was a real person caught in the midst of all this. Yet she was also complicit. As Bill Clinton's chief defender, she helped devise the strategy to deflect the charges they both knew were coming. This strange amalgam defined their political partnership, then and later. She was a victim, yet also in charge of damage control. As a correspondent assigned to the campaign, I knew I needed to report on her role. At the same time, I felt she might have had a point when she talked about trying to maintain the Clintons' "zone of privacy."

When I first started following Bill Clinton in New Hampshire after years of covering scandal on the Hill, I hardly imagined that I would soon be chasing an unending series of campaign scandals. The Arkansas governor seemed like the perfect candidate—bright, smart, a Southern Democratic centrist, and the darling of the liberal elites. For years, he had cultivated the power brokers of Georgetown at dinners carefully orchestrated by friends like Pamela Harriman, a Democratic fund-raiser and the widow of former New York governor Averell Harriman.

The Clintons' first hurdle was their marriage. For years, there had been rumors of his infidelities. In 1988 he had considered a run for the presidency and then backed off, reluctantly accepting the advice that his misbehavior would become an obstacle. The issue was raised by his opponents when he ran for reelection in Arkansas in 1990. So, in September 1991, the Clintons devised a strategy: if they brought it up themselves, they could defuse the fallout from their less-than-perfect marriage. During a celebrated breakfast with Washington print reporters, Bill and Hillary tried to inoculate themselves from questions about their complicated relationship by suggesting that there had been "difficulties" in their marriage and that their relationship had "not been perfect." In Washington, among reporters who lived most of their lives on the road and had experienced their own marital problems, everyone understood what they meant.

Yet the Clintons' relationship remained a legitimate part of the political debate, because as they themselves told the voters of New Hampshire, "Buy one, get one free." They were a team, a package deal, what Hillary called the "blue plate special"—a twofer running for president of the United States. At first, it worked. They were a novelty act. And until Gennifer Flowers, and the appearance of a damning letter a young Bill Clinton had written to his ROTC director about avoiding possible service in Vietnam, he was leading the pack in New Hampshire. The draft issue resurrected the same questions that had dogged Dan Quayle four years earlier. Within a week of the Flowers accusation and the draft controversy, Clinton was trailing former Massachusetts senator Paul Tsongas by eleven points.

We had to cover the marital scandal, yet were unsure what was fact, what was rumor, and how much was payback from his Arkansas enemies. Initially, our network decided not to air Gennifer Flowers's charges because we could not confirm them—a cautious approach that now, only thirteen years later, seems almost quaint. For journalists trying not to get swept up in a feeding frenzy, when does a rumor become news? Clinton was in full denial. But as we now know from books written by some of his closest aides, his campaign staff had long been aware of his "woman problem." For months, they'd been war-gaming how to handle what Betsey Wright, his former chief of staff in Arkansas, had colorfully called, "bimbo eruptions."

The larger issues of how important the "eruptions" were to his qualifications to be president, and to his credibility and character as a human being, were still to be addressed. At NBC, we only mentioned the assertions briefly until *Nightline* devoted an entire broadcast to the allegations. In those days, before Matt Drudge and Internet bloggers, it was Ted Koppel who validated the Flowers story for much of the press corps by doing a program on it.

With the story now in play, Gennifer Flowers held a news conference at the Waldorf-Astoria, broadcast live on CNN. The headline: she had proof, audiotapes, which she played. But what she released were excerpts, with obvious breaks where the tapes had been edited selectively; and though it was undeniably Bill Clinton's voice on them, we could not ascertain his exact meaning from the excerpts. It was evidence of a relationship—but what kind of relationship, and of what duration?

The campaign was in free fall. The Clintons had responded to the Flowers allegation by addressing a huge television audience of forty million on *60 Minutes*, immediately after the Super Bowl. They had appeared side by side, holding hands. It was the first of many occasions when Hillary stood by her man, even while declaring she was not sitting there as "some little woman standing by my man like Tammy Wynette." Hillary was taking charge of the Clinton rescue mission, even as she clearly resented being put in that role.

The Clintons toughed it out, brazenly facing down their critics. For the moment, they succeeded in silencing many of the doubters, but they paid a heavy price. The media accepted their denials of the Flowers affair, but with considerable skepticism. When the president admitted to it under oath in 1998, his credibility suffered a terrible blow. Looking back, it's also clear that those early confrontations with the press in New Hampshire marked the beginning of Hillary Clinton's bitterness toward the national press corps. With this introduction to the media, it would be hard to imagine her feeling otherwise. The seeds were being sown for the Clinton administration's subsequent defensiveness at the slightest hint of scandal. Instead of using the media to help sell his programs, the president and his wife resented most of the reporters assigned to the White House. That became one obstacle to a truly successful presidency.

At times that winter, literally going door-to-door, Clinton pleaded with New Hampshire voters to view the "character issue" as a test of who would help make their lives better, not who had had a perfect marriage. At one emotional rally, he said if the voters would give him a chance, he'd promise to be with them "until the last dog dies." The phrase was so quintessentially Clinton, combining his Southern vernacular with a personal appeal to the voters, that it became the mantra of his campaign.

In one of the great recoveries in American politics, Clinton pulled off a second-place finish in New Hampshire, instead of being demolished by the late-breaking scandal as Gary Hart had been in 1987. Hart, also a married politician, had been caught on the aptly named yacht *Monkey Business* with a young aspiring actress named Donna Rice. His presidential campaign immediately imploded.

In Clinton's case, if you were watching television news, or reading the headlines the next morning, you might have thought he'd won in New Hampshire, instead of placing second. Even before all the votes were counted, Clinton was spinning the results as a victory and calling himself "the comeback kid." In fact, while knocking Bob Kerrey and some of the lesser candidates out of the race, he had still lost to the former Massachusetts senator Paul Tsongas. But Clinton knew that while Tsongas had a unique advantage in New England, he did not have the money or organization to mount a truly national campaign. The Arkansas governor began to look like a winner, and I realized I might be covering the potential nominee.

The Clinton team then moved south, stopping in Georgia to pick up an important endorsement from the state's popular Democratic governor, Zell Miller—who would later turn on his party and gave a fiery convention speech for George W. Bush in 2004. But in 1992, Miller was far more liberal and, in fact, had even had the same campaign strategists—Paul Begala and James Carville—as Clinton. Performing on cue, Miller threw his arms around the candidate and declared, "This old marine corps sergeant is proud to call Bill Clinton one of our own." After the draft controversy, it was a welcome embrace.

But there were more questions about his past. The Clintons had survived the Gennifer Flowers attack, at least temporarily, but a week before the Illinois primary, *The New York Times* raised questions about the role of Hillary's law firm in an obscure Arkansas land deal. It was the first national mention of Whitewater. At NBC, lacking the investigative teams the *Times* had deployed, we started scrambling to catch up, sending our top investigative producer to Arkansas. Then, two days before the Illinois primary, *The Washington Post* added more details about Hillary's law practice and its connections with Arkansas state contracts.

That night, during a debate in Chicago, California iconoclast Jerry Brown, still pursuing a quixotic race for the nomination, challenged Clinton on whether Hillary Clinton's legal work on savings and loan and real estate deals were a conflict of interest.

Bill Clinton drew up in umbrage and said, "I don't care what you say about me. . . . But you ought to be ashamed of yourself for jumping on my wife. You're not worth being on the same platform with my wife." It was a turning point, the highlight of the encounter. By taking the offensive, Clinton clearly hoped to discourage any further scrutiny of their finances.

By now, Hillary was so protected by aides that there was no way to get to her. I knew that the Clintons were going to address rush-hour commuters at the Busy Bee Diner under the elevated train in Chicago at six-thirty or seven a.m. the next morning. I figured that the only way to get a question to Hillary was to get up earlier than anyone else, hightail it to the diner, and plant myself on a stool as just another paying customer before the Secret Service and the advance men roped it off. I sat there, drinking mug after mug of coffee for more than an hour. They couldn't stop serving me, nor could they throw me out. I was positioned so that when the Clintons finally did arrive, I was front and center, able to ask Hillary whether her husband had steered state business her way, as charged.

Outside, Bill Clinton was telling commuters that Brown's attack the night before was "insulting and unfair." In that Southern slang that sometimes sounded self-conscious, or deliberately folksy, he told the Chicago commuters that if someone attacked his wife, "I'm going to jump them back."

Meanwhile, inside the diner, Hillary was on her own, and making news. To my question about a possible conflict of interest, she answered famously, "I suppose I could have stayed home and baked cookies and had teas," adding, "but what I decided to do was to fulfill my profession, which I entered before my husband was in public life." She had stepped into a political minefield for candidates' wives, much as Teresa Heinz Kerry did in 2004 when she inaccurately suggested that Laura Bush never had "a real job."

Instantly, Clinton aides at the diner, especially Paul Begala, knew she had made a mistake. Just as they were trying to soften her image, and make her seem less abrasive—less threatening to homemakers across America—she was putting down all women who bake cookies and serve tea. They quickly took her aside, telling her she had to fix it, and fast—within the same news cycle.

The advance people brought us outside, herding us with a rope like cattle. We lined up as a newly politically correct Hillary came out to declare that of course she was not demeaning women who worked at home. "I'm a big believer in women making the choices that are right for them. And, you know," she said, "the work that I've done as a professional, as a public advocate, has been aimed in part to assure that women can make the choices that they should make—whether it's full-time career, full-time motherhood, some combination, depending upon what stage of life they are at—and I think that is still difficult for people to understand right now, that it is a generational change."

Hillary's off-the-cuff remark was an early example of how important she was going to become, and how controversial: Bill and Hillary were definitely a team. But there was a downside to the teamwork, and they were beginning to realize that she could engender as much hostility among voters as support.

My predawn stakeout at the diner had provoked an incident that became emblematic of the Clinton campaign, Hillary as a lightning rod, and the campaign's attempts to transform her from defiant feminist into Betty Crocker. It was an example of how important it is to cover an event yourself, no matter how routine, rather than relying on a producer or other surrogate. I'd learned that lesson covering

Frank Rizzo in Philadelphia, and then again during the Reagan years. Unfortunately, it gave me a reputation for being very aggressive, for getting in people's faces—not a popular quality with candidates or their aides.

The lesson Hillary drew from the experience was to become even less accessible to reporters—except when she knew she was in control and could charm them, as she did later in her successful bid for a Senate seat in New York. She was, and is, a formidable campaigner. She is now a virtuoso at taking the media attention she attracts and making it work to her advantage. But it took years for her to perfect those skills.

Clinton won easily in Illinois, despite "tea and cookies," but the road to the nomination still had obstacles. Jerry Brown threatened to derail the Clintons in New York's primary. Difficult as it is to imagine now, with Clinton the toast of Harlem and his wife New York's popular senator, in 1992 New Yorkers were not charmed by Clinton's Southern accent. Typically, they didn't hesitate to tell him what they thought. Hecklers harassed him wherever he went, even on a street corner when he went to see a doctor for his chronic laryngitis. In turn, we felt we had to trail him everywhere, in case something unscripted happened, such as this street corner exchange: "Do you pardon all the drug dealers, or just the ones who contribute to your campaign?" one man asked.

"You're a phony, and you're dishonest, and you misrepresented yourself," Clinton shot back, after discovering that the guy had been planted by one of the state's fringe candidates.

People would question Clinton's character wherever he went, even when he was talking about foreign policy. In frustration, he blamed the media, especially those of us in television news, complaining, "Half the voters question whether you have the honesty to be president. What do you say about that? If I had been sitting here watching the television, I would, too."

By the end of March, only a week after declaring that he would not agree to any more debates, Clinton changed strategy and accepted a joint appearance with Brown. Tackling the problem head-on, he hoped reporters would finally focus on how Brown had changed his positions over the years, on everything from taxes to abortion. But at the forum, Marcia Kramer, a local CBS reporter, asked whether Clinton had ever tried marijuana while studying at Oxford University in the sixties. For years, Clinton had evaded responding on the issue, saying carefully he had never broken the drug laws of the United States.

This time he said, "When I was in England, I experimented with marijuana a time or two and I didn't like it. And I didn't inhale." Bang—we had another character issue. As Clinton later wrote in his autobiography, *My Life,* "As the old country song goes, I didn't know whether to 'kill myself or go bowling.'"

To soften the damage, Clinton went on Phil Donahue's television show, where I was sitting in the audience in the press seats. It was a debacle. Donahue peppered him for a full twenty minutes with questions about marital infidelity. The audience was on Clinton's side, but Donahue was relentless. He wasn't the only media heavyweight who was killing Clinton on the air: radio talk show host Don Imus was calling him a "redneck bozo." Showing considerable guts, Clinton went out to Queens to face down Imus and try to prove him wrong—a risky strategy, as any of us who submit to Imus's tender mercies know. That time, it paid off for Clinton. At least back then, before the Monica revelations, Imus was willing to cut him a break, especially after Clinton joked that Bubba—Imus's derogatory nickname for the candidate—was Southern for "mensch."

Clinton also visited another New York political icon, Mario Cuomo. Clinton wanted to make peace with "the oracle of Albany." Their relationship had become strained when, on Gennifer Flowers's tapes, Clinton was heard calling Cuomo "a mean son of a bitch," and said he "acts like" a Mafia figure. The two men also had profound differences on issues like the death penalty, which Cuomo opposed. But with Clinton closing in on the nomination, the New York governor was willing to fake it. He proclaimed, "Bill Clinton will make in my opinion a superb president." Cuomo knew that of all the Democrats, Clinton could mount the most credible challenge to an incumbent president. And Cuomo was not going to be a spoiler.

But nothing Clinton did could appease Jerry Brown. The two men were at each other's throats through the final hours of the New York campaign. Brown simply refused to fade away, even when he lost his press bus because the campaign hadn't paid its bills. Party leaders worried that Clinton would survive the New York primary, but would be so damaged he'd never be able to defeat George Bush.

It was not a misplaced concern. Clinton won the primary, but the exit polls from New York were ominous: only 50 percent of the voters thought he had enough honesty and integrity to be president. And 24 percent of both Democrats and Republicans said they would vote for someone entirely different in November, Ross Perot. Colorful, eccentric, and very, very rich, Perot was not even a declared candidate, but was making waves with his idiosyncratic call for people to "get under the hood" and fix the budget deficit.

Perot had announced on *Larry King Live* that he would consider running as a third party candidate if enough people put his name on the ballot in all fifty states. Rapidly, he made his quirky noncandidacy the liveliest political story around. His sound bites were irresistible to talk show hosts. At the same time, his call for responsible budgeting made him equally appealing to more sober-sided newspaper columnists.

Suddenly, Clinton found himself almost ignored—a Democratic front-runner unable to get top billing on the evening news. Even after Clinton won the California primary and wrapped up the nomination at the beginning of June, the lead story on *Nightly News* was how Ross Perot had hired two nationally known political professionals, Republican Ed Rollins and Democrat Hamilton Jordan, to help run his campaign.

Lisa Myers's report on NBC began, "This morning, official Washington awakened to discover that it was not just a bad dream—Ross

Perot really could be elected president." That day, the billionaire had also proved he would play dirty, saying he "would not go to war to prove my manhood at the expense of young people"—suggesting that Bush had done exactly that with the Gulf War. There was a history of bad blood between Bush and Perot. Perot blamed Bush for preventing him from going to Hanoi five years earlier as an official envoy to negotiate for soldiers missing in action during Vietnam. An extensive Senate investigation had disproved Perot's theories about finding surviving prisoners of war, but he never forgave Bush for denying him the opportunity. Now Bush's campaign manager, Bob Teeter, was pushing the president to fight back.

And what about Bill Clinton? There were troubling signs for the candidate, despite his victories in the final primaries. Even at that late stage in the campaign, the presumptive Democratic nominee was trying to get the American people to give him a second look. Democratic and independent primary voters in both Ohio and California had said they'd defect to Perot in the fall. In national polls, Perot was beating Bush, with Clinton coming in third.

As Clinton struggled to get attention, so did I. I was covering the Democratic nominee, but couldn't get on the air. Clinton was yesterday's news. All the producers cared about was Perot.

At least that gave Clinton time to focus on choosing a running mate. He considered, among others, Senators Bob Graham, Bill Bradley, Bob Kerrey, Harris Wofford, Indiana congressman Lee Hamilton, and, of course, Al Gore. At first, Gore was not the most obvious. He'd been preparing to be president all his life, but he had bombed at a Democratic party conference a year earlier in Cleveland. Instead, a Washington outsider, Bill Clinton, had wowed the crowd. Unlike Clinton, Gore was not a natural politician. And, on one level, even after being chosen for the ticket, he must have resented Clinton, feeling their roles should have been reversed.

They had very different styles: one so straightlaced and disciplined, the other so—well, Clintonesque. They did not have good chemistry. And choosing Gore ignored all the conventional wisdom about seeking geographic balance in a running mate. But during a secret late-night session at a downtown Washington hotel, Gore proved that he could fill in Clinton's gaps in foreign policy and the environment. By the end of the night, it was a done deal.

Defying their past practice, the Clintons now launched an entirely new campaign at the Democratic National Convention in Madison Square Garden. For months, they had pleaded with us for a zone of privacy, especially with regard to Chelsea. Now they needed to sell themselves to a larger audience as the reincarnation of Ozzie and Harriet. Their Hollywood friends, Harry Thomason and Linda Bloodworth-Thomason, created a soft-focus campaign video called "The Man from Hope," in order to generate a new political narrative. Now Clinton was the poor boy who understood the common man because of his humble origins. The Thomasons produced everything but a log cabin.

After months of shielding their daughter from public view, the Clintons permitted *People* magazine to take informal family pictures of them at home with Chelsea. The convention featured a rousing nominating speech from Mario Cuomo, followed by Clinton's surprise appearance at the Garden to thank the delegates. The Democrats had finally learned how to hide their differences behind a façade of great visuals, a skill previously the sole province of Reagan Republicans. To achieve unity, they silenced Pennsylvania governor Bob Casey, denying him a chance to speak because of his opposition to abortion. I scampered through the stands to score an interview with him. But Casey's bitter complaint was an isolated instance of criticism. The party had come together behind Clinton.

On the morning of his acceptance speech, the best news for Clinton was that Ross Perot, his campaign spinning out of control, had quit the race. Perot's campaign manager, Ed Rollins, had resigned the day before, saying the candidate wouldn't listen to his advice about running positive TV ads. And Perot had suffered a serious setback a week earlier, when he gave a speech to the NAACP and referred to African-Americans as "you people," a phrase that was widely perceived to be patronizing and insensitive.

Throughout the convention, I'd been doing triple duty: appearing on *Nightly News,* covering the action on the floor during prime time, and then preparing for live reports each morning on the *Today* program. That meant working into the night in a trailer the network had erected in a vacant parking lot on Thirty-second Street, between Seventh and Eighth avenues. There was a flashlight in case I needed to use the portable john. After writing my morning script and feeding my voice track back to the studio at Rockefeller Center, I'd head to the hotel for a few hours' sleep before appearing on the *Today* show at seven the next morning. I couldn't have gone on if I hadn't had a cheerleader at home, my "constant viewer," Alan. I'd call after every morning live shot to get his reaction. Instantly, I knew whether it was merely okay or really good. He's always been my most constructive critic.

By the last night of the convention, I was barely functioning, and the hard part was just beginning. To launch their general election campaign, the Clinton-Gore team introduced the baby boomer duo and their wives in a novel way—a bus tour across America.

Bus trips have since become a campaign cliché, but for decades, until 1992, candidates had flown from airport rally to airport rally, appearing before preselected, ticketed crowds produced by the local political party. There was nothing unscripted or spontaneous about any of it.

This was different. The morning after the Democratic convention, Clinton and Gore got on the bus and just took off across America. For the networks, covering this rolling campaign was a huge technical and logistical challenge. Our plan was to follow the buses with a satellite truck taking in and feeding out the video, plus a Winnebago outfitted with editing equipment, so that a producer and tape editor could screen the videotape as they drove along. I would ride the bus for most of the day, jumping off to cover Clinton's speeches at each stop, calling my team in the RV on a two-way radio with video cues as I outlined a script.

Later in the day, I'd switch to the Winnebago to finish writing and packaging my report for *Nightly News*. We would edit on the road while we were moving, using early-generation cell phone technology and computers that were constantly losing the connection, and often our scripts. No one had thought to build car seats for this job; seat belts were nonexistent. Most of the time, my producer, Carroll Ann Mears, and I would perch on folding chairs to view what we'd shot, as we rocked down the highway and tried to brace ourselves against sudden stops. By the end of the tour, we were in complete meltdown, physically and emotionally.

Our first misadventure, on the very first day, had nothing to do with faulty computers or our aching backs. It had been a whirlwind: I'd worked the convention floor for Clinton's acceptance speech, written my *Today* show story, covered Clinton's midmorning rally in Manhattan, and boarded the bus. We planned to file for *Nightly News* that night from Camden, New Jersey, where Clinton would make his first stop at a former RCA plant at five p.m. Carroll Ann and our crack tape editor, Wayne Dennis, were following behind in the Winnebago.

I rode the bus down the New Jersey Turnpike to Camden and arrived at the plant at five-thirty p.m., but the NBC Winnebago was nowhere to be found. Frantically, I ran up and down the street, past local and network satellite trucks, but couldn't find our tape editor or Carroll Ann—or, of course, all the videotape we'd shot in New York for that evening's broadcast. How could they have gotten lost between New York City and Camden? It never occurred to me: they'd run out of gas.

In desperation, I found the local NBC truck that was coordinating live shots for the nearby Philadelphia NBC affiliate, KYW, my alma mater. They didn't have any of the New York rally pictures, but they could at least feed my voice to New York. So my first night's story of the general election campaign was a mess—a combination of whatever pictures Carroll Ann could throw together when she finally did arrive in Camden, augmented by the local NBC station's coverage and a hurried narration recorded on the street—proving once again that political coverage was sometimes held hostage to more than the whims of high technology and campaign schedules. Today, the networks pool much of their coverage and feed the raw tape back to Washington or New York in bulk, so that it can be slickly edited into final form. But in those days, we were still doing it ourselves, from wherever we were on the road.

As we struggled to get on the air for *Nightly News,* the Clinton bus moved on. A second NBC team covered the next few stops, while we leapfrogged ahead to York, Pennsylvania, where the campaign was going to spend the night. The moment we arrived in York, at one a.m., but still ahead of the campaign entourage, I sensed that something extraordinary was happening in American politics. The streets were filled with people in lawn chairs, with candles and flashlights, waiting for the Clinton bus to arrive. This was hardly a Democratic stronghold. In fact, the city was in a Republican area of Pennsylvania.

Had something about this new team captured the imagination of Middle America, or was it just that the circus was coming to town? I didn't know, but for whatever reason, the bus trip was already becoming an iconic event. The crowds cheered our Winnebago, thinking we were the candidates. Naturally, we waved back. When Clinton arrived at two o'clock in the morning, despite the hour, there were thousands of people waiting up for him. He and Gore rewarded them with impromptu speeches, and for another hour, tried to shake every hand in sight.

For weeks, we traveled the back roads of America, through Pennsylvania and Ohio and then on to the Midwest, crisscrossing the Mississippi River and rolling into St. Louis for an outdoor rally big enough to fill Busch Stadium on one of the hottest days of the year. Along the way, the candidate made plenty of promises. As I reported on July 20 from Kentucky, Clinton hadn't been specific about how he'd pay for all his new programs, "but name a problem—

he has a program to fix it." There would be plenty of time for budget math later.

The next day, my colleague, White House correspondent John Cochran, reported on the president's own budget difficulties—a projected $399 billion dollar deficit. As John put it: "Even the Republican chairman of the Federal Reserve said today, 'Nothing is more important than cutting the deficit.'" Then he showed Alan warning Congress in his semiannual testimony that the deficit was a "corrosive force," damaging the economy. After such a long stretch on the road, I didn't care what Alan was saying—I was just glad to catch a glimpse of him on television.

On that first thousand-mile trek of the Clinton campaign, the candidate would often stop the bus if he saw ten people at a crossroads. The man loved campaigning so much he would have gone house to house if it meant he could deliver his stump speech. Each time he stopped the lead bus, we had to jump off and run alongside to catch up and cover whatever he was saying to the gathered crowd. One night in Iowa, Clinton stopped the cavalcade so many times— including once for some drunks leaving a bar at closing time—that one of the Secret Service men on the press bus said, "If he stops one more time, and we don't get some sleep, I'm going to become a threat to his safety."

To Clinton, schedules were irrelevant. For a rally organized by Senator Tom Harkin at a county fair somewhere in Iowa, the advance teams had set up bales of hay so that Clinton could give his speech against a scenic backdrop, a stage set made for television. But the candidate stopped so many times along the way that by the time we got to the fair, the sun had set. Still, at least a thousand people were waiting, standing shoulder to shoulder, in the dark. It didn't make great pictures for television news, but it was a rousing campaign event. Bill Clinton was definitely connecting with the voters.

On another night, after pulling into a motel parking lot around two o'clock in the morning, Clinton insisted on giving his entire campaign speech to whoever was still awake. Finally Al Gore just shrugged and went inside to get some sleep. Usually when we arrived somewhere in the middle of the night, my work was just beginning. I had to write a script and get up for the *Today* show, well before dawn. It was brutal.

The campaign became a blur of sleepless nights and endless Bill Clinton speeches. Yet it was exciting, because he was capturing something new, a yearning for generational change—and people were responding to the energy, the youth of the Clinton-Gore team. In comparison to George Herbert Walker Bush, these were very young men. I began to realize that there was a new dynamic, and that Clinton was selling himself, successfully, as an agent of change. No matter how much we focused on the candidates' policies, people were comparing their styles, and Bush was coming up short.

The contrast became apparent during a White House press conference in June 1992, when a reporter asked Bush why he wanted to be reelected.

The president said, "That's what Barbara was asking me a few minutes ago." What was his answer to his wife?

"I'd say, hey, I want to continue this job to help this country. . . . It's worth finishing the job. Nobody likes the primary process." It was hardly a sweeping vision for a second term. There was no energy to his self-presentation; he seemed like a spent force. If he had great ideas for the next four years, he didn't project them. Despite his popularity after the first Gulf War, Bush seemed vulnerable.

As we went through the fall campaign, the Clinton-Gore team seemed to click with their theme song, Fleetwood Mac's "Don't Stop (Thinking About Tomorrow)." The first baby boomer candidates for president and vice president were outfoxing Bush. And despite a serious effort by Jim Baker to talk Bush into dumping Quayle in favor of a candidate who could represent "change," Bush, according to one advisor, was "reluctant to pull the trigger."

—

The contrast between the optimism and hope Clinton had projected at his convention and the weariness Bush was conveying became even more pronounced after the Republicans gathered a month later in Houston. Despite a rousing performance by Ronald Reagan, there was nothing moderate about the party's platform, or the opening night speech by Pat Buchanan, who climbed on board with an attack on Bill Clinton's patriotism, whipping up the crowd with the cry that Clinton was "not the kind of change we can abide in a nation that we still call God's country."

On the floor, moderates like Kansas senator Nancy Kassebaum were dismayed at other speakers like Marilyn Quayle, who was just as harsh as Buchanan. Prominent Republican women, one by one, took me aside, questioning what was happening to their party. It was a warning sign of what was to come on Election Day: moderates and independents, particularly women, would abandon Bush in droves. Campaign organizers were blamed for letting Buchanan speak in prime time. I was told that the candidate's son, George W. Bush, held Secretary of State Jim Baker accountable for resisting appeals to quit his cherished cabinet post before the convention and take control of the campaign.

The mood in Houston that August was ugly, inside the hall and out. One day a fight almost broke out at a downtown restaurant when one hundred Young Republicans besieged Democrats, brought to Houston by party chairman Ron Brown to present opposition "spin." The Young Republican activists pounded on the windows and walls as Brown tried to show reporters new campaign ads. They were too angry to interview, alternately chanting "Libs go home" and "Millie, not Hillie," a juvenile comparison of the president's dog to Bill Clinton's wife. Bush gave a strong speech, attacking Clinton and the Democratically controlled Congress, but the impression the country had was that Buchanan, not Bush, was the face of the Republican Party.

The morning after Bush was nominated, my colleague Maria Shriver offered to give me a lift to Burbank, California, so that I

My parents, Cecile and Sydney Mitchell, on their wedding day, December 8, 1940. (Personal collection)

My older sister Susan and me in the Catskill Mountains in the summer of 1949. (Personal collection)

Susan, our brother Arthur, and me with our dad near our apartment in the Bronx, 1951. (Personal collection)

My first oval office photo op, accompanying Philadelphia mayor Frank Rizzo when he visited Richard Nixon on January 24, 1972. Next to me is fellow reporter Fred Hamilton of the *Philadelphia Daily News.* (Bettmann/Corbis)

A live radio interview in 1975 with a Philadelphia city councilman, Isadore Bellis, in council chambers. (Courtesy *Philadelphia Inquirer*)

Interviewing Mayor Rizzo in Philadelphia on January 26, 1976, at the Bellevue Stratford Hotel, where he allegedly offered a political bribe to the head of the local Democratic party. In a celebrated story, he failed a lie detector test over the controversy. (Courtesy Zacharias/*Philadelphia Inquirer*)

Covering Jimmy Carter on April 8, 1976, during the hotly contested Pennsylvania presidential primary. That day, Carter was apologizing for using the term "ethnic purity" to defend neighborhoods that were resisting integrating. I'm sitting on the floor up front to improve my chances of getting a question to Carter for KYW Radio and TV. (Courtesy McGuinn/*Philadelphia Inquirer*)

Questioning Ronald Reagan with the Air Force One press pool on October 8, 1982 in San Diego. Helen Thomas is standing next to me. (Courtesy Ronald Reagan Library)

Reagan meeting informally with the White House press corps in May 1984. The group included Reagan biographer Lou Cannon of the *Washington Post*, Susan Page of *USA Today*, and columnist James J. Kilpatrick. (Courtesy Ronald Reagan Library)

Preparing to interview Nancy Reagan about her antidrug policy for the *Today* show at the Carlyle Hotel in 1985. It was the start of the first lady's successful effort to improve her image. (Courtesy Ronald Reagan Library)

Sharing a light moment with co-anchor Linda Ellerbee on the set of *Summer Sunday, U.S.A.* before our first broadcast on July 2, 1984. The live prime-time show was a technical nightmare. (Personal collection)

Greeting George W. Bush and his mother at a *Today* show anniversary party on February 24, 1987. (NBC News)

Nancy Reagan greeting me at my first state dinner, one for El Salvador president Jose Napoleon Duarte, on October 14, 1987. Alan had been Fed chairman for two months. (Courtesy Ronald Reagan Library)

Just after our wedding ceremony on April 6, 1997, in the garden of the Inn at Little Washington. We are smiling at our friend, *Washington Post* editor and writer Meg Greenfield. (Photo by Denis Reggie)

On the porch of the inn with our flower girl, my godchild Lauren Hunt, after our wedding. We are looking skyward as it starts to rain. (AP/Wide World Photos)

Getting ready to run in the Race for a Cure on June 5, 1999 with Vice President Al Gore—and sixty-five thousand others. (Personal collection)

My first meeting with Fidel Castro during the custody battle over Elian Gonza-
lez in December 1999. I talked Castro into taking me on a televised tour of
Cuba's medical school, during which he gave his first interview about Elian.
(Personal collection)

Alan and me at the White
House Millennium Dinner
on New Year's Eve, 1999.
(Clinton Presidential Library)

Mikhail Gorbachev signing my notes after I interviewed him
on May 21, 2001 in Washington, two years after he'd been
forced from office. (Personal collection)

An exclusive interview with Elian Gonzalez and his father, Juan Miguel, in June 2001 at Elian's school in Cardenas, Cuba, on the first anniversary of Elian's return to Cuba. (Photo by Felipe Leon)

Interviewing Rudy Giuliani in a live town hall meeting on May 18, 2000. The next day, he dropped out of the U.S. Senate race against Hillary Clinton. (AP/Wide World Photos)

Alan thanking Queen Elizabeth after she knighted him at a ceremony in Balmoral Castle on September 27, 2002. We then had lunch with the Queen and Prince Phillip at the castle. (AP/Wide World Photos)

President George W. Bush, Laura Bush, former president Gerald Ford, Betty Ford, Alan, left, and me, right, visit in the Blue Room during a celebration for President Ford's ninetieth birthday, July 16, 2003. (White House photo by Susan Sterner)

With Alan at a foreign policy conference in Aspen, Colorado, in September 2003. (Alicekoelle.com)

The NBC team in Ramallah for Arafat's funeral. (Photo by ML Flynn of NBC)

At a checkpoint on the road to Ramallah with Brian Williams on November 11, 2004, the morning of Yasser Arafat's funeral. (Photo by ML Flynn of NBC)

With Alan, in July 2006. (Personal Collection)

En route to Beirut with Condoleezza Rice in the middle of the Lebanon War, July 24, 2006. (Photo by Dennis Gaffney, NBC News)

could accept an invitation from Jay Leno to appear on *The Tonight Show.* My producer, Susan Lasalla, and I showed up at the airport not knowing what to expect. It was quite a scene as Maria, her husband, Arnold Schwarzenegger, and their children welcomed us to their gleaming private jet.

As the children played games, Arnold asked me what jokes I had prepared for Leno. Jokes? All I knew was the latest scuttlebutt about Jim Baker and Pat Buchanan. Although I was pretty hopeless, Arnold and Maria spent the rest of the flight coaching me for my *Tonight Show* debut. Much to my relief, when I walked out on the set and was seated on that famous couch, all Jay wanted to ask about was politics. That I could handle.

———

By October, the campaign had gotten mean. Ross Perot had jumped back into the race, declaring that his decision to drop out in July had been a mistake. (He would spend more than $60 million, garner 19 percent of the vote, and fail to win a single state. As Tom Brokaw said on election night, the Texas billionaire seemed to enjoy every dime he spent.) Perhaps it's because most of his support came from voters who would otherwise have supported Bush, with whom Perot had had a grudge match dating back to those differences over how aggressively to keep searching for Vietnam War MIAs.

Knowing Perot was draining votes from him, Bush started lashing out at Clinton in frustration. On October 3, he mocked Clinton's claim not to have inhaled marijuana: "This guy couldn't remember in detail that he didn't inhale twenty years ago, and he can't remember what came out of his mouth twenty minutes ago." Four days later, the president questioned Clinton's patriotism because of a trip Clinton had made while in college to the former Soviet Union and his antiwar activities while a student at Oxford in 1969. "To go to a foreign country and demonstrate against your own country when your sons and daughters are dying halfway around the world, I'm sorry, I just don't like it," Bush said. "I think it's wrong." The themes seem remarkably similar to the attacks on John Kerry's antiwar activities in the 2004 campaign. At the same time, Clinton was excoriating the president for both his economic and foreign policies.

Though Clinton was already ahead, as in 2004, the debates were critical. Of the three debates, the most lopsided took place in Richmond on October 15. Clinton was once again struggling with chronic laryngitis; in fact, he had Hillary stand in for him at one of his campaign rallies. But the format greatly favored Clinton's style of campaigning. The candidates sat on stools, in a town hall meeting setting. When Clinton reached out and walked over to a young woman who had asked a question about people who were unemployed, he instantly communicated his empathy to the larger audience at home. George Bush, not realizing he was on camera, checked his watch to see how much time he had left to frame his answers. The message sent to the voters: the president was bored, and would have preferred to be having his teeth drilled rather than face that live audience.

On October 30, 1992, we started out in Newark on our way to Pittsburgh. It was my forty-sixth birthday, making me one of the oldest reporters in the press corps. In fact, the candidate was one of the few other baby boomers on the plane. At times, on a late flight, we would talk about Vietnam or other events from the sixties, and I'd feel very separate from the rest. They had different cultural icons, different musical tastes. What did they know of George McGovern, or the '68 riots?

As I arrived on this birthday to board the campaign plane for a flight to Pittsburgh, suddenly a guy in a purple jumpsuit leaped out, shaking a guitar. This unlikely apparition was in fact an Elvis impersonator, hired by one of the producers as a joke on me in a campaign where the candidate was often referred to as Elvis (one of his musical heroes). Clinton came down the steps to watch, looking politely amused, although the "Elvis" they'd hired could barely sing.

That day was also memorable because of a later development that George Herbert Walker Bush still believes—along with Alan's interest rate increases—caused him to lose the election. The special counsel investigating Iran-Contra, Lawrence Walsh, won a new indictment from a grand jury against Reagan defense secretary Caspar Weinberger. Most important, in a side note, the indictment resurrected questions about George Bush's role, suggesting that Reagan's vice president may have known more about the arms-for-hostages deal than he'd admitted. Suddenly, the Reagan administration's worst scandal was back in the news, and along with it questions about whether Bush had taken part in the cover-up. Bush aides later told me they had been gaining a point a day in their rolling tracking polls. When the Weinberger indictment hit, their progress slammed to a halt. To this day, the Bushes consider that indictment a Democratic dirty trick, even though Walsh was, nominally, a Republican.

At least the president was flying on Air Force One. How we, or Clinton, survived to reach Election Day is beyond me. Much as I love being on the road, campaigns involve grueling bus trips, terrible press charter flights, no sleep, a diet of fast food, candy, coffee and doughnuts, and rarely, if ever, a hot meal. Even getting from point A to point B is a challenge. One night in Jackson, Mississippi, I had to stay behind to do *Nightly News* and rejoin the campaign, which had flown on to Toledo, Ohio. When we needed to catch up, NBC had been chartering us by jet. But that night, when I got to the airport in Jackson, our assignment desk had ordered a single-engine, small-propeller plane. It resembled something that could have flown combat missions in World War II. The pilot looked as though he hadn't reached puberty.

I climbed in, my fear of flying outweighed by the need to get to Toledo and start preparing for the next morning's *Today* show. The boy pilot tried to start the engine—and nothing happened. He tried again, to no effect. Finally, he got jumper cables, hot-wired the plane to get it started, and hopped in. It was only after we'd started rolling down the runway that I noticed the duct tape holding the window in place.

On the last day, heading out from a Philadelphia diner, Clinton embarked on a final nine-state, cross-country swing to hammer home the image of a younger candidate, as he put it, a "change" agent. Brimming with confidence from polls showing him eight points ahead, he still wanted to outperform Bush in a final burst of energy.

As he crossed the country, each Clinton-Gore rally was more enthusiastic than the last, with thousands of people at every airport shouting, "One more day, one more day." The air caravan, which by then had grown to three planes, followed the sun west before doubling back to Arkansas: forty-one hundred miles from Philadelphia to Democratic strongholds in Cleveland, Detroit, and St. Louis; then on to Paducah, Kentucky; McAllen and Fort Worth, Texas; Albuquerque, New Mexico; Denver, Colorado. Finally, home to Little Rock. By then, we practically had "the speech" memorized.

In stark contrast, there is a still photo from the president's final train trip before the election that captures the mood of the Republican campaign: Bush's political alter ego, Jim Baker, is sitting in a trench coat, staring ahead glumly. It was taken the day Baker was told that the campaign's own polls showed they could not win. At every stop on his final day, the president said that Saddam Hussein planned to hold a victory party if Clinton won. The campaign rhetoric, from both sides, had become so mean that no one found Bush's comment at all remarkable.

On election eve, Ross Perot bought two hours of network television time to repeat his half-hour attack program entitled, "Chicken Feathers, Deep Voodoo, and the American Dream." He did have a way with words.

———

Election night was a sparkling fall evening, unusually cold for Little Rock. Trapped in a huge crowd at the victory rally, I ducked under the press barriers at the Old State House and worked my way to the stage to see if I could get a comment from Clinton or Gore for our broadcast. When the two families finally came out to declare victory, Clinton arm in arm with Hillary and Chelsea, the crowd erupted. Weary campaign workers were hugging and kissing each other. The entire state of Arkansas must have been crowded into the victory celebration. I was hanging on to the edge of the stage when Gore actually leaned down to me; to my mortification, I couldn't think of a relevant question. As I recall, I shouted something dumb, like, "How do you feel?" The newly elected vice president looked at me as though I'd lost my mind. Luckily, the camera never veered my way.

Clinton and Gore had won, but my future was up in the air. I had never asked what the network planned for me should the Democrats reclaim the White House. For one thing, my friend John Cochran was still the White House correspondent, and I didn't want to undercut him. For another, I was superstitious. I'd been down this road too many times. But one morning Tim Russert, our bureau chief, reached me in my Little Rock hotel room and said, "I've got good news and bad news. You are going to be chief White House correspondent."

It was the job I'd always wanted. What was the bad news? After four years, I was losing my coveted slot as political analyst for the *Today* show. I'd been on a weekly panel to talk politics, first with David Broder and Jack Germond, then with Al Hunt and Russert. Tim told me, "We can't have you do political analysis because it would undercut your credibility at the White House." In those days, the boundaries between straight reporting and analysis were hard and fast.

In today's context, it still seems right, but so old-fashioned—the notion that if I were to give my opinions, it would damage my reputation for objectivity as a White House correspondent. Thirteen years later, White House reporters go on talk shows, write blogs, express their opinions on everything.

The other downside about being assigned to the White House was that once again I had to cover a presidential transition. That meant being stuck in Little Rock until January with no direct flights for an easy escape to Washington. By then, Alan and I knew that our relationship was moving in a more serious direction. But we had never really talked about it. Both of our jobs involved enormous concentration and a lot of travel. In contrast to when we first met, when I was away for months at a time while covering Ronald Reagan, now we were a couple. I just didn't know how we were going to manage a relationship if I became White House correspondent and ended up back on the road, traveling for long stretches whenever the president did.

On the morning after the election, I was the pool reporter covering the president-elect's walk from the Governor's Mansion to the home of Carolyn Staley, one of his closest friends from high school, for a victory brunch. In a bad sign of things to come, his press aides kept us so far away we could barely get a picture, much less a question.

They no longer needed us, and wanted us to know it. We did get a group shot of Clinton, his wife and mother, and all their old friends posing on Carolyn's front porch. The Clintons were standoffish, but the president-elect's irrepressible mother, Virginia Kelley, shouted out, "Hello, Andrea." She was a force of nature, strong and invariably friendly. She'd raised her son by herself, and he'd prevailed to become president-elect. Yet she put on no airs and seemingly held no grudges against the reporters who'd been hounding him for months. I liked her a lot, and admired her spunk.

For the next two and a half months, I was in transition hell, focusing almost exclusively on who was or wasn't going to be in the cabinet, instead of on ideas or policies. The competition for leaks was intense. Clinton was forming his cabinet literally at his kitchen table in the Governor's Mansion. Clinton, Warren Christopher, Vernon Jordan, Hillary, Al Gore, Mickey Kantor, and Mack McLarty, Clinton's boyhood friend and campaign advisor, were vetting names and interviewing candidates.

Our only way of finding out what was going on was to stake out the airport, look for private planes, and try to spot people coming in and out. Washington faxed us copies of pictures of potential nominees so our camera crews could chase them down at the airport. It wasn't a fail-proof system. I suspect a lot of salesmen from Memphis and grandmothers heading to Atlanta had their mug shots taken.

We thought we had the whole thing covered, which is why it was pretty remarkable one day at George Stephanopoulos's daily briefing when the Clinton spokesman announced that the president-elect was having lunch with Alan Greenspan. I'd barely seen him in months, but the transition team had managed to sneak Alan into town unnoticed, past all of the cameras. Did they have him slump down in the backseat of his car? Per our understanding about such things, Alan hadn't said a word to me about it.

What was even more interesting was that he and Clinton, whom he'd never before met, really hit it off. What was supposed to be a brief lunch turned into hours of conversation about a wide range of subjects, ranging far beyond monetary policy. Clinton clearly was impressive: well educated, widely read, and a good listener. As *The Washington Post* reported the next morning, "The biggest news out of Little Rock yesterday was that NBC's Andrea Mitchell was caught by surprise when her longtime boyfriend, Federal Reserve Chairman Alan Greenspan, showed up to meet with Bill Clinton." The gossip item was in the same column as a report that Madonna's erotic *Sex* book would be airbrushed for its Japanese edition, providing some cover to the men, but leaving the revealing photos of the women untouched. I was in august company.

The Clintons were attracting plenty of talented Democrats to their Little Rock jobs fair, including people who didn't need or want to move to Washington. The center of all the action, other than the Clintons' kitchen table, where the interviews were taking place, was the bar at the Capitol Hotel. The Capitol was stately, vaguely Victorian with deep burgundy velvet curtains, and featured an enormous guest elevator explained variously as having been built to accommodate coffins or the hoop skirts of Reconstruction-era prostitutes. The bar was a meeting place for campaign aides, reporters, and cabinet prospects, real and imagined.

One night, I ran into Goldman Sachs co-chairman Bob Rubin, looking vaguely uncomfortable in those surroundings. He flashed me that crooked grin of his, and without revealing anything asked what I thought of Clinton and his team.

Where should I start? Clinton's colorful war room regulars (James Carville, Paul Begala, and George Stephanopoulos) had to be experienced to be understood. I certainly didn't think Bob Rubin of Wall Street would understand Carville, aka the Ragin' Cajun, a man so superstitious he wouldn't change his underwear during the last weeks of the campaign to avoid some imagined jinx. But despite their idiosyncrasies, Clinton's advisors were sharp, dedicated, and energetic. And their system of answering any attack with a rapid response made campaign history.

The president-elect was clearly smart, and he knew it. To signal that his laser-beam focus on the economy was not just a campaign slogan, a few weeks after the election he hosted an economic summit in Little Rock. Unlike most such events, which are glorified photo opportunities, Clinton actually listened to the views of the invited experts, hoping to learn something; predictably, most simply parroted Clinton's own positions. It was an early lesson in how difficult it is for a president to get honest advice.

Sometimes, as we struggled to break stories about the players in the new White House, the evidence was right in front of us. I kept running into a little-known Clinton advisor named Ira Magaziner, who was very close to Hillary. He told me he was going to have a very important job in the new administration on health care—little did I realize how important he would be. Ira became the architect of the convoluted health-care proposal that was to preoccupy the new administration for the next two years.

Completing the cabinet took longer than Clinton expected, partly because he was determined to make his administration "look like America" by finding people of diverse backgrounds. White House staffs had always been predominantly male, and white. Not surprisingly, the Clintons wanted a team more representative of their values, and their friends. I remember looking up during a news conference called to introduce the new domestic policy team and noticing that Council of Economic Advisors chair Laura Tyson and EPA administrator Carol Browner both looked like my own friends—women more or less of my generation, from similar backgrounds.

It was striking, after covering all-male administrations for so many decades. I was identifying with them in a visceral way that had nothing to do with politics or policy. I imagined that the symbolism of their selection would resonate with millions of women and girls across the country. Official Washington was going to be very different. And Clinton had chosen Tyson, a well-regarded economics professor from Berkeley, despite a campaign to belittle her by a fellow economist, Paul Krugman of MIT, suggesting she was not up to the job. It was not the first, or last, time a qualified woman would have to overcome sniping by male competitors, in this case by someone thought to want the job himself.

But in their zeal to create a Noah's Ark with at least two officials of every color, from every part of the country, the Clintons trapped themselves with an artificial goal, and an unrealistic Christmas deadline. At times, potential cabinet secretaries, well-regarded men like Bruce Babbitt and Bill Richardson, found themselves parked in Little Rock hotel rooms, not knowing which jobs would be left when the game of musical cabinet chairs ended. If the Clintons didn't fill their diversity goals, perfectly qualified candidates would not make the cut. I'd known some of the cabinet prospects for years, and every few days one or another would call me to ask whether he was in or out. It was more than a little humiliating, and a harbinger of chaotic West Wing decision making in the years ahead.

With his cabinet and staff still unformed, Bill and Hillary Clinton took a victory lap into Washington for the inauguration on a bus from the home of Thomas Jefferson—Clinton's namesake—near Charlottesville, Virginia. Riding the bus one more time celebrated the way their campaign had begun and symbolized their stated commitment to remain connected with Americans outside the nation's capital. In his inaugural address, Clinton declared, "Let us give this capital back to the people to whom it belongs. . . . We have changed the guard. . . ."

The self-proclaimed "change agent" had arrived.

In one last symbolic gesture, on Inauguration Day, Clinton flung open the doors of the White House so that ordinary Americans could line up and shake his hand. It was a deliberate homage to the populist traditions of Andrew Jackson and Teddy Roosevelt. So many people had lined up on the South Lawn, despite freezing weather, that the Clintons abandoned their receiving line inside and rushed out to shake as many hands as they could before sunset.

Despite the auspicious beginning, the new president still faced a more lasting problem. Clinton had spent so much time trying to create a diverse cabinet that he didn't focus enough on how to staff his White House. He didn't think clearly about who was best suited to be his chief of staff and how to organize his communications team. He also hadn't found the right person to be his attorney general, a job that should have been reserved for a trusted advisor. His first nominee for attorney general, Washington attorney Zoe Baird, had to withdraw because of a political firestorm over her failure to pay her nanny's Social Security taxes. Though it was a far cry from the charges that had scuttled John Tower's nomination at the beginning of George Bush's presidency four years earlier, it was a clear signal that the Senate Republicans were not cutting the new administration any slack. Personnel problems became a recurring theme, a leitmotif for Bill Clinton's first term.

The staff difficulties also overshadowed more positive events. On February 5, I prepared a story for *Nightly News* on a significant domestic program, the Family and Medical Leave Act. It was Clinton's first legislation, symbolizing his priorities and fulfilling a campaign promise to guarantee workers unpaid time off when a baby is born or a family member is sick. But late in the day, I confirmed that the president's second choice for attorney general, New York federal judge Kimba Wood, would not be nominated, because of a nanny issue involving an undocumented family worker whom she had employed, although before it was illegal to do so. Quickly, I was told to switch stories.

The Family Leave legislation would be reduced to an anchor "item," a brief mention; instead, I would do a live cross talk about the new team's continuing failure to find an attorney general. Just before air, standing on the North Lawn at our camera position, I spotted George Stephanopoulos headed my way. He made the rounds, stopping at each of the network camera positions, trying to spin us into believing that Judge Wood had never been seriously considered. The only problem was that her husband, New York journalist Michael Kramer, was telling everyone exactly the opposite.

After two false starts, the new president ended up filling one of his most important cabinet posts with a woman he barely knew, Janet Reno, a Florida prosecutor recommended by his wife and brother-in-law. Reno turned out to be one of the least politically astute of his appointments, and one of the least successful. She became mired in endless disputes with Clinton's inner circle. Not having a trusted ally as attorney general became a huge disadvantage when the president was struggling with how to respond to the legal challenges of Whitewater, as well as the Paula Jones and Monica Lewinsky affairs.

Similarly, Clinton later realized that having his childhood friend Mack McLarty as chief of staff had its pluses and minuses: McLarty knew all the players, but was less brutal than an outsider would have been in imposing discipline and cutting their losses. In a key slot at the Justice Department, Clinton placed another Arkansas crony, Webb Hubbell, a former law partner of Hillary's. When Hubbell was later investigated for billing problems from his former law practice, it became a White House problem. As deputy White House counsel, Clinton chose yet another of his kindergarten friends, Vince Foster, with even more tragic results.

———

During the transition, the president-elect was also stumbling over issues that would plague him once he took office. Chief among these was how to handle gays in the military. It was a touchy subject for Clinton because of his lack of military service. He was never comfortable around the military brass, and initially at least, they thought of him as that "draft dodger" who had avoided service in Vietnam. They were also hostile because, during the campaign, he had promised to permit gays to serve—not a popular idea at the Pentagon.

I had a small part in bringing the issue to a head on November 11, even before Clinton took office: I thought Veterans Day would provide a good news peg, and knowing that Clinton would show up for a Veterans Day event at the Arkansas state Capitol, I went early to stake him out.

When you're five foot three, you can't get people to answer a question unless they can see you in a crowd. So just as I'd prepositioned myself up front at the Busy Bee lunch counter to accost Hillary during the campaign, I had to figure out which direction he'd be coming from and plant myself in front of him. That meant arriving early, not letting competing camera crews push me around, and waiting. It isn't dignified, but neither was shouting questions to Ronald Reagan. More to the point, sometimes it worked.

Was this journalism? It depends on your definition. We had a new president with no military experience who had written a controversial letter in 1969 thanking an ROTC colonel for "saving" him from the draft. Now he was about to become commander in chief and had to either renege on his campaign promise to gays, or further alienate the military brass. I thought it was a good test of his decision making on an important, hot-button issue.

When Clinton arrived, I waited for local reporters, who wanted to pin him down about his state pension (technically, he was still governor). Then I asked, "How are you going to handle the opposition of the military to your position on gays and lesbians in the military?"

Clinton didn't duck. "If people who have served our country with distinction, many of them with battlefield ribbons and who have never had any kind of question about their conduct, can be booted out of the military, that is the issue, and I think there are ways that we can deal with this that will increase the comfort level of a lot of the military folks here." Unfortunately, he had no idea how to "increase their comfort level," especially since the most popular man in uniform, Colin Powell, chairman of the Joint Chiefs of Staff, was dead-set against changing the military's policy toward gays.

The issue had come up before with Powell, frequently because of pressure from Democrats like former congresswoman Pat Schoeder of the House Armed Services Committee. During the previous administration Powell had told Dick Cheney, then defense secretary, that the military could not openly accommodate gay servicemen and -women. Powell knew that Cheney was sympathetic to gay rights because of his daughter, Mary, but Powell argued that the military and civilian worlds were very different. Then, after Clinton was elected, Powell and the president-elect met at the Willard Hotel to discuss a long list of defense issues. At the end of the meeting, as the two men stood up to leave without having dealt with the question of gays in the military, Powell strongly urged Clinton to give the brass time to study it, telling him, "I don't think you want to start off with that kind of conflict." Clinton agreed, and Powell left thinking that the new president was not "hell-bent" on taking on the controversy. But within weeks, the White House staff had proposed changing the military regulations. Powell found himself in the uncomfortable position of being on the opposite side of his new commander in chief on a major issue, not where he wanted to be.

I give the president-elect credit for trying to stick to his principles. But he was caught between a campaign promise of equal treatment of gays and his reluctance to alienate the military any more than he already had. The issue also created friction with a powerful player whose support he needed on the Hill, Senate Armed Services chairman Sam Nunn. The Georgia Democrat and Clinton had never been close. I always suspected that Nunn's discomfort with Clinton had similar roots to his uneasiness with John Tower, whose womanizing had also offended Nunn's sense of propriety. As a result, Nunn did the minimum amount for Clinton during the campaign.

Clinton held a news conference on January 29 to announce his decision to delay the decision for six months. It was contentious. I asked if he hadn't thought through the practical problems when he made his campaign promise, and what he had learned from dealing with the powerful members of the Senate and the Joint Chiefs? He stiffened, and glared. You could always tell when Clinton was angry, because a muscle in his cheek would twitch visibly.

I knew I would not win a popularity contest with the Clintons or their aides. At times, it saddened me, because there was a part of me that wanted to be liked, and despite all my years of reporting, I never quite adjusted to the role of skunk at the garden party. But I responded instinctively to any whiff of hypocrisy on the part of politicians. The Clinton people considered me far too tough and edgy—somehow, they expected campaign correspondents to perform as boosters, not adversaries.

I may have annoyed Clinton, but he hadn't lost his sense of humor. When *USA Today* described me in a lengthy profile as "White House watchdog" and a "pit bull," the president's press aides photocopied my picture from the newspaper and attached it to every chair in the briefing room. They then took a picture of the briefing room, populated with "Andrea Mitchell" in every chair, and gave it to the president to sign. He inscribed the resulting photo: "To Andrea Mitchell—Here's my nightmare—They all become clones of you and I vanish under the pressure! One of you is great but sufficient. Bill Clinton."

Assigned to find a way to satisfy everyone on the gays-in-the-military issue, George Stephanopoulos came back with the policy of "Don't Ask, Don't Tell," a compromise first suggested by Powell. But the military was still resentful and the president lost credibility with some of his closest friends, like longtime gay activist and Clinton campaign fund-raiser David Mixner. Mixner was so alienated he was later arrested outside the White House for protesting Clinton's policy toward gays. Because the Senate's Republican leader, Bob Dole, made it sound as though the Clinton White House had focused on nothing else for six months, Clinton lost ground with conservatives as well.

Whether because of arrogance, naïveté, a hostile press—or all three—the first year of Clinton's presidency was sheer chaos for the White House, and unremitting hell for the first couple. For a while, they antagonized us by confining us to the briefing room and closing the corridor to the press secretary's office. That meant that in a crisis, when no one picked up phones, we had no way to get our questions answered. Putting that hallway off-limits also backfired on the Clinton team: what they gained in privacy they more than lost in an early warning system. Press secretaries from the Eisenhower to the first Bush administration had used their press room contacts to get a heads-up on pending disasters. Eventually, they reopened the corridor.

In those first few weeks, the Clintons also misjudged what a revolutionary role they were carving out for the first lady. Hillary Clinton was the first to have a coveted office in the West Wing, where real estate is power. She was the first to lead a supersecret task force to revamp the nation's health-care system. Initially, Mrs. Clinton was given high marks for the homework that she had done. The male politicians viewed it as remarkable that she could do it at all. When she testified before Dan Rostenkowski's powerful House Ways and Means Committee, they were astounded at her mastery of facts and figures. In fact, when she concluded, the members awarded her a spontaneous round of applause.

But the first lady's insistence on keeping the development of her health-care proposals secret—much as Dick Cheney insisted on secrecy for his energy task force in 2001—played into the hands of her critics. Conservative groups filed suit against the first lady, and the *Wall Street Journal*'s influential editorial page campaigned against her. Hillary's health initiative also created divisions within the White House. The president's economic team was deeply distrustful of her top advisor, Ira Magaziner, and nervous about what he and Hillary might produce. Treasury Secretary Lloyd Bentsen, the former Texas senator and vice presidential candidate, didn't know what to make of Hillary's role. Bob Rubin was wary of the economic assumptions her team had reached. After all, they were taking on one-seventh of the nation's economy. What would be the unintended consequences?

With barely a honeymoon, Clinton prepared to make his debut on Capitol Hill at his first speech to a joint session of Congress. That evening, as I waited in our White House cubicle for the advance text of the speech, I received a phone call from Tony Verdi, our director. It was NBC's turn to be the television pool shooting the speech, providing all the camera shots to the media at large. That meant our director received a secret list of the first lady's special guests for her box two hours before the speech was to begin.

Tony asked me if I knew of another A. Greenspan. I didn't. "Brace yourself," he warned. "They have Alan sitting in the place of honor next to the first lady." Though Alan knew he'd been invited, he had no idea he'd been given such a high-profile seat. The new president wanted to signal his commitment to fiscal responsibility, and Alan was as good a symbol as anyone. I felt conflicting emotions: pride that he was so well respected, but at the same time, concern that the exposure would raise new questions about my objectivity.

As I've mentioned, people often wonder how we manage to keep our work separate. When I was covering the Hill, there was less potential crossover. Now, back at the White House, it could become an issue if his monetary policy became politicized. All I could do was continue being blissfully ignorant of his decision making. Since he never discusses anything at home, I learn of his decisions only when they become public. And anyone who's seen him testify knows that Alan can be a sphinx when he wants to be.

Alan was widely criticized in conservative business circles for sitting next to the first lady and seeming to lend his credibility to the new administration. Clearly, he owed the Clintons the respect due their positions. He also felt Clinton's deficit-reducing policies deserved support. But the fact that he could be criticized for appearing with Mrs. Clinton demonstrated how rapidly she had become a polarizing figure.

With Hillary Clinton already under a microscope, when the White House fired seven veteran civil servants from the office that arranged travel for the press corps, reporters leaped at suspicions that she had engineered the coup. "Travelgate" sounded even more like old-fashioned patronage when the media learned that the people taking over the business included a Clinton cousin and other friends of the first family. The Clintons insisted they'd uncovered mismanagement in the travel operation, but it was handled so clumsily that it aggravated the climate of mutual suspicion between the West Wing and the press.

Then there was the two-hundred-dollar presidential haircut on Air Force One by a fancy Beverly Hills stylist, allegedly forcing a ramp delay at Los Angeles International Airport. The White House denied it, vehemently. One of my fellow correspondents at NBC confirmed the flight delays, and Jim Miklaszewski filed the report for *Nightly News.* Later, the Federal Aviation Administration released records contradicting the account, but as we say in the business, the story had legs. White House officials told me Clinton was furious.

Despite his resentment, the president searched for a way to bridge the cultural divide with official Washington. With his approval rating down to 36 percent, he and Hillary sought out David Gergen, a friend from their annual New Year's gathering, Renaissance Weekend. A veteran of the Nixon, Ford, and Reagan White Houses, Gergen would bring badly needed experience and wisdom to the Clinton team, and he would work well with McLarty. But he was a Republican! Hiring him infuriated Clinton's war room veterans, especially since he was going to be big-footing Stephanopoulos. I broke the story during a Clinton trip to Philadelphia.

The announcement in the Rose Garden the next day was painful to watch: six-foot-six Gergen stood on one side of the president; the much shorter Stephanopoulos, his head literally hanging, stood on the other. How could the campaign team, who'd been with Clinton "until the last dog died" in New Hampshire, not resent a man who'd worked for Richard Nixon? In addition, George was being yanked from performing the daily press briefings (not his forte) and replaced by Dee Dee Myers, the role model for C. J. Cregg in the television drama *The West Wing*. Relieved from jousting with the press every day, Stephanopoulos now had time to become a more important advisor to the president. But at first, none of this was apparent. Begala later cracked that only the White House press corps would consider spending less time with them and more with the president a "demotion."

There was also a manic, self-indulgent quality to White House decision making in those first one hundred days. Budget decisions were made during all-nighters resembling college cram sessions, with the president himself presiding over every line-by-line choice. A lot of pizza was consumed. Then, only days after taking office, Clinton and Gore were widely ridiculed for hosting a cabinet retreat at Camp David in which New Age facilitators tried to foster bonding by getting people to reveal personal weaknesses. The president set the example by confessing that as a child he'd always felt ostracized for being a fat boy. Warren Christopher followed by confiding that he liked piano bars. Both Rubin and Bentsen, more than a little horrified at all this self-examination, opted not to play.

More serious crises arose, like the inferno in Waco, Texas, after a protracted standoff between federal agents and cult leader David Koresh. It was a terrible test for Janet Reno, the newly appointed attorney general, one she was widely perceived to have failed. Overseas, the new president faced a growing crisis over ethnic cleansing in Bosnia, which paralyzed both NATO and the United Nations with indecision. The Europeans were once again ignoring slaughter in their own backyard. Determined to do something, Clinton sent Secretary of State Warren Christopher to Europe to propose lifting the arms embargo and launching air strikes against the Bosnian

Serbs. But the NATO countries objected, and Clinton withdrew his support for the military option even as Christopher was flying home. It was a humiliating debut for the new secretary of state, badly damaging his credibility.

An even bigger crisis hit at home, although at the time few people in or out of government realized its significance. On February 26, 1993, a month into Clinton's presidency, a bomb exploded at the World Trade Center, killing six people and injuring a thousand. We now know that it was Osama bin Laden's first attack on American soil, and that he would spend the next eight years plotting to complete the job. But the relatively small number of lives lost lulled the Clinton White House into looking at it as an isolated event. When the smoke cleared, a top Clinton aide told me, "We really dodged a bullet on that one." Neither they, nor we, realized that the nation had entered a new era.

There were so many distractions. Clinton was still running into trouble confirming his top appointees. When law professor Lani Guinier, a personal friend and the president's nominee to head the Justice Department's civil rights division, faced obstacles because of her past writing on voting rights and quotas, Clinton barely hesitated before withdrawing her nomination. It was a painful Oval Office "firing" that friends say she has still not forgiven.

On his first Memorial Day as president, Clinton tried to heal his rift with veterans over his failure to serve in Vietnam. His approach was both diplomatic and symbolic. Coordinating with the White House, Vietnam veterans John McCain and John Kerry, along with military and space hero John Glenn, went to Hanoi to begin talks on the fate of American POWs and MIAs, to help pave the way for normalizing diplomatic relations. In addition to giving Clinton political support for a controversial decision, the trip helped cement the unusual bipartisan friendship between McCain and Kerry.

At the same time, at the Vietnam wall, the president drafted another Vietnam hero, General Powell, to give a stirring introduction to his commander in chief, even though Powell was known to have misgivings about Clinton the politician. I had come early so that I could spend some time walking through the memorial, looking at the reflections of people in the granite, touching the names. It is a place where monument and history combine to make you feel swallowed by the earth, as the wall recedes. There are always families and friends tracing the names of loved ones onto paper, to bring home a more permanent memory. People leave flowers, teddy bears, and ribbons. Even on duty, I can't go to that spot without tearing up. The ability of the young Yale architect Maya Lin to inspire that kind of emotion through such a simple design has never failed to amaze me.

But Memorial Day of 1993 did not bring closure for Clinton. Driving over with Powell, the president was noticeably nervous. He had good reason. Loud protestors tried to drown out his speech, saying he had no place at that wall of honor. Most of the demonstrators were kept out of Clinton's view, but not beyond his earshot. They shouted, "He's a traitor, he's a draft evader, draft dodger."

Another said, "He served the war in Moscow." When he tried to speak, one shouted, "Shut up and get out of here, coward! Coward! Get out of here! Run!"

It was hard to tell whether it was organized or spontaneous. The president replied, "To all of you who are shouting, I have heard you. I ask you now to hear me. I have heard you. Some have suggested that it is wrong for me to be here with you today because I did not agree a quarter of a century ago with the decision made to send the young men and women to battle in Vietnam."

People in the crowd shouted, "Where was Bill? Where was Bill?"

The president went on, "I ask you at this monument, can any American be out of place? And can any commander in chief be in any other place but here on this day? I think not."

It was a gutsy performance, and some of the veterans were impressed. I looked at Powell and Clinton, and thought about the different paths they had taken as young men. At the time, it didn't seem possible that Vietnam would still be haunting American politics more than a decade later, in the 2004 campaign.

Clinton made another high-profile effort to get right with the military during a trip to the DMZ, where I'd gone with Reagan in what seemed like a different era. In driving rains, we went back to the Bridge of No Return, right up to the line where American soldiers face down North Koreans every day. What many people forget is that even though the armistice was signed in 1953, the two sides still stare at each other every day in a tense standoff. We were warned not to raise our arms or make any sudden gestures that could be interpreted as provocative. After all, it was here that a U.S. Army commander and a platoon leader were hacked to death in 1976 by North Korean guards wielding axes. But, given the rain, the mud, and the obvious political agenda of the photo opportunity, it was difficult to treat the entire event seriously. In fact, Gwen Ifill and I snapped photos of each other wearing orange plastic slickers with hoods, posing in front of the rigidly solemn North Korean troops standing guard at the armistice site. I wonder what they thought of us, and our hijinks.

For Clinton, this was an important rite of passage. He posed, as Reagan had, with field glasses looking out over the wasteland separating North from South. Then, in a hangar at Camp Casey, he addressed two thousand cheering troops, and even played the saxophone. It was a big public relations success. But first, we had to carry the video back, and feed it to the networks from Seoul.

The rest of the press corps was busing back directly to the airport, a long drive of several hours. In order to meet television deadlines, the military had arranged to fly the four network correspondents by helicopter to Seoul. When the choppers arrived to pick us up, I thought I'd overcome a residue of acrophobia—a fear of heights, going back to that 1972 helicopter crash that killed my friend Sid Brenner during Hurricane Agnes. Climbing on board with Susan Spencer from CBS, Brit Hume from ABC, and Wolf Blitzer from

CNN, I commandeered one of the outside seats and waited for them to close the door. All of a sudden we were lifting off, and I realized there was no door. I'd flown on Black Hawk helicopters before, but never on one without a door.

With my legs dangling over the edge, the only place for the huge bag filled with the tapes we'd shot that day was between my knees. Could I keep my balance without losing the tapes? Looking down, I got dizzy and began to panic. The choppers were banking across the mountains, as in the opening scene in *M*A*S*H*, except that these mountains looked a whole lot closer. The only thing separating me from them was a shoulder harness and seat belt.

If I'd only taken one of the inner seats, I would have felt safe, or at least safer. Now I was teetering over the edge of this precipice. The wind was lashing my face. With one hand, I held my baseball cap on my head. With the other, I grabbed the colonel next to me, a public information officer, and said, "You don't know me, but I'm hanging on to you for dear life." With my knees, I tried to prevent the bag of videotapes from tumbling overboard. Though the trip seemed endless, it lasted only an hour. I kept asking myself, "Why am I on this crazy ride?"

After we finally got to Seoul and filed our reports, we boarded the buses to go out to the airplane. We would be out of contact for eight or nine hours during the flight to Hawaii, and because of the time difference we would land there only an hour before the evening newscast. It was then that I discovered, in comparing notes with my network competitors, that I had not noticed a telling detail. When Bill Clinton was gazing out over the DMZ trying to look like Ronald Reagan, he had forgotten to take the lens cap off his field glasses. He may have looked like a commander in chief, but he had a little more practicing to do. For at least the next eight hours, all the way to Hawaii, I tortured myself for missing what seemed a big deal at the time. Such are the preoccupations of covering White House photo opportunities.

With the press corps so focused on gotcha moments, it's understandable that the president was often thin-skinned around us. For instance, when he was choosing his first Supreme Court justice, after the retirement of Justice Byron "Whizzer" White, we all wrote that Clinton was considering two possibilities: Interior Secretary Bruce Babbitt or Federal Appeals Court judge Stephen Breyer. Clinton, like all Presidents, hated leaks, so he delighted in the fact that his final choice was a surprise, Ruth Bader Ginsburg.

Ginsburg had a compelling life story, the experiences of a woman who had fought discrimination her entire career. In the Rose Garden when she was introduced, Bill Clinton was visibly moved by her comments. That's probably why he reacted so angrily when a reporter asked if the decision not to nominate Breyer reflected a "zigzag" quality to his decision making.

"I have long since given up the thought that I could disabuse some of you of turning any substantive decision into anything but political process," he said and stalked out.

There would be more anger that summer, and a month later, terrible grief, with the suicide of the Clintons' Arkansas friend, deputy White House counsel Vince Foster. Foster and Clinton had gone to kindergarten together in Hope, and Foster had been one of Hillary's partners at the Rose Law Firm in Little Rock. As deputy counsel, he had been in charge of responding to a litany of accusations, ranging from the travel office inquiry to his own membership in an all-white Little Rock country club. When the pressure, and his growing depression, became unbearable, he drove to a park overlooking the Potomac one afternoon and shot himself in the head.

Foster left behind an anguished note that said he was "not meant for the job or the spotlight of public life in Washington. Here, ruining people is considered sport."

Foster was especially bitter toward *The Wall Street Journal,* which had hounded him with a series of editorials captioned, "Who Is Vincent Foster," questioning his ethics. To the tightly knit clique of his friends in the White House, Foster's death represented all that was most repugnant about Washington. The president and first lady called it the politics of personal destruction: the way petty scandals like Travelgate can get blown up out of all proportion, and personalized; and the way people can be caricatured and demonized by the press.

Inevitably, many of Foster's colleagues, most likely including the Clintons, also felt tremendous guilt for not recognizing his anguish in time to help him. Their anger surely contributed to their defensiveness later, when Whitewater allegations began to reach critical mass. It was the Arkansans against the rest of the world, especially the Washington press corps. What made it even worse for Vince Foster's family and friends were the conspiracy theorists, mostly from the Republican right, who suggested that he had not killed himself, but had been murdered.

Fortunately for Clinton, it was not all pain and tragedy that summer. Congress passed the president's economic plan, a mix of tax increases and spending cuts designed to reduce the projected deficit by a half trillion dollars over five years. It may have been his proudest achievement, helping to transform the American economy. To win the vote, he had to agree to major concessions, giving up some of his most cherished promises for both tax cuts and new programs.

The final House vote on August 5 was a frantic race against the clock. Clinton did not know he would win until the dramatic entrance of Marjorie Margolies-Mezvinsky of Pennsylvania and Pat Williams of Montana, giving him a one-vote margin of victory. (Her vote cost Marjorie, a former NBC reporter, her seat in Congress. In her heavily Republican district outside Philadelphia, casting the decisive vote for Bill Clinton's budget was hardly good politics.)

The Senate vote, the next night, was equally dramatic. After days of arm-twisting, Clinton owed the victory to his old rival, Bob Kerrey. When Kerrey finally committed, it was not with enthusiasm. He rose on the Senate floor and said, "I could not and should not cast a vote that brings down your presidency." Kerrey and Clinton had been uneasy rivals since the New Hampshire primary, but the Nebraska senator knew that if Clinton lost the economic package, he would have no clout with Congress for other priorities. With Kerrey, the president had a fifty-fifty tie, permitting Al Gore as vice president to cast the deciding vote. The White House staff exploded in celebration.

I blended in with the West Wing crowd as they surged toward the North Portico in a spontaneous rally to cheer Clinton and Gore. It reminded me of the bus trips, just after the convention, and election night in Little Rock. For one night, they could forget about Vince Foster's death, Travelgate, designer haircuts, Arkansas land deals, and the fear of scandals yet to come.

———

The other great accomplishment of that first year was achieved without great White House involvement, but Clinton was still able to bask in the success. For months, negotiators for Israel and the Palestinians, including Mahmoud Abbas, had been meeting secretly in Oslo. When they reached agreement, and were ready to sign their first treaty, Yitzhak Rabin and Yasser Arafat agreed to do it at the White House.

As I walked out to the signing ceremony on the South Lawn, I saw everyone who was anyone in foreign policy and Jewish-American causes, meeting and greeting, seeing and being seen. It felt like a Jewish festival, or a bar mitzvah. Normally staid diplomats were practically giving each other high fives in the backyard of the White House. The jubilation was not misplaced—this was the first breakthrough in the Middle East conflict since Jimmy Carter brought Begin and Sadat together at the White House to sign the Camp David accords in 1979. I thought about how I'd covered that pathbreaking ceremony alongside John Chancellor so many years earlier. How many Palestinians and how many Israelis had died in the intervening years?

This time, I was broadcasting from the press platform at the rear of the South Lawn. The speeches were extraordinary, especially Rabin's. It was a heady moment and I have no doubt it inspired Clinton to believe he could broker a real peace before his time in the White House was up.

The very next day, Clinton launched his campaign to ratify the NAFTA fair trade agreement in the East Room, with Presidents Bush, Ford, and Carter looking on. Seeing them together impressed me: despite disagreeing on most issues, they could still come together behind broader principles, like free trade. I wondered how difficult it was for George Bush to lend his presence to the man who had defeated him. Clinton had chosen Bill Daley, son of one famous Chicago mayor and brother of another, to shepherd the controversial trade agreement through Congress.

Daley is a rare combination: a skilled political operative with a deep knowledge of issues, no matter how complex. The NAFTA deal was an unusual example of Washington bridging the usual political divides. It also featured one of Al Gore's most effective performances, when he demolished anti–free trade advocate Ross Perot in a highly entertaining debate. It gave Gore an aura of debating prowess that led people nearly seven years later to assume mistakenly that he would demolish George W. Bush.

But it seemed as though every victory in the Clinton White House was coupled with a disaster, or at least a close call. The staff ricocheted from one crisis to the next. Some were simple mishaps. For instance, that fall the president went to Congress to propose Hillary's giant health-care plan. The plan was a complex scheme to expand access to health coverage by taking advantage of the economic efficiencies of managed care. But it relied on a series of untested economic assumptions about the way the marketplace would respond. And, more fatally, it threatened the profitability of a number of powerful industries.

The night of Clinton's speech, I was standing on the North Lawn, ready to go live. We kept being told they would bring us the prepared text in advance, but the Clintons frequently made so many last-minute changes (even while riding in the limousine to the Hill), that we weren't very surprised when it didn't arrive on time. Without a text to follow, I had no idea that anything was wrong. Only afterward did we learn that the president got to the podium and realized the speech loaded in the TelePrompTer was his previous address to Congress. Clinton later joked, "I thought to myself, that was a pretty good speech, but not good enough to give twice."

Realizing the error, Clinton turned to Al Gore and said, "They've got the wrong speech." It took a full seven minutes to fix the problem. Clinton was so knowledgeable he was able to deliver a complex and detailed speech on health reform extemporaneously, seemingly without missing a beat. I can't think of another politician who could have pulled it off.

Yet his communication skills, and obvious intelligence, could only carry him so far. Preoccupied by domestic conflicts, he seemed unable to prevent foreign crises from becoming full-blown disasters. As early as the fall of 1993, he was juggling twin conflicts in Somalia and Haiti. Clinton had inherited the American peacekeeping operation in Somalia from George Bush, but it was on Clinton's watch that the U.S. lost eighteen soldiers in the murderous incident memorialized in the film *Black Hawk Down*. What began as a mission to provide food to starving Somalians in a country wracked by civil war turned into a seventeen-hour battle, the longest single American military engagement since Vietnam. As a result of a series of bad military decisions, during a poorly conceived daytime raid, Army Rangers in a Black Hawk helicopter were shot down and their bodies dragged through the streets of Mogadishu by the forces of a Somalian warlord. Colin Powell had just retired as chairman of the Joint Chiefs of Staff, and his successor, John Shalikashvili, had not yet been confirmed.

Defense Secretary Les Aspin took some of the blame for not providing armor that had been requested by commanders in the field, but Clinton was devastated by the loss, especially after the families of some of the dead rangers excoriated him at a posthumous Medal of Honor ceremony. It revived all of the resentments over his lack of service in Vietnam. From then on, the president was uncertain about using military power, even when he needed to; and Congress tried to limit his authority to use force in future conflicts in Haiti and Bosnia.

What is still unclear about these early foreign policy failures is how much the president was already distracted by Whitewater. All the newspapers were pursuing investigative leads, and in November we broke some new ground: in his first television interview, a former Arkansas judge named David Hale suggested that as governor Bill Clinton had pressured him to help his Whitewater partners. Hale said that Clinton had asked him if he could approve a loan for Jim and Susan McDougal, Clinton's friends and partners in the land deal.

The president denied ever having had the conversation, and Hale was at the time under indictment in an unrelated case. Clinton's deputy White House counsel Bruce Lindsey, the first line of defense whenever scandals arose, called me to try to debunk Hale's claim. Who was telling the truth? We couldn't tell, but other sources backed up Hale's account. We laid out the charges and countercharges, including Hale's claim that Clinton had pressed the McDougals to hire Hillary as the attorney for a savings and loan they had run. The government had subsequently forced the S&L to shut down.

Was there a conflict of interest? The Clintons had always denied it. But Vince Foster had discovered that the Whitewater partnership had not filed federal or state tax returns for three years. I reported that the day before Foster died, a judge in Little Rock had filed a search warrant enabling the FBI to raid David Hale's offices. Then, for the first time, the controversial land deal began to merge with allegations of a new sex scandal. Several Arkansas state troopers told a conservative magazine they had helped line up women for Clinton when he was governor. Hillary was furious. Both *The New York Times* and *The Washington Post* pressed for the appointment of an independent counsel.

The pressure increased daily, including January 6, the morning the president's mother, Virginia Kelley, died of breast cancer. As Hillary Clinton later recounted, when she and the president turned on the *Today* show a few hours later, Bob Dole and Newt Gingrich hammered the point home. "It to me cries out for the appointment of a regulatory, independent counsel," Dole said. Their appearance had been scheduled previously, but much later the Clintons said the insensitivity of Dole's comments, given the timing, was crushing to them.

After only a few days, Clinton traveled to Moscow, physically exhausted from the scandals, grieving the loss of his mother, and facing his first summit with Boris Yeltsin. There was perhaps one remaining chance to defuse the Whitewater issue. Len Downie, the executive editor of *The Washington Post,* proposed that the White House turn over all its Whitewater documentation to prove there was nothing to hide. Dave Gergen and Mack McLarty both advised the Clintons to let the newspaper have the material. They argued that it was probably the only way to avoid a special counsel, but Hillary and all of the White House lawyers adamantly refused. They thought it would lead to a fishing expedition and not stop the demands for more information.

With most of the White House press corps focused on Whitewater, Clinton tried to carry on at his first European summit. Following tough three-way negotiations with Russia and Ukraine, he was able to announce Ukraine's agreement to eliminate its entire stockpile of nuclear weapons. The world's third-largest arsenal, a total of eighteen hundred warheads, including 176 long-range missiles plus bombers and cruise missiles, would be disassembled. The warheads would be shipped to Russia, where the uranium would be extracted by U.S. contractors and sold for peaceful use in nuclear reactors around the world. Ukraine, desperately in need of cash, would profit by one billion dollars. At the time, I didn't realize how important the disarmament arrangement would be: it helped guarantee at least a decade of nuclear safety after the end of the Cold War.

I reported on the deal from Prague, struggling to edit my piece in a smoke-filled cubicle. Having fought over the years to eliminate smoke from the White House press room—a battle that was led, successfully, by Sam Donaldson of ABC—it was tough to be working in Europe, where everyone still smoked. My eyes burned, and I could barely breathe. We finished filing for *Nightly News* at two in the morning, and before dawn left with Tom Brokaw and Tim Russert on a small charter flight to Moscow in order to prepare for Clinton's arrival in the Russian capital that night.

Unfortunately, that meant leaving Prague hours before Clinton, on the day he finally responded to a growing chorus demanding that he appoint an independent counsel. All of his political advisors said it was the only way to clear the air. Mrs. Clinton, and Dave Gergen—who had lived through Watergate as a member of Richard Nixon's staff—countered that, once unleashed, a prosecutor could destroy Bill Clinton's presidency. Against the advice of his wife, who had organized a conference call the night before from Washington to try to talk him out of it, Clinton capitulated. After we left for Moscow, the White House announced the decision, with Stephanopoulos explaining that "the controversy was becoming too much of a distraction." In Prague, Clinton gave interviews to the network correspondents for the first time in months.

When my colleague Jim Miklaszewski asked about Whitewater, Clinton made news. Clearly testy, the president blamed the mess on the media, telling Mik, "Basically the press has editorialized and pressured the politicians into saying, 'Here's a guy that, as far as we know, hasn't done anything wrong; nobody's ever accused him of doing anything wrong. There's no evidence that he's done anything wrong, but we think the presumption of guilt—almost—should be upon him. He should somehow prove his innocence.'"

With that, the president got up and walked out. As *The New York Times* reported the next day, he also cancelled a scheduled interview with Ted Koppel, whose show *Nightline* had been promised access to Clinton every day of his trip.

Years later, he and Hillary both said that agreeing to an independent counsel was their biggest mistake. Though they started with Robert Fiske, a moderate Republican prepared to pursue a defined, relatively contained investigation, when he was replaced, they wound up with Ken Starr. What started as an investigation into the Whitewater land deal became an exploration into everything they had ever done.

Almost ignored in the furor over Whitewater was the administration's failure to mobilize action to stop the slaughter in Bosnia. NATO was threatening air strikes because of renewed Serb shelling of Sarajevo, which claimed more victims and again interrupted vital UN relief supplies. Even the British, reluctant to permit air strikes that would endanger their peacekeepers on the ground, were about to give in. But the allies were still not ready, and NATO's threats sounded feckless to the leaders of the Bosnian Serbs.

By the time we arrived in Russia, I was having trouble keeping up. What most people didn't know was that I'd had major surgery a few weeks earlier, and against the advice of colleagues, had insisted on making the trip. I just couldn't imagine missing Clinton's first Moscow summit. But before leaving Washington, one of my White House producers had warned that if I went, he wasn't going to carry my bags—something I never would have asked. I was determined not to show any sign of weakness, or cut myself any slack.

On Clinton's first morning in Moscow, in a heavy snowfall, my producer assigned me to cover a pool that was departing at six-thirty a.m. It meant boarding an unheated bus, being driven to the Russian foreign ministry for a security check, switching to a Russian vehicle for the ride to the Kremlin, and then waiting a few more hours for the leaders. There was very little to show for the effort. All we got to see was Clinton and Yeltsin—by then, calling each other "Bill" and "Boris"—walk toward each other, shake hands, and depart for their private talks. It's the kind of inconsequential photo opportunity that producers now cover, especially if correspondents have to stay up and report live until two-thirty each morning (and do it by climbing up to the hotel rooftop, in the snow, the only location with a scenic backdrop). I should never have taken the early-morning assignment, especially not to observe a routine handshake.

When the Kremlin event finally ended, the situation only got worse. The White House forgot to send a bus to pick us up. By then it was snowing heavily. Loaded down with equipment, the camera crew and I waited in the snow, hoping someone would remember and come get us. In those days, before cell phones were in wide use, there was no way to reach anyone for help. Finally, in desperation, we started walking. My feet were frozen. Not having prepared for outdoor duty, I didn't even have gloves. At times that morning, I wasn't sure I would make it. I felt completely overwhelmed, physically and emotionally.

What I really wanted to be focusing on was the political story we'd come to cover. It was a fascinating time to be in Russia. The Soviet Union had collapsed, but Yeltsin had not consolidated his power. It was not at all clear that he or his reforms would survive. Clinton was practically doing acrobatics to confer legitimacy on him. During the brief summit, the Americans reached into their diplomatic bag of tricks to produce agreements, even symbolic ones. One declaration targeted each country's missiles toward the sea, no longer aiming them at each other. They could easily be repositioned in a crisis, but it sounded good. Yeltsin also tried to persuade Clinton of his own popularity, ephemeral as it was. Despite every sign to the contrary, he offered a rosy view of his new parliament, even as the militia had to be brought in to break up a fistfight in the lower house provoked by the controversial nationalist Vladimir Zhirinovsky. Democracy was still a raw experiment in Russia.

It was hardly the time, or place, for the president to make a snap judgment about whether to appoint a special counsel to investigate Whitewater. Looking back, I realize that he must have been thinking that he couldn't win for losing—a hero in Russia, vilified back home.

Could the train wreck that became the Whitewater investigation—ultimately, the legal process that led to impeachment—have been averted? I think it could have, if the Clintons had been more forthcoming when they had the chance. Yet by the time Clinton took office, the lines between traditional reporting and the tabloids were already blurring. This trend had started earlier with coverage of scandals in Congress and the Gennifer Flowers revelations. Now it was poised to explode.

I think Bill and Hillary's resistance to cooperating goes back to that early feeding frenzy in New Hampshire, which persuaded them that they'd never get a fair break from the media. It's also true that the president and first lady had good reason to stonewall. The president didn't want to admit to past flirtations during his Little Rock years, and by then, Clinton had gotten into a defensive posture about almost everything. If he wasn't going to be open about issues as trivial as Travelgate, he was hardly going to admit to propositioning Paula Jones.

Why did official Washington give him such a rough time, having ignored the peccadilloes of his predecessors? One reason may have been that Clinton never really became a part of Washington. When he tried, he could charm any of the "cave dwellers," the local term for the ruling hostesses of Georgetown. But he didn't often try. The Clintons probably would have done a whole lot better had they tried to engage more. Strangely, they became almost as isolated as Jimmy Carter, who was widely criticized for being a Southern hick who didn't know his way around the Capitol.

Occasionally, the first couple tried to reach out by holding small dinners for a variety of guests, including journalists. We attended one of their dinners, held upstairs in the Yellow Oval Room. There were several tables, and I was seated next to the president. We talked about Vietnam, the antiwar years when we were both in college, the civil rights movement, and Bosnia. Born only two months apart, we had taken such different paths. When he was in the antiwar movement and law school, I was already a reporter, adjusting to the challenge of running into college friends and acquaintances on the other side when I covered demonstrations. Reminiscing with the president of the United States about the sixties, as we watched the sun set from the Truman Balcony—well, as has often been written critically of the Washington press corps, it's harder to slam the president when you've been drinking his wine the night before.

On another occasion the president invited the four network correspondents in for coffee. His hospitality included a tour of the small study off the Oval Office, where he kept souvenirs. He showed us his collection of putters. At the time, we thought it a useful way of seeing him in a relaxed setting, and learning more about his thinking, even if it was off the record. But we do trade a measure of independence for that kind of personal exposure to the chief executive— and we didn't learn much, given what we now know about his activities in that retreat.

The Clintons' highly conflicted relationship with the media is perhaps best captured by one frantic April afternoon that spring as the president tried to handle the escalating crisis in Bosnia, finally threatening the Serbs in Bosnia with a wider war. Only an hour after he held a news conference signaling his new tough approach on the Balkans, a big headline on any normal day, the first lady invited us to the State Dining Room. She wanted to respond to new charges that she'd made a one-hundred-thousand-dollar windfall on cattle futures because of a sweetheart deal with an Arkansas businessman and friend, Jim Blair.

Mrs. Clinton did not routinely hold news conferences, and never answered questions about anything the least bit controversial. The network immediately decided what our priority would be, telling me to turn over the Bosnia story to Jim Miklaszewski and head to the State Dining Room for Hillary. We always referred to it afterward as the "pretty in pink" news conference. Wearing a pink sweaterdress, seated under the famous Lincoln portrait, she calmly answered questions for more than an hour about Whitewater, the death of Vince

Foster, and her Arkansas commodities trading. After avoiding the press for two years, Hillary seemed contrite, blaming any mistakes on "inexperience" with the ways of press relations in Washington. Although she had been widely criticized for making an improbable killing on the complex commodities market until then she had refused to acknowledge that her profits were unusual. To her, investigations into her finances were unfair and intrusive, even though it was obvious that the deal looked like a conflict of interest.

It was a flawless performance, but the first lady still would not admit to any errors of law or judgment in her financial dealings. And behind her calm gaze, I saw a woman still enraged that people would even question her ethics. But pragmatism had overcome her stubbornness. Now that both *Time* and *Newsweek* had stories about her finances on their covers, she sweetly said that after guarding her "zone of privacy" for so long, she had been "rezoned." She was in full damage-control mode.

The first lady's decision finally to go public after nearly two years of silence almost eclipsed what had just happened down the hall, the president's threat to bomb the Bosnian Serbs. Most of his staff had expected the media to focus on Bosnia, a major foreign policy decision. Those in the dark about Hillary's intentions included almost the entire White House brain trust, including Dave Gergen, George Stephanopoulos, and Dee Dee Myers. The lack of coordination showed once again how deeply divided the White House was.

Although the Hillary story got a lot of attention—a full transcript ran in *The New York Times* the next day—the news conference was timed carefully for a Friday afternoon, the burial ground for all administration bad news (fewer people read the Saturday papers). And the Clintons knew a secret: Richard Nixon had fallen into a coma. Within a few hours, both Clintons' appearances were overshadowed by the death of the thirty-seventh president of the United States.

Hillary's press conference did help ease some of the public's doubts about her. At the time her approval rating had dropped to 40 percent, alarming the White House political team. But now her appearance of candor—rattling off facts and figures while looking feminine and nonthreatening—was all part of a calculated strategy. Just as Mike Deaver has said that if Ronald Reagan had been a shoe salesman, Nancy Reagan would have made sure he sold more shoes than anyone else, it is also true that Bill Clinton would never have been president without Hillary. But there's no question that her health care initiative, and her defensiveness over Whitewater, damaged his first term.

Hillary's limited admissions did not stop the momentum of the Whitewater investigation. The scandal began to affect the core goals of the Clinton presidency. A group of moderate Republican senators who'd been considering a health care compromise now saw that the president had been seriously weakened by the scandal. Bob Dole signaled that there was no longer any need to make concessions to the White House. The Republicans were mobilizing, but the Clintons, living in their parallel universe, didn't seem to realize it.

———

With his domestic priorities in trouble, Clinton tried to show he could dominate the international stage. But in those years, he sometimes seemed too small to fill the part. In June of 1994 we went to Normandy for the fiftieth anniversary of D-day. Before crossing the English Channel, we visited the cemetery at Mildenhall Air Force Base, near Cambridge, England where almost four thousand American airmen and soldiers from World War II were buried. It was a foggy morning, with mist hovering over the headstones. Overhead, a retrofitted B-17 "Flying Fortress" bomber flew low over thirty acres of headstones. A band played "Moonlight Serenade," "In the Mood," and "American Patrol," in honor of Glenn Miller, who had never returned from a flight across the channel after entertaining the troops.

In that somber setting, one of the surviving pilots of the war, Treasury Secretary Lloyd Bentsen, gave a remarkable speech. Quietly, Bentsen re-created what it felt like to be flying in the chilly cockpit of his unheated B-24 as he and his crew headed out on their thirty-five bombing runs: "They squeezed that oxygen hose to break up frozen breath, clogging their face masks, and they cranked down the landing gear by hand because the hydraulic lines had been shot out. Scared? Of course, and anyone who wasn't was either a fool or didn't have any imagination." A half century evaporated, and we were flying with him to hit a target we could barely see through the frosted window of his lumbering bomber. In contrast, the forty-eight-year-old president of the United States, the first to have been born after World War II, looked callow. Nothing he could say would be half as memorable.

Only a handful of reporters in the tight pool covered Clinton the next day as he sailed with the queen from Portsmouth on the royal yacht *Britannia,* before transferring to a U.S. aircraft carrier for the rest of the channel crossing. But we had our own adventure, a trip across the channel on an enormous ferry. Only one element was historically accurate. The rough seas were almost as stormy as they'd been on that night fifty years earlier. For a few hours, we tried to get some sleep, in tiny staterooms. (Typically, I stayed up most of the night worrying that I'd miss the alarm, and the landing.)

The more carefree members of the press corps found another diversion, gambling in the ship's casino. In the predawn hours, I looked out my porthole and tried to imagine the terror of being one of those kids in 1944, pitching through black waters on a battleship and having no idea whether they'd even survive the landing. How did they summon the courage to face the onslaught that lay ahead?

June 6 dawned rainy and cold. Our logistics seemed complicated, but they were really very simple. We had to find our locations; prepare for the live broadcast, in what had become a sea of mud; and find the right words to re-create the drama of what had taken place a half-century earlier. We were only pale imitations of the previous generation. They had saved the world. We simply inherited it. It was hard not to feel small in comparison.

Whatever the president was thinking or feeling, his image makers saw an opportunity to enlarge his presence. They staged what they thought would be the perfect television picture: Bill Clinton, looking pensive, winding his way in a solitary walk past the headstones of the American Cemetery at Colleville-sur-Mer. Instead, he looked self-conscious, the walk studied.

Perhaps Ronald Reagan was only acting ten years earlier when he'd delivered his speech at Pointe du Hoc—although I doubt it. Again, the network newscasts focused on how some of the World War II veterans resented the young president for not serving in his generation's war. That 1969 letter to Colonel Holmes of the Arkansas ROTC was still haunting the middle-aged Bill Clinton.

In one of those unexpected twists that define our business, I ended up reporting that night from Normandy Beach on a completely different subject, North Korea's threat to reprocess spent nuclear fuel, potentially the first step toward developing a nuclear weapon. The issue was important because Pyongyang had kicked out the United Nations's nuclear inspectors three months earlier, and no one knew what the secretive kingdom was doing. But after experiencing the D-day commemoration, I was frustrated that I couldn't write about it, and share the stories of the men I'd met that day.

I didn't finish my live report on Korea for *Nightly News* until one in the morning. The network then had someone drive me to Paris to catch up with the rest of the press corps, who had long since filed their reports on tape and gone back for a hot shower and a good meal. By the time I got there, tired, dirty, and hungry, I'd been up for twenty-four hours.

The rest of the trip was pure nostalgia. Bill Clinton, the former Rhodes scholar, went back to Oxford. Ironically, the onetime anti-war protester had to cancel some of his appearances because of student protests over tuition increases and neofascism in Europe.

I hadn't been there since my college years, when I'd visited friends. While Clinton went to a few closed events, we had some downtime and I went for a walk through some of the colleges, reflecting on how close I had come to pursuing an academic life. What if I had done graduate work in English literature at Cambridge, where I'd been accepted after graduating from Penn, instead of taking that copyboy job at KYW? I knew I would not trade the travel and excitement, and yes, the celebrity, of my life in journalism. But part of me was still the English student who loved literature, and imagined myself a college professor.

The European trip was only a brief respite from Whitewater and an array of domestic problems. By the end of the summer, a conservative three-judge panel had fired independent counsel Robert Fiske on a legal technicality. The court ruled that Fiske did not meet the standard of an independent counsel, because he owed his appointment to Clinton's attorney general, Janet Reno. The court replaced Fiske with Kenneth Starr. We didn't know at the time that all the players for an historic showdown were now in place.

———

The political opposition to the Clintons and their programs was well funded and well organized. Hillary, especially, in her role as health-care czar, gave them a lot of ammunition. A more traditional first lady is a lot easier for the public to accept. Even Nancy Reagan paid a heavy price for exercising her power over the West Wing. Other presidents' wives, like Barbara Bush, wielded enormous power behind the scenes, but they didn't telegraph it. They avoided arousing too much critical scrutiny.

Hillary Clinton was more up front about her power, but that became part of her undoing. Late that summer, the president was asked at a press conference whether, having been elected with only 43 percent of the vote, he was exceeding his mandate with his legislative ambitions. Was he trying to do too much, too fast? It was a telling question. The other factor was unspoken: was he also permitting his spouse to take on too big a political role, on too important a domestic issue?

At the end of September, George Mitchell, the Senate majority leader, officially declared health care dead, telling a news conference, "It is clear that health insurance reform cannot be enacted this year." He couldn't marshal the sixty Senate votes needed to cut off an inevitable Republican filibuster. It was a terrible blow to both Clintons, but especially the first lady. It also emboldened Newt Gingrich to try to nationalize the midterm elections, challenging the entire Clinton legislative agenda with a revolutionary "Contract with America." Gingrich and his troops were clever, promising balanced budgets and a new breed of "citizen legislators" who would serve briefly and return to the private sector.

It was a rout. The Republican victory on November 8 gave the minority party control of both houses of Congress, for the first time in nearly half a century. High-profile election night victims included the speaker of the House, our good friend Tom Foley, defeated in his own district. Tom shares a birthday with Alan and, as part of an informal club of other March 6 birthday boys, celebrates with him each year. Tom's loss added to the sense that a revolution had in fact taken place in Washington.

Clinton was in shock, clearly depressed. It was the first time I saw him completely overwhelmed by a political loss. He knew that by losing the House to Gingrich, he was going to be beleaguered for the rest of his term. The self-proclaimed "change agent" was unable to achieve his most important goal, reforming the health-care sysem, and to many in the White House, the first lady was to blame.

———

The White House and Congress were undergoing a wrenching change, and so was my little world. The new president of NBC News, Andrew Lack, had fixed problems he'd inherited at the *Today* show and *Dateline,* and eventually focused on *Nightly News.* He wanted to put a rising star destined to be the network's next *Nightly News* anchorman, Brian Williams, at the White House. I had mixed feelings, of course, but knew that the timing was right. I wanted to cover more foreign policy, and moving out of the White House would take me further from any potential conflict with Alan, a presidential appointee. To make it more interesting, Tim Russert created a new beat for me, encompassing national security and the intelligence community, as well as the State Department and diplomacy.

I'd be able to cover foreign policy from a broader perspective than had been done previously, with a mandate to travel.

The issues were familiar: North Korea and its nuclear threat; ethnic cleansing in the Balkans; the conflict between Israel and the Palestinians; the desperation of Haiti; the spread of global terrorism; Castro's Cuba; and, of course, Iraq. The challenge would be to get out of the State Department and make these stories come alive for our viewers. I was excited, but realistic enough to know that I had to create my own breaks. There would no longer be the White House stage, nor the NBC team of producers to perform their logistical magic.

Before I left the White House, the first lady invited me to a farewell tea. I quickly realized that she had more in mind than making a kind gesture to a departing correspondent. After chatting about my plans and her projects, she revealed her real agenda by asking, "What do we do about Chris? Would it help if we got him a TV coach?"

With unusual candor, Mrs. Clinton was confiding her concern that the secretary of state, Warren Christopher, wasn't a good enough communicator to sell the president's policies. The Clintons felt that their problems could be fixed if "Chris," as he was known, could be a more effective spokesman on the Sunday talk shows. The administration was focusing on public relations, not substance. I soon learned from friends of the Clintons that the first lady and her husband had also raised the issue with advisors inside and outside of the White House. In fact, it had gone even further: Clinton intimate and Washington superlawyer Vernon Jordan had already approached Colin Powell to see if he would accept an offer to be secretary of state. Powell had turned it down.

Shortly after arriving at the State Department, I collected more information about the president's dissatisfaction with his secretary of state from other sources, enough to file a story for *Nightly News*. Unfortunately, it was painful to Warren Christopher, who probably deserved more loyalty from the Clintons than he received.

Clinton was, by this point, becoming better liked and respected by foreign leaders. For Boris Yeltsin, Clinton was a lifeline. Similarly, Clinton and Germany's Helmut Kohl, also a man of large appetites, seemed to enjoy one another's company, especially over a big meal. On one visit to Washington, Clinton took Kohl to lunch at an Italian restaurant in Georgetown, where the chef informed them, "There is no spa cuisine here, our motto is *abbondanza.*" Abundance. What an understatement.

As Maureen Dowd of *The New York Times* reported, the two leaders, whose combined weight was around five hundred pounds, each ate cold and hot antipasti; fried calamari; and ravioli stuffed with veal, cheese, and spinach, and topped with marinara sauce. In addition the president had a Tuscan soup with white beans, tomato, and spinach. They washed down the repast with a full-bodied Brunello di Montalcino, and followed with a dessert of zabaglione and berries. An aide was seen taking a chocolate cake back to the White House—perhaps for an afternoon snack?

In contrast, Secretary of State Christopher was rail thin, a man of intense discipline and no obvious bad habits. The State Department was not going to be nearly as colorful, or as much fun, as the beat I was leaving. It was more buttoned down than the scrappier White House, and much more careful about responding to questions. At the same time, the people at State were thoughtful, and, mercifully, the assignment kept me off the firing line of reporting on the president's sexual adventures when the Monica Lewinsky story broke a few years later.

———

During the Clinton years, my own personal life took a dramatic turn. Alan and I had been dating since 1984, and by the mid-1990s we were committed to each other. Most of our friends were wondering why we didn't take the legal step to "sanctify" our relationship. It just was so much easier to keep things unofficial, given the challenges of marriage between a correspondent and a public official.

We'd known each other and dated before he was in government, so I felt our relationship was outside the boundaries of our new roles, as long as we kept our professional lives separate. Obviously there were times when they overlapped. I once bumped into Lloyd Bentsen, then the treasury secretary, outside the Oval Office, on a morning after he'd been at our house for dinner. Some of the other reporters were a little startled when he said, "Oh, Andrea, I was going to write you a note; we had such a good time last night." Clearly it was an awkward moment for the other reporters as well as for me.

Alan and I both traveled a lot, but given our respective schedules, rarely together. I did begin attending the annual Federal Reserve conferences in Jackson Hole, Wyoming, each summer. People were becoming accustomed to us being together, but I'm sure it was off-putting in some circles that we weren't a legal couple.

In October of 1996, Alan gave me a surprise birthday party at one of our favorite Italian restaurants and made a lovely, affectionate toast. Few of our Washington friends had ever heard him speak so emotionally or sentimentally. Our close friends Elaine Wolfensohn and Jim Lehrer, who were seated next to each other, thought that he was about to propose in front of everyone. Elaine still says it was Alan's basic proposal; it was just that none of us, including me, recognized it at the time. We were heading toward marriage, but I'm not sure I realized it, even then. My birthday gift? A diamond ring, though not in a traditional engagement setting. I still didn't get it.

That Christmas Day, we joined Judy Woodruff and Al Hunt and their children for breakfast and to open gifts, as we always do. Later, back home, we were sitting in the den when Alan asked whether I wanted a big wedding or a small one. Finally, even I understood what was up. That was as close to a proposal as he came. I guess you could call it an evasive proposal, as ambiguous as some of his testimony before government committees. As he once told Congress, if you think you have understood me, you must be mistaken. He thought it was more fun to propose in Greenspeak, as I call his testimony. He swears that he had asked me to marry him three previous times, and that I hadn't understood what he'd been saying.

By then, Judy and Al and the children had already left for Vail, as they do every year on Christmas Day. We reached them there that night to share our news, but didn't tell anyone else except family. We had invited friends for dinner later in the week—Kay Graham, Sally Quinn, and Ben Bradlee, among others—on the twelfth anniversary of our first date. With everybody sitting in the dining room, we told our friends we were engaged. Kate Lehrer was at home sick, but Jim was there, and he jumped up and ran to the telephone to tell her. Kay Graham shrieked. No one had imagined that we'd ever become respectable.

The next challenge was finding time in our schedules to get married. Should it be before or after Alan's semiannual testimony to Congress? And how to plan a wedding, when the State Department gave reporters so little advance notice of foreign trips? At Alan's suggestion, we decided to get married in April at the most romantic place we knew, the Inn at Little Washington, in Virginia. We had a wedding lunch, on a Sunday afternoon. It was small by design, because we knew that between NBC and the Federal Reserve, we had too many friends from work to accommodate everyone. The occasion was very celebratory, with just our closest friends and family. My sister, Susan Greenstein, was my matron of honor and my goddaughter Lauren Hunt, was our flower girl. She was terrified. Ruth Bader Ginsburg agreed to perform the ceremony, making it that much more meaningful. Our friend Oscar de la Renta designed my dress.

We wanted to get married outside, in the Inn's garden, but when the day dawned, bright and sunny, the forecast was still for rain. We had ordered a tent, and reluctantly agreed that it should be set up. I made one last call to our local NBC weatherman, Bob Ryan, who confirmed that it would, in fact, rain. But I was so eager for a garden wedding that at the last minute, I called ahead and told the Inn to take the tent down. As Alan and I drove out through the Virginia countryside, it started to sprinkle. As he nervously rehearsed our vows, he looked up impishly when he got to "in sickness and in health," and said, "in rain and in shine." The weather held for another hour, but just as we were being declared husband and wife, it started to pour. I'm told it's good luck.

We weren't planning to go on a honeymoon, because we both had too much work to do. But the festivities continued the following evening, when our friends Elaine and Jim Wolfensohn gave us a beautiful wedding reception at their Washington home so we could include many friends who'd not been to the ceremony. The next night, we went to a state dinner, our first as a married couple. I wore a black lace gown, also designed by Oscar, and although the dinner was in honor of the prime minister of Canada, it felt as though we were still celebrating our marriage.

I was seated at the president's table, next to Dan Aykroyd, and across from Marylouise Oates, a writer and political activist who had been in the antiwar movement with the Clintons in the 1960s. At some point, Aykroyd, the president, and Marylouise all started singing the Beatles song, "I Saw Her Standing There." Looking around, I tried to reconcile the cultural dissonance of a group of baby boomers—including the president of the United States—singing anthems of our youth, beneath the solemn portrait of Abraham Lincoln in the State Dining Room.

At the dinner, Marylouise and her husband, political consultant Bob Shrum, were shocked that Alan and I had not taken time off to go on a honeymoon. "You should go to Venice," they suggested.

So we did. Typically, we did it a little differently: instead of taking a leisurely trip, we tacked our honeymoon onto a previously scheduled monetary conference in Switzerland where Alan was speaking. How many brides get to listen to German chancellor Helmut Kohl give a luncheon speech on their honeymoon? And how many travel with a security detail?

We spent our honeymoon weekend at the luxurious Cipriani Hotel in Venice where I had covered Ronald Reagan at the 1987 economic summit, exactly ten years earlier. Alan's security agents from the Federal Reserve tried to give us as much privacy as they could, but it was impossible to be anonymous. We even saw Shrum and Marylouise, along with her sister and nephew. By the end of the weekend, our little traveling party had expanded to include the Shrums, their family, Alan's agents, and assorted other friends. It was a wonderful trip, possibly because we did it in such a casual way.

Except for our stays at a tennis retreat in California each summer, we don't often plan vacations. One of the things I regret most is that we haven't seen much of the world together. Because we each travel so much for work, when we have time with each other, we really don't want to be on the road. Instead, we'd rather be at home doing easy things, like reading, watching baseball on television, or listening to music. Not surprisingly, we're both news junkies.

Once I married Alan, it was hard for me to know if people viewed me differently. There is a glamorous side to our life together, but it often conflicts with the demands of my job.

For instance, on New Year's Eve in 1999, we were invited to the Millennium Dinner in the Clinton White House, but I couldn't primp because I'd been at work since five o'clock that morning covering events on the Mall. Still, how many people who love music are fortunate enough to spend New Year's Eve at the White House with musicians like Pinchas Zukerman? On another occasion, Yo-Yo Ma even offered to come to Washington and play chamber music with us if Alan and I would once again practice our instruments. Alan had occasionally picked up his clarinet, but after so many years away from the violin, I'm afraid even to play for myself, much less perform with the world's greatest cellist. I often tell myself that someday, if I ever stop chasing news stories long enough to take lessons, I'll see if I can still play.

Of course, after so many years covering the White House, it's a completely different experience to go to events as a guest with my husband. But as grand as White House social occasions are, even they pale in comparison to a truly royal event, when Alan received a knighthood from Her Majesty, Queen Elizabeth. The private ceremony took place at Balmoral Castle, the royal family's summer residence in Scotland. The schedule was typical Greenspan. Alan and I flew to London overnight, where he gave five separate speeches in one day. After a night's sleep, we flew to Scotland, drove to the castle, had the knighting ceremony, lunched with the queen, drove back to the airport, flew to Heathrow, and switched planes back to Washington. All in forty-eight hours.

The Palace had briefed me on what to wear. A suit would be appropriate. I had fussed over every detail, and learned the required protocol. Not surprisingly, the most important caution was to avoid discussing anything political. When we arrived, the welcome was much warmer and less formal than I'd anticipated. The queen was dressed comfortably, in a kilt and cashmere sweater set. We played with her Welsh corgis, met her special breed of "dorgis" (a dachshund-corgi mix), and were invited to lunch with her, Prince Philip, a favorite cousin, and a few other guests from the Foreign Ministry and British Treasury. Also interesting was the castle itself, one of the queen's personal residences that had been built as a retreat for Queen Victoria and Prince Albert.

The rules were very clear about not talking to the press afterward. But CNBC had sent a camera crew from London to try to get Alan to comment outside the Balmoral grounds. Much to my discomfort, given that I work for the same network, we had to drive by without stopping. I later learned they'd been waiting since before dawn. In fact, during lunch, the queen complained that her ride around the estate that morning had been ruined when lights from a television crew frightened her horse. I was mortified.

The queen's estate was certainly a great distance from the Jewish neighborhood in East London where my father's family had lived in the nineteenth century. But while my life is sometimes a bit of a fairy tale, there are downsides to being married to a public figure. A week after our wedding, on a Sunday morning, Alan was playing golf and I was straightening the house when I heard a huge ruckus outside. We live on a narrow, winding road, but when I looked through the front window, there were five buses out front, and hundreds of people jamming onto our walkway and front porch.

They were community activists from Chicago, in town for a convention, targeting Alan—unfairly—for his community investment policies, which they misunderstood. They papered our quiet little neighborhood with fliers featuring a photocopied picture of Alan in white tie and tails. The caption? "Alan, while you're on your honeymoon, we're being screwed."

I was vaguely amused, until they tramped through my flower garden. Alarmed, the neighbors called to see if I needed help. Their kids had run inside to say, "Guess what, the Greenspans are having a party." Some party.

Aside from occasional protestors on the front porch, marriage means having a best friend, a partner in times of celebration as well as when times are tough. No matter how unpredictable my schedule because of breaking news, Alan has never complained—to me—about my last-minute schedule changes, or midnight arrivals from the office. His mantra is, "Your work comes first." Sometimes I wish he were more demanding—it might inspire me, occasionally, to turn down an assignment!

My one regret is that I can't share enough of what Alan does because he can't discuss his work. There are long stretches when I have no idea what he's even thinking about. When he was fresh to this job, I found it difficult, not being able to ask him about his work at the end of the day, especially since I'm a reporter, and by nature nosy. But I make it a practice never to put him on guard or make him uncomfortable. I know he will explain what he's been doing, once it becomes public.

Then, of course, we have to deal with the challenge of media coverage. For a while, CNBC would track Alan's arrivals at the Fed on days when the Federal Open Market Committee was meeting to set interest rates. The business network had what they called their "briefcase index," predicting either a rate hike or a cut depending on the size of the briefcase he was carrying that day. A thin briefcase meant lower rates. A fat briefcase meant a rate increase. It was very funny, but clearly they didn't know the score. I had bought him two briefcases for Christmas, and if he was carrying a lot of books, he took one, and not the other. It had absolutely nothing to do with monetary policy.

It was all done in good fun, but Alan became more and more of an icon, especially after Bob Woodward's book about economic policy making in the Clinton White House, *Maestro*. Woodward's book characterized Alan as a central character in Clinton's decision making, which probably assigned Alan too much credit and, perhaps, set him up for those who then wanted to bring him down a peg or two. Woodward's book certainly made Alan even more widely known— and frankly, that makes him slightly uncomfortable.

The real secret about Alan is that he does not take himself, or anyone else, very seriously. When I'm a guest on *Imus in the Morning,* Don often refers to Alan as Crazy Al. Somehow, it seems to fit.

The dialogue goes: "Where is Crazy Al?"

Because it is usually seven in the morning, or even earlier, the true answer is, "He's in the bathtub," because it is Alan's habit to soak in the tub in the morning, which helps him to concentrate on his reading. It started out when he had back trouble years ago, and it's been his daily habit ever since.

Don then says, "Well, put him on; let me talk to him."

All of us know that if I put Don Imus and Alan Greenspan on live radio together, it would be a disaster—economically, maritally, and professionally. This is a man who has not given an interview since 1987 to anyone, on either radio or television. If he were to go on *Imus in the Morning,* Lord knows what the impact would be on the financial markets.

For reasons of loyalty and friendship, he did give one interview immediately after getting the Fed job, to David Brinkley for his

Sunday morning program. It did not go very well. I think Alan hadn't yet adjusted to the difference between being a frequent guest and commentator, as he had been for years on these talk shows, and being Fed chairman. The markets interpreted his comments in one fashion, and the newspapers another. After that, he decided that the simplest thing was not to do any interviews, a rule he has maintained.

For people who think I have some inside track to Fed decisions, my most embarrassing rejoinder is what happened in December 1996. Alan was giving a speech and told me it would be a retrospective on the history of the Federal Reserve, but that I might find it interesting. Of course, it turned out to be the famous speech by which he was attempting to puncture, in part, the stock market bubble by speaking of "irrational exuberance." To my chagrin, when he returned to the table from the podium and asked me what was the most important thing he'd said, I had completely missed the lead. It's a good thing he doesn't rely on me for fiscal or monetary advice.

Few people know how funny and sweet my husband can be. Except for our close friends and family, people might think him aloof. In fact, he is constitutionally shy. But he is constantly amusing, invariably curious, and always emotionally and intellectually supportive. All of which was important when I left the confines of the Clinton White House and embarked on a series of adventures as a foreign correspondent.

CHAPTER 7

Foreign Correspondent

Of all the tough leaders I've encountered, Hafez al Assad is the only one who managed to shut me up, much to the amusement of the president of the United States. Bill Clinton flew to Damascus in October of 1994 because of signals from Syria that Assad, Israel's implacable enemy, was finally rethinking his refusal to consider peace. The president's first meeting with Assad, nine months earlier, had created an opening for serious contacts. Separately, peace talks between Syria and Israel at a lower level were followed by secret negotiations. Now Assad's former patrons in the Soviet Union were gone. The United States, with a coalition that included Syrian troops, had defeated Saddam Hussein in the first Gulf War. Israel and Jordan had just signed a peace accord, and, for the first time, the Syrian dictator seemed willing to consider an opening to the West.

I landed in Damascus on Air Force One, accompanying Clinton as the pool reporter for the American networks. The rest of the press corps, on a larger charter plane, would not arrive for hours. Being the sole broadcaster covering the president in a country like Syria requires you to be more uncompromising than you might otherwise be: you have to insist on access to all public events, despite obstacles.

To do otherwise would be to deny your colleagues information that is rightfully theirs. But being the pool reporter in a country run by a dictator like Assad presents special challenges.

No American president had been to Damascus in two decades. It was too risky, diplomatically and politically, because of Syria's support for terrorism and its domination of Lebanon. Assad has been compared to Machiavelli or a Mafia boss. I think his talent for political survival was more particular to the Middle East. In a region of bullies, he had figured out how to be the toughest guy on the corner. For fifteen years, he had incited rival Lebanese groups to kill each other. When they didn't rise to the bait, he sent his agents to assassinate their leaders. He'd driven Yasser Arafat out of Tripoli into exile in Tunis. After years of reporting on terror attacks linked to Assad, I had no idea what to expect. But as it turned out, the Syrian strongman had no idea what to expect from me, either.

A realist, Assad knew he would eventually have to make peace with Israel. Now the White House believed he was ready to deal, if Israel would withdraw completely from the Syrian territory it had occupied since 1967 on the Golan Heights. Israel's prime minister, Yitzhak Rabin, agreed that the signals were promising and encouraged Clinton to go. So one day after participating in signing ceremonies for an historic peace agreement between Jordan and Israel, Clinton headed to Damascus to meet the Syrian leader on his own turf.

Assad had not survived for so many decades without protecting himself from internal and external enemies. Clearly, the American press corps represented a real and present danger—at least, that's what you'd have to conclude from the way his security treated us when we arrived. Syrian police went through everything in our bags, and I mean everything. Our personal hygiene products were taken apart. Medication was analyzed. In my case, contact lens fluid was viewed as highly suspicious. Since this was long before such searches became routine at American airports in the wake of 9/11, it seemed extraordinarily invasive, especially when applied to a handful of reporters who'd just disembarked from the security bubble of Air Force One.

The drive to the ceremonial palace where Clinton and Assad would meet was not any more welcoming. The White House advance man told us how the landscape along the highway had been transformed in the previous week. Decrepit housing had been torn down, trees planted, the ground painted green to appear lush. At sixty miles an hour, it looked pretty real. It was another Potemkin Village, as we'd seen years earlier during Ronald Reagan's trip to the DMZ in Korea. Dictators, it seemed, were very good at creating stage sets.

After the high-speed motorcade ride, Assad's enormous white marble palace loomed at the top of a hill, dominating the landscape. It was monolithic, forbidding, and sterile, since it was used only for ceremonial events. Once inside, past another security barrier with a full pat-down body check, we were given our marching orders by the Syrian equivalent of a presidential press secretary—that is, if they'd had a press corps covering their president. We were told there would be a press opportunity, but only for cameras. No writers would be permitted. As the only representative for the networks, I told the White House that we would not allow our cameras to cover the meeting without an editorial presence to report the facts and surroundings—standard rules. After huddling with their Syrian counterparts, Clinton aides told us Assad's men had backed down, but only if I pledged not to ask a question. I made no such promise, as they knew I wouldn't. Just before I entered the room, the Syrians reminded me once more not to say a word. I simply smiled.

Clinton and Assad's meeting earlier in the year in Geneva was during a stopover on the president's return from his Moscow summit. At the time, Clinton was facing a storm over Whitewater at home, but squeezed in six hours of talks with Assad to set up what he hoped could develop into a new peace track between Syria and Israel. During their joint news conference, Assad had given the White House new hope of a breakthrough by declaring that Syria could have "normal peaceful relations" with Israel if a treaty were negotiated. But he avoided spelling out what "normal" meant. Now Clinton was in Damascus to see what Assad might be willing to deliver.

I lined up with the camera crew, mentally rehearsing possible questions to ask. Even if I got lucky, there would be only one opportunity at best. Should I try to get Assad on the record about Israel or terrorism? If I dared to ask a question, what would happen to the camera crew? Assad and Clinton were sitting in armchairs, on either side of a coffee table, not unlike the arrangement in the Oval Office. I waited just long enough to make sure I was not interrupting their small talk, and asked the Syrian dictator why he still supported terrorism—hoping to provoke any kind of response.

The White House and Syrian presidential aides were flabbergasted. No reporter, and certainly not a woman, had ever dared ask Hafez al Assad a question at a photo opportunity. To my amazement, instead of ignoring me, he began to answer, vigorously challenging the premise of my question. As he did later in a joint news conference with Clinton, Assad denied that anyone could name one incident in which Syria had committed a terrorist act. But before he could finish, I suddenly felt myself being lifted off the ground. With the cameras safely focused on the presidents, two burly Syrian security men had come up from behind, grabbed me under the elbows, and were carrying me out of the room. To my amazement, Assad continued to answer my question, but effectively, I was silenced. If I'd protested against what the thugs were doing, I would have interrupted Assad, and ruined the photo opportunity for all of our later broadcasts.

Watching me be ejected so ignominiously greatly amused Clinton, who doubled over with laughter. He later told me that he'd finally found a way to shut me up. Perhaps, but it didn't last long. As I'd learned with Frank Rizzo, Don Regan, and assorted scoundrels, "talking back" to presidents and dictators was second nature to me. No matter how much they meant not to, sometimes they responded, in spite of themselves.

Clinton's visit to Damascus did not create the breakthrough he'd sought. In private, Assad agreed to condemn terrorism, a commitment Clinton wanted before he would agree to peace talks. But in public, afterward, Assad denied that terrorism had even come up. The president had put his prestige on the line, as he did repeatedly during his two terms in pursuit of a Middle East peace, only to be disappointed. After the hope and optimism of witnessing the treaty signing between Israel and Jordan a day earlier, Syria brought Clinton back to the grinding reality of Middle East diplomacy. It was never going to be easy.

My trip to Damascus that fall was my last foreign assignment as a White House correspondent. Soon I discovered the new challenges of traveling on my own, without the communication gear and assorted spear-carriers that accompany the White House. Perhaps I could have started with an easier venue, like Paris. For whatever reason, for my debut as a solo actor the news gods chose the poorest and least-developed country in the Western hemisphere, Haiti.

———

Haiti is the kind of place that grabs your heart, and never lets go. It is not only poor; it has been ravaged by corrupt politicians, ruthless generals, and a small group of ruling families that have left it polluted, violent, and desolate. The disparities between the elites and the rest of the population are overwhelming. The rich live elegantly in villas draped in bougainvillea and other luxuriant plants. The rest of the people are among the least educated, most superstitious, and most victimized in the region.

I flew into Port-au-Prince in February 1995, five months after twenty thousand American troops had deposed Haiti's military dictators and restored the elected president, Jean-Bertrand Aristide. An experienced NBC producer, Joe Alicastro, had organized a team on the ground, but for the first time in many years, I was traveling outside the cocoon of the White House press corps. When you land in a Third World country with the president of the United States, advance teams from the White House and the networks have already installed computer lines, direct-dial telephones to the States, computerized video screening and editing equipment, TV monitors—the works.

To maintain security, the White House travel office—the same office the Clintons had purged when they first arrived—makes all the other arrangements. Fax machines? Copiers? Printers? Ready to go. The networks and print media jointly pay for all this. It is in the interest of both sides to work together: the White House wants the president's activities to be reported; the news organizations want to transmit their stories instantaneously from remote locations. But all this proximity can breed too much coziness for our own good.

My first night in Haiti was in sharp contrast to the ten years I'd spent on the White House beat. U.S. troops had established martial law, but gangs still roamed the streets. Our NBC team had found rooms in a run-down guesthouse called the Hotel Idéale. The conditions inside were anything but. For starters, it had neither running water nor its own generator. Undressing in the dark, longing for a shower, I wondered what I'd gotten myself into. I had flashbacks to my first foreign trip for NBC almost two decades earlier in Guyana, when I was still trying to figure out the basics, like how to get my stories filed. Surely, I had learned enough in the intervening years to handle this.

By morning, we'd started to figure out how to rise to the challenge. NBC flew in a gas generator to power our equipment so that we could edit our stories. Joe Alicastro and I huddled over TV monitors with flashlights to screen the video our camera crews had shot. As the deadline for *Nightly News* approached each evening, two Haitian drivers, Andre and Sergo, rocketed down the rutted streets of Port-au-Prince to get us to the satellite uplink. Along the way, we had to dodge chickens, dogs, protestors, and streams of raw sewage, sometimes all at the same time.

When you arrive in Port-au-Prince, the first thing that strikes you is how vibrant the colors are. Buses, buildings, fences, clothing, everything is brightly painted in primary hues. On closer inspection, you see the reality behind this brightly colored landscape: a dark, grinding poverty, the worst in the Western hemisphere. Everywhere you look, there are barefoot children, unpaved streets, filthy alleys, and ramshackle houses. Quickly, you're hit by the smells—fumes from open sewers make you gag. This was true a decade ago, before the economy was further starved by additional years of local and international neglect. It is difficult to imagine what could be left after killer hurricanes slammed into Haiti in 2004. What additional plague can be brought upon the heads of these people?

We relocated to a real hotel that had everything you'd want except a computer connection. There was one pay telephone with long-distance service. In those days, before wireless connections, if you timed it correctly you could manually pulse-dial the laptop to send scripts to New York. Occasionally, it worked. The capital city itself was a cauldron of political intrigue. Jean-Bertrand Aristide, the populist poet-priest who had spent his exile courting politicians in Washington, was safely reinstalled at the Presidential Palace. Rival political factions plotted against each other, reflecting the sharp class differences that divided Haiti's masses—Aristide followers—from the mercantile class and the military.

As often happens in Haiti, first impressions can be misleading. While we waited for President Clinton's envoys, former president Jimmy Carter, Senator Sam Nunn, and former chairman of the Joint Chiefs of Staff Colin Powell, we passed a parade in the main streets near the Presidential Palace. Was it to celebrate the return of the trio that had helped negotiate the departure of Haiti's dictators and restore Aristide to power five months earlier? To the contrary, it was to protest Carter's call for what would be the country's first democratic elections. Aristide's followers didn't want elections or any part of representative democracy. They took to the streets, chanting that they wanted to make Aristide "president for life."

Carter, Nunn, and Powell offered intriguing contrasts in diplomacy. When the three had first gone to Haiti the previous fall to negotiate the departure of the generals, White House officials told me they'd sent Powell to make sure Carter didn't cut too easy a deal. They thought of it as "babysitting" Carter, reflecting the president's suspicion that Carter would compromise too quickly. Despite similar backgrounds, the two presidents were not close. Clinton did not even want Carter to attend the Democratic convention in 1996. The tension between them had deep roots. Clinton had long resented Carter for relocating Cuban boat people to Arkansas when Clinton was in his first term as governor. He lost his reelection, he thought, because of voter anger over a prison riot by these unwelcome immigrants. (At the dedication of Clinton's presidential library in Little Rock in the fall of 2004, Carter said he wanted to apologize, acknowledging, "I made some mistakes in 1980 during the Mariel boat lift, and the presence of Cuban refugees in Arkansas may have cost him his reelection.")

The friction between these two Southern Democrats worsened after Clinton became president when Carter took it upon himself to go to North Korea to resolve a crisis over nuclear inspections. For more than twenty-four hours, despite attempts by the National Security Council to reach him, he kept the president and vice president in the dark. Not hearing from the former president, they couldn't answer our questions about how the negotiations had gone. When they finally found out, it was only by watching Carter live on CNN, the network owned by his close friend and benefactor Ted Turner. Clinton did not quickly forgive Carter's breach of protocol and common courtesy.

The Clinton administration wanted to get out as fast as it could, even if it was before Haiti was stable. American troops would depart on schedule and be replaced by a smaller, less-experienced force of United Nations peacekeepers. Badly burned by his experience with the American deployment in Somalia two years earlier, Clinton had only reluctantly agreed even to send troops to Haiti. He remembered all too well how, during his first year in office, armed Haitians had blocked a U.S. troop ship, the USS *Harlan County,* from docking in Port-au-Prince. The ship's humiliating retreat became a metaphor for the president's continuing struggle to be accepted by the military, and to be seen as a strong commander in chief.

Now, despite his promise to stay long enough to restore electricity and other services, Clinton was planning to pull out U.S. troops. The country still had rolling blackouts, and without reliable power and telephones, businesses would not return. Seventy-five percent of the people were unemployed. Hunger was rampant, traffic impossible, garbage everywhere. To provide additional security, Clinton national security advisor Tony Lake, Aristide's chief supporter within the administration, had advised the Haitian leader to retain some of the country's military officers. But fearing another coup, Aristide defied the White House and fired the entire army.

That left the country with no military, no functioning police force, and virtually no criminal justice system. I went with Nunn and Powell to Haiti's national prison, where only eighteen inmates of 580 had even seen a judge. Criminals were simply warehoused. People waited months, even years, before being charged. On a micro scale, and without the challenge of a well-armed insurrection, it was not unlike trying to create order out of chaos in Baghdad today. To accomplish this, the administration imported an experienced police administrator, former—and future—New York City police commissioner Ray Kelly.

Kelly, a tough, take-charge Irishman with the crew cut of a former marine, was undaunted by the chaos of Haiti's streets. One day, he took me with him as he made his rounds in Port-au-Prince during Carnival week, Haiti's version of Mardi Gras. The celebration seemed to get more frantic as we moved into the more desperately poor areas of the city. At one point Kelly pushed through a mob to prevent a crowd from lynching a bicycle thief. Haitians had developed their own kind of instant justice. "You can't do this in Haiti anymore," shouted the marine translator in Haiti's vernacular Creole patois.

My expert cameraman, Maurice Roper, captured the entire incident: Kelly grabbing the accused thief with one arm while shouting at the screaming lynch mob to get back. The scene encapsulated the chaos of the streets. You could see the terror in the face of the Haitian victim, surrounded by a threatening crowd of thugs. Yet, somehow the mob backed down under the sheer moral force of a single law enforcement official. The confrontation was captured on tape, a vivid example that violence could erupt at any moment. At the same time, the populace was prepared to respond to authority, but the American soldiers would not be there long enough to assert it.

Kelly's multinational force had eight hundred police from twenty-seven countries, including Jordan and Pakistan. For their governments, "blue-helmet" duty in a multinational force was a good source of income. The UN paid a healthy stipend for the use of foreign troops. But flying north with Kelly on a helicopter tour of outlying towns, we learned that food for the police had not been delivered, and they wouldn't be paid for another two weeks. Kelly needed to resolve the problem quickly. An earlier police pay dispute had become violent, turning into a riot. In that incident, Kelly had also waded in to rescue the victims, helping to evacuate the wounded and retrieve the bodies of the dead.

In a northern town, we saw the depth of the squalor and degradation of Haiti's scandalous prison system. Behind the gates of a stone and iron enclosure, inmates crouched on mud floors in buildings nearly two centuries old. If they had committed murders, the inmates told us, it wasn't of their own volition. They were under a spell cast by voodoo spirits.

A month later, the United Nations took over, and Ray Kelly's work was done. He had given up electricity and plumbing and seeing his family for six months in order to give the Haitians a head start toward creating some civil order. Did he succeed? No outsider could have in such a brief period. When I returned a year later to cover Haiti's first elections since the military coup, I saw that the political and economic divisions between Aristide and the elites had deepened. Unable to run again by law, Aristide couldn't succeed himself, but he could undermine the chances of his successor, Rene Preval.

An agronomist who was serious about transforming Haiti's economy, Preval was quiet, disciplined, and utterly lacking in charisma. I interviewed him the morning after his election, and he promised to take on the tough economic issues that Aristide had ignored.

To my surprise, Preval tried to deliver, challenging the ruling families who had been running Haiti's few lucrative industries as private monopolies for generations. He refused to fuel inflation by printing money, tried to privatize state businesses, opened the country to competition, and enforced the tax code. On a trip to Washington, he quickly impressed Clinton and his national security team.

But Republicans, led by Jesse Helms, viewed him as no improvement over Aristide. Haiti was a convenient way of attacking Clinton's foreign policy. Helms blocked millions of dollars in aid until Preval investigated dozens of political killings that had occurred during Aristide's reign. But without friends, Preval had little authority to investigate anything, and none of his predecessor's mass appeal. With Aristide undercutting him at every turn, the new leader couldn't form a cabinet or pass his austerity program. Without the required economic reforms, Haiti would not be able to qualify for $1.2 billion from the World Bank and International Monetary Fund that might have brought it back from disaster.

The Clinton administration had lost interest in Haiti's continuing nightmare. Boat people were no longer washing up on Miami's shores, and the White House no longer felt pressure to find a solution. Haiti was abandoned until its next crisis.

I felt guilty about our short attention span, and worried that we had left the story too quickly. Two years later, I talked the network into sending me back to cover Haiti's first legislative elections under the new regime. Little had changed. Mounds of garbage still blocked the streets. Unemployment remained at 80 percent. Pollution was rampant. Hunger, disease, and illiteracy were still the worst in the

Western hemisphere. The U.S. and international aid groups had helped spark riots by demanding painful budget cuts, government layoffs, and other economic reforms. Investors were still reluctant to return because of continuing violence, despite America's best efforts to train a new police force. The head of the State Department's Agency for International Development told me it was "a little like the Wild West" in our country—and it would take more time to develop a system of laws.

In legislative elections, fewer than 10 percent of the people even bothered to vote. Why should they trust the ballot box? American election observers told me tally sheets were altered. Ballot boxes were stuffed. In half the provinces the police ordered people to vote for their favorite candidates. After so much promise of reform, democracy was still a distant hope. Without U.S. troops on the island, it was difficult to persuade the network that Haiti's plight was a story of interest to an American audience. After filing a few reports, I was told to come home. I left our Haitian staff, Andre and Sergo, with a real sense of failure and loss.

In 2004, Haiti blew up again. By then Aristide was back in power, after sitting out one term. But the man who had inspired so much hope a decade earlier had come full circle. His dictatorial style of governing was inspiring the same kind of rebellion that had helped him replace the military dictators. Aristide's former supporters turned against him and were marching on the capital. Even Jimmy Carter, Aristide's most prominent American supporter, concluded that the Haitian leader had become politically corrupted. And over the course of the past decade, Haiti had become a serious strategic threat to the United States, a major transshipping point for millions of dollars of cocaine destined for the United States. U.S. investigators believed 8 percent of the illegal drugs arriving in this country came through Haiti, but Aristide's government had not arrested or prosecuted a single major drug trafficker in more than a year.

Aristide was now threatened by a rebel army approaching from the north and a student movement for peaceful change demonstrating in the streets of Port-au-Prince. Secretary of State Colin Powell signaled the Haitian leader that he should consider stepping down peacefully. In Port-au-Prince the U.S. ambassador, James Foley, carried out back-channel negotiations. Under heavy U.S. pressure, Aristide agreed, but only after the Americans promised to help him escape with his family, his bodyguards, and, State Department and Haitian officials claim, a considerable fortune. Even his departure was controversial. Once safely in temporary exile, Aristide told members of the Congressional Black Caucus that U.S. officials had kidnapped him and even dictated his letter of resignation.

An angry Powell told me it was absurd, "absolutely baseless," and that Aristide had left voluntarily after negotiating his own terms. In fact, Powell had made fifty calls between ten o'clock Saturday night and eight o'clock Sunday to meet Aristide's financial and security demands. Even after all that, no one wanted to take him in. Aristide and his family were in the air for an hour and a half while Powell and other officials frantically called foreign leaders to find some place for him to go. As soon as I reported these telling details, I received a furious call from one of the leaders of the Black Caucus, California congresswoman Maxine Waters. She and Aristide's other longtime supporters, including Senator Chris Dodd, remain convinced that the United States had deposed the Haitian leader. But with Aristide gone, Haiti finally qualified for international aid that had been frozen since 1997 because of the continuing political chaos.

My experiences in Haiti had given me confidence that I could find a way to combine my Washington experience with more first-hand experience on the ground. Over the next few years, I had remarkable adventures in Vietnam, Afghanistan, China, the Middle East, and Cuba. It was not as easy as having a more narrowly defined beat, like Congress or the White House. It was often more difficult to "sell" the stories to the New York producers. But the pictures were compelling, the stories were important, and above all, I felt that I was stretching myself, growing stronger and more confident as a correspondent. And the knowledge I had from covering foreign policy briefings and hearings on the Hill was now enriched by experience on the ground in all parts of the world.

———

Traveling for NBC has had the added benefit of giving me a chance to learn from some of the network's premier producers and camera crews, men and women who have a different set of skills than those of us assigned to Washington. They wouldn't necessarily know the difference between an authorization and an appropriations bill, but they can land anywhere in the world, figure out how to tell the story, and find a way to feed it before deadline.

Charlie Ryan and Mike Mosher are typical of their generation of network producers—smart, tireless, wonderfully competent. I worked with both of them at different times in Vietnam and Taiwan, among my favorite assignments in Asia. The joy of going to Vietnam was that my first visit was not during a crisis, and not under the pressure of deadlines. In August of 1995, Warren Christopher, then secretary of state, was going to Hanoi to establish diplomatic relations. What would the normalization of contacts between two former enemies mean? *Nightly News* bought my suggestion that I go a week earlier and learn about Vietnam's gradual transition to a more capitalist economy.

My arrival in Ho Chi Minh City was not auspicious. I had flown via London and Bangkok, carrying a change of clothes so that we could start interviewing people as soon as I landed. As it turned out, my extra shirt and slacks were a fortunate addition because my bags never made the transfer at Heathrow. It took a week for them to catch up to me. In the interim, I learned that Vietnamese women were a lot smaller than I, and that their traditional garb didn't exactly work in my on-camera appearances.

Over the next week we interviewed American and Vietnamese business executives, politicians, and workers about the evolving politics of Vietnam, first in Ho Chi Minh City, then in Hanoi. The South was overrun by Asian, European, and American businessmen trying to get a foothold in what everyone thought would be the next Asian tiger. But unlike Korea, Thailand, and Malaysia, Vietnam was still ruled by an aging communist politburo. We were shadowed everywhere we went by a "minder" assigned by the Foreign Ministry to watch us and translate our interviews—and not, coincidentally, intimidate anyone who might have otherwise offered an opinion contrary to the official view.

At least superficially, Ho Chi Minh City was very Western, a bustling capital of commerce. Far more surprising was Hanoi, which was less French than I'd expected, and exuberantly friendly toward Americans. With our Foreign Ministry "spy" in tow, we approached Hanoi across the Red River Bridge, which was flanked by two giant Coke bottles advertising that most American of products. I had a flashback to footage I'd seen of the same bridge being strafed by American bombers during the war. There were other dramatic contrasts between my mental images of Hanoi then and now. As I walked through the city, along the shore of the lake where John McCain had crashed and been taken captive, people would stop to chat, hoping to practice their English. Everyone was studying it, often at night classes held in the basements of office buildings where the only teaching tools were giant boom boxes blasting American songs, like the oversized radios you used to see on the streets of New York.

We did a series of interviews with American businessmen, including oilmen from Mobil who'd had to give up their promising offshore fields during the Vietnam War and were now trying to recapture their investment. But Vietnam was struggling with its ambivalence toward permitting private investment. The people wanted Western consumer goods, but the aging communists who ran the country were not ready to loosen the reins on either political thought or economic power. Almost immediately, our tape editor, Steve Sung—sent over for the trip from our Burbank bureau, and familiar with a little Vietnamese—figured out that our friend from the Foreign Ministry was not accurately translating our interviews. (Steve was also one of the few survivors of the Jonestown murders, having been the soundman on our camera crew in Guyana. He still bears the scars from that shooting.)

Fortunately, one of the businesswomen we met loaned us her secretary. In the hotel room at night we would retranslate the interviews, discovering entirely new shades of meaning. It was all I could do to be polite to our Foreign Ministry guide the next morning, but polite we were, given that he monitored every single word and picture before it was sent out via government satellite. He also held us up for a king's ransom every time we fed our reports, demanding thousands of dollars more than any Western country charges for similar satellite time. Capitalism may be triumphant in most of the world but communism was not dying without getting its cut.

Seventy-two million Vietnamese were hoping to become Asia's next economic miracle. Only ten years earlier, people there were starving, forced to import their own largest crop, rice. The government provided jobs but little was produced, and inflation hit 800 percent. In desperation the Communist party started welcoming foreign investors, but only to partner with government-run companies. Asian businesses rushed in to take advantage of the country's greatest strength—low-wage, highly educated workers. But everyone was waiting for the Americans who would arrive when diplomatic relations were normalized.

There was an advance team of a few gutsy entrepreneurs willing to risk doing business in a country that did not recognize private property or contract law. One was a young African-American named Eugene Matthews, who had bought a Vietnamese yogurt factory. He and his friends were full of hope and expectations despite the frustration of doing business with the Hanoi bureaucrats. There were also a few Vietnamese benefiting from the transition. One family we interviewed, the Kims, were already millionaires who owned five Mercedes. Kim used to move supplies down the Ho Chi Minh Trail. Now he showed off his karaoke equipment, manufactured clothes, and talked about his plans for selling his products to America.

One day I was wandering through Hanoi's congested streets when a young woman engaged me in conversation. In halting English, she sought to learn everything about my work, education, and family.

On an impulse she invited me up to see her home. Taking off my shoes, I climbed a narrow staircase above a souvenir shop to reach her family's living space, where the ceiling was so low that it was impossible for me, at five foot three, to stand. She introduced me to her parents, grandmother, and siblings. We had tea and dumplings. It was a completely open and spontaneous encounter, remarkable to me as a child of the sixties who had experienced Vietnam only as a foreign war, not a real place.

On the night before Warren Christopher and the State Department press corps' morning arrival we were editing a *Today* show story in Steve Sung's hotel room, when Charlie Ryan got very quiet. He stretched out on the bed, and told me to finish producing the spot. I didn't realize for a while that he was desperately ill, perhaps from some chicken soup he'd had for lunch. I called the consulate, but couldn't find a doctor and didn't want to entrust Charlie to a Vietnamese hospital. He toughed it out, but was dangerously dehydrated and a lot sicker than any of us had originally thought. Every once in a while Steve and I would hear a faint voice from the bed saying, "Make sure you let that shot last a few frames longer." We probably could have edited the piece in an hour if we'd been on deadline. But having fallen in love with the pictures and interviews we'd shot, we fussed over every scene, barely finishing in time to cover Warren Christopher's arrival. Fortunately, by morning Charlie was starting to recover.

That day, twenty-two years after the last American bombing raid over Hanoi, the American secretary of state landed in his white-and-blue jet to restore relations with Vietnam. It was no accident that Warren Christopher's first official act was to accept recently recovered remains, believed to be those of four American servicemen. There were still critics back home, like Jesse Helms, arguing that there should be no official contact until Hanoi had resolved the 1,619 remaining cases of men missing in action during the war. Joint American and Vietnamese teams had been digging for clues throughout the country.

While the United States focused on the MIA issue, all the Vietnamese wanted was economic aid and trade. But Christopher told them they would not get full trading rights until they enacted further economic reforms, such as contract laws, a tax code, and property rights. Still, even without a trade agreement, there was a sweet sense of closure for Christopher. He had begun grappling with the Vietnam issue thirty years earlier as a young negotiator for Lyndon Johnson. But for many families of the missing, Christopher's visit brought no relief from a lifetime of unanswered questions.

For years afterward Vietnam's hard-line communist leaders stalled any progress on trade agreements, disappointing Eugene Matthews and my other American friends in Hanoi. In 1999, I returned to Vietnam, this time with a different secretary of state, Madeleine Albright. In contrast to the adventure of traveling independently, now I was part of the State Department press corps. The Vietnamese were still hungering for American goods. A new motorbike was more important than ideology. But economic progress was much slower than most people had expected.

Vietnam's offshore oil and gas fields never produced the finds Mobil was seeking. Most of the wells they drilled were dry, and there were legal challenges from China, which claimed territorial rights over potential fields in the South China Sea. Eugene Matthews had to close his yogurt factory and return to the States. And Mr. Kim was not exporting his inexpensive suits to American markets. But while economic progress had stalled, there was one bright spot in America's tentative new relationship with Vietnam, the joint exploration for MIA remains. Slowly, painfully, the United States and Vietnam were reconciling and, when possible, burying their dead. Representing America at the repatriation ceremonies was a Vietnam War hero and former prisoner in the Hanoi Hilton, Pete Peterson, appointed as the first postwar U.S. ambassador to Vietnam. With the help of other Vietnam War heroes, including John McCain, Bob Kerrey, and John Kerry, Clinton had taken the first steps toward closing one of the most painful chapters in U.S. history, or so we thought at the time.

But, as we learned in the 2004 campaign, as long as there are Vietnam veterans, or people who protested the war, Vietnam will remain an unresolved part of America's political history. It cost Lyndon Johnson his presidency and, arguably, made an embattled Richard Nixon more prone to the political abuses that led to the Watergate scandal. It animated McCain's political career and nearly ended Clinton's before it started. And in the 2004 campaign, Vietnam service again became a touchstone issue in the contest between John Kerry and George W. Bush.

———

My coverage of Vietnam resonated because so many Americans still think about the war and its political fallout. Unfortunately for those of us fascinated by foreign policy, the slow tending of economic or political relations that is the day-to-day job of diplomats rarely makes news headlines, in print or on television. There are too many crises, especially during times of war, interfering with a sustained examination of quiet diplomacy.

During the 1980s, when the world was both simpler and slower, NBC viewed the State Department as one of its premier assignments. One of my predecessors, Marvin Kalb, reportedly had an extraordinary clause in his contract entitling him to appear on the flagship *Nightly News* broadcast three times a week, even if the producers didn't want his stories. It was a benefit granted by Bill Small, who became president of NBC News after years of working with Marvin at CBS. Marvin's guaranteed exposure was a measure of the status foreign news used to enjoy. But that was a different time and place, during the Cold War and before domestic issues began to dominate news coverage in the 1990s. By the time I came to the beat, that era of devotion to foreign news had long since passed. My challenge was to find new ways to tell interesting stories, and make viewers want to know more about places they'd never thought were relevant to their lives.

Taiwan was such a place, when China threatened the island nation with live-fire military exercises, a policy of intimidation in advance of Taiwan's first direct presidential election. Taiwan's president, Lee Teng-hui, was trying to raise his nation's profile, which is what infuriated the mainland in the first place. The situation appeared close to exploding when I arrived in Taipei in the spring of 1996, looking for a fresh way to convey this David and Goliath story. We found it on the island of Quemoy, in the middle of the Taiwan Strait.

As my producer Mike Mosher and I started digging for some kind of new insight into the confrontation, we began to realize how heavily invested Taiwan was in the mainland, particularly in the southern Fujian Province directly across the Strait. The frontline Taiwanese islands of Quemoy and Matsu had been lightning rods in the 1950s for a heated debate over America's commitment to defend Taiwan should the mainland attack. Their defense came to symbolize a firm stand against Communism during the 1960 campaign between Richard Nixon and John F. Kennedy. Vaguely remembering that history, we flew to Quemoy without a game plan but eager to discover some ground truth. Driving around the island, we found a fishing village that turned out to provide most of the fish eaten in the capital of Taipei. But on further inspection, we learned that the fishermen who ventured out into the Strait each day never cast a net. Instead, vastly outnumbered by the fleet of boats from the mainland, the islanders simply motored out to a point midway between Quemoy and the mainland to meet their counterparts and buy their catch. The fishermen from Taiwan had the money. The fishermen from mainland China provided the fish. Anchored side by side it was a simple exchange, reflecting their mutual codependence. Stunningly simple, this two-way trade in fish made me realize how unlikely it was that China and Taiwan would ever engage in a real firefight. It was the perfect metaphor to explain the story on *Nightly News.*

In the next few years, I traveled to China several times, both accompanying Madeleine Albright when she became secretary of state and on my own. While I was in Hong Kong on vacation in 1997, attending World Bank meetings with Alan, NBC called and said I should go immediately to the mainland to prepare a story for the upcoming visit of China's premier to Washington. Leaving Alan on a moment's notice—which has become a pattern of our marriage—I headed to Beijing. True to character, Alan encouraged me, predicting it would be a great adventure.

It was. During that visit, I got a chance to meet Chinese people more easily than on previous trips, in all sorts of settings. We went to food markets and factories, college campuses and housing projects. I discovered more and more people who spoke English and who were willing to talk on camera to an American television reporter. It was a fascinating contrast to the closed, suspicious society I'd first encountered when I'd gone to China with Ronald Reagan more than a decade earlier.

China lurched forward, still groping for answers to its economic transformation. A visit to Beijing University captured how much progress the Chinese had made, and how far they still had to go. Business students flocked to hear a speech by Treasury Secretary Bob Rubin. They treated him like a rock star, hoping for clues to the American economic miracle. Those I talked to afterward wanted a road map to the way businesses grow and prosper in the United States, an easy way to adapt American rules to their system. Very few understood that the differences between our two economic models were a philosophical and moral gulf not easily bridged.

To compare the life of Chinese steelworkers with their American counterparts we went to an enormous steel plant in the capital city. It was vast, but hopelessly outdated. Compared to the new technologies now utilized in American plants, the Chinese equipment was obsolete and dangerous. The plant had more than one hundred thousand workers, many of whom spent grueling hours in front of open furnaces. Some wore hard hats, but few had protective eyewear. Iron shavings were everywhere. The air was so thick with smoke it was almost impossible to see even a few feet ahead of us.

We were permitted to ride home with one of the workers, who came from three generations who had been assigned to that factory. All lived in the same three-room apartment in a company housing complex. Admittedly, it was a controlled setting, arranged through the local factory committee, but the visit was a perfect illustration of how dependent Chinese workers were on guaranteed jobs and cradle-to-grave benefits, including housing. It was going to be very difficult for the Communist Party's Central Committee to lay off millions of workers from state jobs, as it believed it had to do over the next five years in order to reduce government subsidies and modernize the economy.

China was even beginning to think about legalizing some forms of property rights to facilitate the development of a market economy. But Beijing's experiment with capitalism stopped when it came to individual rights. Despite astonishing changes in the years since Reagan first went to what he called Red China, Chinese leaders still had an iron grip on political reform. Successive American presidents focused on what they considered the more pressing concerns to the United States of China's role as a military and economic power. They ignored China's Laogai, its extensive system of forced-labor camps. In a diplomatic and political tap dance, Bill Clinton even managed to separate progress on human rights from Congress's annual renewal of China's trade privileges in 1994. But in the summer of 1995, China's human rights abuses became impossible to overlook when China arrested a prominent Chinese-American activist, Harry Wu.

Harry Wu was a naturalized U.S. citizen who had spent nineteen years in Chinese prisons before coming to the United States in 1985. He had previously returned to China to investigate prison abuses, without incident. In Xinjiang Province, he uncovered evidence of labor camps with thousands of prisoners toiling in the remote desert. Despite warnings that his forays were becoming too dangerous, on June 19, 1995, he tried to enter China once more, at a remote border crossing on China's frontier with Kazakhstan. This time he was arrested and imprisoned at a secret location.

Wu's arrest created a convergence of events that instantly elevated the subject of China's behavior to the front pages and lead stories on network news. Tension between China and Taiwan had already exacerbated relations between Beijing and Washington. The administration, bowing to Republican pressure from Congress, had offended the Chinese by granting a rare visa to Taiwanese president Lee Teng-Hui to attend a college reunion in the United States, contrary to decades of agreed-on policy to hold Taiwan's leaders at arm's length.

Global communications made Wu's story accessible to all of Beijing's trading partners. He was well known to members of Congress and the news media because of his past writings and testimony at hearings. And Hillary Clinton was planning to attend a United Nations' women's conference in Beijing that September. When, during a visit to the White House, Wu's wife, Ching Lee, said that the first lady would "certainly" boycott the conference if Wu were still in prison, one man's story became an international political soap opera.

The White House hadn't planned on linking Hillary's trip to Harry Wu's release, but now the administration was boxed in. We were told the first lady would not go to China if Wu were still in prison. As the situation dragged on through the summer with no signal of Beijing's intentions, I went ahead with a planned trip to California with Alan. We arrived at our favorite vacation retreat in Carmel Valley on August 23. The very next day my beeper went off while we were on the tennis courts, midmatch. The Chinese were releasing Harry Wu, and *Nightly News* wanted me to go to San Francisco to meet him when he arrived. The other players, mostly vacationing Californians, thought I was nuts.

I already knew from my years of covering Reagan's western White House in Santa Barbara that there is a different rhythm to life in California than in Washington or New York. This time, even I couldn't completely understand why I would agree to leave Alan on a tennis court during my only week of vacation for the entire year. I headed off to shower and change, telling Alan I'd be back in a day or two, and got the next commuter flight to San Francisco.

When I arrived at the San Francisco Airport, the first challenge was to find out when and where Wu would be arriving from China.

I figured out that his fellow activists, especially in the U.S. labor movement, would be flying in from Washington to meet him. So I staked out every plane arriving from Dulles, hoping to intercept someone who would know his schedule. Finally, I spotted a union leader who knew what time Wu was arriving. From years of flying in and out of San Francisco, I also knew some of the local security officials. It wasn't difficult to spot them and find my way to Harry Wu.

The payoff was the first interview with Harry Wu for *Nightly News,* and the chance to get to know better one of those rare individuals willing to follow his ideals no matter how difficult the course. Harry and other activists are often dismissed or barely tolerated by official Washington. Their protests can be "inconvenient" when they disrupt the normal patterns of super power diplomacy. But Harry had been both toughened and inspired by his years in prison before coming to the United States. He was passionate about saving tens of thousands of fellow prisoners who were still being incarcerated. He wanted the Chinese prison system to become as well known to the world as the Soviet gulags that Ronald Reagan consistently elevated to the top of the U.S.-Soviet summit agendas. As often happens, Harry's release produced a flurry of attention—international awards, testimony in Congress, an appearance on *The Tonight Show*—and just as quickly, he disappeared from our newscasts. But thanks to him, human rights would now have to be the centerpiece of the first lady's trip to Beijing.

————

I had returned to spend a few days with Alan playing tennis, but with Harry's release, there was no longer any political obstacle to Hillary's trip. Soon I was detouring to Hawaii to join her entourage. It turned out to be a much better story than any of us had expected. This was not going to be a "tea and cookies" visit. Harry Wu's vivid account of conditions in China made it inevitable that the first lady do something rarely done by any of her predecessors with the possible exception of Eleanor Roosevelt——she was going to have to tackle the human rights issue head-on.

Flying to Beijing, we were briefed on security issues. The White House assumed that our rooms would be bugged. Among other tips, we were told to turn on the shower and steam up the bathroom mirror. If there was a spot that did not fog over, that was likely the bug. It wasn't the kind of information that made you feel warm and cozy about relaxing in your hotel room. Anticipating the focus of the conference, Hillary's speech equating women's rights and human rights, the Chinese were already tense.

On the very first night, after flying for twenty-four hours, I wrote my story, recorded my voice track for New York, and prepared to go out and tape my on–camera stand-up. Unfortunately, the senior producer returned to the office late that day, and decided he wanted an entirely different approach. By the time we'd written a new version, it was four in the morning, local time. The streets were pitch-dark. There were no lights still on to illuminate a suitable backdrop for my on-camera appearance.

The crew and I headed out in a van, looking for any kind of setting. The only place that was lit up was Tiananmen Square, off-limits to foreign journalists since the uprising in 1989. Desperate, and getting close to our deadline, we decided to chance it. It turned out to be a very bad idea. As soon as we set up, the police descended. I had only enough time to roll off one take, pop the tape out of the camera, and hide it under my jacket. As we tried to get another version taped at the last minute, the police moved in. When one put his hand in front of the camera, I started arguing and telling him he had no right to interfere with our camera. The resulting video is pretty funny. I'm doing my best imitation of an outraged schoolmarm, lecturing this Chinese police officer on the finer points of freedom of the press. Knowing we had at least one good take, my cameraman hustled me out of there before the police could examine my coat pockets, or worse.

Only hours after I'd finished filing for *Nightly News,* and with barely a nap, I watched Mrs. Clinton open the conference with a dramatic challenge to the Chinese human rights record. Startling her hosts, she condemned China's population control policies and equated women's rights with human rights, declaring, "If there is one message that echoes forth from this conference, let it be that human rights are women's rights. And women's rights are human rights, once and for all."

Without mentioning China by name, her message was unambiguous. She was condemning Beijing's policy of one child per family, a policy that led to widespread forced abortions and sterilizations. At the same time, she strongly criticized China's decision to exile a parallel gathering of twenty thousand women from international nongovernmental women's organizations to a suburb thirty-five miles outside Beijing. Hillary had been walking a political tightrope between antiabortion groups who were opposed to her even attending a conference that they viewed as "antifamily" and human rights leaders who feared she would soft-pedal their concerns. Both sides ended up applauding her speech. For a first lady, even one as outspoken as Hillary, to venture beyond traditional first lady diplomacy was unprecedented. The Chinese were braced for some criticism, but hardly expected Hillary Clinton's blunt attack on their policies. Their leaders were furious. The best measure of how threatening her message was to the status quo? China's official media devoted only two seconds to it—literally.

For those of us covering her trip the real trial was the next day, when the first lady led the delegation to the unsanctioned women's gathering in Huairou, an hour outside the capital. We arrived in a driving, monsoonlike rain, riding in a press bus along with several members of the official delegation: Health and Human Services Secretary Donna Shalala, State Department official and former senator Tim Wirth, and former New Jersey governor Tom Kean. The Chinese security men were waiting for us. Most likely because of her tough speech the previous day, Hillary's delegation was going to get a very "special" welcome.

The security men blanketing the conference let the first lady's car enter, but then stopped the rest of the vehicles in her motorcade.

With the barricades about to close, we jumped off the bus into the drenching rain and ran toward the entrance. Donna Shalala, all five feet of her, pushed forward like a miniature fullback. I tried to shelter her with my umbrella as we practically wrestled with the guards to get through the gate. The Chinese police pushed back. Tim Wirth tried to hold them off, but it was Tom Kean who emerged as the true hero of our predominantly female group.

Kean, a usually laid-back college president—who later distinguished himself as the chairman of the 9/11 Commission—shoved the Chinese guards back while simultaneously dragging Shalala and me through the barricade. The gates then closed behind us, shutting out the rest of the group, including even Hillary's press secretary, Lisa Caputo. Soaking wet, badly shaken, but giddy with our victory over the uniformed thugs, we arrived at a conference devoted to women's rights. Hillary told the crowd, "I want to pay tribute to your perseverance," applauding those who had overcome the phalanx of Chinese soldiers, as well as the local audience that had spent years resisting harassment and intimidation. The conference provided a rare opportunity for women to make connections with each other. Given China's human rights policy, it was remarkable that the meeting was even being held.

From Beijing we flew to the most exotic country of any previous White House itinerary, Mongolia. It was a strikingly gentle contrast to the authoritarian experience we'd had in Beijing. Aside from being tourists, there was a diplomatic reason for the stop: previously communist, Mongolia was holding its first democratic elections and the State Department wanted to reinforce its leaders' commitment to reform. But especially after the tension of our visit to Beijing, it was simply exhilarating to see children racing their horses bareback across the steppes in displays of expert horsemanship. A nomadic family, a man named Zanabaatar and his wife, Haliun, invited the first lady into their domed canvas tent known as a yurt or ger. To avoid offending her hosts, Hillary stepped gingerly over the pail of cow dung they used as fuel and politely sampled an offering of curdled mare's milk and horse cheese. It smelled awful, and must have tasted worse. "It tastes like what we call yogurt," she said with a wicked grin, as she tried to pass it along to us; she found no takers.

There were a few other awkward moments, including a luncheon performance in the first lady's honor featuring adolescent contortionists, girls whose bodies had been completely manipulated so that they could tie themselves in knots. For a woman who'd just been criticizing the abuse of girls, it was not a comfortable experience. There was little hard news, but a lot of color; however, getting anything on the air was going to be a big challenge for technical reasons. Mongolia was not exactly geared for a White House trip, and, understandably, the first lady's press corps traveled with a lot less support than the president's. I was on my own, without a producer. Most frustrating, the phone lines were not capable of transmitting computer data to upload the script, and because of the time difference, there was no way to talk to my producers in New York and tell them what I could offer. So to transmit my story, I commandeered the only dedicated telephone line I could find, which happened to be connected to the fax machine at the U.S. embassy.

Some reports are not fated to get on. Just before airtime, word came from Washington that an embattled senator, Bob Packwood, had finally resigned in the face of long-standing sexual harassment accusations. The late-breaking Packwood story bumped all of us from the evening news. Wryly, I thought, "How fitting, Bob Packwood has screwed yet another group of women." Not that it was the most important story I've ever offered, but I dearly wanted to be able to sign off with the exotic dateline, "Andrea Mitchell, NBC News, Ulan Bator, Mongolia."

We were a ragtag bunch on the flight home. Hillary came to the back of the plane to visit us and her photographer took a class photo. We must have shared a private joke, because there is a picture of the two of us, with really bad hair from our Mongolian adventure, laughing our heads off. It was a rare moment in which she seemed completely at ease, without her usual wariness of the press corps.

The next year I accompanied Hillary to Greece, Turkey, and Bosnia, where she and Chelsea visited the troops during the war. Except for one evening in an Athens restaurant, and another at a party in Turkey organized on a yacht in the Bosporus, we rarely saw the unofficial side of the first lady. It was a caution bred of the rollercoaster ride of the early White House years and her growing belief that she and her husband were being victimized by what she came to call "the vast right-wing conspiracy." She had been burned badly by the health-care debacle, Whitewater, and of course her husband's scandalous behavior. In some ways she was still a bit tentative, almost ambivalent about her role. As good as she was, she still lacked the experience and self-confidence that would come later, after her election to the Senate.

———

The visit to Bosnia was my first, having not covered the war, often to my frustration. Instead, I was tracking the tortuous diplomacy that eventually led to peace talks in Dayton, Ohio, and a treaty signing in Paris. Bosnia marked a watershed in U.S. relations with the United Nations. Instead of viewing the UN as a useful diplomatic tool, the Clinton administration felt hamstrung by the complex relationships within the Security Council. Finally, the president turned to NATO to lead the operation. As a result, when the conflict erupted in Kosovo, the same model was followed. The U.S.-led mission was coordinated with NATO, not the UN.

That set the stage for my own adventure in Kosovo. On March 31, 1999, the Serbs took three American servicemen prisoner. Without even tacit approval from the White House, the Reverend Jesse Jackson, once again casting himself in the role of international troubleshooter, flew over to try to rescue them—with us in tow to make sure every dramatic moment was recorded. On our first night in Belgrade, I found myself on the floor—thrown out of bed. A small

276 • *Talking Back*

earthquake had hit Belgrade. I'd barely gotten back to sleep when NATO launched the biggest air attack of the war on the capital city. I felt reasonably confident that we were safe since I was sure the Pentagon knew where American reporters were staying. It's a good thing I didn't know about the mapping error that would later lead the U.S. to mistakenly bomb China's embassy in Belgrade.

Jackson had done this kind of cowboy diplomacy before, during the Reagan years, and successfully; now he was roiling the diplomatic waters for Bill Clinton. By putting the media focus on the three prisoners, he gave Slobodan Milosevic an opportunity to control the agenda, and distract from NATO's hard-fought-for unified front. It became a propaganda bonanza for the Serbs. They brought Jackson, and our cameras, to inspect civilian damage from the air strikes. He held hands with the Serbian dictator and, paraphrasing Isaiah, said: "If a lion and a lamb can lie down together, we can all lie together and find the elusive peace that connects families again, between our nations and around the world." Critics said it was a travesty. But the flamboyant civil rights leader also managed to see the prisoners, and pray with them, as well. Military officials did not permit questions about the war or politics, but the men were allowed to send messages home. For the first time, their families were able to see that they were healthy, and they were able to send their love to their wives and children.

Ignoring objections from National Security Advisor Sandy Berger and Secretary of State Madeleine Albright, Jackson held running news conferences, repeating the Serb bargaining position: a halt to the bombing, no withdrawal of Serb forces from Kosovo until after NATO forces withdrew from Albania and Macedonia, and no NATO participation in an unarmed UN peacekeeping force. Jackson's freelancing was turning U.S. diplomacy upside down, and we were giving him the platform. At the same time, he was succeeding in his primary mission. On May 1, while standing in the hotel lobby surrounded by reporters, an emotional and exhausted Jesse Jackson got word that the prisoners would be released. Using my cell phone as a microphone, we carried audio of his announcement live on MSNBC. And Jackson played into Milosevic's hands by calling for a bombing halt.

The POWs—Specialist Steven Gonzales, Staff Sergeant Andrew Ramirez, and Staff Sergeant Christopher Stone—were released to Jackson on a Sunday morning. It was late at night back home, long after our broadcasts, but once again we were able to carry audio of the event live on our cable network via my cell phone. Then I turned the phone over to the servicemen so they could call their families. Jackson took a call from the president, but also challenged Clinton to show what Jackson called "moral responsibility" and consider Milosevic's demand for a cease-fire.

We marched across the border into Croatia, with the three former POWs shouting in unison, "Free at last, free at last, thank God Almighty, we are free at last." It was an emotional homage to Dr. King that was surely done at Jackson's prompting. *Meet the Press* was just going on the air. I put Jackson on the phone to answer Tim Russert's questions. As we drove toward a NATO base where the men would be returned to their commanders, they drank Coke, ate doughnuts, and complained about how bad they looked in news magazine pictures of their capture. It was a happy ending for the three servicemen, but it was left to Defense Secretary Bill Cohen to remind the world that Milosevic's gesture in releasing the men should not diffuse the intensity of NATO's resolve to win the war. From Carter to Jesse Jackson, over the years Bill Clinton had his hands full with freelance diplomacy.

———

Often, explosive foreign policy issues erupt on a president's watch with no warning. Such an instance was the arrival of a five-year-old child, clinging to an inner tube, who washed ashore in Miami on Thanksgiving Day in 1999. Elian Gonzalez had survived the physical travail of being at sea for two days as well as the horror of watching his mother and at least ten others on their seventeen-foot boat die. He was about to become the central figure in an international custody dispute that forced both Cuba and the United States to retreat even further from any accommodation with each other.

Miami's Cuban-American community claimed Elian as the poster child for their opposition to the Cuban dictator. All of America seemed to fall in love with this doe-eyed little boy. As the custody dispute gained emotional force, Fidel Castro's government organized enormous anti-American demonstrations in Havana to counteract the outpouring of anti-Castro sentiment in Miami. The story was being covered almost completely from Miami's point of view. Danny Noa, NBC's director of foreign news and a Cuban-American, agreed with our bureau chief in Havana that we had to find a way to report the Cuban perspective as well. Elian hadn't been hatched at sea, as many Americans seemed to feel. He had a father, grandparents, a pet parrot, a dog, and schoolmates. What was his childhood like in communist Cuba? Why had his mother been so desperate to flee that she would risk her life, and her son's, in a seventeen-foot boat? We wanted to tell that story.

I had never been to Cuba, and now NBC ordered me to Miami to catch a charter flight. We were in a hurry, trying to get to Havana in time to broadcast live for Brian Williams's nine p.m. cable newscast on MSNBC. But when I arrived at the airport to meet the camera crew, we discovered that our foreign desk had lined up a one-engine prop plane, with only one pilot. Both were violations of standard network practice. I was willing to take the chance, but felt I couldn't order the camera crew to risk it. And the weather in Havana, we were told, was turning ugly.

A call to network headquarters confirmed that we should ask for a second pilot. After a lot of phone calls and scurrying around, one turned up, out of uniform. Only when we were taxiing down the runway did my cameraman point out to me that the copilot wasn't even wearing a headset. I imagine he was the pilot's brother-in-law, or a buddy who ran the local gas station. In any case, he had no idea how to fly a plane.

In a blinding rainstorm, we arrived in Havana, opening a new and important chapter in my life. In the years since, I have returned many times. Cuba, with all of its contradictions and tragedy and potential, has become part of my bloodstream. It is open and mysterious, embracing and sinister, exuberant and rigid. I love the people, the food, the architecture, and all the rhythms of Cuban life captured so vibrantly in their music.

Entering Havana from Miami separates you immediately from the Canadian and European tourists Cuba courts so assiduously. Flights from the United States arrive in Havana's oldest terminal, and passengers are subjected to special scrutiny, targeted as suspicious by Cuban immigration officials. But we were on deadline, and as I've discovered over the years, Fidel's secret police are no match for the hurricane force of NBC's Havana bureau chief, Mary Murray. She practically dragged us through the gates, overriding all objections.

Mary is from a working-class background in New Jersey, half Irish, half Sicilian, and has lived in Cuba for more than a decade. She has a warm embrace, but her maternal appearance is deceiving. When she's chasing a story, Mary is one of the purest journalists I've ever known. If she worked in Washington, she would stand out for being so unyielding to pressure or compromise. Living in a totalitarian society as she does, her gutsiness is nothing short of a badge of courage. If anything, going up against Cuba's maddening bureaucracy has toughened her, rather than softened her edges. She is the kind of instinctive reporter who spots a phony a mile off. Nothing intimidates her, not even the bearded icon Cubans call *Commandante*.

After sweeping us through customs and immigration, Mary raced through Havana's insane traffic to get me to my live shot downtown. By the time we arrived, we were barely minutes from our broadcast. The protestors were still marching in the rain. Over their shouts, I did my first report from Havana, the first correspondent from the

States to cover the story from Cuba. Mary and I had barely had time to say hello. But in a way, we didn't need introductions. We share a love for the excitement of chasing a story, especially in a hostile environment. We both thrive on adrenaline, chocolate, and very little sleep. That first broadcast, under deadline pressure, was the beginning of our adventures together, and the start of a friendship that continues to this day.

Fidel Castro was staying out of sight, trying to give Bill Clinton enough leeway to extricate himself from the Elian mess. But on the eve of the 2000 election campaign, there was no chance of that. Cuban-American relations in the Clinton years had taken many fateful turns. Early in the administration the president's top national security officials had thought they could take on the Cuba issue and lift the embargo that had separated the two countries for four decades. But in February of 1996, Cuban MIG fighter jets had shot down two planes piloted by anti-Castro activists belonging to a group called Brothers to the Rescue.

In the middle of a reelection campaign, Clinton had to retreat from his secret back-channel overtures to Havana and accept even tighter restrictions demanded by Congressional hard-liners Senator Jesse Helms and Congressman Dan Burton. Later, White House officials acknowledged to me that they had not read the fine print of the new law. They had been badly outmaneuvered. From that point on, the sanctions could be lifted only by a majority vote of Congress, instead of a simple presidential executive order.

In those early weeks of the Elian crisis, American immigration officials were insisting on interviewing the boy's father, who lived in a small fishing village two hours from Havana. But Juan Miguel Gonzalez was unwilling to submit to U.S. authority. It was now up to Fidel. Mary and I started pressing for an audience with the Cuban leader. His aides told us to wait, that a summons might come. Each night we stood by, dressed and ready at any moment for a call from the palace. When it finally came, we were told to come for dinner at eight that evening.

We arrived at Fidel's palace and were greeted by his top aides and told to wait. Looking around nervously, I noticed that the furnishings seemed to have a strong Bauhaus influence—leather chairs, glass tables, wood paneling, more like a 1960s New York office building lobby than what I'd expected in Havana. When Castro arrived, I was even more surprised to see him wearing a dark brown, double-breasted business suit instead of military fatigues. Except for the beard and his long fingernails, characteristic of Latin men of a certain generation, he looked like an elderly diplomat. He greeted me halfway across a narrow footpath crossing an elaborately landscaped indoor garden with a small waterfall and gurgling brook.

For almost an hour we exchanged small talk, while they offered us orange juice or potent mojitos. Though I was dying to take notes, I knew it would be rude. When he finally escorted us in to dinner, the long banquet table was set with the first course, the largest grapefruits I'd ever seen. There was a lot of talk about healthy diets, and his decision years earlier to give up cigars. He told us he still enjoyed red wine, which was good for his heart. He didn't like treadmills but exercised by walking for miles each day around his convention center, a palatial complex. This was a man very conscious of his physical health.

That first conversation lasted seven hours. Castro was sizing us up, deciding whether we would be a suitable vehicle for any statement he wanted to make about Elian and U.S.-Cuban relations. Of course, I was also forming my own impressions about him. While fierce about his politics, in demeanor he was courtly, paternal, old-fashioned. In some ways he was surprisingly modern: the aging leader stayed up nights surfing the Web. He read constantly on the Internet, although he interpreted what he read through the filter of his communist ideology. Still, he was up-to-date, knowing at least a little about many contemporary events, especially economic developments.

In other ways, Castro was frozen in time, a captive of his Cold War mentality, and paranoid about the overwhelming power of the Goliath to the north. (That said, sometimes paranoids have reason;

after all, Fidel had survived several assassination attacks, including the ludicrous CIA plot during the Eisenhower administration to kill him with an exploding cigar.) The dinner had its moments of comedy. Poor Mary, sitting to my left, had a sudden allergic attack. She was trying to cover up her sneezes, I was slipping her handkerchiefs under the table, and Fidel, who misses nothing, ordered his foreign minister to get her some nasal spray.

He also showed me his personal notebook, in which he had transcribed a *Meet the Press* interview with Madeleine Albright. He told me that he had been advised to watch these interviews for hidden messages to him from Washington. Typically, he did not leave it to an aide to transcribe the shows for him. Castro was his own note taker. When it came to the case of "the child," as he referred to Elian, he knew every detail, including the relevant U.S. case law. I remembered that before becoming a revolutionary, he had graduated from law school.

Our longest conversation that first night involved one of his pet projects, the Medical University of Latin America. Cuba was inviting students to come from all over the region to study medicine in Havana, tuition-free, as long as they agreed to return to their countries after graduation to practice medicine in urban or rural poor communities for several years. It was his version of the Peace Corps, guaranteed to do good while polishing Cuba's relations with its neighbors. Although he did not want to do an interview on camera about Elian, to preserve his diplomatic options, I thought this might be a way to get him to go on camera. I suggested he give us a tour of the medical school.

Two other comments got my attention. In the middle of a lengthy discussion about Cuba's faltering economy, Castro mentioned my husband. He said, "I've read a lot about him on the Internet. He seems to be a serious person who does a good job. The only issue on which I would disagree is, why did he bail out Long Term Capital?"

I couldn't believe that I was sitting at dinner with one of the world's last committed Communists, and he was asking me why the

Federal Reserve Board of New York had intervened to help negotiate a settlement for a troubled multibillion dollar hedge fund.

Castro's other unusual comment involved Elian. He predicted that
the custody fight would become a huge political controversy that
would tie up the American courts for months. He guessed that the
child would not be returned to his family until May or June. How
could this custody fight drag on for that long? We thought that he
was crazy.

The next night, we were invited back for a five-course dinner
that didn't start until two in the morning. Castro was known among
foreign visitors for his late-night dinners and lengthy conversations.
To stay awake, I found myself digging my fingernails into the palms
of my hands. This time, Fidel was wearing his more familiar combat fatigues. Clearly, he had something important to communicate.
Squeezing Mary's arm for emphasis, he said he needed someone
young to go to Cardenas, Elian Gonzalez's family's village, at dawn
the next morning. If she was there, she might see something very
interesting. We realized that the stalemate that had continued for
weeks, with the boy's father refusing to be interviewed by American
officials, was about to break.

Not only was Castro giving us a huge tip, he jokingly told us he
would act as our producer. He told us Mary should arrive at exactly
the right hour and since she would have to travel at night, he would
have his driver take her over the difficult roads. We assured him that
that would not be either necessary or appropriate. He also agreed to
give us a tour, on camera, of his medical school the next day, and do
a sit-down interview. We were going to be the first American reporters to question him on camera since the Elian story had erupted.
Castro had also been very wary of American television interviews
over the years. He had done a lengthy interview with Barbara Walters decades earlier, and more recent interviews with Dan Rather for
CBS and Maria Shriver for NBC. But the access we were being
given was extraordinary.

I stayed behind at dinner while Mary left to get the camera crew and prepare for the trip. For hours into the night, Fidel talked about the case, about his conflicts with Washington, and the American presidents he had observed from his island citadel. Whom had he respected the most? John F. Kennedy, he said, despite the fact that JFK had tried to kill him. But he thought Clinton was smart, and seemed eager to see if there was still a chance to reach out to him. If he wanted better relations, then why had Cuba shot down the two planes from Miami four years earlier? He told me that he had repeatedly warned the White House that the Miami "spies," his term for anti-Castro Cuban-American activists, were going to try to invade Cuban airspace and that Washington had ignored his concerns. Incredibly, he also refused to take responsibility for the shoot-down, saying his military commanders had not consulted him—an assertion I found difficult to believe.

Castro's denials were in direct conflict with everything I knew about the incident. When the Miami planes were shot down, the United States presented chilling evidence to the United Nations that Cuba had known it was firing on unarmed civilian planes. Madeleine Albright, then the U.S. ambassador, had distributed a transcript of the conversation between the Cuban ground controllers and the military pilots. From audio intercepted by American intelligence, the transcript proved that the ground controllers had informed the pilots four times that they had permission to shoot down the civilian planes. The transcript also showed that the pilots were gleeful about firing at the Cessnas. After the first missile was fired, the MIG-29 pilot shouted, "We hit him! *Cojones!* We busted his *cojones!*"

MIG-23 pilot: "This one won't mess around anymore."

After releasing the transcripts, Albright said, "Frankly, this is not *cojones*. This is cowardice." Many of her fellow diplomats were shocked at her language but the White House was impressed. She was certainly a lot tougher, and more colorful, than Secretary of State Warren Christopher. That single moment made her a hero in

Miami, and helped her win the job of secretary of state in Clinton's second term.

Castro knew all of this, and that Albright would not be sympathetic to Cuba's concerns if the dispute over Elian became a full-blown crisis. I wondered if the man who looked to *Meet the Press* for hidden messages from Washington was now trying to send signals back through me. By the end of the dinner at five in the morning, I was exhausted from the balancing act of trying to counter his arguments while being suitably respectful to his office and conscious of his hospitality. On subjects like his country's attack on the Miami planes, Castro had his own set of facts, and we would never be able to agree.

Bleary-eyed, I went straight to work on a story for the *Today* show. Mary called in from Cardenas that the immigration officials had in fact shown up to interview Elian's father. We were the only network there, and were able to report exclusively that the logjam was broken. That night we broadcast the details and our exclusive video on *Nightly News*. Bone tired, we both fell asleep, with no idea what we had missed.

The next day, we went to meet Fidel so that he could escort us to the medical school for our shoot.

"Did you rest well?" he asked pointedly.

I rode with him in his car, while Mary followed with his aides. She was mortified to learn that the palace had called the night before to ask us to come back for more conversation. In her sleep, she had answered the phone, said she was tired, and hung up—without remembering any of it.

No one in Havana can recall Castro ever jumping through hoops for American television as he did that day at the medical school. He let us put a wireless microphone on him, had his entire medical team brief us on what the young doctors were accomplishing, and did a walking tour of the classrooms and laboratories while hundreds of students crowded around. Afterward, we did an interview about the medical school for a feature report and, more urgently, about Elian.

In Miami, the boy's relatives were showering Elian with gifts. The media were camped in the front yard in what could be described only as a carnival atmosphere. Compared to the child's simple life in a small Cuban fishing village, it was very seductive. Deeply suspicious of American motives, Castro told us, "The Americans want to delay the return of the child, to be able to change the child's mentality, to destroy his identity."

"Are you concerned that the child will say that he wants to stay in the United States, that he will be seduced by all these toys and trips to Disney World?" I asked.

"They are trying to simply baffle the child with all these things. According to the father, the boy has been coerced. They feel that their boy is antinational."

"You know that some people in the United States say that the father is coerced by the government and can't speak freely?"

"And how could we prove that that is false? Would we have to take the father to Miami to prove that there is no coercion here?" It was clear that Castro had taken personal charge of the crisis, and was micromanaging the negotiations to get the child back.

By the time we finished taping it was dark, and we were approaching yet another television deadline, this time for Brian Williams's cable show. Fidel dropped me at my hotel and suggested dinner. I had to decline in order to file my story. He said he had never had anyone refuse a dinner invitation two nights in a row.

For the next six months, I covered Elian's story from Washington for all of NBC's broadcasts, while anchoring a nightly cable show on MSNBC devoted to coverage of the 2000 political campaign. Throughout January, Elian's Miami family fought to retain custody of the boy, and kept losing rulings from the immigration officials and Attorney General Janet Reno. The custody battle was a huge issue in Florida, and Al Gore was becoming increasingly worried about its impact on his candidacy. Elian's grandmothers came to the

States to appeal for the child's return. Their arrival in New York was carried live on cable television. Thanks to Mary, who flew up with them, I got the only interview they granted while in the United States.

The Miami family appealed to the courts to grant the boy political asylum. But how could you argue that a child whom Fidel had transformed into a Cuban national hero would face political punishment should he be returned home? Castro understood that Elian Gonzalez could serve as a symbol of Cuban nationalism, a rallying cry for a population eager for distractions from their economic privation. The case was a useful political safety valve for the government, and its leader made the most of it.

In April, Juan Miguel Gonzalez and his new wife and child, along with Elian's teacher and pediatrician, arrived in the U.S. Juan Miguel, an unsophisticated man with a privileged government job as a waiter in a seaside beach hotel, was emotional and angry. Fortunately for him, Cuban diplomats had retained one of Washington's most skillful attorneys, Greg Craig, to navigate the corridors of power, defend the father's legal rights, and in his spare time, make sure Juan Miguel presented a sympathetic face to the American media. Craig had gone to law school with Bill and Hillary Clinton. He'd worked for Ted Kennedy in the Senate. Now a partner in the Washington law firm of Williams & Connolly, he knew everyone in Washington, especially in the Clinton White House and Justice Department. If anyone could win an international custody case fraught with political overtones for the Democrats in a presidential election year, it was he. And he had American public opinion on his side: an NBC News/*Wall Street Journal* poll found that most Americans favored returning the boy to Havana, by an overwhelming 62 percent to 24 percent.

The final showdown between Miami and Washington took place in the early morning hours of April 22, on Easter weekend. INS officials stormed the house in Miami's Little Havana. In an unbearable flash of light, a still photographer captured Elian's terrified face as

U.S. marshals took him, at gunpoint, from the closet in which he was cowering. The nation was transfixed. Juan Miguel was finally reunited with his son, but had to wait in Washington for two more months while the custody case worked its way up to the Supreme Court. Finally, on June 28, the High Court refused to consider the appellate court's ruling. The boy who had arrived on an inner tube on Thanksgiving Day flew home on a Learjet to a hero's welcome, and promptly disappeared, reabsorbed by his small village and protected from further scrutiny by Fidel Castro's patronage.

———

A year passed with no attention paid to Elian except for the occasional "whatever happened to" stories on key anniversaries—and speculation about how Florida's critical presidential vote that November might have been influenced by Cuban-American anger at the decisions of the Clinton-Gore Justice Department in the Elian case. Then, in June of 2001, Cuba came back into my life suddenly, when I least expected it.

Alan and I were going to an annual conference hosted by President and Mrs. Ford in Beaver Creek, Colorado. A group of senators and members of Congress were also flying out for the weekend, traveling, as we were, with the vice president and Mrs. Cheney. The Cheneys and Alan got their start together in government in the Ford White House. Their friendship is rooted in those shared experiences, and loyalty and gratitude to the Fords.

When we arrived in Beaver Creek, it was already after dinner. We sat and chatted with the Fords and the Cheneys for a while, unpacked, and went to bed. After breakfast Saturday morning we all headed to the conference, where the vice president was to be the first speaker. I sat in the back of the room, in a row of spouses. No sooner had Dick Cheney begun to speak than my beeper went off. Dialing the network desk from a phone booth, I reached my editors, who conferenced me with Mary Murray in Havana. Fidel had collapsed during a speech delivered in a blazing sun, while wearing his heavy combat fatigues. He had already gotten back on stage to reassure the sobbing crowd of loyal Cubans that he was fine, and promised to complete his speech on Cuban television that night. Mary was sure it was simple heat exhaustion, but New York was afraid that he was seriously ill, a major story. They ordered me to fly immediately to Havana. I had been in Beaver Creek for less than twelve hours.

It seemed terribly unfair: I had been looking forward to spending two free days with Alan. The last thing I wanted to do was leave before the weekend even started. We got back to the Fords' to collect my things. Betty took one look at my face and said, "Sit down and visit with your husband while I pack your bag." I was embarrassed and grateful, all at the same time. It was also hard to explain to my hosts why a fainting spell, even by Fidel Castro, was more important than a weekend with my husband, at the home of a former president, with the sitting vice president and his wife as fellow houseguests.

I didn't have a visa to go to Havana, and no time to negotiate for one. Mary talked to someone in the Foreign Ministry who said they'd let me in. It was immediately apparent that Fidel was fine, but we needed to show that to American audiences. It was also days from the first anniversary of Elian's return. Could we capitalize on my unscheduled trip and score exclusive interviews on both stories?

The next day, after filing a story from the satellite facility at Cuban Television, I noticed a lot of security around the building. Fidel was there for his nightly broadcast. Why not stake him out? Mary laughed and explained that reporters didn't do "ambush" interviews in Fidel Castro's Cuba. I was determined to try. We sent a note up the chain of command to see if he'd see us, without a camera, and waited for a response. Finally, they ushered us into an empty studio. A rush of security men signaled the Commandante's arrival.

"I'm going to punish you," he teased Mary. "Why have you brought her back to bother me?"

Turning to me, he asked, "What do you want this time?"

I explained that I wanted two things: an interview with him to show America that he was still in charge. And an opportunity to show Cuba's critics in the United States that, after a year, Elian Gonzalez was leading a "normal" life. Castro said any decision about Elian would be up to Juan Miguel, who was zealously guarding the boy's privacy. We both knew that Juan Miguel would do whatever Castro wanted, but I promised that I would not question the child, only the father, as long as I could visit Elian at school and home and show how he was doing.

With Castro's permission, and a minder from the Foreign Ministry, we drove to Cardenas two days later. Per our agreement, first I met with Juan Miguel in the town's new Elian Gonzalez Museum (so much for the simple life) and persuaded him that we would be sensitive to the trauma the boy had already experienced at the hands of the news media. With the father's concurrence, we went to the Marcelos Celado Elementary School to see Elian. At first, I couldn't pick him out of the lineup of seven-year-olds playing in the yard. Then I spotted him. He looked like a typical kid, playful, even mischievous. His teachers said he was getting good grades, and liked Spanish and math. His favorite pastime was playing baseball, practicing after school with his two-and-a-half-year-old brother.

For all their celebrity, the family—including a new baby—still lived in a modest house. All shared the same bedroom. But could life ever be normal for a boy who had witnessed his mother die at sea? There were pictures of her around the house, and Juan Miguel said on Mother's Day and her birthday Elian kissed her picture. He was not afraid of swimming, but never talked about what had happened in the water. Juan Miguel insisted that the decision to return to Cuba was his, not Castro's. Most surprising, the father said his son's readjustment had been relatively simple. Why did he think so? "Because the boy returned to what he has always been. He was not born to be a symbol."

In Cuba, there is no way to know what is real and what is staged, but the day we spent with Elian Gonzalez and his family persuaded me that his story had had the least "bad" ending.

We drove back to Havana to put together our story. The next night, we stayed up waiting for word that Castro would deliver on the second part of his bargain, an exclusive interview with him. Though we stayed up for hours, with a chartered plane sitting at the airport ready to take us, and our tapes, back to the States for editing, nothing happened. We kept calling Castro's aides, pleading for an answer, reminding them of Fidel's personal commitment. Finally, we gave up and went to sleep.

Early the next morning, our New York producer, Phil Alongi, took the tapes and left. The Cubans assumed I was with him. When Mary called them later that day, Roberto de Armas of the Foreign Ministry asked, "Was she very angry not to get the interview?"

I grabbed the phone and said, "I'm back."

I could hear him screaming to his boss, in Spanish, "She's still here!" I had become their worst nightmare.

That night, Fidel came through. We were brought back to one of his many offices, where he usually worked until dawn. We talked for three hours, brief by Castro's standards. Despite the awkwardness of asking him about his health after the fainting episode, I found him ready with details about his blood pressure, pulse (sixty per minute), cholesterol readings (375), and weight. Who would replace him? For the first time, he revealed his plans for succession. Cuba's next leader would be his brother Raul, head of Cuba's armed forces but only five years younger than he. Had he thought about having a younger generation carry on his legacy?

He said, "Raul is very healthy. Undoubtedly, he's the comrade who has the most authority after me, and has the most experience. Therefore, I think he has the capacity to succeed me."

He was even open about what had happened when he fainted. "Perhaps I was sweating too much. I was really drenched in sweat. All of a sudden, I don't remember what happened. I did realize I was being carried away."

"You passed out?" I asked.

"Yes, perhaps I passed out for fifteen seconds. It was like going to sleep, like falling asleep, like sometimes when you are watching TV. If instead of fainting, it had been a heart attack or a stroke, which is not very likely, not for the time being, because my blood pressure is between seventy and one-ten, which is very normal. But it is not something that I am worried about, my succession."

At that point Fidel Castro had antagonized ten American presidents, and was not worried about dying. Now he was ready to spar with George W. Bush, especially because of his family's long connection with Florida's anti-Castro Cuban-Americans. Did Fidel see any chance of better relations with this president?

"He was not elected, he was appointed president of the United States," was his response.

I pointed out that Bush would say that Castro hadn't been elected either. Castro was combative when I pressed him on Cuba's lack of free elections and asked why he wouldn't release political prisoners. I had clearly pushed him as far as I could. Behind me, I could hear his aides rustling papers. I knew that meant the interview was over. When we stood up, Castro asked me to join him across the hall to meet his young leaders, gathering in his cabinet room at midnight to give him a nightly report on "polling" in the provinces. For more than an hour, they each stood and gave him the public's reactions to his nightly broadcast on Cuban television. More than a thousand people had been "questioned." Who knew that Fidel Castro had his own focus groups!

There was one more remarkable episode during that visit. After getting all of that exclusive material, just before we were to go live on *Nightly News* from the rooftop of Cuban TV the next evening, an enormous storm blew in. Within minutes, just before my report, it started pouring, threatening to knock us off the air. I could imagine all our efforts being washed away. Suddenly, the staff from Cuban TV started appearing on the roof, dragging poles, a ladder, brooms— anything they could get their hands on to help erect a tent. They'd been watching from the control room, had seen the storm blow in, and without being asked had raced to the roof to make sure I got on the air—fellow broadcasters who probably didn't like what I was saying about their government, but knew the show must go on.

———

I went back to Havana a year later to cover Jimmy Carter's landmark trip to deliver a human rights lecture on Cuban television. He was the first American president, in or out of office, to visit Cuba since Castro had seized power in 1959. Carter and Castro had a long history. As president, Carter accepted thousands of boat people trying to flee Cuba, but Castro used the exodus to unload hardened criminals and mental patients. It embarrassed Carter, and contributed to his defeat in 1980. Now, on the eve of Carter's trip, which the Bush administration approved only grudgingly, the State Department's hard-line arms controller, John Bolton, charged that Castro was hiding a biological weapons program. And Cuban dissidents, emboldened by Carter's trip, advertised their Varela Project, a drive to collect eleven thousand signatures petitioning for free elections. Castro was furious.

Fidel quickly seized the initiative, taking Carter on a tour of the suspect biological sciences laboratories. American intelligence officials told me there was nothing to the State Department accusations, though Jimmy Carter was certainly in no position to reach a judgment either way. Castro claimed the labs were developing a meningitis vaccine in a joint venture with the American firm GlaxoSmithKline. The Cubans easily deflected the Bush administration's concerns about weapons. And although Carter was able to meet with dissidents, there was no spontaneous outpouring by Cubans demanding free elections. Castro's regime had too tight a hold on his people for that. As Castro had calculated, Carter had more of an impact in calling for an end to the U.S. embargo on Cuba than in sparking a groundswell for democracy. The Cubans I talked to were more interested in economic reform than political change.

I interviewed Carter, but Castro refused all requests, not wanting to distract attention from his visitor. But as soon as Carter's plane took off, Castro marched back down the red carpet and stood in front of my camera. Unfortunately, the roar of Carter's jet on the runway drowned out what he was saying. As Castro left, and the camera crews started putting away their equipment, one of Fidel's top aides came to get me and escort me inside the terminal. I was brought to a private room, where Fidel waited. We talked for forty-five minutes, and I extracted a promise that he would do another interview if I returned in six months to cover a conference commemorating the fortieth anniversary of the Cuban Missile Crisis. With that, he took me to my plane.

Little did I know how badly it would all turn out. A week later, Alan and I were in New York at a small dinner Barbara Walters was giving. She asked me to tell the group about my Cuban adventure. Unwittingly, I talked about my plans to cover Castro's October conference, which was going to reassemble all the surviving players of the era: Robert McNamara and Ted Sorenson from the Kennedy administration, the Russian generals, and, of course, Fidel. Barbara and I are friends, and she has been unfailingly kind and encouraging to me over the years. We also share an unusual personal history, since she dated Alan in the 1970s, and remains close to him. But nothing gets between Barbara and a "get." It is why she is, was, and always will be, the most indefatigable television journalist, male or female, in the business. In the following weeks and months, she proved it once again by talking Cuba's young foreign minister, Felipe Perez Roque, into promising her an interview with Fidel during the Cuban Missile conference. Even worse, she insisted it be exclusive. He couldn't keep his commitments to the other networks.

The Cubans had planned to give interviews to Dan Rather, Barbara, and me. The *Today* show built two days of scheduled broadcasts around the event, flying in a plane loaded with equipment so that Matt Lauer could anchor from Havana. Everything was pegged to the Castro interview. I got to Havana, only to learn from a story in the New York tabloids that Barbara was getting the only interview. The foreign minister came to my hotel to apologize, explaining that he hadn't realized how competitive the television news business was. Indeed! While we appealed the decision, the network was going crazy. The *Today* show urgently needed to know whether or not to send Matt. New York executives were calling by the hour to remind me of how much money I was wasting.

Furious, Dan Rather's people pulled out, but I stayed at least to cover the conference. It reminded me of the classic film *Rashomon*. Each side replayed its version of history, producing new evidence of how dangerously close they had come to a nuclear showdown. On the last day, the palace asked me to stop by and say good-bye to the president.

He wanted to make amends. When Mary and I walked into his sitting room, he offered us "a very good California merlot" he'd gotten during a trade show in Havana. So much for the embargo! The situation could not have been more ridiculous. He asked me if I was still angry. I said I was, because he'd wasted our money and embarrassed me with my bosses. Trying to appease me, he said Barbara had only gotten what he called a "celebrity interview" and that if I came back, he'd give me better access than ABC had had. With that, he drove me to my plane. With Castro squeezed in the backseat of his armored limo between me and his trusted aide Juanita, I asked how the Russian generals had impressed him, after the passage of so many years. He said he was struck by the fact that they had no sense of humor. It was all I could do to retain mine.

Fidel delivered on his promise to give me a special interview. I returned in December and we spent a week traveling all over the island. At my request, Castro took us to see the biomedical laboratories that had been the subject of so much State Department suspicion. We went to Lourdes, the Soviet-era spy station Castro was converting into a computer science school. We went to schools for the arts, for disabled children and for inner-city teenagers. We visited a port facility where Cuba was refining American grain. And finally, I got my interview.

We talked for so many hours that at one point, I'm told, I nodded off. It wasn't an easy conversation. With so much talk in the U.S. about the possibility of war with Iraq, Castro got cranky when I pressed him on his attitude toward Saddam Hussein. He was noticeably concerned about the possibility of war because of Cuba's enormous dependence on foreign oil and the likelihood that war in the Gulf would cause shortages and higher prices. Once again, I pressed him about his own mortality and his plans for succession. We filed a series of stories for the broadcast and cable networks, and produced an hour-long, prime-time special for MSNBC.

I left Cuba concerned about the country's uncertain future, fears that were born out only a few months later when Castro ordered a major crackdown, arresting seventy-five dissidents, including many of the people I had interviewed. We applied for another visa, in order to cover their trials. This time Castro nailed the gates shut to American broadcasters. I argued that we could do a better job of reporting all sides of the story from down there, but the Cubans refused. So Mary stuck her neck out and gathered as much material as she could in Havana, while I did interviews in Washington. I talked to Cuba's very effective representative in the United States, Dagoberto Rodriguez, along with Senator Chris Dodd, a longtime opponent of the embargo who was reevaluating his position because of the arrests, and Cuban dissident Oswaldo Paya, who was visiting the States. Combining all of these elements, we did a series of tough reports on the crackdown. Castro was furious.

I returned to Cuba to argue that we could tell their side of the story more completely if they granted us access. But all of Castro's aides were angry about our coverage. During a meeting that turned into a virtual show trial of my work, the foreign minister even played a video they'd made of my reports on the human rights issue, cataloguing their complaints. I asked, "Who suddenly made you a professor of journalism?"

In succeeding years, with Florida once again central to a presidential election campaign, and in reaction to Castro's crackdown, the Bush administration tightened the embargo and all but eliminated cultural exchanges. Cuban-Americans can no longer return home each year. There were many unintended victims of the new policy. For instance, we profiled a Cuban-American soldier in Iraq who came home to Miami on leave, hoping to fly to Havana to visit his teenage children from a previous marriage. He missed out by one day. The new restrictions had just gone into effect. He is back in Baghdad, and has still not been able to see his kids.

———

My adventures in Havana taught me a lot about "talking back" to dictators. There can be no compromise with freedom of expression. You can debate American policy, but you can't justify "a little bit of repression." It's difficult to defend a regime that throws its critics in jail, no matter how demonized it is by its opponents. Fidel was willing to engage in a dialogue, but he had his limits. Over the years, I've bumped up against them every time I've pushed him hard on human rights. Still, if you can compare one totalitarian regime with another, I've been to other places that were far scarier. None was more frightening than Afghanistan, accompanying then–UN ambassador Bill Richardson as he tried to persuade the Taliban to agree to stop providing sanctuary to Osama bin Laden.

The Taliban had first imposed strict Islamic law when they took power in 1996. Women were for the most part confined to their homes. Men had to wear beards of a certain length. By the time we arrived in April of 1998, they had imposed such severe prohibitions on women traveling without a male relative that even the United Nations was withdrawing its mission. At the airport, Taliban representatives lined up to greet our small UN plane. We weren't sure whether we could even shoot video of the black-turbaned greeting party. It was against their interpretation of Islam for any living creature to be photographed.

Bill Richardson had a deserved reputation as an international troubleshooter: before becoming UN ambassador, while still a member of Congress he had managed to win the release of Americans imprisoned in North Korea and Iraq. Now, he would be the first American official of cabinet rank to visit Afghanistan since Henry

Kissinger in 1974. His stated mission was to broker a cease-fire between the Taliban and Afghanistan's feudal warlords. The real purpose was to see if the Taliban would give up bin Laden.

I had started writing about Osama bin Laden several years earlier, when American intelligence first began linking him to several bombings of U.S. servicemen in Saudi Arabia—charges later discredited. In one of those early reports for *Nightly News,* I had called bin Laden "the new face of terror, the renegade son of a Saudi billionaire. Elusive. Mysterious. And now, wanted worldwide." My producer Robert Windrem and I reported that bin Laden recruited his followers by investing millions of dollars to improve conditions in countries like Sudan and then opening training camps to mold the young radicals into strike forces ready to disperse to other countries. Already, U.S. investigators were linking him to Ramzi Yousef, one of the masterminds behind the 1993 World Trade Center bombing. And for the first time on American television, we had video, pictures of bin Laden climbing in the mountains of Afghanistan and meeting in his tent with his closest aide, Ayman al-Zawahiri.

How did we get the video? Bob and I had been at a background briefing with government officials in advance of writing our story. I asked if anyone had ever seen a picture of this guy. They showed us a paperback book, in Arabic, that had one photo, and said the original was in the New York Public Library's Middle East division. We had a researcher fax us the entire book, in Arabic, along with a translation. To our amazement, once it was translated, we realized the back cover offered a companion video! Our Cairo bureau chief, Charlene Gubash, tracked down the producer and bought a copy for thirty-two hundred dollars. It may turn out to be one of the biggest bargains NBC News ever got. In the years since, we have used those pictures over and over again, followed by every other network. Those images are how the world was first introduced to Osama bin Laden.

When we filed our first stories on him, the idea of a terrorist from a fabulously wealthy Saudi family who had fought alongside CIA-financed mujahideen to drive the Soviets from Afghanistan sounded far-fetched, and even a bit romantic. Some of my producers thought my focus on bin Laden was obsessive, that I had been spending too much time covering the CIA. But it wasn't long before the agency had established a top secret bin Laden "station" headed by Michael Scheuer. Scheuer recently came in from the cold and identified himself as the author who, as "Anonymous," wrote *Imperial Hubris,* a book sharply critical of the Bush administration's war on terror. He subsequently resigned from the CIA.

The Taliban told Richardson that bin Laden was their "guest" in Kandahar, and untouchable. As a small gesture to the visiting ambassador, they at least postponed that day's public amputations and executions in Kabul's sports stadium, their form of criminal justice. Having made no headway on terrorism, Richardson would have to settle for a promise on another front, that the Taliban would hold cease-fire talks in the civil war. On a final issue, the role of women, he won no concessions at all.

Behind their burkas, the women of Kabul floated through the dusty streets like ghosts, robbed of all identity. Before the Taliban, they were able to work as doctors and teachers, filling essential jobs in a society whose male population had been decimated by more than a decade of civil war. Now, barred from holding jobs, many were committing suicide. On the streets, religious police patrolled in black pickup trucks, on the lookout for anyone who bared too much ankle, or dared to talk in public to a man.

I was approached by two young men, brothers, who huddled on the filthy floorboard of my car to avoid detection so they could tell me about their mother and sister. Eighteen-year-old Shoaib said his mother had been a school principal, his younger sister a star student. Now both were housebound, virtual prisoners. He and his brother pleaded with me to tell their story so that the world would know of their plight. What would their future be like? They told me they both wanted to be journalists so that they could report on Afghanistan's struggle. I was afraid of putting them in danger and didn't dare record their appeals on camera.

We traveled north to Shibergan, one of the few cities then still free of the Taliban's hold. We were greeted by cheering throngs, including a group of women doctors. The contrast to the profound silence of Kabul could not have been more striking. Abdul Rashid Dostum, the local warlord and leader of the Uzbeks, welcomed our small traveling party with elaborate pageantry and the performance of bazkashi, a polo-like game played by Uzbek horsemen tossing the head of a goat. Somehow, I got separated from the rest of the motorcade and had to run across the playing field, dodging horses—and the goat's head—until I reached the safety of the stadium seats.

In the chaos of our arrival, the National Security Council's top Middle East expert, Bruce Riedel, tripped and fell into an open pit carrying sewage, slashing his leg. Blood was pouring out of the gash on his calf. I ran to get my producer, who was carrying a first aid kit. To my amazement, he knew how to sterilize a needle and confidently stitched up Bruce's leg. For years afterward, Bruce jokingly told me NBC had probably saved his leg, if not his life.

Richardson negotiated what he thought was a successful cease-fire, halting the civil war and laying out a timetable for peace talks to come. Details still needed to be worked out, but he ran out of time: in order to fly out that night we had to leave before sundown—there were no lights on the airstrip. As we prepared to leave, Dostum ordered his men to pile Afghan carpets into a truck, one for each member of the official party. All I could think of was what the load of heavy carpets would do to the lift, on a dirt runway no less, of that small prop plane.

I never saw what happened to the rugs, but as we took off, we saw spectacular bursts of antiaircraft fire. The cease-fire was already broken and the two sides were once again shelling each other as our pilot took evasive action. I buckled my seat belt and practically held my breath until we had crossed the mountains into Pakistan.

My departure from Islamabad was delayed as thousands of pilgrims tried to get on flights to Saudi Arabia for the annual hajj. When I finally did get back to New York and put together my stories, I had no idea that the region would become such a tinderbox, and so important a part of our universe. Only one month later, Pakistan's government set off a nuclear test, triggering a tense arms race with India in one of the world's most dangerous flashpoints. Shortly after that, a secret indictment handed up by a grand jury in New York charged Osama bin Laden with terrorism in connection with the killing of eighteen U.S. soldiers in Somalia in 1993 as well as the attacks on U.S. military personnel in Saudi Arabia and the 1996 al Qaeda fatwa ordering Muslims to kill Jews and Christians anywhere they could be found.

Later that summer Osama bin Laden attacked two American embassies in Africa. Bill Clinton retaliated against suspected training camps in Afghanistan and a possible bin Laden–related chemical plant in Sudan, but critics said the intelligence was faulty, and the response too little, too late. The president could have been distracted: he had just testified to the grand jury investigating the Lewinsky affair and acknowledged, finally, what he had long denied. He had had what he called an "inappropriate relationship"—what other people would call "sex"—with "that woman Miss Lewinsky."

Under the strain of the terror attack and their personal turmoil, the president and his wife led the nation in mourning the victims from the embassies in Kenya and Tanzania at a memorial service at Andrews Air Force Base. It was our first chance to observe the Clintons since their painful retreat to Martha's Vineyard after he confessed his marital infidelity. They had aged dramatically since those first days in the snows of New Hampshire.

Standing at Andrews, I watched the flag-draped coffins being carried from the planes and thought of all the other victims of terrorism who had been eulogized during the years since the Beirut bombings during the Reagan administration. None of us had any idea that this tragedy, as awful as it was, was only the first of many worse still to come. Bin Laden and al Qaeda were already plotting an assault on America more devastating than anything we had yet contemplated.

CHAPTER 8

Peace on Earth

The millennium dawned peacefully. Despite billions of dollars spent in anticipation of a technology crash, computers worked. Trains ran on time. Planes landed with no interruption in air traffic control. None of this had been forecast. At the Federal Reserve, top officials had been up all night manning command posts to pick up any hint of a breakdown in the electronic global check transfer system. The FBI and Canadian authorities were working around the clock to preempt a millennium bomb plot. At NBC, correspondents and producers were positioned around the world on terror alert. Nothing happened.

The only two NBC reporters permitted to have fun on New Year's Eve were Fred Francis and me. Fred had sweet-talked the producers into assigning him to Las Vegas, one of his favorite haunts. And after doing live reports all morning for the *Today* show from Washington's Mall, I had been given the night off to attend the president's black-tie White House Millennium Dinner.

At the White House that New Year's Eve, as one century was ending and another beginning, the Clintons had assembled stars from every profession, along with a large contingent of campaign contributors. Democratic chairman Terry McAuliffe bragged that they raised $16 million that night. The lure was the venue and a spectacular and eclectic guest list: among others, Bono, Sid Caesar, Muhammad Ali, Robert De Niro, Mary Tyler Moore, Jack Nicholson, Will Smith, and Elizabeth Taylor, who arrived last, wearing enormous diamonds, and walking—with difficulty and two escorts—to her seat. For the first time in my memory, the unusually large guest list of 360 was seated in two rooms, the East Room and the State Dining Room, both festooned with white orchids and roses topping silver velvet tablecloths. The president alternated between the rooms as the chefs served beluga caviar, lobster, foie gras, rack of lamb, and a dessert of chocolate and champagne. Addressing the assemblage, including artists, musicians, actors, and political contributors, Bill Clinton raised his glass and said, "I cannot help but think how different America is, how different history is, and how much better, because those of you in this room and those you represent were able to imagine, to invent, to inspire."

Guests were told they could bring their children, who ate in a tent in the Rose Garden. Then they were able to join six hundred others for fireworks and a performance in front of the Lincoln Memorial on the Mall, produced by George Stevens, Jr. Die-hard partygoers were invited back to the White House for breakfast and dancing till dawn. There were so many celebrities, the stars themselves were craning their necks to see which pop icons might be seated at the next table. As a lapsed violinist, I was especially delighted to find myself sitting with Pinchas Zukerman.

While we were partying, national security officials were congratulating themselves on having thwarted a deadly plot. Two weeks before, they had arrested an Algerian man, Ahmed Ressam, completely by chance. An alert customs inspector had stopped him at Port Angeles, Washington, north of Seattle, after he arrived on a ferry from Canada with more than 130 pounds of bomb-making chemicals and four homemade detonators hidden in the trunk of his car. He admitted being part of a conspiracy to blow up Los Angeles International Airport. Officials soon learned that the millennium plot was indeed part of a much larger operation. The United States announced it had broken up terror cells in eight countries, with the help of Jordanian intelligence, almost certainly preventing numerous attacks.

In a foreshadowing of changes that have now become routine, U.S. airports tightened security after Ressam's arrest, a dramatic response to what officials called a "heightened terror threat." But while we were eating foie gras at the White House, Tawfiq bin Attash, aka Khallad, one of the planners of the embassy bombings and a key operative in the group already plotting 9/11, flew from Kuala Lumpur, Malaysia to Bangkok, Thailand and on to Hong Kong. According to intelligence sources and the *9/11 Commission Report,* he carried a box cutter in his toilet kit to test airport security. At the Bangkok airport, screeners opened the kit but let him continue. Along with Khallad and others, on January 5, 2000, Nawaf Alhazmi and Khalid Almihdhar arrived in Kuala Lumpur for an al Qaeda summit. They were already discussing a bold plan to hijack airliners and crash them into American targets. Two years later, they flew American Airlines flight 77 into the Pentagon.

The CIA knew about the Kuala Lumpur meeting, but not its significance. Intelligence was scanty, and follow-up minimal. The news media were similarly unfocused. After all the warnings about millennium terror proved unfounded, there was a sense that the intelligence community had been crying wolf. Like most Washington reporters, my attention was rapidly shifting to the upcoming election. I was also handed an entirely new professional challenge. NBC wanted me to anchor a nightly broadcast on our cable station, MSNBC, a show they wanted to advertise as NBC's "political newscast of record" for the campaign year. It was a great opportunity, but I worried about losing my traction on the foreign policy beat, and disappearing from *Nightly News.* The cable show would air every night at six p.m. *Nightly News* went on at six-thirty p.m. I would be facing almost simultaneous deadlines on broadcast and cable, often on entirely different stories.

Facing a career crossroads, I sought out Tom Brokaw. His advice was to seize the opportunity. He assured me that he and the producers would help me overcome the logistics, and that the chance to do a political show was worth it. As it turned out, he, and David Doss, our executive producer at the time, kept that commitment. Although in the past there had been a caste system at the network, with *Nightly News* obligations taking precedence over everything else, everyone on Tom's team, especially our foreign editor, ML Flynn, jumped through hoops to help me make my cable deadlines. It made me realize that the fledgling cable news operation was becoming a critical part of our company's long-term strategy. The challenges of functioning in two worlds simultaneously remained daunting.

At the time, though, I never even considered whether adding a second full-time job on top of covering foreign policy and politics for *Nightly News* could overload my personal system. Alan and I saw it as an opportunity and a challenge, not a burden. We didn't discuss how it might affect our free time because it never occurred to either of us that there was a choice. When offered a chance to do something new, the only conceivable answer was yes. Once again, as I had my entire working life, I leaped off a cliff. But despite the best of intentions, the cable network had no one to catch me.

The show was initially called *Decision 2000,* but within a few weeks became *The Mitchell Report.* It had no format, no executive producer, a tiny budget, and a remote control room in New Jersey. In some ways, nothing had changed since *Summer Sunday,* sixteen years earlier, when NBC let Linda Ellerbee and me play at doing television. Initially, the idea was to feature NBC political correspondents and our colleagues from *Newsweek* and *The Washington Post* in a reporter's roundtable. Quickly, the show morphed into an interview program, with top-flight political guests.

On the first broadcast, we covered a debate between Al Gore and Bill Bradley, debriefed reporters Claire Shipman, Jonathan Alter, and Dan Balz, interviewed Andrew Cuomo about a potential New York Senate race between Hillary Clinton and Rudy Giuliani, and did a cross talk with Tim Russert. We had so many people appearing in boxes, it looked like *Hollywood Squares.*

We did improve, and became a cable destination for political junkies. NBC let us take the show on the road to all the primary states and the debates. In New Hampshire, we latched on to John McCain's "Straight Talk Express," which had captured the imagination of the political press corps. And I caught up with George W. Bush, whom I hadn't covered since his days as campaign "enforcer," when he was riding herd on his father's more laid-back campaign managers.

Doing the show was fun, but best of all was being back in New Hampshire, where politics is the home-team sport. One morning, I chased down Al and Tipper Gore in a doughnut shop so we could open our show with an exclusive interview. Running around to all of these events drove my producers crazy. They were just trying to put on a talk show. But I wanted to get out in the field and break some news. No matter how unbalanced the early primaries and caucuses are, with states like Iowa and New Hampshire carrying so much weight, that kind of "retail," front-porch politics where candidates have to sell themselves door-to-door is as good as it gets for political reporters. It's the only time of the campaign year when candidates mix with small groups of people, and advertisements are less important than first impressions, face-to-face. In a presidential campaign year, nothing beats New Hampshire in January.

We also had a few "firsts." In July, the biggest unknowns were each candidate's running mates. NBC had a proud tradition of breaking vice presidential running mate stories: in 1980, Chris Wallace was the first to report that Ronald Reagan had chosen George Herbert Walker Bush. In 1988, I had broken the Quayle story. Now Claire Shipman broke the news that Joe Lieberman would run with Al Gore. And on July 21, while we were also busy covering the president's Camp David summit with Ehud Barak and Yasser Arafat, we got the first word from Lisa Myers that Dick Cheney would be on the ticket with George W. Bush.

Lisa's scoop is a tale of smart reporting, as well as missed opportunities. In March of 2000, Bush had asked Cheney, who was vetting possible running mates for Bush, whether he would put himself on the list. Cheney, who had become the chief executive of Halliburton, the energy services giant, declined, saying he was enjoying the private sector after all those years in government. But on July 3, over the holiday weekend, Cheney visited Bush at his ranch in Crawford, and Bush asked again. This time, Cheney said he'd think about it.

The next night, the Cheneys were back in Washington and came to a Fourth of July party Alan and I give each year for Federal Reserve families and our other friends. It's a Fed tradition established by Alan's predecessor, Paul Volcker. Staff and other friends bring their children for a picnic supper, and after dinner we have the greatest entertainment possible, courtesy of the city—fireworks, directly across the Mall from the Fed's rooftop balcony.

That year, the Fed's dining room was buzzing with speculation about the campaign and the vice presidential contenders. The rumor mill had speculation about Governors Tom Ridge, George Pataki, and Frank Keating; Senators John McCain and Chuck Hagel; even former senator John Danforth. Cheney, the only person with real information, was like catnip for a room full of reporters. I didn't want to impose on our friendship to ask any "work" questions, but I noticed that just about every other reporter was sidling up to him.

The next day, Republican pollster Bob Teeter, an old friend and coleader of NBC's polling team, was on my show to talk about vice presidential choices. Chatting afterward, we talked about how Cheney was better qualified than any of the others on the list. Teeter, who had been friends with Cheney since the Ford White House, may have been sending me a signal, but I didn't pick up on it.

The following week, on July 18, our Senate producer Roberta Hornig was told that Cheney was going to be Bush's running mate. She passed the information on to Lisa Myers, who started digging for confirmation from the Bush camp. It took three days, but the tip-off was when Lisa reached the Teton County clerk in Jackson, Wyoming, and discovered that Cheney, then a resident of Dallas, where Halliburton was headquartered, switched his registration to vote in Wyoming. The only possible motive would be to avoid constitutional problems that would arise if both the presidential and vice presidential candidates came from the same state of Texas.

As soon as Lisa got word of Cheney's change in registration, she came on my show to break the story. The newspapers picked it up the next day, putting Cheney at the top of the list of contenders, but there were still boomlets for McCain, Danforth, and others. The weekend talk shows were filled with false leads. For instance, on Monday, Dan Rather reported on CBS Radio that the president and his father were in heavy negotiations with Colin Powell to take the job. None of the rumors was true. On Tuesday morning, Bush called Cheney and made the offer, which was instantly accepted.

Most of the pundits praised Bush's choice. Cheney was considered a seasoned statesman, with foreign policy experience, and it was thought that George W. could use a little seasoning.

A week later, we took the show to the Republican convention in Philadelphia. I anchored *The Mitchell Report* on MSNBC and worked as a floor correspondent, doing interviews during our prime-time coverage on NBC. Over the years, as the political parties changed their primary and caucus schedules to pick their nominees by late winter or early spring, modern conventions lost their nominating function. They have become extended televised advertisements for the political parties, uninterrupted by any controversy, even a contentious platform issue. Occasionally, though, developments do take us by surprise, such as Pat Buchanan's red-meat speech in 1992 that divided the Republicans and sharpened the divisions between the two parties, or John Kerry's decision in 2004 to silence all attacks against George Bush and focus almost entirely on his Vietnam record. But for the most part, conventions have become entirely predictable. Floor fights over party rules or policies are history. The diminished network coverage reflects that new reality.

With the networks now devoting only one hour a night to broadcast coverage, there is much less airtime to report from the floor. That greatly increases the pressure to compete for A-list guests. Booking "gets," to use the slang of our profession, is my least favorite thing about modern convention coverage. None of us likes it, because often you plead with a cabinet secretary or governor to appear at a precise time, then search for that politician among thousands of people milling about on the convention floor, only to discover that the producers have changed their plans for that segment. When you're standing next to a governor whom you've begged for a live interview and the live shot is canceled, it is painful.

On the second night, the convention paid tribute to Gerald Ford. Having just visited the Fords that June in Colorado, I was able to get an exclusive interview with the former president. But as soon as we went on the air, it was apparent that something was wrong. His speech was slurred, and he explained that he'd been suffering from a sinus infection and was taking antibiotics. I was concerned enough to call Alan from my cell phone as soon as the interview was over. He was also worried, having noticed the same problem with the former president's speech.

Still, the eighty-seven-year-old former president stayed in his VIP box until eleven that night, when the session ended. I waved goodbye as he and Mrs. Ford walked out slowly together, declining a staff offer of a golf cart to ease their way. When I got back to my hotel at one a.m., I heard a radio bulletin that Jerry Ford had been taken to the emergency room of a local hospital. Despite my concerns for him, I felt I had to do my job. Calling in to MSNBC, I did a phone report about my impressions of his health earlier that evening. Then I ran to the hospital.

By the time I got there, Ford had already been treated and released. As he headed back to his hotel, he pointed to his head to indicate that he thought it was a minor problem. The doctor had given him medicine to clear his ears so he could fly back to Colorado later in the day.

The next morning I had to report President Ford's condition for the *Today* program, appearing from a camera location outside his hotel on Rittenhouse Square. It was the same park I'd walked through thirty-two years earlier as a kid reporter covering the night beat for KYW. Suddenly, there was a commotion behind me. The former president was heading back to the hospital. This time, they got the diagnosis right. He had suffered two small strokes.

He was all right, but Betty was understandably distressed. She agreed to do an interview with me to talk about her husband's condition and to reassure people that he was going to recover fully. He had, up until that point, been in remarkably good health, with the exception of two knee replacements. I'd watched his daily routine of swimming laps at their home in Beaver Creek. He also still played nine holes of golf on Colorado's steep courses. And both Fords strongly resisted suggestions that Colorado's thinly oxygenated mountain air put them at risk. But they also knew that the effort of getting to Philadelphia had been too much for them, and that after a lifetime in politics, this would be their last Republican convention.

During the convention, other advisors who later became major players in George Bush's administration had big parts to play. I interviewed Condoleezza Rice, who was tutoring Bush on foreign policy. She stressed the "compassionate" side of his conservatism, and promised that, if elected, he would make sure the administration was more representative of America. In contrast to Rice, Colin Powell delivered a provocative speech, which included an endorsement of affirmative action, a hot-button issue. He scolded the delegates, saying, "We must understand the cynicism that exists in the black community, the kind of cynicism that is created when, for example, some in our party miss no opportunity to roundly and loudly condemn affirmative action that helped a few thousand black kids get an education, but you hardly hear a whimper when it's affirmative action for lobbyists who load our federal tax code with preferences for special interests. It doesn't work! It doesn't work. You can't make that case."

As Powell spoke, I could hear a rumble from the delegates. They were actually jeering him—he, a war hero, and easily the most popular Republican in America. This was a man who was too liberal for his national party. It was an early sign of how out of sync the new secretary of state would later be with the neoconservatives in the White House and Pentagon. Powell has always defined himself as a Republican because of the party's tougher stance on all things military. He is much more comfortable with the Republican vision of how a superpower behaves in the world than with a Democratic foreign policy. That led to difficult moments during the Clinton years, when Powell was chairman of the Joint Chiefs of Staff. At times, the general openly criticized some cabinet officials—particularly Madeleine Albright—who he thought were naïve on defense issues. But while Powell thought of himself as a Republican, he identified more with the moderate, internationalist policies of the first President Bush than with the tougher, more confrontational philosophy of the second Bush administration.

Powell was clearly the cabinet's best-known figure and I anticipated that if Bush was elected, the new secretary of state would dominate the foreign policy team. That would mean that a Bush White House would, like Powell, be reluctant to use military force unless it was absolutely necessary, and then only with a broad coalition of allies. But most of us hadn't paid enough attention to what Dick Cheney, Don Rumsfeld, and their circle of advisors had been saying during the years they were out of office about the importance of overthrowing Saddam Hussein. Nor did we imagine that when policy disputes arose, Powell, although secretary of state, would be the odd man out.

In fact, during the 2000 campaign, it was far from clear that foreign policy would be very different under Bush than Clinton. In a pre-9/11 world, no one discussed world events very much. During the second presidential debate that year, there were only a few questions even tangentially related to foreign policy. Bush was asked about nation building, and flatly rejected the idea. "Maybe I'm missing something here. I mean, we're going to have kind of a nation building corps from America? Absolutely not. Our military is meant to fight and win war. That's what it's meant to do. And when it gets overextended, morale drops."

In that same debate, he was asked how he would project the United States around the world, as president. He said, "If we're an arrogant nation, they'll resent us. If we're a humble nation, but strong, they'll welcome us. And our nation stands alone right now in the world in terms of power, and that's why we have to be humble. And yet project strength in a way that promotes freedom."

Few people paid enough attention to that answer. Even in the years since, critics of the Iraq war have made much of the seeming inconsistency between candidate Bush promising to have a "humble" foreign policy, and President Bush's doctrine of preemptive action. That ignores what he was saying before he took office. In that second debate, he made it clear that he believes great nations have an obligation, almost a religious requirement, to promote freedom by projecting their strength. It is a bedrock view, a core philosophy that is as fundamental to Bush as any of Reagan's essential principles was to him. You can disagree with the way George W. Bush has conducted his foreign policy, but you'd at least better understand his intentions.

Bush was judged lacking foreign policy skills because he flunked a pop quiz when asked to identify foreign leaders during a local TV interview in Boston. Critics dismissed him as stupid or, at least, unschooled in foreign affairs. But experience may be a poor measure of how a leader will perform. Most people overlooked the fact that George W. Bush had strong views about America's place in the world and, if elected, was determined to act on them.

———

My job that summer soon got even more complicated. In addition to hosting a daily political broadcast while covering the presidential campaign and foreign policy, I was assigned to follow the hottest

Senate race in the country—Hillary Clinton's race in New York. It was the first time a first lady had run for public office. Most people didn't know what to make of it. How would she succeed in appealing to voters in New York, instead of her birth state of Illinois, or her adopted Arkansas, especially since she was trying to replace a political icon, Senator Daniel Patrick Moynihan? And how could she perform her duties as first lady if she was spending all her time in New York?

Hillary had played many roles over the years: loyal wife, political victim, and political savior. As she saw her husband's White House years drawing to a close, she and her friends argued that it was her turn. Bill had damaged his legacy with Monica and impeachment. After twenty-five years of helping him, it was time for her to have a political career of her own. She could strike out on her own, instead of being the "wronged wife," and make sure people remembered her for more than a failed health-care initiative. Her aides were telling me, "Don't expect joint appearances with that other Clinton. She has to establish her own identity. Let him stay home and run the country."

By March of 1999, she was drawing crowds and news coverage befitting a presidential candidate. Three months later, she was dropping local place names like Queens and Elmira into almost every sentence to deflect criticism that she was nothing more than a carpetbagger. Her unofficial staff was hunting for campaign headquarters as she organized her New York makeover. The Clintons would plan a summer vacation in the Adirondacks, or the Finger Lakes, instead of Martha's Vineyard. She'd visit Cooperstown, the birthplace of baseball. And she would launch her campaign on the historic Moynihan farm upstate.

Alan and I had spent a weekend there with Liz and Pat Moynihan the previous summer. Their farm was set on a thousand rolling acres not far from the town of Oneonta. This was where Pat retreated to write books in a nineteenth-century one-room schoolhouse on the property—an unlikely place to hold a campaign event with hundreds of reporters and camera crews. Liz had personally managed Pat's races since he was first elected in 1976 on budgets of thousands, not millions, of dollars. Now Hillary's big-money operation was coming to a rural crossroads called Pindars Corner.

Pat and the Clintons had always had an arm's-length relationship. For instance, three days before Bill Clinton went to Congress in September 1993 and called for universal health insurance, Moynihan had gone on *Meet the Press* and said there was no health care crisis. He also dismissed Clinton's claims of $91 billion in projected savings from Hillary's health-care proposal as "fantasy." But now Hillary needed Moynihan's blessing to help win over New Yorkers, and he obliged her. There was huge national interest in the race. In fact, her campaign kickoff drew a bigger crowd of reporters to that upstate farm than had shown up at the Texas statehouse when George W. Bush announced he was running for president.

The first lady had some big advantages, like an air force jet and the Secret Service to help move her from one location to the next. But she was facing a difficult race, because her likely opponent was New York City's tough-talking mayor, Rudy Giuliani. Appreciating a good political fight, Moynihan told me, "It's going to be a wonder to watch."

For the next few months, it was. Rudy crisscrossed the state taking shots at Hillary for being a carpetbagger. Both were polarizing figures. Polls showed that people either loved them or hated them. In a contest limited to one-liners and photo opportunities, he even popped up one night on her old turf, at a Cubs game at Wrigley Field, telling reporters, "I don't even live in Peoria, Illinois. Here's the idea, maybe you should run in a place that you don't know anything about." To rub it in, he scheduled a fund-raiser in Little Rock.

Hillary also gave Rudy some openings. At one point, she went to the Middle East—an attempt to use her position as first lady to curry votes with New York's Jewish community. It backfired. Not yet fully aware of the sensitivities of New York's ethnic voters, she hugged Yasser Arafat's wife, Suha, during a joint appearance, and even smiled diplomatically after Mrs. Arafat (without any evidence) accused Israel of using poison gas on Palestinian children. Hillary waited a full day to respond, and then blamed the translator for not explaining what Mrs. Arafat had said in Arabic. New York's tabloids had a field day.

A bigger challenge was how to appear more authentic to women voters, who should have been her biggest supporters but were telling pollsters they didn't know who the "real" Hillary was. Her advisors were informing her that white female voters favored Giuliani by eighteen points, a potentially fatal gender gap. Why were they so hostile to her? Some women said she was arrogant. Others said she wasn't independent enough, had sold out. And to many, she had an identity problem. Was she the "stand by your man" Hillary of 1992, the scorned wife of the impeachment scandal, or the "buy one, get one free" copresident and sometime health care czar?

The campaign had to reinvent the first lady, and that meant tackling the issue of her troubled marriage head-on. After months of self-imposed silence about the Lewinsky affair, Hillary spoke out in an interview with writer Lucinda Franks for Tina Brown's *Talk* magazine. In the article, Mrs. Clinton blamed her husband's pattern of infidelities on psychological damage he'd suffered as a child. We had come a long way from her angry comments on the *Today* show a year earlier, when the Lewinsky scandal first broke, about a "vast right-wing conspiracy."

It was a calculated gamble. Although some people said she was trying to excuse her husband's misbehavior, she hoped to forestall questions by talking about her marital problems herself. There was another motive. She was about to move out of the White House to establish residency in New York for her Senate campaign, and her advisors wanted to avert any suggestion that the first couple was splitting up. They weren't, but the move to address the matter directly was another White House first.

A friend had already scouted a house for them in Chappaqua, a Westchester County bedroom community an hour from New York City. On January 4, 2000, a moving van pulled up to the front door.

It wasn't your typical suburban move-in. Instead of the local Welcome Wagon, all the networks trailed the van's progress live, in "white Bronco" fashion, by helicopter. The first lady was now legally a New Yorker.

Rudy Giuliani pointedly told us, "I feel very, very proud of the fact that people from all over the country want to come to New York, including people from Arkansas."

The Clinton-Giuliani race had enough tension and drama for three soap operas. By March, the Republican-controlled Congress was opening hearings into whether the first lady was improperly using taxpayers' money to finance her campaign. They called it Air Hillary—a campaign kept aloft partly through subsidized flights on military jets. Democrats countered that all first ladies use military jets, and that the hearings were just a stunt to help Giuliani's campaign. We reported that the New York mayor also had taxpayer help: no plane, but an official car, and security men to clear his way.

Fortunately for Hillary, Giuliani had his own problems, many of them self-inflicted. For weeks, he refused to show any sympathy for the Haitian family of Patrick Dorismond, an unarmed man shot by New York's undercover police. He excused the police, blamed the victim, and even released the man's confidential juvenile police record. And this was only the latest in a series of controversial police shootings causing tension with minorities.

Suddenly that April, Hillary leaped ahead in the polls. After months of the race being a dead heat, now she was up by eight points statewide, and by an overwhelming forty-two points in New York City, where Giuliani was known best. The election was still seven months off, but Giuliani had to confront a growing impression that he was too mean even for the United States Senate. Looking for a forum to present a more human face to the public, Giuliani agreed to sit down with me for a town hall meeting, to be carried live on MSNBC in prime time. It was a roll of the dice: not only couldn't he control my questions, he had no idea what a live audience might ask.

But before we could do the show, the campaign took another dramatic turn. In a stunning announcement, Giuliani revealed that he was suffering from prostate cancer. New York's tough mayor, who had made his reputation as a prosecutor busting the mob, was now in a very different kind of battle, fighting cancer while undergoing a very ugly split from his wife. He was evaluating treatment options, and relying heavily on the woman he would later marry, Judith Nathan. This was a man reevaluating his life in front of our eyes.

At midnight the night before our town hall broadcast, Rudy's brain trust came to my hotel for a meeting. Clearly, the campaign was in crisis. His closest advisors did not know whether he was going to stay in the race. They wanted to cancel the broadcast, but weren't sure if that was the best strategy. Finally, they agreed he would keep the commitment.

It was a contentious interview, especially on the subject of police brutality by New York's police. This was before 9/11, when Rudy's courageous response would elevate him to the status of "America's mayor." Until then, he was just a middle-aged politician suffering from prostate cancer who had a reputation as a cad for going on television to notify his wife he was leaving her for another woman— not the most sympathetic character.

But that night, in a rare display of remorse, Giuliani expressed regrets for his handling of controversial police shootings. "I made a mistake. I should have conveyed the human feeling that I had of compassion and loss." He acknowledged he was "readjusting" his priorities in life. He was almost thinking out loud about his future.

This Senate race was turning into the best running story I'd been on in years. That is, until the next morning. I was at our New York studios in Rockefeller Center when I got a tip that Rudy had decided to drop out. We interrupted the network to break the story, and then carried his announcement live. Emotional but strangely calm, Giuliani was passing up a good political battle for the first time in his life, having decided that fighting cancer was more important than trying to defeat Hillary Clinton. Giuliani said, "I used to think the core of me was in politics. It isn't. When you feel your mortality and your humanity, you realize that the core of you is, first of all, being able to take care of your health."

Hillary's new challenger was a little-known Republican congressman from Long Island, Rick Lazio. Without a real contest, the first lady figured she had nothing to gain by talking to the national media, so she avoided us. It was far easier to deal with local reporters who might ask her about farm prices upstate or the dairy compact. The contest was dead even when the two finally faced real questions, in a debate moderated by Tim Russert. In the confrontation, Lazio tried to take Hillary on, crossing over to her podium and demanding she pledge to refuse contributions from political action committees. To millions of women across the state, he looked like a bullying husband demanding to see the credit card bill. Somehow Lazio had done what all of Hillary's campaign advisors had failed to accomplish—turned her into a sympathetic figure, especially to women.

Hillary had proved the skeptics wrong. She could operate outside of the White House, although she brought a lot of the White House infrastructure with her to pull it off. She dug down into local issues, particularly in rural, Republican areas upstate. After getting off to a bumpy start, she had shown herself to be an agile, adaptive politician, and a tireless campaigner.

To keep up with her Senate race, I had to anchor more and more of my shows from New York City, instead of from Washington. We used a *Today* show studio across the street from the *Nightly News* offices at 30 Rockefeller Center. To accommodate both deadlines, I frequently wrote and recorded my *Nightly News* script at five p.m. and then raced across the street to prepare for the six p.m. cable show. If I had time, I'd record my closing stand-up for *Nightly News* from the set. If not, I'd record my stand-up during a commercial break. It all depended on split-second timing, and having no technical glitches. This was not a drill for the faint of heart.

Even more challenging was to keep the show going while I juggled the other part of my job, covering foreign policy. In July, President Clinton held round-the-clock talks between the Israelis and Palestinians for fifteen days at Camp David, talks that ended badly. Despite intense pressure from the president, Yasser Arafat balked, refusing to accept the terms offered by Israel's prime minister, Ehud Barak. Clinton at times reminded me of a very bright, but undisciplined, college student who left his studying until the last minute, and somehow aced his courses. His all-nighters had worked when he needed votes for a landmark budget deal in 1993. Now, with time running out, why couldn't his powers of persuasion produce a miracle on that most intractable of problems, Middle East peace?

But the two sides had deep, historic differences that couldn't possibly be overcome, even by the sheer force of Bill Clinton's will and personality. The administration had not properly prepared the region for the July summit. The United States failed to bring the so-called moderate Arab states on board, especially Egypt and Saudi Arabia. Without their endorsement, Arafat had no political cover, and no pressure from his own constituency to do anything but stonewall.

Summits, like Camp David or the Bosnian peace talks in Dayton, Ohio, earlier in the administration, are very difficult to cover. The network's appetite for information was enormous, but the White House had imposed a "news blackout"—no briefings or substantive announcements to help us update our stories. Of course, that didn't stop the delegations from holding secret briefings for favored reporters in their own traveling press corps. Both sides played the rumor and leak game relentlessly, making it especially important for reporters to be wary of disinformation. The only way to separate rumor from fact was to call the negotiators on their cell phones when they took breaks and try to piece together an accurate picture of what was going on inside.

On July 19, reports leaked through the Israeli press that the summit had collapsed and the president was heading back to the White

House to declare it dead. Bags were packed, motorcades lined up with their engines running, and planes rolled out onto the tarmac to await the departing delegations. But just before midnight, people involved in the talks told me that under heavy pressure from Clinton, the two sides had agreed to keep talking. The president had to break away to attend the annual economic summit in Japan that weekend. But Arafat and Barak would stay behind and continue negotiating with the secretary of state until Clinton could return.

Clinton's maneuver extended the diplomatic marathon for another few days, but the negotiators never reached the finish line. After Clinton returned from Japan, Arafat still wouldn't compromise; the Israelis insisted they had made their best offer. After fifteen days of fruitless negotiations, the final breakdown came at three o'clock in the morning. As always, the deal breaker was who would control Jerusalem, a city claimed by both Palestinians and Israelis. U.S. negotiators blamed Arafat and other Arab leaders who had told the Palestinian leader to hold out for a better deal.

Two months later, in September, a new Palestinian intifada erupted against Israel. The White House blamed Ariel Sharon, the most powerful of Israel's conservative cabinet ministers, for provoking it by leading a march to the Al-Aqsa Mosque, one of East Jerusalem's most disputed holy sites. Palestinian youths, outraged, poured into the streets, throwing rocks at the soldiers accompanying Sharon. Over the next two days, the violence escalated quickly. Arab men and boys stoned hundreds of Jews who were praying at the Western Wall on Rosh Hashanah, the Jewish New Year; Israel retaliated with considerable force. Israel later claimed the outbreak had been long planned, and deliberately ignited. In any case, the chances of a political dialogue became even more remote.

A month later, the administration faced an even worse crisis. On October 12, suicide bombers attacked a U.S. warship, the USS *Cole,* in the harbor at Yemen. Seventeen sailors were killed; thirty-nine others were injured. Almost immediately, intelligence officials told me that the bombing had all the hallmarks of al Qaeda. According to the report of the 9/11 Commission, on November 25, 2000, National Security Advisor Sandy Berger and his deputy, Richard Clarke, wrote President Clinton that although the FBI and CIA had not reached formal conclusions, they believed a large al Qaeda cell was responsible. Still, the Clinton administration did not retaliate. Clinton and Berger later testified to the 9/11 Commission that they did not think the case was solid enough to go to war. And by then, the 2000 election recount was under way. Bill Clinton did not believe it wise to launch a military strike at a time when the nation's political leadership was so unsettled.

Only five days after George Bush was sworn in, CIA director George Tenet briefed the new president about al Qaeda's likely role in the *Cole* attack. Clarke recommended military action, but nothing was done. Bush told the 9/11 investigators, according to their report, he was concerned "lest an ineffective air strike just serve to give bin Laden a propaganda advantage." Two American presidents had been urged to take action against Osama bin Laden and neither had. It was nine months before 9/11.

Despite setbacks that would have discouraged most leaders, Clinton still didn't give up on the Middle East. That fall, with time running out on his presidency, he rushed to an emergency summit in Sharm el Sheik, Egypt, for one last effort to broker the agreement that had eluded him for eight years. There was little time to prepare, and the combination of the new intifada and the attack on the *Cole* created an ominous backdrop as the world leaders gathered to discuss peace. I went along, eager to see whether Clinton could make any headway, despite the escalating tensions. The setting for the meeting was in sharp contrast to the mayhem in the streets of the West Bank and Gaza. We arrived at a lush Red Sea hotel that could as easily have been a resort outside Phoenix or near Palm Springs. To add to the sense that we were disconnected from the real events in Israel and the Palestinian territories, this final summit of the Clinton years was held on a golf course carved out of the desert called the Jollyville Golf Resort. No summit venue could have been more poorly named.

For the next few days, I juggled covering the peace talks for *Nightly News* with taping interviews for my cable show. There were low expectations for the peace talks, and they were fulfilled. Once again, Arafat refused to budge. I flew back overnight on the White House press charter so I could anchor my show in Washington the next day.

Despite the newest reversal, in January, with only eighteen days left in office, Clinton summoned Arafat for one last round of White House talks. For Clinton, it punctuated eight years of frustrating peace efforts. It was clear where Clinton placed the blame. After he left office, he told me that Arafat had misled him. According to Clinton, the Palestinian leader had promised that if the president devoted time and political capital to the issue, the Palestinians would compromise. Clinton invested the time. Arafat didn't deliver.

What angered Clinton most was that with time running out on his presidency, he could have focused on either the Middle East or North Korea, but not both. Based on Arafat's assurances, he had foregone the chance to follow up on a diplomatic overture from Pyongyang that might have led to normalized relations with North Korea. It was a decision he deeply regretted. Clinton thought, perhaps too optimistically, that if he had met Kim Jong Il in person, he could have won acceptable terms for establishing diplomatic relations for the first time.

Were the North Koreans really ready to open up to the West? It was difficult to imagine, given what I had experienced that fall in Pyongyang. The communist country was a major exporter of missiles, was still designated by the State Department as a terrorist state, and was reportedly developing nuclear weapons. Its million-man army was considered enough of a threat to have warranted the deployment of thirty-eight thousand American troops on its border for the last half century.

In a surprising breakthrough that October, two weeks before the 2000 election, Madeleine Albright was going to have the opportunity to meet with the Korean dictator, Kim Jong Il, and see if there was an opportunity for diplomacy. She would be the first American secretary of state to visit the North in fifty-five years, since the communist state was first created. I had seen the country only from afar, through binoculars from U.S. military outposts along the border of the demilitarized zone, during separate trips with Ronald Reagan, Bill Clinton, and Albright herself. Now Albright was going to get to the North Korean capital, and I'd have a chance finally to explore the "hermit kingdom" that had long been closed to American journalists.

———

North Korea had sent an emissary to Washington with a letter inviting the president to Pyongyang. The State Department felt that North Korea was ready to deal, and Clinton ordered Albright to explore the possibilities. The North had lost millions of people to famine in the nineties. Now, it was also suffering from the ravages of a recent typhoon. The UN's World Food Programme was feeding almost eight million people there with a bare minimum of food. The need for more aid was massive. North Korea's economic plight was the only plausible explanation for the regime's willingness to reach out to the United States, even to the extent of tolerating a press entourage to accompany Albright. But while the North Koreans may have thought in the abstract that they were ready for media coverage, they—and we—were completely unprepared for the encounter.

We landed in North Korea at dusk. Already, the streets were dark. I don't think I'd ever been in another major city of two million people where there were no lights of any kind. No streetlights, traffic signals, or illuminated signs, and few if any pedestrians or other signs of life. By the time we got to the hotel, it was pitch-black. The hotel lobby was lit with a few bare lightbulbs hanging from the ceiling. As we soon learned, even those few lights were there to impress the Western press. Electricity was scarce, which is why they had a dusk-to-dawn blackout. Whatever resources they had were plowed into their oversized military, not into raising the standard of living for average Koreans.

Understandably, since I was the first NBC correspondent to get into Pyongyang in years, the *Nightly News* producers wanted me to roam the streets and capture a sense of what life was like in this secretive place. Unfortunately, that's exactly what the North Koreans didn't want us to do. We were all assigned "minders" from the Foreign Ministry, who functioned as censors. We could go only where we were told, and were escorted to places where there was nothing to shoot. The system worked perfectly, for them. They showed us a lot of Stalinist-style monuments and empty parks, but we never saw any people. Our video could have been an outtake from a horror movie, the kind with nightmare sequences of empty cities and no signs of human life.

Here I was in the forbidden kingdom, and all I could show was the official architecture of Kim Jong Il's capital. My producer in New York kept saying, "I want to see people in the street; I want to see stores—give us a sense of what life is like." It was a perfectly reasonable request, but there was no way to accomplish it without breaking the rules.

After hours of being told I could not take pictures of our surroundings, I was desperate. As soon as my minder went to lunch, I sneaked out of the hotel with a small handheld camera, along with another reporter. Wandering through the streets on our own, we walked for blocks, grabbing pictures when we could. We were able to show a traffic policeman going through an elaborately choreographed series of moves as though he were directing traffic. Except that there was no traffic to direct. There were few if any cars, and if there had been vehicles, they wouldn't have had gasoline. That didn't stop the policeman from waving and pointing as though there were. Perhaps he performed this elaborate charade because, in the North Korean system, once assigned to a job, you made sure you did it. As we walked on, the few people on the streets looked at us strangely, but left us alone.

No one stopped us until we wandered into a barbershop to see if people would chat. As soon as we tried to ask the patrons a few innocuous questions about everyday life, they ran. We knew we were in trouble. Moments later, they returned with two soldiers who'd been patrolling nearby. We were arrested, brought back to our hotel, and turned over to furious North Korean officials.

Right away, the North Koreans tried to take the tape, but I hid it inside my clothing and insisted that they let me call Albright's aides. They were staying separately, in an official guesthouse, but came quickly to bail me out of trouble. I was able to surreptitiously swap the tape for a blank, which I happily turned over. We saved our real tape, and were able to get it out on the satellite. I did reports for *Nightly News* and our cable show, showing our viewers more of Pyongyang than any Westerners had ever before seen.

Later that day, the same helpful State Department officials got me into the press pool that was going to cover Albright and Kim's historic meeting. The CIA had been profiling Kim, the eccentric son of North Korea's founder, for years. I never knew whether their reports of a scotch-drinking xenophobe with a taste for Swedish actresses and porn movies was real intelligence or copied from an old James Bond movie. We did know that he had a taste for Western food and good wine, and that he was afraid to fly. When he had to travel it was in a lavishly appointed railroad car.

We were told to wait in an elaborate, ceremonial hallway. The carpets were luxuriously thick. The ceilings glowed with the light from enormous chandeliers. North Korea couldn't feed its people, but it still had money for pomp and ceremony. There we waited for the much-anticipated photo opportunity between the American secretary of state and the communist leader known to his people as the Dear Leader.

When Kim finally walked in, I thought of *The Wizard of Oz*. He was wearing a khaki military-style suit, but what made the situation so comical were his feet. The diminutive dictator was wearing elevated lifts on his shoes. Combined with his pouffed hair teased into a mini-beehive, the lifts added several inches to his small stature making him appear almost at eye level with the American secretary of state. As I scribbled rapid notes, a separate voice in my head was saying, "This is amazing. I am standing a few feet away from one of the world's most notorious tyrants, and he's smiling and shaking hands like the host of a dinner party."

Kim proceeded to engage Albright and her delegation in what they later described as a polite, serious conversation. They had been expecting a monster, and were stunned when he behaved normally, exchanging diplomatic niceties such as, "If both sides are genuine and serious, there is no thing we will not be able to do." Encouraged that they might be receiving a peace overture, Albright hastily accepted Kim's invitation to what she thought would be a simple May Day celebration.

Instead, sitting at Kim's side in an enormous Olympic-sized stadium, Albright was treated to a display of military might that had all the trappings of a rally in Nazi Germany. There were one hundred thousand performers, and twice that number in the stands applauding on cue. Children danced, people flew in on small rockets, soldiers performed with their bayonets. As Albright has described it in her memoir, *Madam Secretary,* the show's finale was a display simulating the launch of North Korea's most threatening weapon, the Taepo Dong missile—the very weapon she had hoped to persuade Kim to eliminate from his arsenal.

Still, Kim invited Clinton to visit Pyongyang himself before his term expired that winter. Albright felt there was a possibility to achieve a diplomatic breakthrough, but the president was tied down with the Middle East negotiations. The moment of opportunity with North Korea passed. During the transition, I learned from members of the incoming Bush team that Condoleezza Rice felt very strongly that the U.S. should not negotiate with North Korea. Either she was reflecting the new president's point of view, or he hers. But early in the new administration, in the spring of 2001, his decisions about North Korea became an early signal that hard-liners were in control of his foreign policy team. Bush overruled his secretary of state, Colin Powell, who had wanted to follow up on Albright's initiative.

Powell was humiliated. It was his first major setback, and a very public one. Later, the Bush White House discovered that North Korea had been cheating on an agreement they'd signed with the Clinton administration calling for North Korea to give up its nuclear weapons program in exchange for money for fuel and power plants. The hard-liners felt vindicated. By the following year, all talk of diplomacy was dead. North Korea became a charter member of the president's "axis of evil."

———

Two weeks after the North Korea trip, on election night, I was back on Hillary duty in New York. I waited for the returns in an overheated ballroom at the Grand Hyatt Hotel near Grand Central Terminal, perched on a riser with hundreds of camera crews jammed onto a wooden platform. The early exit polls had made it clear that she was going to win big, and by the time I arrived after *Nightly News,* her supporters were already celebrating. It was a mob scene, but a happy mob.

The crowd was even more buoyed by word that Florida was looking good for Gore. The drama began in the twelve-minute period between 7:50 and 8:02 p.m., when the major networks awarded Florida's twenty-five electoral votes to Al Gore. But within the next ninety minutes, the Voter News Service, which at the time conducted the exit polls for most of the nation's news organizations, warned the networks that the information was wrong. The networks discovered that the actual vote in several sections of Tampa was less Democratic than the exit polls had projected. At the same time, the Bush campaign—armed with data from Florida's governor, the Republican nominee's brother—was raising hell with the networks, trying to roll back their Florida projection.

At 9:50, the Democratic stalwarts at Hillary headquarters got very quiet as one by one the networks started reversing their calls. Florida was back in play and the people near television screens began passing the word. By then, the president and Hillary were on stage for her victory speech. I climbed down from the camera platform and pushed my way through the crowd to the foot of the stage, to see if Clinton had any inside information about Gore's situation. As I reached up with my microphone, hoping vainly that I could somehow get his attention, he saw me and said, "How's Al doing in Florida?" If he didn't know, I surely didn't have a good answer.

Clinton had been a peripheral figure in the Gore campaign, much to the president's annoyance and frustration. Some Clinton aides still think that if Gore had used Clinton as a campaign surrogate in Arkansas, Gore would have won the state, and hence, the election. But Gore was so angry about the Lewinsky affair, and concerned about its political fallout, that he had decided to keep the president offstage.

With the presidential race still undecided, at midnight I left Hillary's happy warriors and walked back to Rockefeller Center. As I wrote my *Today* show story on Hillary's election, the numbers in Florida were flipping back and forth. Having been wrong once, no one wanted to be wrong again. The networks waited until shortly after two a.m. to give Florida, and the presidency, to Bush. The Gore camp was understandably outraged. No one went to bed. Worst of all, we became the story, because of the premature call of the Florida race. As Tom Brokaw said so memorably at dawn, the networks have "not just egg on their face, but a whole omelet."

The next thirty-four days were a kaleidoscope of dangling chads, legal briefs, and spin. The American political process was being tested as it hadn't been for almost two centuries. Battalions of legal warriors descended on Florida. Al Gore brought in a team led by former secretary of state Warren Christopher, along with David Boies, one of the nation's most successful litigators. But as it turned out, the postelection contest was less a matter of legal skill than a game of defining the battleground. And there was no one better at the political ground game than former president Bush's longtime advisor, James Addison Baker III.

Although the most senior veteran of the Ford, Reagan, and Bush administrations, he had for the most part sat out this campaign. While the younger Bush was eager to surround himself with some of his father's advisors, like Dick Cheney, he seemed to resent others of that generation, particularly Baker and his father's national security advisor, Brent Scowcroft.

Baker and the younger Bush had an uncomfortable history dating back to the 1992 campaign, when Bush felt his father might have won reelection had Baker taken charge before the convention. Now the stakes were too high to dwell on past disagreements. Baker was in his car when he got the call from Bush's campaign chairman, Don Evans, asking him to head to Florida. The biggest thing on his schedule was a hunting trip in Britain with former president Bush. Suddenly, loyalty to the elder Bush called for a change in plans. Baker flew to Florida, bringing along his trusted lieutenants, Robert Zoellick and Margaret Tutwiler.

Washington was a strange place during those thirty-six days. I had friends in both camps, and relationships were strained. At private dinners, members of the Supreme Court were clearly agonizing over their role and wishing it had not landed on their doorstep. Programming a nightly political program on cable was a nightmare. It didn't matter whether we were in midsentence with the leader of the Senate—if a clerk walked out of a courthouse in Florida to announce a bathroom break, the network would break away to carry it live. There were nights when my show was squeezed into a brief segment or two between commercials.

When it was over, we all praised Al Gore for being statesmanlike, and promptly started focusing on the new administration. What gets lost, often, is the personal drama behind the election results. Gore, whom I'd known since he was a young congressman, was devastated. Out of respect for him, and to be supportive, Alan went to New York to speak to one of his classes at Columbia, where Gore had started teaching. That April, three months after Gore left office, he and Tipper invited us for dinner at their home in Arlington, Virginia, on a Saturday night.

The Gores had moved back to Tipper's childhood home, where they'd lived while he served in Congress. They still had Secret Service protection for another few months, but aside from men lurking behind trees, it was a normal suburban setting. We were just two couples sitting out on the deck on a spring night, checking out the hot tub the Gores had installed in their wooded backyard, having a lovely meal with some very good red wine. It was difficult to believe how close he had come to the presidency, and I admired how he was carrying on with his life. I don't know whether Gore ever regretted his decision to refrain from challenging the final outcome. However, he must have wished he'd pursued a different legal strategy in Florida, challenging the statewide vote instead of "cherrypicking" the four counties he thought would give him an edge. A consortium of news organizations who reviewed the disputed Florida count a year later found Gore might have won if the courts had ordered a full statewide recount of all 175,000 rejected ballots.

A few weeks after our April dinner, Gore called to say that he wanted to surprise Tipper for their thirty-first wedding anniversary. He had scored tickets to the hottest show in New York, *The Producers,* and invited us to join them. His plan was for us to show up at their hotel for cocktails as part of the surprise. When we got there, he had organized champagne and hors d'oeuvres in their suite. She was still getting dressed and had no idea she was in for an evening of us or Nathan Lane. At the theater, the audience erupted in an ovation as the Gores were spotted going to their seats. They were clearly touched by the response. Al Gore had been in public life since he was barely back from Vietnam, and now he was making a tough adjustment, but gracefully.

His poignant isolation was in sharp contrast to the hubbub surrounding the beginnings of the new Bush administration. My immediate assignment was the secretary of state, Colin Powell, by far the most popular member of the new cabinet. I'd known him since he was the deputy to the national security advisor in Ronald Reagan's White House and considered him a friend. I genuinely liked him, and had very warm feelings toward his wife, Alma. They had both been guests at our wedding. Now, as often happens in Washington, a former official was rotating back into government. I had to take a step back and figure out how to be a little more distant, and tough when necessary. It was going to be a difficult balancing act.

———

Powell's first diplomatic mission overseas in January 2001 was to the Middle East, but, significantly, not to broker peace between Israel and the Palestinians. Rather, it was to make the case against Saddam Hussein to Arab leaders. Immediately, he ran into a wall of opposition from Egypt's president Hosni Mubarak. He and others in the region were outraged by a decade of U.S. air strikes against Iraq and economic sanctions. Mubarak didn't even show up for a joint news conference with Powell. Instead, as a sign of his displeasure, the Egyptian president sent his foreign minister to deliver an unvarnished criticism of America's Iraq policy.

The next day, we went to Kuwait, where Powell, the president's father, Margaret Thatcher, and other leaders from the first Gulf War were gathering for a tenth anniversary celebration of their victory over Saddam Hussein. Filmmaker Michael Moore would have had a field day. Half the former officials were now in business with Kuwait on lucrative investment deals. Powell, Schwarzkopf—the men who had decided not to go to Baghdad, and left Saddam in power—were now back warning that the Iraqi leader still could not be trusted.

While American and Kuwaiti troops performed war games in the desert, just fifteen miles south of Iraq's border, former president

Bush pledged, "We are never going to betray our responsibilities to continue to help preserve the peace of Kuwait. We fought too hard. Too many died."

Powell's words were tough, and in retrospect, prescient: "Iraq the aggressor sits stranded, trapped in a prison of its own making; its people and children put at risk by a regime that also puts at risk the people and children of the entire region by threatening to rebuild its army and manufacture weapons of mass destruction."

It was a moment of sharp contrasts still imprinted on my memory—a blazing desert sun, a colorful parade of troops, and the slightly aged Gulf War victors once again hurling invectives at Saddam Hussein. The new administration was barely a month old. And the saber rattling wasn't coming from some secret cabal of administration hard-liners, but from the supposedly moderate, dovish secretary of state. But while Powell, at least then, was claiming Iraq wanted to restock its weapons, that night I reported that the CIA had secretly reached a completely opposite conclusion. At least then, the agency had found no direct evidence that Saddam was rebuilding nuclear, chemical, or biological weapons. The administration's intelligence on Iraq was already in conflict.

After he left Kuwait, Powell's attempt to build support for Bush's Iraq policy was rebuffed by yet another Arab leader, Syria's president Bashar Assad—son of the late dictator whose security men had dragged me out of a palace event. Powell wanted Assad to stop buying millions of dollars of Iraqi oil that was being smuggled out each day in violation of the UN embargo. Assad wasn't about to give up his cheap oil, nor do any favors for the American diplomat.

The trip proved that the region's leaders were not going to give the new president any kind of honeymoon. One of Powell's aides told me wryly, "We started out with low expectations, and we met them."

At the beginning of Bush's presidency, before 9/11, terrorism was only one of several national security concerns. In fact, if the Bush administration was focused on any foreign policy objective, it was Iraq, not terrorism. During the new president's first major speech to

Congress that February, the only reference to terrorism was a two-sentence proposal about developing missile defenses—a program favored by Defense Secretary Donald Rumsfeld. Tom Brokaw described the speech as "more prose than poetry" with a lot of emphasis on civility and reaching across party lines.

But as we later learned from the *9/11 Commission Report,* that winter, counterterrorism officials were already picking up repeated, but fragmentary, threat reports. By summer, the system was "blinking red." In May, I did a story with *Nightly News* senior investigative producer Robert Windrem on America's continuing vulnerability to terror. We reported that top Bush administration officials feared that they could not prevent a terror attack, despite six years of training and disaster drills.

In that report, we showed a draft executive order the president was considering that would create an Office of National Preparedness under FEMA, the Federal Emergency Management Agency, to coordinate responses to chemical, biological, or nuclear attacks. It would link more than forty agencies and put Dick Cheney in charge of planning a national response to terror.

Mayors, governors, and Congress had been complaining that money and time were being wasted. We also showed a satellite photo that military experts said revealed a chemical weapons laboratory built by Osama bin Laden in Afghanistan. Paul Pillar, a deputy chief of the CIA's Counterterrorism Center, told us that the United States would still be the most vulnerable terrorist target "simply because of who we are, how big we are, how open we are." Paul Bremer, who chaired a commission on terrorism (and who later became our viceroy in Iraq) said that night, "There is a threat of terrorism escalating now to higher levels of casualties." We raised the question of whether the Bush plan to expand FEMA's reach was enough to deal with the expanding terror threat.

But no one in or out of government connected the dots. In fact, a widely read *New York Times* article in 1999, a year after the embassy bombings in Africa, had discounted suggestions that bin Laden was even a terrorist leader. There was little consensus in government or journalism about the nature of the threat. As the *9/11 Commission Report* points out, the intelligence community did not produce a new consensus report on how it assessed the risk of terror attacks (known as a "national intelligence estimate") during the entire three-year period leading up to 9/11. Former National Security Council official Richard Clarke has testified that the new administration did not begin reviewing their counterterror policy until April 2001, three months after they took office. Condi Rice and other top officials have vigorously disputed Clarke's charge that they were inattentive, but the record shows they did not agree on a counterterror plan until September 4, one week before bin Laden struck.

More recently, while covering the postmortems in the aftermath of 9/11, I've asked myself whether we could have sounded more alarms about Osama bin Laden. During the spring of 2001, Bob Windrem and I continued to talk to intelligence officials and file occasional stories on bin Laden, but we were also assigned to other stories on a variety of subjects. I analyzed Bush's first one hundred days on environmental policy and health care. After the president decided to limit federally sponsored stem cell research during a week when I was substituting for Tim Russert on *Meet the Press,* I learned everything that I could about stem cells. And during the first few weeks in April, the president had his first foreign policy crisis: a U.S. spy plane collided with a Chinese jet fighter that was trying to force it to land on an island off the mainland. For a while, the crew was held in what could have turned into an extended hostage situation. The U.S. ambassador negotiated a deftly worded agreement, and the administration was given high marks for artful diplomacy.

In May, I got to chase the hottest political story of the moment when we learned that Vermont senator James Jeffords would be defecting from the Republican Party. With Republicans barely controlling the Senate, his decision would put the Democrats in charge. Not surprisingly, the Republicans were furious. Overnight, all of the power and patronage that came with their committee chairmanships were going to evaporate. Within an hour, I was grabbing a change of clothes and scurrying to catch the same commuter flight Jeffords was taking to Vermont, where he would be making his announcement the next day. The airport scene reminded me of the crush of reporters chasing Bill and Hillary Clinton through New Hampshire in 1992. Jeffords and his beleaguered wife could barely get to the gate as the media pack pursued them for a comment. Then the throng of national, and even international, reporters descended on Burlington, Vermont.

It was a circus, but also a great political story that fit perfectly with Vermont's history of independent thinking. The state had been the first to outlaw slavery, to elect a socialist to Congress, to produce politically correct ice cream, and to legalize same-sex civil unions. Vermonters like to say they're not liberal or conservative, just independent. Polls there bear that out, showing independents consistently outnumbering Democrats or Republicans by two to one.

Still, there was a lot of fallout. Jeffords's defection made the president look weak. Senate Republicans, especially those who were losing committee chairmanships, were furious over their fall from power. Moderate Republican senators, like Olympia Snowe of Maine, didn't hesitate to blame White House arrogance. She told me Republican moderates had tried repeatedly to meet with the president to air their policy complaints, but couldn't get past his palace guard.

At the same time that spring, the Israeli–Palestinian conflict was spinning out of control. A task force led by former Senate majority leader George Mitchell reported that Israel should stop building settlements on Palestinian land and should reopen borders Israel had closed between its country and the territories. The closures were creating serious hardships because Palestinians in the territories could not get to their jobs in Israel. On the other hand, the Mitchell group said Palestinians should stop firing on Israeli areas, and should condemn violence. The report was ignored by both sides. Israel's prime minister, Ariel Sharon, knew that George Bush would not pressure him to comply. And Yasser Arafat was still offering no sign that he was prepared to crack down on terror.

By August, Prince Bandar, the veteran Saudi diplomat, delivered a tough message to Condi Rice. As paraphrased in *A Time of Our Choosing: America's War in Iraq* by Todd S. Purdum and the staff of *The New York Times,* Bandar told Condi that the president's uncritical support for Sharon was leaving the Saudis with no choice but "to pursue policies based on our own national interest, regardless of their impact on you."

In the final months leading up to 9/11, I filed stories ranging from the violence in the Middle East to Dick Cheney's energy task force and the crippled status of nuclear power in America, twenty-five years after Three Mile Island. I went to Cuba to interview Fidel Castro and visit Elian Gonzalez and his family on the first anniversary of the child's return home. I did stories for *Nightly News* on the death of Maureen Reagan and the exploits of the Bush twins. But above all else that summer, the tabloid world was obsessed with the story of a congressman and his missing intern. We went along with the pack.

To many people, there was something irresistible about the behavior of Gary Condit and Chandra Levy. Her disappearance, most likely while out jogging, was probably the result of a random crime, but the coincidence of her connection to a married politician was too enticing to be ignored. Immediately, the police zeroed in on Condit because they believed he had been less than forthcoming about the relationship when they first interviewed him.

Understandably, the young woman's parents, frantic with worry, rushed to Washington from their home in California seeking media attention to spark a wider search. Soon camera crews were trailing them everywhere, including back to California. How could this possibly have a happy ending?

Gary Condit was an obscure congressman who had briefly appeared on my radar years earlier, when we interviewed him for a story on the unhealthy mix of politics and money. Then he was just another politician from the Agriculture Committee attending an inaugural party financed by lobbyists. Now he was the reluctant lead player in a summertime soap opera. Network camera crews set up housekeeping on his front step. At the Capitol, producers chased him down corridors and through underground tunnels, and even into the men's room.

The news media feeding frenzy is hardly a new phenomenon, but when you're caught up in it, it can be relentless. Now the network couldn't get enough of Gary Condit and Chandra Levy. During a three-month period from May to June, I did twenty stories on *Nightly News* about the search for the missing intern.

Why was I assigned? Most likely because there was a declining appetite for stories about foreign policy or intelligence gathering. With so much rumor and innuendo about the Chandra Levy story floating around the Internet and cable shows, they wanted a senior correspondent on the case to sort through all the rumors and false reports. To check out leads, we had a team of producers tracking developments. Although the story was a family tragedy for the Levys, for the news media it was the journalistic equivalent of junk food, or a bad beach novel. Inevitably, the story raised echoes of that other Washington intern. But this time, a young woman had gone missing, representing every parent's nightmare.

Still, that does not excuse the disproportionate attention the case received on television. We rationalized it by talking about the public policy implications of possible misbehavior—or worse—by an elected official. But Tom Brokaw, who was away on a ten-week sabbatical that summer, got it right. Even though he was not responsible for the decision making, he has since called the Condit summer one of the periods he most regrets at *Nightly News*. I also wonder what leads we might have stumbled across on bin Laden and his nineteen hijackers if we hadn't been so absorbed in searching for the missing intern.

———

On September 10, 2001, I reported on a hidden scandal, runaway teens selling their bodies for drugs, food, or money in Portland, Oregon. A new report estimated that 325,000 children in seventeen cities were being sexually exploited at home or sold for sex to strangers each year. It was a disturbing story, and a serious subject. But it would not compare to the horrors we were about to experience.

The next morning, I was only a few blocks from work when the office called and told me a plane had slammed into the World Trade Center. My first thought was that a small plane must have lost its way. Perhaps the weather was bad in New York. By the time I parked and ran into our bureau, we were already on the air, on both the broadcast and cable networks. None of us had any idea that we would continue broadcasting live on all NBC networks, uninterrupted by commercials, for four days.

At 9:03 a.m., the second plane crashed into the South Tower. Instantly, we all realized that the first plane had not been an accident. America was under attack for the first time since Pearl Harbor. As I watched the top floors of the Trade Center in flames on the television monitors, I felt sick to my stomach. I remembered that al Qaeda had had a plot in the Philippines in 1995 involving hijacked airplanes to be used as weapons. Part of me wanted to call my parents to give and seek comfort. But at the same time, something inside me kicked into gear. It is the automatic response mechanism of a reporter reacting to a story; to a certain extent, no matter how great the horror, the mechanism works. I knew my job was to call sources and find out who was responsible, and why. It sounds cold, but that is what we do. The emotional part comes later, when we pause, take a deep breath, and are hit suddenly with the impact of what we've been reporting.

Already, intelligence officials had only one suspect: Osama bin Laden. By 9:32, less than a half hour after the second attack, I had enough sources to report that bin Laden's organization was the most likely group capable of that kind of simultaneous, highly coordinated attack on America.

Like the rest of the country, and our government leaders, we had no idea how extensive the plot was, or what target might be next. Air traffic controllers froze all takeoffs and tried to account for aircraft already in flight. At ten a.m., Tom Brokaw, Katie Couric, and Matt Lauer sat and watched, trying as best they could to explain the unexplainable, as the horrifying images unfolded live in front of our eyes. In the Washington newsroom we were grabbing phones, frantically calling sources, speed-dialing to find out if there were any other missing planes. A few minutes after ten, my colleague Jamie Gangel reported that intelligence officials said the explosion and fire at the Pentagon had been caused by a plane diving into its west wing.

We were piecing together information to try to get a handle on what had happened. No one knew how big a plot was still under way. By then, barely an hour after the first plane hit, Brokaw was able to identify the specific flights that had gone into the Trade Center towers. Government offices in New York were being evacuated. Katie asked me to describe what was happening in Washington.

I reported, "The State Department has been evacuated. There was a meeting going on in the operations center. Other top officials were in the situation room at the White House. Colin Powell is in Lima, Peru, on a two-day trip." Then I reported a major problem with the FBI's ability to respond to the attacks. The FBI had been conducting a massive hostage rescue exercise in California involving all of their top teams and a lot of critical equipment. They had been scheduled to fly back on 9/11, commercially. Now all of those people were out of place, and with phone lines down in New York City, no one could reach the top FBI antiterror team headquartered there.

There had been a rush by terror groups to take responsibility for the attack. Katie asked, "Andrea, is the State Department taking this claim of responsibility from the Democratic Front for the Liberation of Palestine seriously? Are they giving any credence to that? Or are they dismissing it? Or how do they feel about who might have been responsible for this?"

I answered: "They have one instant reaction, as you know, and it could be wrong. But their immediate reaction in a case like this would be to look toward Osama bin Laden and the collateral groups connected to him, simply because he has proved with the embassy bombings in Africa that he is the one terror leader who's capable of this kind of highly coordinated attack. When bombings went off in Tanzania and in Kenya almost simultaneously, it was extraordinarily well coordinated. They proved their case to a jury effectively, and have managed to develop a great deal of information from sources, from in fact turning some former members of his network. So they believe that he is the most likely person, but it's far too early to say anything."

The White House had been evacuated right after the attack, on the assumption that it was the next likely target. The chaotic decision making later described in the *9/11 Commission Report* did not seem crazy to us at the time. We didn't question why the president spent seven minutes reading *The Pet Goat* to that class of children, or flying around the country before finally returning to Washington. All of us were confused, and at the time, we didn't expect a lot more from the White House. It was only later that we started asking questions.

I was on automatic pilot, reporting the information I was gathering to update the broadcast network and, separately, our cable viewers. One side of my brain heard that the FAA was diverting incoming foreign flights to Canada. Then, more than an hour into the attack, I remembered that Alan was flying back from Switzerland that day and approaching Dulles Airport in Washington.

Over the next few hours, I became quietly frantic as flights landed and all were accounted for except his. His office felt they must have diverted his plane elsewhere, but they had not landed in Canada. Logically, it was impossible for another plane to have been hijacked without someone knowing it. Unable to reach him, I tried to concentrate on my job, calling sources to keep updating information and get it on the air.

Finally, his office got word that his plane had been sent back to Switzerland. Still, I was desperate to hear his voice. Then, just before three p.m., I was getting ready to summarize everything that had happened that day with Brokaw at the top of the hour. My cell phone rang, and it was Alan. They'd run out of landing space in Halifax and sent his plane back across the Atlantic to Zurich. He had just landed and wanted to know, "What is happening to America?"

As I held the cell phone to my ear, our special events producer in New York, Phil Alongi, almost shouted through his microphone into my earpiece, "Andrea, Tom is coming to you, are you ready?"

All I had time to say to Alan was, "Listen up." Still connected to him in Zurich, I put the cell phone in my lap so he could hear my report, took my cue, and recounted the day's developments up to that point. That's how the chairman of the Federal Reserve got his first briefing on 9/11.

In fact, with Alan out of the country, the Fed's vice chairman, Roger Ferguson, took emergency steps to keep money flowing to the markets and make sure the banking system was safe from attack. All of the regulators and their emergency planning performed flawlessly. The nation had taken a body blow, but our financial systems proved they could withstand an enormous shock.

That night, back in Washington, the president outlined what was to become known as the Bush doctrine. It reflected core beliefs few people knew he had. Here was a man with so little curiosity that he rarely traveled outside the United States before becoming president. Now, in the wake of the attacks on New York and Washington, he told the rest of the world, "We will make no distinction between those who planned these acts and those who harbor them." You were either with us, or against us. There was no room for nuance or straddling.

In our bureau, we were bringing in a stream of former government officials and other experts to provide commentary. At the top of the list for Brokaw to interview was James Baker, the former secretary of state, who was visiting from Texas. With government officials too busy to discuss the attacks, Baker—with his wide range of government experience—was an important voice. Chatting with them, I learned that he and his wife, Susan, had been stranded in Washington when all flights were canceled. Baker and the president's father had both been attending the annual board meeting of the Carlyle Group, a global private equity firm, during the days preceding 9/11. Even more interesting was the fact that one of the other Carlyle investors stuck in Washington when the nation's airspace shut down that day was Shafig bin Laden, Osama's half brother.

Later, we were the first to report that the FBI helped the Saudi ambassador, Prince Bandar, get all the bin Ladens—including several dozen college students around the country—out of the U.S. on chartered planes as soon as the ban on flights was lifted. That, of course, became a controversial decision for conspiracy theorists, and figured prominently in Michael Moore's movie *Fahrenheit 9/11*.

Like everyone else in the country, all I wanted was to be with the people I loved, which in my case meant Alan and my family. But my parents were in New York, and Alan was on the other side of the ocean. Still not knowing whether there was a larger conspiracy, my husband's staff took him from Zurich to a NATO base to spend the night and wait for transport home. The White House organized a military flight and he came back the next day on a refueling plane, with a handful of other government officials who'd been out of the country when the terrorists struck. When they approached the East Coast, the pilot flew over the gaping wound that had been the Twin Towers. Alan could not believe what he was looking at. He had worked on Wall Street, only a few blocks from the Twin Towers, for more than thirty years. He had been in the air himself during the attacks and the immediate aftermath, unable to watch what most of the world was watching. To this day, he has not been able to bring himself to look at those first images.

But I didn't know that until later. All I knew at the time was that I had a job to do. For the next 144 hours, we broadcast as many facts as we could accumulate, even those that were difficult to absorb. It was exhausting, but no one complained. America was on a war footing, and so was television news. We were juggling different programming on NBC's three networks, simultaneously. Tom Brokaw, Brian Williams, and the other anchors were drawing twenty-hour shifts without a break. The networks lost hundreds of millions of dollars in advertising revenue for cancelled commercials. But everything we did was dwarfed by the sacrifices of the people of New York, in Shanksville, Pennsylvania, and the military and civilian personnel at the Pentagon. By the afternoon of 9/11, according to the *9/11 Commission Report*, Defense Secretary Rumsfeld was already wondering if Iraq was involved and should be targeted, along with Afghanistan.

By Thursday night, Colin Powell confirmed that bin Laden was a prime suspect. That night, I filed a report asking how, with so many leads now being developed, could the terrorists have operated successfully right under our noses. And why didn't the billions of dollars spent on intelligence give us an early warning?

Powell acknowledged to us, "We did not get the cueing we needed. We did not get the intelligence information needed to predict this was about to happen." The problem, experts were telling me, was too much information, too little smart analysis. I closed the report by saying that the more alarming possibility was that our spies would never be able to guarantee it wouldn't happen again.

Within twenty-four hours of the attack we were identifying the failures highlighted later by the 9/11 Commission, not because we were so smart, but because the problems were so obvious. Brent Scowcroft told me, "We're getting to the point where our ability to collect information far exceeds our ability to analyze it. We need some help." Scowcroft, who led the president's Foreign Intelligence Advisory Board, proposed giving the director of central intelligence control over all of the intelligence agency budgets—which meant taking power away from the secretary of defense. But Donald Rumsfeld, not surprisingly, was fiercely opposed to this suggestion. As a result, Condi Rice didn't even send Scowcroft's plan to the president. I was told she wanted to make sure the president was sheltered from any criticism for killing the idea. It is a great irony that eventually the president did end up creating a director of national intelligence, but within a structure quite different from what Scow-croft had recommended. Scowcroft had wanted to expand the authority of the CIA director. Bush's eventual solution did exactly the opposite.

As draining as it was for those of us in Washington, I knew my colleagues in New York had been hit even harder. Most of them were personally connected to victims. Yet all of us, even those who had been near the Trade Center when the planes hit, responded the same way. The story came first. And in ways large and small, we found ourselves reaching out to help each other. We pooled information, updated each other's scripts, and produced an hour-long *Nightly News* broadcast each night, twice as long as usual. Adrenaline kept me going, and working long hours prevented me from thinking too deeply about the events I was covering. But I couldn't get out of my mind the ghostly skeletal silhouette of Ground Zero and the constant grinding of the forklifts and bulldozers clearing the debris.

———

Three days after the attack, the president led a memorial service at the National Cathedral. Ushers passed out red, white, and blue ribbons to pin on our lapels. I had been to weddings at the cathedral, and funerals, most recently for Katharine Graham, but no service was as deeply moving as this. Usually, even in times of tragedy, friends hug each other, or tell stories about the deceased. This was different, on a scale so enormous that people seemed unable to comfort themselves, or each other. It was a horror beyond comprehension.

With his parents and all the other former presidents, except Ronald Reagan, joining him in a show of solidarity, George Bush led the mourners in prayers of consolation and sorrow. Seeking God's blessings, the president evoked the wrath of a vengeful nation and vowed "to answer these attacks and rid the world of evil." Sitting several pews back with Alan, I began to realize how much the attack had burdened the president, and how profoundly it had changed his worldview. "War has been waged against us by stealth and deceit and murder," he said. "This nation is peaceful, but fierce when stirred to anger. This conflict was begun on the timing and terms of others. It will end in a way, and at an hour, of our choosing."

Sitting in the congregation with so many members of the military, I kept looking around and wondering what these people might have to order their troops to do. What missions would they have to deploy? How many of these people have lost colleagues and friends and loved ones already? Right behind me and across the aisle was Theodore Olson, the solicitor general of the United States, whose wife was on American Airlines flight 77. She had called twice from the plane between 9:16 a.m. and 9:26 a.m. on 9/11. Calmly, she had told him the plane was being hijacked and asked what she should tell the captain to do. Now, only three days later, I couldn't imagine how he was handling his emotions. I had interviewed both of the Olsons on Inauguration Day. Walking out, he saw me and we hugged.

I came outside in the wake of a throng circling Bill Clinton. Suddenly, he appeared diminished in comparison with Bush, now a wartime leader. And Al Gore, walking out alone with Tipper, was almost ignored. It was a hint of how 9/11 would enlarge the new president's standing. We had broadcast the service as part of our live coverage. Now, on my return to the bureau, I was told to go on the air with Brokaw and give a first-person account. As I sat down in front of the camera, I quickly unpinned my mourner's ribbon. Somehow, it felt inappropriate to wear it on camera. It was all right to participate in the religious service, but now I was retreating back behind the lines, to the role of observer. Journalist.

Tom asked me what it felt like inside the cathedral, surrounded by the country's secular and spiritual leaders at a time of national mourning. I said that it was an extraordinary moment, because all of these very powerful people were simply humble servants unable to fathom the enormity of what had happened, and searching for answers. The most stunning moment was when the Reverend Billy

Graham, frail but having risen from his sickbed to preach, was greeted by a thunderous wave of applause. You don't often hear ovations in church.

That same day, the president flew to New York to see Ground Zero for the first time. Standing on a charred fire truck that had just been dragged from the debris, he found his voice, forever altering his presidency. With a flag in one hand and a bullhorn in the other, he vowed to "rid the world of evil." When a rescue worker shouted, "George, we can't hear you," the president delivered his memorable declaration: "I can hear you. The rest of the world hears you. And the people who knocked these buildings down will hear all of us soon!" I wondered how a civilized nation, following the rule of law, could win a fight with fanatics.

I had still not been home to see my parents, who had been badly shaken by 9/11. Lifelong New Yorkers, they were in their eighties and had lived through two World Wars and the Great Depression. My mother still talked vividly about the Holocaust as though it had happened to her. Now, like many New Yorkers, they were trying to absorb the horror of an attack on their own city. NBC encouraged me to take time off and accompany my father to synagogue on the Jewish New Year, one week after the attack.

It was my first visit to New Rochelle, where my father still attended services, in quite some time. What had been a very traditional service when I was growing up had become much more relaxed in the intervening years. Thanks in part to my father's influence, women could now participate, something unheard of when I was a child, and now the rabbi invited me to take part. I've been on many stages in my life and broadcast to millions of people. Nothing made me more nervous than walking up the steps to accept the honor of opening the ark on Rosh Hashanah in my father's synagogue.

Before I returned to my seat, the rabbi asked me to address the congregation with some thoughts about the terror attacks. I spoke about the outpouring of humanity around the world for Americans in the aftermath of 9/11, and took the opportunity of the Jewish high holidays to remind the gathering that Osama bin Laden did not represent either Muslims or the Muslim faith. I recalled my experiences in Afghanistan, and how brutal the Taliban regime had been, especially toward women. But along with a warning against the excesses of religious fundamentalism, I concluded with a message of hope. I still thought our nation, and the world, could learn from the tragedy and the way the world had responded.

A week after 9/11, just as our NBC colleagues in New York City were recovering from the initial shock of the terror attack, a letter containing anthrax arrived at our 30 Rockefeller Center studios, addressed to Tom Brokaw. Tom's longtime assistant, a valued friend and colleague, fell ill as a result of having opened the tainted mail. On the same day, another letter containing anthrax, carrying the identical Trenton, New Jersey postmark, arrived at the offices of *The New York Post*.

At our headquarters, the *Nightly News* staff was evacuated to temporary quarters on a different floor for weeks while the entire newsroom was sterilized. Leaders from GE and NBC, along with *Nightly News* executive producer Steve Capus and Brokaw, kept people from panicking, and the staff got through it, but not without a great deal of emotional pain, at a time when people in New York were most vulnerable.

No perpetrator was found for that attack, or for other, fatal attacks in Florida and Washington, D.C. But before the spate of anthrax letters subsided, five people had died. The offices of two Democratic senators, Tom Daschle and Pat Leahy, had also received contaminated letters. The Hart Senate Office Bulding had to be closed for three months. Post office facilities in New Jersey and suburban Washington, D.C. had to be sterilized. Federal investigators determined from the text and style of the letters that they did not originate with al Qaeda. And some of the victims never fully recovered the life they'd known before being infected by the anthrax.

———

As frightening as the anthrax attack was, it still paled in comparison to what happened on 9/11. In the days afterward, the nation mourned, but also expected a strong military response. But against whom? A year before 9/11, CIA drone Predator planes flying over the Afghan desert had sent back images that could have been bin Laden, but by the time the pictures were analyzed, the suspect figure had moved on. Picking targets in Afghanistan was going to be a military challenge.

At Camp David on the first weekend after the terrorists struck, the president and his war council began planning for the invasion of Afghanistan. But Deputy Defense Secretary Paul Wolfowitz argued that they were better prepared to attack Iraq than Afghanistan. As Bob Woodward has brilliantly documented in *Bush at War* and *Plan of Attack,* the president vetoed the suggestion—for the moment. He and Dick Cheney were reluctant to take on too many military challenges at once. There would be plenty of time for Iraq later.

The CIA was the first to go into Afghanistan, but they had lost a key asset. The only Afghan leader capable of challenging bin Laden or the Taliban had been attacked two days before 9/11 on bin Laden's orders. Ahmed Shah Massoud, the Afghan opposition's greatest war hero, died a week later, killed by two suicide bombers posing as a television camera crew. Massoud was legendary, a tribal leader known as the Lion of the Panjshir. He'd been on the CIA's payroll for a decade, and Bill Richardson had tried to meet him when we traveled to northern Afghanistan in 1998. To the UN ambassador's considerable disappointment, Massoud hadn't shown up. His death left Afghanistan, a country carved up by tribal fiefdoms, without any single individual strong enough to command loyalty across groups. In this patchwork quilt of feuding tribes, the Taliban, who were largely ethnic Pushtuns, still controlled most of the country. The rest was divided among ethnic Uzbeks, Tajiks, and other minorities. In the resulting power vacuum, the Taliban and bin Laden reigned supreme.

To build international support for the invasion of Afghanistan, Colin Powell began putting together an unlikely coalition—not only moderate Arab states, but Sudan, Yemen, and Syria. Even Libya's Khaddafy said the United States had the right to respond to terror. Powell's strategy was to make temporary alliances with countries that also felt threatened by Islamic extremists. Now it was time to sign up the most important player for achieving victory over the Taliban—Pakistan.

On September 18, 2001, I started reporting from the United Nations, now barricaded by dump trucks filled with sand to thwart potential suicide bombers. It was the perfect metaphor for the fear and isolation that would poison the Iraq debate to come. France was already questioning whether action against Afghanistan had to rise to the level of war. That night, Powell launched a long, complicated negotiating strategy that succeeded in the short run in building alliances, but ultimately left the U.S. isolated when it came time to attack Iraq. In the final analysis, his diplomacy was a tragedy of crossed signals and missed opportunities.

The UN is one of the most frustrating institutions I cover. As a child, I visited it on Girl Scout field trips and wrote school essays about its lessons of peace and internationalism. The reality is very different. Although often maligned, unfortunately it gives its critics plenty of ammunition. Despite repeated efforts at reform, it is far too bureaucratic. Its global assistance projects are often the only lifeline for people suffering from hunger or disease. But in Rwanda, with American complicity, it utterly failed to prevent the slaughter of millions. And in the Balkans, only NATO's belated intervention saved the UN from complete disgrace.

The UN now became the fulcrum for American diplomacy, but that set up an inevitable conflict with a White House more used to going it alone than asking for help from lesser powers who had votes on the Security Council. (Or even cooperating with more traditional allies like France and Germany, as evidenced by Donald Rumsfeld's dismissive reference to them a year later as "old Europe.") Immediately after 9/11, the United States had enormous sympathy from around the world for military operations against the Taliban. But only three weeks into the operation, critics on the left and right began questioning whether we had gotten ourselves into a quagmire. The operation was being judged by unreasonably high expectations for rapid military victories, fixed in the public's mind by the success of the first Gulf War. Eventually, the Pentagon strategy disproved the networks' armchair commentators, or "Rolodex generals," as Powell and Richard Armitage called them, dismissively. The combination of CIA paramilitary units, inserted covertly prior to the invasion, and indigenous Afghan forces in the Northern Alliance, succeeded in wresting control of the country from the Taliban.

By November, the Taliban were in retreat. They were officially replaced in Kabul a month later by an interim regime, 102 days after 9/11. But Afghanistan, even without the Taliban, was still a feudal state ruled by warlords. Its nominal leader, Hamid Karzai, had more charisma in the West than real power at home. And Osama bin Laden was nowhere to be found. The CIA believed that he crossed into Pakistan by mule on December 16.

With Pakistan now critical to the hunt for bin Laden, and tense border disputes between Pakistan and India, both nuclear powers, Colin Powell headed to the region. I went along, describing it at the time as "mission impossible." The trip was high-risk: the Taliban had infiltrated Pakistan's security services. So to maintain secrecy for Powell's arrival time in Islamabad, we were told we could not tell our networks where in Europe we were refueling on the flight over and were not permitted to use our cell phones en route. The night landing in Pakistan was unlike anything I'd ever experienced. Cabin lights inside and exterior running lights were turned off. We were told to brace ourselves as though for a crash landing. The military pilots of the secretary's 757 then dove down to land with almost no glide path on the approach, minimizing the time terrorists could target the plane with stinger missiles.

Powell didn't get a very warm welcome. Just as he arrived, India raised the stakes, hinting that its submarines were already armed with nuclear warheads, a threat Pakistan couldn't match. India was posturing because it still wanted satisfaction for a suicide bombing attack on its parliament a month earlier that most likely had been staged by Pakistani terrorists. It was in this highly charged atmosphere that Powell undertook his mission to get Pakistan's leader to take on al Qaeda.

Pakistan is ten hours ahead of New York, so when we landed we had to go right to work. My first challenge was to go to the roof of our hotel and appear on a cable show with the host, Ashleigh Banfield. Ashleigh had moved to Islamabad to cover the war, and achieved some celebrity back home for dyeing her blond hair brown, to better blend in to the Muslim world. Just off the plane, I sat next to her on her set, on the roof of the Marriott in downtown Islamabad, feeling very blond. I didn't finish my report for *Nightly News* until 7 a.m., just in time to turn in my bags for the flight to India, our next stop. I longed for a bath, if not a nap, but it didn't matter. The rundown hotel we'd been billeted at on the Rawalpindi Road—called the Dream Motel—didn't have running water, and it was time to leave for New Delhi.

Our departure was similar to our arrival, only in daylight, and was even scarier. This time, the pilots gunned the engines, roared down the runway at full speed, and screeched to a stop. Then, to throw off any would-be attackers, they did a 180 degree turn, accelerated rapidly in the opposite direction, and lifted straight up. I don't know if it fooled the Taliban, but it certainly made us sick to our stomachs.

I didn't have a producer with me, but NBC hired a local stringer to help out in New Delhi. I had to stay up to write a report for *Nightly News* and then find the satellite transmission point to feed my story to New York in the early hours of the morning. A few hours later, we left for Afghanistan. We flew into Kabul on a cargo plane capable of evasive maneuvers, escorted by F-14 fighter jets and an

AWACS early warning radar plane. The visit was brief and largely symbolic. Its aim was strengthening Karzai's tenuous grasp on power.

The city, devastated long before the current war by years of uprisings against Soviet and then Taliban rule, was in ruins, but you could see small signs of renewal. I had not been there since my trip three years earlier with Bill Richardson. This time, we went back to the American embassy compound that had been shuttered since 1989, when the United States withdrew. Powell awarded a commendation to an Afghan caretaker, an embassy employee named Ahmed Zai, who had voluntarily guarded the U.S. property during all those years of occupation. Zai told me he did not regret the sacrifices he'd made for his service to America. It was a proud moment for the man and his family as Powell saluted him, and the Stars and Stripes were once again raised over the reopened embassy in Kabul.

All of our attention was still focused on unfinished business in Afghanistan, but the president had another war in mind. He had secretly asked General Tommy Franks, the head of U.S. Central Command, to begin planning for war with Iraq. His hidden agenda became more apparent at his State of the Union speech at the end of January. That night, I was at the Russell rotunda at the Capitol watching the speech and preparing to offer analysis afterward. Heralding successes in Afghanistan four months after 9/11, the president declared that the war on terror was only just beginning.

———

None of us was prepared for what came next. Bush accused Iraq of supporting terror, and of having plotted "to develop anthrax and nerve gas and nuclear weapons for over a decade." He went on to say that states like Iraq, Iran, and North Korea "constitute an axis of evil" that pose a "grave and growing danger" should they share weapons of mass destruction with terrorists. He added, ominously, "The United States of America will not permit the world's most dangerous regimes to threaten us with the world's most destructive weapons."

This was the Bush doctrine of preemptive action, a policy the president spelled out more fully eight months later. He was underscoring that the war against terror was not limited to al Qaeda. My immediate reaction was that he had shut down what some State Department officials thought was a promising attempt to cultivate Iran. Clearly, that overture was dead. But the real signal was Iraq. As Bob Woodward reported in *Plan of Attack,* the White House had sent drafts of the speech to the State Department three or four days earlier. Powell and his deputy, Richard Armitage, did not have any problem with the phrase, only questioning whether the speech was too "bleak" and needed more uplifting language at the end. More poetry was added to lighten the prose. George Tenet also raised no objections.

What is remarkable is not that the phrase "axis of evil" worked its way into a Bush speech, but that the Bush team was so accustomed to the president's tough thinking no one thought it would be controversial in the rest of the world. It was just another catchy speechwriter's phrase to please the political team. Even Powell and Armitage were tone deaf to the likely reaction from Europe. There was criticism from some Republicans, like Senator Chuck Hagel of the Foreign Relations Committee, who afterward told me, "Words have meaning, and meaning has consequences." Hagel believed the "axis of evil" phrase would make it harder for Iranian reformers. But the president had already given up on them. He felt the hard-liners had won, and Iran would not live up to any agreements. A month earlier, an Iranian ship smuggling weapons to Yasser Arafat had been intercepted in the Red Sea. Intelligence showed that Iran was also trying to destabilize Hamid Karzai's fragile interim government in Afghanistan.

What is most revealing, however, about the mood at the time was the reaction of the Democratic leader, Tom Daschle. The majority leader said that Congress would back military action against all three of the axis of evil states if the president decided to launch military strikes against them. "If it takes preemptive strikes, (if) it takes preemptive action, I think Congress is prepared to support it, but obviously we want more details," he told ABC. In post-9/11 Washington, there would be no strong challenge from the loyal opposition.

That winter, favorable world opinion of the American effort in Afghanistan began to wane after pictures were released showing al Qaeda suspects bound and kneeling in their prison at Guantánamo, Cuba. In a foreshadowing of the Abu Ghraib prison scandal in Iraq two years later, a visibly annoyed Donald Rumsfeld shot back at critics: "The treatment of the detainees in Guantánamo Bay is proper, it's humane, it's appropriate, and it is fully consistent with international conventions."

The subject was still sensitive a week later when we went to a dinner our friends Elaine and Jim Wolfensohn were hosting in honor of Kofi Annan. Also attending were the Rumsfelds, several senators and their wives, and a number of prominent journalists. Given Washington's "off the record" rules about that kind of social occasion, none of us ever disclosed what happened. But two years later, Al Hunt, who had not attended and so was not bound to keep the secret, wrote about it in *The Wall Street Journal*. As Al revealed, an argument erupted between Annan and Rumsfeld over whether prisoners at Guantánamo deserved protection under the Geneva Conventions. When one of the guests challenged Rumsfeld, he got up and left in the middle of dessert. It was an early warning of a growing chasm between the administration and the UN.

—

The arguments over war and foreign policy began to dominate our lives, in and out of the office. These were not small political debates that could be laughed off over a drink. This was big stuff, and people were passionate. Perhaps Washington was like this during Vietnam, before I'd arrived in town. But this was more serious than anything I'd ever covered. I have repeatedly gone back over our reporting in those years to better understand how we, along with the intelligence community, much of Congress, and leaders in the United States and Great Britain got it so wrong.

My stories reflected a variety of viewpoints, but many of the people interviewed came to the weapons debate with erroneous assumptions about Saddam Hussein's motives. From those misunderstandings flowed critical errors about Iraq's weapons program. In a report I filed for the *Today* show on April 10, 2002, I interviewed Charles Duelfer, a dedicated former United Nations weapons inspector who had shown singular independence at the UN. Later, Duelfer went back into government and helped the CIA determine that Saddam had not resumed weapons production. But two years earlier, in the debate before the war, he told me, "Right now we would face chemical and biological weapons. Those are bad enough, but they are things that we can deal with. If he gets a nuclear weapon, when he gets a nuclear weapon, then all bets are off."

In that same report, former Clinton defense secretary William Cohen, one of the nation's most thoughtful military experts, said he suspected Iraq started rebuilding weapons of mass destruction almost four years earlier, when it kicked out UN inspectors. "That's my strong suspicion, that since the time that they have kicked out the inspectors, that they have continued on their program to develop chemical and biological weapons."

When I try to recapture my own mind-set by going through notes, scripts, and tapes, I come to the conclusion that some of these assumptions were based on overly simple logic. If Saddam had no weapons, why would he continue to suffer from economic sanctions, when he could so easily come clean and regain control over his country's economy? There was also Saddam's history of lying to hide his weapons before the first Gulf War, and using them against Iran and the Kurds. Duelfer, in one of our reports that April, said, "I myself have spent an evening in 1995 listening to them describe how they weaponized a biological agent."

At the same time, there were powerful voices of caution. Senator Joe Biden, after a series of exhaustive Foreign Relations Committee hearings in August 2002, said, "One, we don't want to do this alone if we can avoid it. Number two, when we go, if we go and take down Saddam Hussein, we're going to have to be there for a while, and it's going to cost a great deal of money."

I had talked to enough senior officials that summer to know that going to war with Iraq was only a matter of time. If anything, the president would accede to appeals from Tony Blair and Colin Powell to go to the UN first as a useful delaying tactic. The military needed more time to get our troops in place and would not be ready for war until early spring.

Brent Scowcroft, national security advisor to the president's father during the first Gulf War, and Condi Rice's mentor, clearly read the internal politics the same way. He weighed in with a column in *The Wall Street Journal* that August, cautioning, "There is scant evidence to tie Saddam to terrorist organizations, and even less to the September 11 attacks." He added that there was virtual consensus in the world against attacking Iraq at that time.

Scowcroft's column was widely viewed in Washington as a thinly veiled message from Bush's father, who had decided not to oust Saddam when he had the chance, to the son, who seemed hell-bent on finishing the job. Everyone was playing armchair psychologist and interpreting the president's decisions through an oedipal lens. To counteract Scowcroft, Cheney gave a major policy speech, rare for late August when official Washington vacations, to the Veterans of Foreign Wars. The vice president used the speech to challenge the value of UN inspections and declare categorically, "Simply stated, there is no doubt that Saddam Hussein now has weapons of mass destruction (and) there is no doubt that he is amassing them to use against our friends, against our allies, and against us."

In Cheney's view, the risk of being wrong about Saddam was simply too great to take the chance of letting him get a nuclear weapon. Others in the administration arguing for war were also emboldened by what they viewed as the initial success, and relatively

low casualty count, of the military operation in Afghanistan. In going to the UN to satisfy Blair and other key allies, the president was
buying into a process for which he had little regard. His and
Cheney's obvious contempt for the UN diplomacy only fueled the
continuing debate with Powell over how to proceed.

The president's speech to the General Assembly that fall set the
stage for the confrontations to come. After a ferocious internal argument, the president committed to ask for a war resolution, but
somehow that sentence didn't appear in the version of the text
loaded in the TelePrompTer. Powell, listening from the front row of
the audience, was mortified. But, a few lines down, the president realized the sentence was missing and ad-libbed it. Was the omission in
the text provided to the president just an accident? I still wonder
whether someone in the White House was trying to subvert the
policy decision.

Going to the UN helped the president win a resolution in Congress, with critical help from House Democratic leader Richard
Gephardt. John Kerry, as is well known, went along. At the time, it
was the most politic course for a man with presidential ambitions,
and not an unreasonable vote. But he never developed a coherent
enough explanation of that vote to satisfy the Democratic Party's
antiwar base.

Kerry was not alone. Most Democrats, other than Biden, were
simply not asking tough questions about the administration's underlying case against Saddam and neither were the Republicans. Unlike
the debate led by Sam Nunn before the first Gulf War, there was no
longer a bipartisan group of Senate intellectuals willing to take on
the issue, no matter where the facts led.

When the Iraq resolution came to a vote in the UN that November, we were on the air live. Suddenly, U.S. Ambassador John
Negroponte rushed to the chamber holding a cell phone to his ear.
What was up? I reached a source who told me the Syrian ambassador, representing the only Arab state in the Security Council, had

called to say he would vote with the United States. It was unanimous, a huge personal victory for Powell. But there was an underlying problem. Each side had a different interpretation of what the resolution meant. Powell interpreted its warning that Iraq would suffer "serious consequences" for not complying as a mandate for war. But the language was ambiguous enough to mean something entirely different to France.

To this day, Powell insists that he had a personal commitment from France's foreign minister, the dashing—and politically ambitious—Dominique de Villepin, that this was a final ultimatum to Iraq. Powell said he even took a call from de Villepin as the secretary of state was about to walk his daughter down the aisle, delaying the wedding to hammer out the interpretation of the war resolution. It is one of the reasons why he viewed France's later opposition as such a personal betrayal.

As part of the resolution, Iraq was required to disclose how it had disposed of its weapons. Saddam produced twelve thousand pages, overwhelming the UN inspectors with detail. As I reported, former UN weapons inspectors David Kay and David Albright both suggested it was a rehash of previous claims, not a true accounting. U.S. officials immediately dismissed it as inadequate, but we had no independent way to verify either side's claim. The United States said Iraq had failed the test and was in violation of the UN's ultimatum. Except for Tony Blair, the rest of the Security Council disagreed.

Now the case for war rested on Colin Powell. I knew how skeptical he was about many of the administration's arguments. So when he went to CIA headquarters and personally vetted the intelligence community's case against Saddam before presenting it to the UN, his word carried a lot of weight. The State Department also made sure we knew he had personally eliminated some of the White House and Pentagon claims linking Iraq to terrorism, a connection he considered tenuous. To give his presentation the CIA "Good Housekeeping" seal of approval, he insisted that George Tenet sit behind him, visible in every frame.

Powell's audio and visual display included satellite photos that we could not possibly analyze for ourselves. Few experts challenged the documentation. When Tom Brokaw interviewed Lee Hamilton, the highly respected former House Intelligence Committee chairman called it "impressive." Hamilton, who later co-chaired the 9/11 Commission, said, "The administration's most persuasive advocate who has the greatest credibility in the world, the dove in the administration, makes the case. He's backed up by the head of the Central Intelligence Agency. Secondly, the intelligence capabilities of the United States came through this presentation powerfully, just showing to all the world what we know about what's going on."

Only now, after several investigations by Congress and a presidential panel, do we know that U.S. intelligence agencies misinterpreted the satellite photos, relying on a discredited source. In fact, three key charges—that Saddam had imported aluminum tubes designed exclusively for nuclear fuel production, that he had mobile biological weapons labs, and that he had unmanned aerial vehicles capable of delivering biological or chemical weapons—were completely false. The CIA's assessment about the mobile labs was based solely on an Iraqi defector code-named "Curveball" provided by the German intelligence service. But American officials ignored warnings as early as May 2000—three years before Powell's UN presentation—that "Curveball" was unreliable. Red flags were raised about "Curveball" repeatedly during those years, but neither the Defense Intelligence Agency nor the CIA ever circulated what the agencies call a burn notice about his false information, and no one alerted Powell. A second defector, the source for the erroneous claims about the aluminum tubes, was also a known fabricator. Dissenting opinions from the State Department and the Energy Department about the tubes were relegated to a footnote. The air force's doubts about the unmanned vehicles were suppressed. Powell has said since that he regrets the errors in his presentation to the UN, but not the outcome—the decision to go to war and remove Saddam Hussein from power. But he is known to fear that he will always be remembered, fairly or not, as "the guy who made a bad case to the UN."

At the time, Powell's reputation went far toward convincing American audiences that what the CIA said should be accepted at face value. But many members of the Security Council, heavily lobbied by the French, were deeply skeptical. Even Powell admitted at the time that there was no smoking gun.

But the White House was all too willing to believe any "evidence" it could find about Saddam's weapons capability. Only a week earlier, the president had asserted in his State of the Union address that "the British government has learned that Saddam Hussein recently sought significant quantities of uranium from Africa."

At the time, it was just one more administration accusation about Iraq's efforts to shop for nuclear weapons fuel. No one challenged it. It wasn't until March, a week and a half before the war started, that Mohamed El Baradei, director of the International Atomic Energy Agency, said that charge was based on fraudulent documents. By then, war was inevitable. It took another four months for the simmering feud between the White House and the CIA to boil over because of those sixteen words in the president's speech.

———

Long before the president issued his ultimatum, there was no turning back. We were all at our stations in the newsroom, ready to begin continuous coverage, but when the war started, it was still a surprise. Acting on information from a spy in Baghdad, the president had moved up the timetable and ordered an air strike against one of Saddam's compounds, hoping there was a chance to take out the Iraqi leader and his top advisors.

We had assembled a team of retired generals and other expert commentators from all of the services to guide us, and our viewers, through the military maze. For the first time, our correspondents were embedded with the troops, reporting live as they advanced toward Baghdad. They were all heroic, but what will forever be imprinted in my memory of the war is the reporting of David Bloom.

It was David's inspiration to retrofit a tank recovery vehicle, known as an M88A, and combine it with a mobile Ford uplink truck so that he could report in real time as he rolled through the desert. His cameraman, Craig White, rode with him, using a high-quality broadcast camera instead of the more primitive videophone being used by other reporters. The pictures were astounding. Viewers were taken deep inside the armored division. Their guide to the Third Infantry Division was a man they'd known previously as an impeccably groomed White House correspondent and Sunday morning anchor. Now he was a modern-day Lawrence of Arabia, driving hard through the desert with bloodshot eyes and hair clotted with sand. Instead of a camel, he had what we called the Bloom-mobile.

At times Brokaw cautioned us, and the audience, not to get distracted by the gee-whiz toys that were bringing the war into our living rooms. In one breathtakingly poignant interview, Nancy Chamberlain, mother of U.S. Marine captain Jay Aubin, quietly told Tom, "I truly admire what all the network news and news technologies are doing today to bring it into our homes. But for the mothers and wives who are out there watching, it is murder. It is heartbreak. We can't leave the television. Every tank, every helicopter, 'Is that my son?' And I just need you to be aware that technology is great. But there are moms, there are dads, there are wives who are suffering because of this." Mrs. Chamberlain's son died on the third day of the war, when his Sea Knight helicopter crashed during a sandstorm.

Bloom's genius was that he never lost sight of the human story. He was a newsman's newsman, in Brokaw's words, "a warrior, fearless, hard charging, always eager for the next difficult assignment. He'd arrive on a story and within twenty-four hours have a notepad full of the secret cell phone numbers of the best sources." He was such a life force that it was inconceivable that David, who outhustled the rest of us on every story, would not be at the other end of a satellite or a telephone saying with rapid-fire enthusiasm,

"Hey, buddy, here's what I've got." David started having severe leg pains as he rode through the desert with his knees propped up in the compact vehicle, but apparently did not want to stop telling the stories of the soldiers in his unit long enough to get medical help. It is a determination that all of us understand, completely. He was heading toward Baghdad, doing the best reporting of his life. Two weeks later, David, only thirty-nine years old, collapsed from a pulmonary embolism. He died only days before his unit, the Third Infantry Division, entered Saddam's capital. The doctors assumed the clot had formed in his leg because of the cramped conditions inside the tank recovery vehicle. Retired general Montgomery Meigs, one of our analysts, likened him to Ernie Pyle, telling war stories for another generation of soldiers. Irrepressible and full of life until the abrupt end, David's last call to the NBC news desk was to check on the scores of the Final Four basketball play-off games.

On April 8, two days after David's death, coalition troops—led by the Third Infantry Division—pushed into Baghdad. Iraq's infamous information minister, Mohammed Saeed al-Sahaf (ridiculed in the American press as "Baghdad Bob"), gave his last briefing. In an unconscious echo of Al Haig after Ronald Reagan was shot, Saddam's spokesman told reporters, "We are in control." The next day, with the Third Infantry Division rolling through the Iraqi capital, Saddam's statue was toppled and pulled to the ground by what appeared to be a jubilant crowd. Few of us had predicted that Iraq's capital would fall so rapidly, and with so little resistance.

In fact, the entry of U.S. troops into Baghdad was so unexpected that until the last moment I had been planning to fly with Alan that morning to the Reagan library in Simi Valley, California. Alan was scheduled to give a lecture, and Nancy Reagan was hosting a dinner. Instead, I stayed behind to track reaction here to the dramatic fall of Iraq's capital. From the narrow perspective of the video being fed back, the streets of Baghdad seemed to erupt in celebration. Perhaps

Washington's war hawks had been right all along. But even then, we knew that it was far too early to celebrate a victory for American policy makers. The furthest thing from our minds was that no weapons would be found. Instead, the fear was that Saddam would use chemical weapons on our troops and set fire to his oil fields.

None of that happened. Now, with American troops inside Baghdad, administration officials hoped they'd finally discover Iraq's stockpiles of weapons. David Kay, our dogged weapons expert, left NBC to lead the CIA's hunt for the weapons. But Iraq is a large country. At first, Kay thought that some of the evidence, both documents and weapons, might have been destroyed during looting immediately after the invasion. No one had any answers, and before long Washington was in full battle cry over whether the administration had deliberately misled the American people and Congress about Saddam's weapons.

The CIA and the National Security Council were each blaming the other. Then, on a Saturday night in July when I was preparing to fill in for Tim Russert on *Meet the Press,* the show's executive producer, Betsy Fischer, called to alert me to a column in the next morning's *New York Times.* Joseph Wilson, a former ambassador, revealed that he had traveled to Africa for the administration a year earlier and told them that charges that Iraq had tried to purchase uranium from Niger were untrue—long before the president repeated that claim in his State of the Union address.

We called Wilson and added him to our show. Already appearing were Senators Carl Levin and John Warner from the Armed Services Committee and, importantly, columnist Robert Novak, a frequent guest. To my knowledge, Novak had never met Wilson before arriving that day in our greenroom, or since. That meeting had far-ranging ramifications.

On the program, I asked Wilson whether the administration was politicizing the intelligence to justify the war. He said, "Either the administration has some information that it has not shared with the public, or yes, they were using the selective use of facts and intelligence to bolster a decision in the case that had already been made."

The president was traveling in Africa, but the White House was forced to acknowledge its error. Condi Rice's deputy, Stephen Hadley, who later replaced her as national security advisor, stepped forward to take the blame. So did George Tenet, for not having caught the mistake before the president's big speech. After a week of bloodletting, the White House struck back. In his syndicated column, Robert Novak quoted two anonymous administration officials who seemed to be suggesting that Wilson had a political agenda because his wife, Valerie Plame, worked at the CIA.

Wittingly or not, Novak had revealed the name of a covert agent. Plame had the deepest kind of cover, a false identity carefully created over years so that she could safely and secretly perform her missions. *The Washington Post* reported, erroneously, that in addition to Novak, I was one of six other reporters to whom the administration had tried to leak Plame's identity in order to discredit Wilson. That was not the case. Someone in the administration had steered me in that direction, but only after Novak's column appeared. The consequences for Plame were severe—she could no longer travel overseas or work undercover. For at least a year afterward, the subsequent criminal investigation into the leak seemed to focus more on reporters than government sources. The net effect was to intimidate other officials from talking to journalists, especially those targeted by the prosecutor. And in a twist worthy of *Alice in Wonderland,* at least two of the reporters swept up in the probe hadn't written a word about Plame or anything related to the case.

The Wilson affair damaged the CIA's standing in the White House, despite the president's close personal relationship with George Tenet. Within the vice president's office and the National Security Council, officials questioned the judgment of sending Wilson on such a sensitive mission in the first place. Worse yet, no weapons of mass destruction had been found, Saddam Hussein was still at large, and the agency badly needed a victory.

———

Even Washington pauses during the Christmas season. On Saturday, December 13, Alan and I were going to a holiday party at the Rumsfelds'. I was juggling all my roles: I'd just been to trustee meetings at the University of Pennsylvania and had rushed home to decorate the dining room and set the table for a dinner we were giving the next night for Federal Reserve officials. At the Rumsfelds', everyone seemed especially jolly. The defense secretary was almost bouncing on his heels. The vice president and my husband huddled in a corner. George Tenet was cracking jokes. At one point, Tim Russert told the CIA director that he'd dreamed Saddam had been captured. Tenet looked startled, but laughed it off.

We got to bed late, but that was all right, because it was Saturday night. The phone rang at five a.m. The Iranian news service was reporting that Saddam had been captured. Turning to Alan, I asked, "Was that what you and the vice president were talking about last night?" He said, "Don't ask me that question."

I jumped out of bed, called two sources to get it confirmed, and did a phone report for the network. By five-thirty a.m., half an hour later, I was dressed and in the newsroom helping to report one of the biggest stories of the decade. It was not too much to hope that Saddam's capture would mean the beginning of the war's end. The insurgency would collapse, and our troops would start coming home. It was the holiday season and there was no reason not truly to celebrate peace on earth.

CHAPTER 9

Red/Blue Nation?

W e knew we were getting through to our audience the night a man jumped onto the outdoor set for *Hardball* in Herald Square during the 2004 Republican convention in New York and tried to take out Chris Matthews. Was this an illustration of how divided we were as a nation, or just a passing drunk looking to pick a fight? Television news had indeed come a long way from "Good night, Chet. Good night, David."

With the nation at war, perhaps it was inevitable that our politics would inspire so much passion. Vulnerable to terrorists at home, fighting an invisible enemy in Iraq, Americans were angry, or at least worried. In polls, large percentages of people claimed the country was heading in the wrong direction, usually a bad indicator for an incumbent president. Protestors in New York wanted to be heard. When security barriers prevented them from getting anywhere near the Republicans at Madison Square Garden, we were the next best target.

Our outdoor broadcasts, produced in front of live audiences in all kinds of terrible weather, quickly turned into a media circus. One night, thousands of demonstrators massed across the street, separated from us only by a line of mounted police. After a while, you tune out the madding crowd. If the convention speakers went on long enough, we would even grab a hamburger and eat on the set, since that was the only chance we'd get. Once, when I tried to figure out what the protestors were chanting, I was startled to realize that it was, "How can you eat while this is going on? How can you eat while this is going on?" It was not my best New York dining experience.

Most memorably, on the third night of the convention, Georgia senator Zell Miller, a renegade Democrat, challenged our anchorman, Chris Matthews, to a duel. Fortunately, the senator was at Madison Square Garden, where he'd just delivered the keynote address for the Republicans, and was presumably unarmed. We were several blocks away at Herald Square. The televised exchange, over the senator's attacks on Kerry's past support for defense cuts, escalated quickly when Miller said, "Get out of my face. If you're going to ask me a question, step back and let me answer. I wish we lived in the day where you could challenge a person to a duel."

The crowd surrounding the set was part of the problem, alternately booing and cheering so that Miller couldn't quite be sure what he was hearing. Sitting just to Chris's left, I tried to quiet the audience, but that seemed only to make them yell more loudly. Chris tried to persuade Miller to come over so they could continue the debate face-to-face. Miller refused, but Jon Meacham, our panelist from *Newsweek,* pointed out that Miller had already made history. He'd issued the first threat to kill in presidential politics since Andrew Jackson threatened to shoot Henry Clay and hang John C. Calhoun.

The campaign was probably more passionate than any since 1972 because it was playing out against a backdrop of escalating violence in Iraq. How did a lightning-quick war turn into what some feared was becoming a nightmare occupation? Critics said there were several key mistakes, despite plenty of warning. One issue was too few troops. A month before the war, then Army chief of staff General Eric Shinseki told Congress it would take several hundred thousand troops to keep the peace in Iraq. Instead, the Pentagon planned a postwar occupation with only 110,000 forces, not enough to prevent widespread looting or a wider insurgency. For that, Shinseki was humiliated by the Pentagon's civilian leaders and driven to retire early.

The second issue was the decision to disband the Iraqi army. Coalition leader Paul Bremer had let Iraqi soldiers go home with their weapons, instead of using them to create a new security force. Before the war, former general Anthony Zinni had told Congress the United States would need five thousand police trainers. But top Pentagon officials ignored that recommendation, as well as many others, from a prewar State Department report that filled thirteen volumes.

The White House insisted that the media were overlooking the good things that were happening in Iraq: schools were reopening, oil was being exported, Saddam Hussein's old currency was replaced without a hitch by a new monetary system. But the threat of attack made it almost impossible for foreign journalists to risk roaming far enough to cover those "human interest" stories. And the security situation was so perilous for civilian contractors that a year after the occupation, the American-led coalition and its Iraqi partners had spent barely a fraction of the $18 billion Congress had appropriated for reconstruction. The United States was still bearing 90 percent of the costs, taking most of the risks, and suffering almost all the casualties.

Earlier in the 2004 campaign, anger over the war among Democratic activists, as well as innovative Internet organizing and fund-raising, had briefly propelled Vermont's former governor, Howard Dean, into the front ranks of presidential candidates. Seven weeks before the first caucus voters would even vote in Iowa, Al Gore had stunned the political world by endorsing Dean. Gore hadn't even given a heads-up to Joe Lieberman, his former running mate, who was also seeking the nomination, albeit from the back of the pack. At the time, Dean looked formidable with his double-digit lead over John Kerry in New Hampshire. Democratic campaign activist

Donna Brazile underscored this, telling us, "Howard Dean is on his way to winning the Democratic nomination."

At the time, John Kerry's aides were fairly confident that they would win Iowa. They had poured in money and volunteers, and campaign advisor Bob Shrum had sharpened the message and shortened Kerry's speeches. The crowds were building, and Kerry was connecting. Through sheer luck, the campaign also picked up an emotional endorsement from Jim Rassmann, whose life Kerry had saved in Vietnam. Kerry's other advantage was that Dean was making mistakes, and his campaign began collapsing. As *Newsweek* later reported, Dean's iconoclastic campaign manager, Joe Trippi, was by then more committed to the cyberspace movement he'd invented than to Dean's candidacy.

On caucus night, Kerry trounced Dean and Dick Gephardt, the presumed Iowa front-runners. John Edwards came in second. Dean's "primal scream" to rally his troops was so bizarre—and the media response so negative—that his campaign was virtually over.

With the administration struggling in Iraq, Democrats wanted a candidate with foreign policy credentials and military experience. At the time, they thought that this campaign would be the first since 1972 to focus on war and peace, not the economy. Who better to lead the party than a decorated Vietnam veteran like Kerry, with decades of experience on the Senate Foreign Relations Committee? One week later, Kerry won New Hampshire, as well.

———

I'd been covering prewar planning, the search for weapons of mass destruction, the investigation into 9/11—all issues that were now front and center in the presidential race. With so much focus on the war, there were half a dozen investigations examining prewar intelligence. By then, no weapons stockpiles had been found and the search wasn't likely to produce any. In fact, the administration had been forced to shift resources from the CIA's weapons hunt to the more pressing problem of fighting the insurgency.

On January 28, five days before the Democrats would hold primaries in seven states, there was a shocking declaration from the head of the CIA weapons search, David Kay. The prewar intelligence had been wrong. Iraq had not had large stocks of weapons of mass destruction. Had the administration misled the world, or was the rhetoric before the war the result of poor intelligence? And why had we in the media failed to uncover the real facts before the U.S. invaded?

To better understand what went wrong, it is instructive to look at the role of David Kay. He had spent years disarming Iraq for the UN after the first Gulf War, and then, partly on my recommendation, had become NBC's weapons analyst before this war. In that role, his confidence that Saddam was hiding weapons had helped shape my reporting. Then, in June 2003, Kay left NBC to return to Iraq, this time for the CIA. At first, he believed they would find clues to the whereabouts of the weapons by interviewing Iraqi scientists and translating thousands of pages of documents now available to them. Instead, a very different picture emerged. Some of the scientists claimed they themselves had exaggerated their progress toward developing illegal weapons to placate Saddam. Others suggested it was all an elaborate sting by Saddam to fool his neighbors into thinking he was more dangerous than he was—in a sense, a ruse like the secret plan of some Reagan advisors to persuade the Soviets that the United States was building strategic defense systems against their missiles, long before a program had even been designed.

Whatever the truth, Kay now delivered a searing indictment of prewar weapons analysis. He told the Senate, "We were almost all wrong, and I certainly include myself here." Saddam Hussein had not deployed militarized chemical and biological weapons, did not have biological laboratories, and had not reconstituted a full-blown nuclear program. I had to count myself among those who had thought the logic of Saddam's behavior indicated he likely did have weapons.

Even if the world was better without Saddam Hussein, Kay's bold testimony destroyed the administration's original justification for the invasion. And if U.S. intelligence couldn't be trusted, how could the president pursue a policy of preemptive action under his Bush doctrine? That night, in an interview for my report on *Nightly News,* former defense secretary Bill Cohen asked, "Were there any qualifications to the assumptions (about the intelligence)? Did those get airbrushed out of existence over a period of time so that the statements became much more categorical and self-confident?"

It had been a year since Colin Powell, with George Tenet right behind him, had firmly described Iraq's weapons to the Security Council. Repeatedly, I have asked myself then, and since, whether we ascribed too much credibility to both Powell and Tenet because of their prior reputations for independent thinking and their relationships with many of us in the media. While I used the conventional journalistic caveats to distance myself from their conclusions, and sought out the French foreign minister and others for alternate points of view, phrases did creep in to my reports—"Powell's powerful presentation to the Security Council"—that sounded like an endorsement of the secretary's weapons argument. Again, I relied on sources, not only David Kay, but other former weapons inspectors and dissidents within the State Department, to test the official assumptions. This was a case, however, where the established wisdom overshadowed the critics.

Now, a year later, Tenet tried to explain to Congress what had gone wrong. Under a hail of questions from the Senate, the CIA chief snapped, "We're not perfect. But we're pretty damn good at what we do and we care as much as you do about Iraq and whether we were right or wrong, and we're going to work through it in a way where we tell the truth as to whether we were right or wrong."

This was no explanation, and as we now know, there had been plenty of prewar hype. In October of 2002, a classified CIA paper said Saddam was "capable of quickly producing and weaponizing" anthrax and delivering it by "bombs, missiles, aerial sprayers, and covert operatives." The agency's public, unclassified version was even more alarming. In it, the CIA added that Iraq could also use the anthrax "against the U.S. homeland" even though air force experts told the CIA that was unlikely. At the same time, the president and Condoleezza Rice also warned ominously about the need to prevent a "mushroom cloud." And Donald Rumsfeld said, "There is no doubt in my mind that he has weapons, chemical and biological weapons, and has been working on nuclear weapons."

Now, after the postinvasion search provided scant evidence of an ongoing Iraqi weapons program, the president started backing off. Suddenly, Saddam was only a "gathering" threat. With the administration already under attack, the Abu Ghraib scandal made a bad situation even worse for America's credibility abroad, especially in the Arab world. Both *60 Minutes II* on CBS and Seymour Hersh in *The New Yorker* got the horrific details. The press, demanding that someone be held accountable, was running wild with stories that Rumsfeld was going to be fired. I doubted it. Alan and I had been invited to a small dinner at the Rumsfelds' to take place two days after the prison abuse story had broken. When we arrived, quite late because of my *Nightly News* duties, there was a motorcade idling outside. Inside, George Bush's presence was a silent signal that Rummy was still his man.

———

John Kerry was positioned perfectly to capitalize on the administration's troubles. Yet even with the White House on the defensive over both the failure to find weapons and the prison scandal, Kerry could not seem to turn the president's policy errors to his advantage. On March 16, the democrat was in West Virginia when a heckler pressed him on why he had opposed funding for the troops. Kerry lapsed into Senate-speak, saying, "I actually did vote for the $87 billion before I voted against it." He was referring to legislative procedures in which several votes are taken before an issue is decided.

But in the process, he had given the Bush team the ammunition it needed to reinvent Kerry as a flip-flopper who was "soft" on defense. It was the political equivalent of friendly fire, a moment as self-destructive as when Michael Dukakis climbed into that M1 tank in 1988.

Months later, Kerry was still sending mixed signals when he tried to explain his vote against the spending bill and for the war. During an ill-fated photo opportunity in the Grand Canyon, he was asked if he'd still vote for the war, knowing what he knew now. Ceding the antiwar position he'd tried to stake out, he said, "Yes. I would have voted for the authority. I believe it was the right authority for a president to have." It was an honest answer, but far too nuanced for that stage of the campaign. Now he was committed to supporting the war and the president, whatever his reservations might be. Clearly, it was a turning point for the campaign, although his advisors may not have realized it at the time.

I've long thought that both candidates were much too sheltered from the give-and-take of press questions. In an April press conference, the president seemed petulant, refusing to concede mistakes. It didn't hurt him in the polls—in fact, his stubbornness may have been an asset with the voters—but it was the same impulse to appear smug and impatient that hurt him later in the first debate. Bush had had fewer press conferences than any of his recent predecessors except Ronald Reagan. But Kerry also avoided the national press. For a senator who had made his reputation mixing it up with reporters every day, it was an odd retreat, and one that hurt him as a candidate. When you're used to daily combat, as Bill Clinton was during his 1992 campaign, it prepares you mentally for anything the opposition can throw at you.

The Kerry camp was painfully disorganized, but drew false confidence from the many problems the White House was experiencing. The war was going badly, and even Republicans in Congress were openly critical of the administration. When the Senate Intelligence Committee finally produced a major report on prewar intelligence, only weeks before the Democratic convention, the verdict was unanimous. The Republican-led panel called it a colossal failure. President Bush had gone to war on false assumptions about Iraq's weapons of mass destruction. And, despite repeated and recent suggestions by the administration, the report found no formal terror connection between Iraq and al Qaeda. The Republicans discounted any political pressure on the CIA, but in a strong dissent, Jay Rockefeller, the group's top Democrat, said, "A veteran of many years there said that the hammering on (CIA) analysts was greater than he had seen in his thirty-two years of service."

In June, George Tenet announced that he was resigning. I had known George as a Senate staff member and a member of Bill Clinton's National Security Council. He had always been a straight shooter and I couldn't fathom how this had happened on his watch. I also felt that he and the agency were not getting credit for their considerable accomplishments in Afghanistan. There, CIA special operations forces had laid the groundwork for the invasion. Tenet's mentors, some from his years in the Senate, warned him that he should quit immediately after the Afghan success, before the Iraq invasion. But George had become obsessed with achieving the one major goal that had eluded him for years: finding Osama bin Laden.

For seven years, ever since he'd taken over the agency, Tenet had gone to bed every night worrying about what he didn't know. Since 9/11, he was surprised each morning that he'd gotten through one more day without America coming under another attack. He had come a long way from waiting tables at his parents' diner in Queens, and had wanted desperately to capture the top al Qaeda leader. That was not to be, and now seven proud years of service were ending badly.

The day after Tenet's departure, the administration started a counteroffensive against the scorching Senate report. Appearing at a Tennessee weapons lab in front of a display of nuclear equipment retrieved from Libya, the president said, "I had a choice to make. Either take the word of a madman or defend America. Given that choice, I will defend America every time."

Of course, the White House was setting up a false choice, but it was an effective political tactic. At the same time, Condi Rice went on cable networks, saying, "We did the right thing in removing Saddam Hussein." The implication was that if you criticized the White House, you had to be supporting Saddam (whom the president had called a madman that same day). And, in the battleground state of Pennsylvania, the vice president accused Kerry of developing a "convenient case of campaign amnesia" by forgetting that he had voted for the war. Kerry rose to the bait, replying, "The United States of America should never go to war because we want to. We only go to war because we have to." The problem was, of course, that he had voted to authorize the use of force.

———

In a dramatic courtroom drama that July, we saw Saddam for the first time since he had been dragged out of his spider hole. He appeared before a Baghdad judge shortly after eight-thirty a.m. eastern time, right in the middle of the *Today* show. The former dictator was gaunt, but defiant. When the judge asked him his name, he drew himself up and proclaimed, "I am Saddam Hussein al-Majid, the President of the Republic of Iraq." He challenged the judge's credentials even to hear the case, and demanded immunity. Ridiculing the tribunal, he told the court, "Everyone knows this is theater by Bush, the criminal, in an attempt to win the election." The hearing, similar to an arraignment in this country, lasted only twenty-six minutes.

Seeing and hearing the former dictator for the first time since his capture was electrifying television, but somehow, through a combination of errors, NBC was late in putting Saddam's hearing on the air, and the people involved were embarrassed. NBC needed to erase the bad publicity quickly with a win. That is when I decided we had to break the next big story, John Kerry's choice of a running mate.

———

Kerry would be making his decision within a few days and announcing it in the morning, when the *Today* show was on the air. Every newspaper, magazine, and television network was chasing the story. I was determined that we would find out first and give the *Today* crew some bragging rights.

Kerry knew that in an election as close as the 2004 contest, he needed to find someone who would give him a competitive advantage. Only one person was a big enough political celebrity to meet that standard: John McCain. For weeks, Kerry had been courting McCain, even to the point of offering him a bigger portfolio—he could be vice president *and* defense secretary at the same time, running the Pentagon and foreign policy.

It was an impossible sale, largely because, despite their past disputes, McCain believed George Bush was a better war president, and likely wanted to prove his party loyalty by campaigning for Bush in order to run himself in four years. He also knew Kerry would have a difficult time turning over foreign policy to his vice president, no matter what had been promised. A similar proposal had been floated once before, in 1980, when Ronald Reagan briefly flirted with the idea of making former president Gerald Ford his vice president and virtual "copresident" on a fusion ticket. Alan and Henry Kissinger had played a part in those negotiations, but in the end, both Reagan and Ford balked.

Now, as then, a fusion ticket or copresidency was a nonstarter. So who would Kerry choose? Often, when we are chasing a big story, we have to juggle. That weekend, over the July 4 holiday, I was also substituting for Tim Russert on *Meet the Press*. Tim has made the show "must-see TV" for people who follow politics, building on a long tradition—the program first went on the air in 1947 and is the longest-running television show in history. It has always been rigorous, but Tim has made his preparation an art form. His sequence of questions is built as carefully as an architect's model. Grown men and women cringe when he produces a quotation or, worse, a video clip, with a contradictory or incriminating statement. Sometimes, they've forgotten they even said it until Tim comes up with the evidence.

I've learned from hard experience that the only way to get ready for *Meet the Press* is to do your homework. That means spending days reading and selecting the issues, then honing the questions and choosing which quotations to put up on the screen. And, as I'd learned a year earlier when the Joe Wilson story broke late Saturday night, you have to be ready to switch directions at the last minute if news happens. Fortunately, Tim and his producer, Betsy Fischer, have the best team in television news.

Our guests on the Sunday before Kerry's announcement of a running mate were Senators John Warner and Joe Lieberman and former national security advisor Sandy Berger, all on Iraq, and a segment with Ralph Nader about his quixotic quest for the presidency. I've known Nader for years, and respect his brains, if not his judgment. What many people don't know is how secretive he is about his movements. For a profile about him for *Nightly News,* we had to meet at a restaurant. When bringing him to the studio for a show, you have to pick him up on a street corner. Under questioning, he's just as hard to pin down. He refused to concede that his candidacy in 2000 had taken more votes from Al Gore than George Bush, and insisted that if anyone were the spoiler this time, it would be Kerry, not him.

I also had another role that weekend. That Sunday was July 4, and as Alan's wife, after *Meet the Press* I should have been preparing for our annual Independence Day party at the Federal Reserve. But instead, I spent most of the day calling every source I knew, trying to winnow the list of Kerry's possible choices. In a significant development that day, ABC had reported that Kerry had had a secret meeting with his likely choice in Washington the previous Thursday at the home of Madeleine Albright. Since Edwards was known to be on vacation with his family at Disney World, ABC concluded erroneously that the meeting had been with Dick Gephardt. We started speed-dialing our sources. During a series of conference calls led by our political director, Elizabeth Wilner, and our New York producers, Wilner and I both concluded that ABC was wrong.

Monday was a federal holiday, part of the three-day weekend. I was told that John Edwards was still in play, but that Kerry was also taking a late look at Florida senator Bob Graham. Graham made a lot of sense from an Electoral College standpoint. He was enormously popular in his home state, having served as its governor. He'd led the Senate Intelligence Committee and had plenty of foreign policy experience. But he'd not shown a great deal of skill as a national campaigner in his own race for president, and had dropped out the previous October.

To cover all bases, the *Today* show had correspondents prepare reports for Tuesday morning on all the possibilities. In addition to Edwards and Graham, the list included Iowa's governor Tom Vilsack and Missouri congressman Dick Gephardt. I was assigned to profile Gephardt. He was clearly the safest choice, and I wrote the story, but all day Monday I was picking up signals that he had been eliminated. The argument for Gephardt was that he could appeal to voters in the Midwest, especially labor groups long loyal to him. But labor's support had not brought him success in Iowa. And it wasn't even clear that he could help the ticket carry his home state.

Edwards was a much riskier pick. Kerry and Edwards had clashed repeatedly during the primaries, although Edwards was always careful not to let it get personal. But four years earlier, Kerry had been openly dismissive of Edwards when they were both finalists on Al Gore's short list of running mates. At that point, Kerry told people that Edwards was unqualified to be a heartbeat away from the Oval Office because he had only been in politics for two years.

But Sunday night, I was told that Kerry's feelings about Edwards had warmed. Edwards had, in fact, been the suitor Kerry had met with secretly the previous Thursday. Edwards had interrupted his Disney World vacation to fly back to Washington. Kerry had waited until the reporters outside his home left for the night, had sneaked out a back door, and then walked the two blocks to Albright's house, where Edwards was waiting. The meeting had gone well, greatly improving Kerry's comfort factor with the younger man.

As Monday evening approached, I kept working the phones until I reached someone who told me it was Edwards. But it was a single source. To prevent leaks, Kerry was not going to call the "losers" until the next day. Until he did, he could always change his mind. I called New York and we had another conference call, this time with Elizabeth Wilner; Brian Williams; our top New York producers, led by Mark Lukasiewicz; and Neal Shapiro, president of NBC News.

To the world outside television news, it may seem like a silly competition, but in our business, it was the World Series and the Super Bowl combined. We all became journalists because we love to chase stories, and this was a story worth chasing. Kerry's decision would open a window into how he perceived his own strengths and weaknesses and whether he had enough self-confidence to risk being upstaged by a better campaigner. Trying to puzzle this out was also like a giant game of Clue. The dirty little secret of journalism is that it's fun, like being hooked on detective novels. All those Nancy Drew mysteries I'd read as a child weren't that far off the mark.

That night, Brian's sources told him that Secret Service agents had arrived at an airport in North Carolina, Edwards's home state, and were putting together a motorcade. But we decided even that wasn't enough proof. They could have been doing the same thing for all the potential choices, and we just didn't know it. One of our best "embedded" campaign reporters, Felix Schein—who had started his career as my researcher—was working the story hard in Pittsburgh, where Kerry was huddled with his wife and advisors. An Internet site was reporting that the campaign was restenciling the candidate's plane to include Edwards's name. But Felix couldn't get into the hangar to confirm it.

For hours, we debated whether we had enough to go on, and if so, how and when to break into the network's entertainment programming. As it got later, there were fewer remaining "windows" during prime time. At that point, after Jay Leno and Conan O'Brien were off the air, I took a break and went home to change clothes and clean up for the *Today* program. It was too late to get any sleep.

Tuesday morning, we felt confident enough to hint broadly at the choice of Edwards at the top of the *Today* show. At 7:01, I reported, "John Kerry is very likely to pick John Edwards as his running mate." But to play it safe, the program still ran a previously scheduled segment on all the other possibilities. Then, twenty minutes later, Katie Couric came up with another source. We finally had it cold, and were able to break the Edwards story just before seven-thirty a.m. Speaking to Katie, I said, "My understanding is that John Edwards is the pick, that John Kerry decided that he wanted to choose John Edwards and felt that in a series of meetings he increased his comfort level (with Edwards)." We pointed out that the two men had been competitors during the primary, but that Edwards appealed to Kerry because "He's got a lot of sizzle, he's got pizzazz. He is a very good vote getter." Kerry had planned to announce it in an e-mail to supporters, and then appear together with his choice at a nine a.m. rally. We had beaten him to it.

In picking Edwards, Kerry was acknowledging that he had to add some spice to the ticket. Edwards was a vibrant, young face, and as a Southerner might appeal to swing voters in those crucial states. He also had a compelling personal story and a beautiful, young family. At the same time, it was a stretch. He'd been in politics only six years. He'd have to go head-to-head with Dick Cheney in a debate. He was a trial lawyer, an unpopular profession with many voters. And he still had to prove that he could keep his ambitions in check and not overshadow John Kerry. But party leaders like Ted Kennedy really wanted him. He polled well, and was a favorite of congressional Democrats, even though Gephardt had been their leader.

Breaking the story was even sweeter because that day *The New York Post* had a screaming front-page headline: KERRY'S CHOICE: DEM PICKS GEPHARDT AS VP CANDIDATE, with file pictures of Kerry and Gephardt grinning at each other so affectionately they looked as though they were about to lock lips. It wasn't quite DEWEY DEFEATS TRUMAN, but it was close. *The Washington Post* media story the next day was headlined, NBC BEATS THE PACK; N.Y. POST GETS BOOBY PRIZE. The flip side of feeling good about our work was what happened that morning with Bob Graham. As part of checking whether Kerry had notified the others on his list, I'd called Graham, who picked up the phone breathlessly. He had not yet heard from Kerry, and I was in the awkward position of telling him that he would not be running for vice president. He was crestfallen, but could not have been nicer. I felt truly lousy.

———

With Iraq still at war, and so much happening on my foreign policy beat, for the first time I didn't get out as much as I'd have liked to cover the candidates in the field. Still, I discovered that not being one of the "boys on the bus" gave me some useful distance from the day-to-day tumult. Helped immeasurably by the research of Libby Leist, a rising star at the network, we were among the first to dig into the so-called 527 groups, the supposedly independent groups that circumvent spending limits mandated by the McCain-Feingold campaign finance law by exploiting a loophole. At first, it was largely Democrats who figured out how to beat the Republicans at the money game. Eventually, the Republicans caught on. But none of these groups had as much impact as a previously unknown organization called Swift Boat Veterans for Truth.

Perhaps Kerry set himself up for the attack when his fellow swift boat veteran Jim Rassmann showed up in Iowa, validating the candidate as a Vietnam hero. By "reporting for duty" at the convention in Boston, he was making his campaign all about his past, not about Bush's record or America's future. The Democratic nominee was ripe for the Republicans' counterattack. We traced the group's organizers to some of the same players who'd hit John McCain with anonymous attacks four years earlier when he'd run against Bush in the primaries. The shadow campaign of the 527 groups, in both parties, was now totaling more than $100 million. Before it was over, the election would cost $1.2 billion, an obscene amount of money unless you were a campaign consultant or a local television station raking in the ad dollars.

While filing these carefully researched and scripted stories for *Nightly News,* I had another, more freewheeling, job on cable as an occasional sidekick to MSNBC's political anchor, Chris Matthews. Chris and I have known each other since my days as a young reporter in Philadelphia, Chris's hometown. As a result, we understand something about each other's political DNA. I'd known him when he worked for Tip O'Neill on the Hill and as a columnist for *The San Francisco Examiner.* Now he was putting his encyclopedic knowledge to use as the anchor of all our campaign coverage on cable.

With his frequent interruptions and rat-a-tat style, Chris is inimitable, except when Darrell Hammond is doing him on *Saturday Night Live.* MSNBC's president, Rick Kaplan, figured out that the best way to let Chris be Chris was to turn him loose with a live audience, building on the success Chris had had four years earlier when he hosted a *Hardball* College Tour from campuses across the country. Kaplan's genius was to put Chris outside on the street where he could get down off his set and interact with passing crowds.

From the first night, our coverage of the Democratic convention in Boston was raucous and unpredictable. Rushing over from the convention, where I'd been doing interviews all day, I was afraid I'd have trouble finding the set outside Faneuil Hall. I needn't have worried. In the center of the square, held back from the set by a few police barriers, a huge crowd was cheering Chris. Executive Producer Tammy Haddad, the energetic ringmaster of this circus, was juggling panelists and guests.

On the set, Chris had assembled an eclectic group: former San Francisco mayor Willie Brown, MSNBC talk show host Joe Scarborough, and Howard Fineman from *Newsweek.* I slipped into my chair and occasionally got in a word, but it was a tough crowd—especially after Teresa Heinz Kerry's speech, which Scarborough immediately panned as "too long." He added that people close to Kerry were "horrified that there's going to be that one Teresa Heinz Kerry moment that's going to alienate a lot of people in middle America."

All I could say was, "Now you know why there's a gender gap."

The atmosphere got even more interesting later, when Cheers and the other pubs bordering the square emptied out. We had a large live audience, but I doubt that very many of them were sober.

Over the next few months, different players joined the set as our traveling road show crossed the country. At times, the panelists included Ron Reagan, actor/activist Ron Silver, Pat Buchanan, former congressman J. C. Watts of Oklahoma, and, with his special gift for politics and history, Jon Meacham of *Newsweek*. Through the conventions and the debates, there was no shortage of opinions. We were also encouraged to blog, in a melding of mainstream and new media. It was an informal way to give the public a behind-the-scenes look at the convention. On August 30, I posted a blog about the difficulties involved in even getting into Madison Square Garden each day during the Republican convention because of ever-changing security checkpoints.

It was stream of consciousness, but in an unstructured way, the blogs captured some of the color and chaos of the circus that is a political convention. As Nicolle Devenish of the Bush campaign said, blogs had become what talk radio used to be. Information, both accurate and inaccurate, was now flying through cyberspace faster than candidates, or reporters, could either absorb it or test its accuracy.

Without knowing the source of a blog, there was no way to determine whether you were being manipulated by an organized advocacy campaign. In a further blurring of lines, Joe Trippi, Howard Dean's former manager, liked to call the bloggers "cyber journalists." The new media were exciting additions to the campaign's rhythms, but I still resist calling an anonymous blogger a "journalist" unless I know more about the writer's dedication to the truth, as well as reporting skills. True journalism involves seeking new facts, testing them with conflicting points of view, and presenting them in a balanced fashion. Blogs are something very different. That said, the bloggers instantly became important players in September 2004 when they quickly debunked the documents *60 Minutes II* used to attack the president's National Guard service. The bloggers were the first to figure out that the CBS documents were probably created on a computer and couldn't have been written during the Vietnam era, as Dan Rather's story had claimed. The resulting exposé severely damaged CBS's credibility, and Rather's reputation. They later struck again, helping to force the resignation of a top CNN executive after compromising comments he made at the World Economic Forum in Davos. These episodes helped establish the bloggers as a new factor in the national debate.

———

With the advent of twenty-four-hour news, our deadlines had already become constant. Now, with the Internet, there was no escaping a torrent of political information. The Internet had also become a powerful organizing tool for campaigns, helping the candidates compile vast lists of contributors and volunteers. Both sides were sending out nonstop e-mails to challenge opposition claims. In particular, the Republicans were adept at circulating instantly what they claimed were Kerry's goofs. The Democrats, in turn, were quick to figure out how to raise money on the Net. But what we all missed, because it was so hard to find, was an even more important developing story: how the Internet had become the Bush camp's secret weapon to get out the vote, particularly in Ohio. As far as I can tell, it didn't surface in local news reports, either.

Kerry was running a far more traditional Democratic campaign, depending on the union movement, campaign workers, and volunteers to urge people to vote. But since the highly effective Democratic get-out-the-vote effort in 2000 (much admired by the Republicans, even though Al Gore did not get elected), White House strategist Karl Rove had been working on a Republican alternative. Nearly invisible to the national news media, the Republicans ran an underground voter mobilization effort, largely organized on the Internet. And the Republicans had enough money to finance their grassroots organization from regular campaign funds, unlike the Democrats, who had to set up parallel groups to circumvent campaign spending limits. The Republican effort was therefore far more efficient, and more difficult to spot. They mobilized their base with a simple get-out-the-vote message—well-targeted and highly effective.

I'd first gotten a hint of the new Republican initiative from the vice president during a dinner conversation on August 9, the thirtieth anniversary of President Ford's swearing in to replace Richard Nixon. The alumnae of the Ford White House, including Alan, were gathered in Statuary Hall at the Capitol to honor the former president. In talking about the campaign that night, Dick Cheney told me that the Bush organization had been badly beaten four years earlier by the Democratic ground campaign, and this time was trying to compete by fielding a much more sophisticated grassroots operation.

Until 2004, big turnouts usually indicated a Democratic victory. In the Bush-Kerry race, conventional wisdom was turned upside down. In Ohio and other battleground states, the Bush campaign used computerized databases to leapfrog over the Democrats and seek out Bush supporters, or those leaning toward the president. Millions of rural Bush voters were carefully identified and then, in the last seventy-two hours, marched to the polls. By Election Day, 1.2 million Republican volunteers had reached 1.8 million people. Another advantage for the Republicans: most of the Bush volunteers were residents of the states in which they were working; the Kerry volunteers were often college students from out of state, less likely to win the confidence of potential voters as they went door-to-door.

All this was done without most political reporters even noticing. We were paying attention instead to the thousands of Democratic field-workers who had flooded into Ohio from blue states where Kerry didn't need them. But the Republican effort effectively neutralized the extensive field operations by those 527 groups, especially in Ohio, which gave George Bush his electoral margin of victory. At a Harvard conference after the election, Zack Exley, online communications director for Kerry-Edwards, said, "The right is beating the left at what used to be our game: grassroots politics, real democracy." Exley admitted that his campaign did not harness the energy of the volunteers it recruited and deploy them effectively. Perhaps Exley had in mind that the Republicans were able to tap into local volunteers to spread their message. The Democrats relied instead on importing volunteers from "blue" states who often failed to connect with "red" state voters.

That August night at the dinner for Betty and Jerry Ford, I knew the vice president was telling me something important, but I didn't realize how critical it would be. Sitting in the heart of the Capitol, I found the gathering especially poignant. For years, the Fords had been returning every summer for a reunion of their former Cabinet and White House staff. Given their declining health, the trip had now become too strenuous. We toasted the president's service, and his ninety-first birthday, knowing he was unlikely to return to Washington.

Holding the dinner at the Capitol was especially appropriate. Ford had always loved Congress more than any other institution he served, and said he considered himself "a man of the people's house." This accidental president, who had done so much to restore our nation's honor and dignity, still regretted not having become speaker of the House of Representatives.

We had spent a weekend at the Fords', along with the Cheneys, earlier that summer while attending an annual political and economic conference hosted by the former president. Alan's term as Fed chairman was about to expire at midnight that night, and the Senate had just voted to reconfirm him for a fifth time. We were waiting to find out whether the president had signed the legislation at Camp David so that Alan could be sworn in. Late Saturday afternoon, word came from the White House that it was official. Alan took the oath of office that evening, standing in front of the fieldstone fireplace at the Fords' home in Beaver Creek, Colorado. Dick Cheney administered the oath, and I held the Bible. The setting could not have been more meaningful, since it was Jerry Ford who had first given Alan the opportunity to go into government service exactly thirty years earlier.

———

Ford had become president suddenly, in the poisonous aftermath of Watergate, but it strikes me that that was still a gentler time in our country's politics. Today, the breakneck speed of communication gives us volumes of information, but also coarsens our political discourse. In the years since Jerry Ford was president, the rapid pace of radio and cable talk shows has contributed to a chorus of opinion. The faster we talk, the harder it is to listen. I sometimes wonder how much the harsh way we express our opinions has contributed to the sense that we are divided, perhaps even more than the colors on the electoral map do.

In a nation of people increasingly informed by talk show rant on the right and the left, facts are incinerated in a blaze of rumor and accusation. If the accumulated charges burn brightly enough, the resulting smoke obscures any real truths. Lost in the haze of left- and right-wing polemics is real journalism. As the line between reporting and opinion becomes blurred, so do the definitions that used to be the touchstones of my profession. Recent scandals have sullied traditional news organizations, along with their imitators. Who can be surprised that readers and viewers are confused? Michael Moore creates entertaining films, but he is not a journalist. In the traditional sense, neither are talk show hosts like Bill O'Reilly, nor Al Franken, and certainly not Armstrong Williams, with his pay-to-play ethics, who secretly took money from the federal government to promote the Bush administration's programs. And with the proliferation of so many broadcast channels and twenty-four-hour cable news, individual programs can differentiate themselves only by being edgier than the competition. The morphing of television interview programs into verbal food fights is now nearly universal. For an anxious nation in a post-9/11 world, the media have become an echo chamber, reinforcing our misconceptions and exaggerating our differences, real and imagined.

We had come a long way since NBC took away my assignment as a *Today* show political analyst in 1992 to avoid confusing viewers who would see me reporting from the White House lawn. In those days, network executives said a White House correspondent should not also do political analysis. No longer. In the 2004 campaign, my dual roles—covering the news while at the same time analyzing events on our cable shows—were a careful balancing act, especially when surrounded by some of the most opinionated men in television. Fortunately, Chris Matthews was also sensitive to my plight, and steered me through the difficult moments.

Augmenting the chattering classes in the 2004 presidential election was a flood of political advertising—$1.6 billion worth. After all the money that was spent, what did voters in six battleground states remember when asked by Election Day pollsters? Only three television ads, all produced for the benefit of George Bush: the Swift Boat Veterans campaign; "Ashley's Story," showing the president comforting the daughter of a 9/11 victim; and "Wolves," a metaphor for the terror threat. People responded emotionally to these powerful video images, even while saying they were paying close attention to the issues. In fact, three-quarters of Americans said they were fully engaged and interested in the election, a sharp increase from previous presidential years. This first election since the attacks on New York and Washington revolved around how much confidence Americans had in who would better protect the nation from terror threats.

———

To report and analyze the outcome of this national debate, on election night in 2004 our broadcast and cable teams were arrayed on the ice rink in front of NBC, renamed Democracy Plaza for the occasion. The entire square block was gussied up with an electoral map painted on the ice and streamers on the face of the GE Building at Rockefeller Plaza to signify the rising electoral vote count. We had lights, cameras, and plenty of action. It was a truly splendid display. Surrounded by a festive crowd of New Yorkers, we were celebrating democracy with a street fair. We broadcast for twelve hours, sneaking M&M's for quick sugar hits, and poring over the numbers for clues to the future direction of our nation.

Our election analysts had warned us that the outcome would be too close to call, despite an inaccurate first wave of exit polls early in the afternoon indicating that John Kerry would win. We were also working under new guidelines NBC had developed after the terrible mistakes all the networks had made four years earlier when calling the Bush-Gore race in 2000. Four years later, we were not going to project the winner until a candidate had accumulated a majority of the electoral votes available. Throughout the night we watched the numbers flow in, calling sources during commercial breaks to compare notes on what they were hearing from the field. With the election so evenly divided, neither a Bush nor Kerry win would have surprised me. By early morning it was clear that Ohio would decide the outcome. Bush had more votes, but we delayed "calling" the state for several more hours since the returns were still being tallied. Finally, the signals from the Kerry campaign were clear. Despite the continuing count in Ohio, Kerry's advisors told us they would not be able to close the gap even if they were to win all of the disputed ballots outstanding. George Bush had been reelected. The final exit polls painted a portrait of an electorate so intensely partisan that most people had decided relatively early and stuck by their choices. In a striking departure from other years, no more than 6 percent of the voters made up their minds during the last few days—compared to 12 percent normally.

At five-thirty a.m., I got off the air and crossed the plaza to watch Tom Brokaw's election night farewell. We'd all been together for so many years that there were few dry eyes as he told our viewers that it was nothing short of "awe-inspiring" to sit at that desk and share information with them on how our nation peacefully, if emotionally, decides our elections.

————

With Tom's decision to step down from the anchor desk, I thought about the arc of my own career. When that bell rings, I still spring into action in the middle of the night. After all these years, I still love the chase for news. I want to know why people behave as they do, and why they choose one leader over another. What makes one state red, and another blue? Or, do the news media overgeneralize, overlooking several shades of color within states to fit a preconceived narrative framework? I also wonder whether the country is really that sharply divided, or, as I suspect, are people simply viewing the same world through slightly different prisms? The electoral map shows a sea of red except for the coasts, but the true margins within each state are close enough that we are not really living in such a sharply polarized nation. Nor is a divided America a new political phenomenon. We've seen bitter disputes since the first days of our history, starting with the Federalists and Anti-Federalists, and later between the North and South. Today, despite all that's written about deep divisions, most voters think of themselves as somewhere in the middle. It's the political class, not the majority of voters, that have become more sharply ideological.

Once again, I learned that for all its satisfactions, and they are numerous, the demands of this profession are relentless. On that morning after the election, after briefly taking time to change clothes and eat breakfast, I came back to the outdoor set at Rockefeller Plaza. Replacing the all-night election team, Don Imus and his merry band were now holding forth, broadcasting *Imus in the Morning,* the popular radio program now simulcast on MSNBC. Don, Charles McCord, and Bernard McGuirk are irreverent, smart, and, occasionally, wickedly mean. Appearing on *Imus in the Morning* is challenging enough after a good night's sleep. It's downright dangerous after working all night. I was so tired that as I left the stage, I tripped, fell down the stairs, and landed unceremoniously on the sidewalk. With both my dignity and knee badly bruised, I limped upstairs to find an ice pack and start thinking about that night's assignment for *Nightly News,* a report on how the Democrats were reevaluating after losing their second consecutive bid for the White House.

The defeat extended beyond the presidency. The Democrats, who until 1994 had dominated the House of Representatives for nearly a half century, were now reduced to their smallest number of congressional seats in fifty years, and held only twenty-two governorships. The morning after losing their bid for the White House, what kind of post mortem were they conducting? Were they examining why, according to the polls, so many rural voters found Democrats too smug, too urban, and too elite? And what role did "moral values" actually play in determining how people voted?

Except for John Kennedy, in modern times only Southern Democrats have been able to bridge America's cultural divide and build support in enough diverse constituencies to win the White House. Howard Dean was so desperate to appeal to Southern whites, he once said he wanted to be the candidate "for guys with Confederate flags in their pickup trucks." He didn't even realize how offensive that would be to large numbers of other voters.

Did Democrats really lose because only voters in red states understand moral values? I think not, but that is certainly the impression many pundits communicated to their viewers. Yes, 22 percent of voters said that they reached their decision based on "moral values." But whose values? The question asked by postelection pollsters was open-ended and subjective. Individual voters could have been defining "moral values" very differently. Were they really delivering a verdict against gay marriage, or did they see moral values instead as a commitment to patriotism, family, and neighborhood? Or were some defining their vote according to another possible meaning of "moral," as a protest against the deployment of troops in Iraq? It is very hard to say, but neither red states nor blue states have a monopoly on family values or patriotic fervor. This is as true since 9/11 as it was before. Interpreting voters' motivation is a cautionary exercise for pundits and party strategists.

What 9/11 did affect were the issues on which people voted. In the first national election since the attacks, 34 percent of voters said they based their decision on either Iraq or fear of terrorism. They told pollsters they were motivated by anxiety for securing their homes from attack and, perhaps, more broadly defined concerns about national security. What the postelection instant analysis often overlooked was that clearing the national security bar was as big a hurdle for Democrats as proving they could master the language of God, guns, and NASCAR.

———

When *Nightly News* ended on November 3, the night after the election, I went back to the hotel to finally get some sleep. All I could think of was getting home the next morning, but my love for breaking news was about to be tested. At five a.m., the assignment desk woke me up. Yasser Arafat had taken a turn for the worse. I felt like saying, Why is that my problem? There are moments on this job when you are so tired, it's hard even to answer the bell. This was one of them.

The *Today* show needed me right away. As soon as I was off the air, my producer, Libby Leist, and I hurried to the airport, again trying to get home. This time, the call from the desk came just as we were boarding the plane. The word from the Paris hospital was that Arafat did not have much time left. They wanted me to get off the shuttle and head back to the studios in case he died during the next few minutes.

I persuaded them that it was a short flight, and I would be far more useful back in Washington. They agreed I could fly home, as long as I stayed on the air phone with the producer in the control room for the entire flight. The phone bill came to $238. When I landed an hour later, the president was about to hold a news conference. NBC had set up a live camera near the ticket counter at Reagan National airport so I could be hooked up for our special reports.

Back in the Washington bureau, I worked on an Arafat story for *Nightly News*. All I could think about was that the show would be over by seven p.m. and I'd finally see Alan. The call from the head of our news operation came midafternoon: Arafat could die at any moment. They wanted me to leave right away for the Middle East, to help cover his funeral.

I had interviewed Arafat many times over the years, in Ramallah and in Washington. At times, he had yelled at me, in two languages, and I had "talked back" as best I could. At the height of his power, he was awarded a share of the Nobel Peace prize for signing an historic treaty on the White House lawn. A decade later, the Palestinian leader was under siege in his West Bank headquarters, with Israeli guns pointed at his head. He and Israel's prime minister, Ariel Sharon, were two aging enemies, locked in a lifelong feud.

I thought back to the years when Arafat was held prisoner in his own headquarters, in Ramallah. I'd gone to Israel with Colin Powell in April 2002 when he had tried to negotiate a cease-fire. On his first day in Jerusalem, a female terrorist had set off a bomb in a crowded market, killing herself and six Israelis and wounding scores more. When the bomb exploded we were only a few blocks away, about to lift off for an aerial tour of Israel's tense border with Lebanon. Powell ordered his helicopter to divert to first survey the terror scene; we watched emergency vehicles rushing to rescue victims. The attack strengthened Sharon's resistance to Powell's arguments that Israel pull back from the West Bank.

Two days later, the secretary of state drove to Ramallah to try to make peace, taking a road cratered by Israeli tanks and artillery fire to reach Yasser Arafat's nearly demolished headquarters. We rode in armored vehicles and were instructed on how to abandon the motorcade and run if we came under attack. When we got to Arafat's besieged headquarters I volunteered to be the pool reporter representing the networks inside. The two men met for three hours.

Arafat and his men had been holed up in a few small rooms with fetid air, bad food, and little sleep. I wondered what his bodyguards were taking to stay awake. What were the chances one of them would get jumpy, fire a gun, and set off a three-way shoot-out among Powell's security force, the Israeli army on the doorstep, and the Fatah militia guarding Arafat?

All of these memories were flooding over me as I tried to figure out how to get to Ramallah in time for the Palestinian leader's death. I hadn't been home in weeks and now had to finish *Nightly News* and get on another plane. Libby helped get my things together, and Alan raced home so we could at least see each other on the way to the airport. In New York, Brian Williams was getting the same summons. He would be anchoring our live coverage of the funeral.

After a twelve-hour layover in Frankfurt, I got to Israel and met Brian at our NBC bureau on November 5, three days after the election. We had dropped everything to get there in time; now the deathwatch over Arafat dragged on for ten more days.

True to form, the call that Arafat had died came in the middle of the night, when I had only just fallen asleep. A desk editor in Washington tried to wake me up. I had no idea what she was saying and hung up the phone. The next call was from the control room, patching me in for a live phone report on MSNBC. Before I could explain that I was still half asleep, I found myself on the air. The anchor was Pat Buchanan, the hard-driving former Nixon speechwriter and presidential candidate who had delivered a strong challenge to George W. Bush's father in New Hampshire in 1992 and actually won the New Hampshire primary four years later.

I was on for what seemed like twenty minutes. Fortunately, Pat knew the subject, and kept the conversation going. At the time, it didn't even strike me as odd that I was doing a phone report from bed, with a man I'd covered in the Reagan White House and as a presidential contender, who was now a talk show host on cable news.

All night, the Palestinians used bulldozers and backhoes to prepare the gravesite for their leader, polishing the stone by hand. The courtyard of Arafat's headquarters had been piled with tires, rubble, and abandoned cars to barricade against the anticipated Israeli invasion. Now the rubble was cleared and leveled to create a landing zone for the Egyptian helicopters that would bring Arafat's body home.

The funeral was the next day. Two of our best New York producers, Phil Alongi and John Zito, had found rooftops with camera angles on all sides of Arafat's walled compound. Camera crews had flown in from NBC bureaus all over Europe and the Middle East. In the dust of buildings that had been shelled repeatedly for years, our Palestinian team had created a satellite village.

The air was black with the acrid smell of burning tires, a traditional signal of defiance, as thousands of mourners began to fill the streets. Brian opened the broadcast from a second-story rooftop with me standing at his side. An hour later I went out on the street, trying to appear inconspicuous as I pushed my way through a sea of men to get to our second location. We had a perfect view of the burial, directly across from the main gate.

As we went on the air, the mourners started shooting their AK-47s in the air. Thousands of men and boys were massing at the gate and scaling the wall to get inside the yard. Security was nonexistent. Palestinian soldiers in olive-drab uniforms reached down from their perches on top of the wall to help them climb over. Suddenly, the crowd surged forward, filling the helicopter landing zone and firing more rounds of ammunition. The air was thick with gunpowder and rubber from the burning tires. At one point, I looked in my hand mirror and saw that my face was covered in soot. Somehow, the helicopters landed, but the frenzied mourners wouldn't let them lower the stairs so that they could carry out the coffin.

On MSNBC, Don Imus was on the air as I reported in from Ramallah. I told him how the al-Fatah youth brigades were marching below, shouting that they were going to drink the blood of the man who poisoned Arafat. Imus asked, "Are you safe there?"

I replied, "Oh, yeah, I'm on a rooftop, I'm fine," although I didn't really believe that myself.

Don asked, "Is that gunfire, Andrea?"

I said, "Yeah, it is. It's traditional to shoot into the air with AK-47s, but of course, these bullets can come down, so we're getting down behind the satellite dish now. We're pulling our people down, Don, but I hope you can still see these pictures. They're firing rounds in the air. This is mostly a celebration. It's to honor Arafat. He's a military hero to them. This is traditionally done, so this is not an outbreak of violence."

Imus observed to Charles McCord, sitting across from him, "Bullets come down somewhere, don't they, Charles?"

I answered, "Yeah, that's occurred to me."

Brian offered some hard facts: in the case of automatic weapons fire, bullets spiral down at 120 miles per hour. That's all Alan, watching from home, had to see and hear. During a commercial break, I called him on my cell to reassure him that I was safe. I didn't know who was going to reassure Brian and me.

We were on the air for five hours that day, nonstop. The only thing that prevented a worse riot was the approaching deadline for the end of the Ramadan holiday. By sundown, the men had to be home to break fast. The crowd began to disperse. I went down on the street to tape a stand-up for *Nightly News,* trying to wipe the gunpowder off my face and reapply makeup discreetly, hoping not to offend the sensibilities of the Palestinian men.

Surrounded by so much emotion from Arafat's followers, I started thinking about the broader issues his death might trigger. Would his passing now create a real opportunity for peace? Not without a new commitment by the United States to mediate the dispute, according to Palestinian leaders I spoke to that night. President Bush and Ariel Sharon were waiting for Arafat's successors to prove they could control the violence before the United States would reengage. But the

Palestinians told me they would not be able to hold elections and control the dozen or more militias that Arafat had supported, without American help.

At a surprise fiftieth birthday party for Condi Rice, at the residence of the British Ambassador the night I returned, however, the president would tell me he first wanted to see the Palestinians control the violence and prove they are reliable partners. Bush said if I really wanted to understand his thinking on the conflict, I had to read a book by Natan Sharansky, *The Case for Democracy*. Sharansky, the former Soviet dissident who has served as a cabinet minister in several Israeli governments, opposes any compromise with the Palestinians until they fully accept a Western-style democracy. His writing has, in fact, also influenced the president's thinking beyond the Middle East. As expressed in Bush's second inaugural address, and echoed by Rice when she became secretary of state, Sharansky and the president see America's vital mission as advancing the spread of democracy to oppressed peoples around the world. In this, George W. Bush is parting company with conservative realists—like his own father—who place a higher priority on achieving stability through strategic alliances, not idealistic causes like the advancement of liberty.

Bush was already thinking deeply about the region, but had not yet shown he would take the political risks necessary to play intermediary. Nor was he willing to acknowledge how much the criticism over his "benign neglect" of the Israeli-Palestinian stalemate had already poisoned his relationships with other Arab leaders. Circumstances and history would now make reengaging in the Middle East one of the first tests of his second term. That was already clear on the night of Arafat's burial, as we prepared to leave Ramallah and begin the journey home.

But before I could leave the West Bank, I was told that an NBC producer in Jordan might be able to secure an interview with Arafat's controversial wife, Suha, if I now flew to Cairo. Suha Arafat had lived a life of luxury in Paris for years, while her husband was a virtual prisoner in Ramallah. When he died, she attended the services in Cairo, but was warned not to come to the burial in Ramallah, where she was so hated by Arafat's followers, that if she showed up, she might not get out alive.

I desperately wanted to go home. It had been a long election, and then a difficult trip to the Middle East. There was no guarantee Mrs. Arafat would grant the interview, and I might end up waiting in Cairo for weeks. But I honestly didn't know if I could turn down the chance. We decided to head back to Israel, the first step toward either flying home or catching a flight to Egypt. Phil Alongi and I piled into a car with a Palestinian driver, along with our bags, computers, and other gear. One hundred yards from the Israeli checkpoint, he suddenly stopped and told us to get out. It was not safe for him to approach the Israeli line. We'd have to walk the rest of the way and hope our Israeli driver was on the other side of the barrier, at least a mile away.

It was pitch-dark. I saw the silhouettes of the Israeli Defense Force, guns ready and on hair-trigger alert. I thought how ironic it would be if, at this point, they mistook me for a terrorist. I would have survived that hail of gunfire at Arafat's funeral, only to die alongside the road at Checkpoint Petunia. I reached for my cell phone to call Alan.

"I'm almost out," I said. "But now they want me to go to Cairo and find Suha Arafat."

Once again torn between my job and my personal life, I was too weary to decide which road to take. For the first time since I've known him, Alan told me what to do. He said firmly, "Get on the plane and come home."

Afterthoughts

On January 20, 2005 I stood on the steps of the U.S. Capitol and watched George W. Bush take the oath of office for his second term. It was the eighth time since becoming a Washington correspondent that I had covered this rite of passage, and the ceremony was no less inspiring than when I'd first arrived from Philadelphia three decades ago. For the same reason that walking through the gates of the White House used to imbue me with a sense of awe, I still become emotional during political rituals. On that day, from my perch just behind the cabinet and special guests, I had a perfect panoramic view of the Mall and its monuments, including the new World War II Memorial dedicated only six months earlier.

Interspersed with the applause were the dissonant shouts of protestors. Looking out over the crowd, I thought of all the demonstrations I'd covered since I'd come to Washington, from the farmers and the Native Americans in the 1970s to the Nation of Islam's Million Man March in 1995, as well as the historic marches for civil rights and against the Vietnam War that had been imprinted in my memory during adolescence. Washington had been the incubator for so many political movements, struggles that changed the way we live, work, and vote. In 1963, John Lewis was marching with Dr. King. Now he was a veteran congressman. At this inaugural, I was one of four NBC women correspondents with major roles. Forty years ago, there weren't any. Today I am part of an accepted generation of women journalists. In 1969, I was stopped at the press room door in the Pennsylvania state capitol, at a time when women broadcasters were still rare and unwelcome.

Now, surrounding me on the inaugural stage, I saw a virtual photo gallery of images from my life as a reporter. There were the presidents: Carter, Clinton, and both Bushes, father and son. The senators: Clinton, McCain, Frist, Kennedy, and Specter. John Kerry, wearing a forced smile and a wistful expression, no doubt imagining what might have been. And in the VIP section were those other Washington notables, including cabinet members past and present, greeting each other warmly, even though they were often bitter rivals.

In a prominent seat, next to the CIA director, was Alan—wearing a Yankees cap because I'd worried about him going hatless in the cold. As his wife, I could have sat with him among the official guests instead of covering the event as a reporter. But for me, this was a dream assignment: we had a live broadcast, hundreds of prominent politicians with no way out, and no one stopping me from snagging interviews. Libby and I roamed the stands, lining up everyone from Rudy Giuliani to Arnold Schwarzenegger, Karl Rove to Barack Obama, and Bush's speechwriter, Michael Gerson. Knowing me as he does, Alan understood that it wasn't even a close call. But looking across the way at him, I was struck by how different our roles were on days such as this: he was inside, looking out, while I was outside, looking in. I caught his eye across the crowd; he waved and gave me a thumbs-up. As the president declared, "All who live in tyranny and hopelessness can know: The United States will not ignore your oppression, or excuse your oppressors. When you stand for your liberty, we will stand with you," I wondered where rhetoric left off and policy began. If we had learned anything about George W. Bush during the previous four years, it was that he views the world in sharp contrasting colors rather than shades of gray. Whether realistic or not, when Bush pronounced the country "tested, but not weary" and "ready for the greatest achievements in the history of freedom," he meant it. As a reporter covering foreign policy, I knew that the next four years were going to be busy.

Inaugurations are also political celebrations for the victors. After the swearing-in ceremony, I climbed onto a flatbed truck to broadcast the Bushes' progression along the parade route from the Capitol to the White House. It was as close as Washington ever gets to a hometown event, at least in the years since the Redskins won the Super Bowl. I've seen so many of these grand occasions: the bittersweet inauguration day a quarter-century earlier when the American hostages were released from Iran, but too late for Jimmy Carter. The departure of Ronald and Nancy Reagan from their "little cottage" on Pennsylvania Avenue after one of the most consequential presidencies in modern history. And Bill Clinton's exit a dozen years later, following two terms of political triumph and scandal. I have been an eyewitness to all of these histories, personal and political, but in the role of observer, not participant. To me, that remove is still the price of admission for a front-row seat, despite the revolution that has turned politicians into anchormen and activists into bloggers.

Along this journey, I have made sacrifices I sometimes regret, although none so important that I would take the path not chosen. As I was warned so many years ago, this is indeed a course for a long-distance runner. If asked what qualities helped me earn whatever success I have had in this venture, I'd have to list endurance near the top. It is what drove me to the finish line of the New York City Marathon in 1996, two days before the election, and still carries me through assignments in remote regions far from family and friends. But perhaps even more important is an insatiable curiosity about the way other people live their lives—their hopes, disappointments, privations, and triumphs. Those are the stories that inspired me to want to be Brenda Starr, "girl reporter," imagining an adventurous life then available only to women in comic strips.

For all the social progress, technology presents new dilemmas for my profession. In an age of instantaneous news, major news organizations have sometimes put speed above accuracy, sacrificing fairness in the process. Is it acceptable to recycle rumors for which we have no proof simply because they are on an Internet website? Does a questionable story become fair game simply because the subject has been forced to deny it? How many correspondents still require two sources before going on the air? And how many broadcasters, to say nothing of bloggers, are even trained in these fundamentals? The stakes are high: after struggling to find truth in competing claims about war, weapons, and terror connections, we are still left with more questions than answers. In my memory, there has never been a time when our coverage of foreign policy or domestic politics was as important or as difficult.

This journey through America and its foreign entanglements has rewarded me in ways both material and emotional. It has also left me in constant wonder over the decency of humankind, along with our awful ability to inflict pain upon one another. I still search for answers to the horrors of 9/11, or the execution of *Wall Street Journal* newsman Daniel Pearl, or the genocide in Rwanda. But I am equally fascinated by the other side of human nature: by the courage of amputees in Ward 57 at Walter Reed Army Medical Center who still believe in miracles; of the Afghan boys who risked so much to tell me about their mother's and sister's plight; of the Cubans, who still dare to speak and write; of the Israeli mothers who put their children on public buses. And by the hopeful spirit of the Palestinian families who welcomed me to share their Ramadan feasts, so that I could better understand their yearnings for peace.

These are the stories I still want to tell. There is so much joy and excitement in being a reporter, I often wonder how I got to be so lucky.

INDEX

FOR THE BEST IN PAPERBACKS, LOOK FOR THE 🐧

In every corner of the world, on every subject under the sun, Penguin represents quality and variety—the very best in publishing today.

For complete information about books available from Penguin—including Penguin Classics, Penguin Compass, and Puffins—and how to order them, write to us at the appropriate address below. Please note that for copyright reasons the selection of books varies from country to country.

In the United States: Please write to *Penguin Group (USA), P.O. Box 12289 Dept. B, Newark, New Jersey 07101-5289* or call 1-800-788-6262.

In the United Kingdom: Please write to *Dept. EP, Penguin Books Ltd, Bath Road, Harmondsworth, West Drayton, Middlesex UB7 0DA.*

In Canada: Please write to *Penguin Books Canada Ltd, 90 Eglinton Avenue East, Suite 700, Toronto, Ontario M4P 2Y3.*

In Australia: Please write to *Penguin Books Australia Ltd, P.O. Box 257, Ringwood, Victoria 3134.*

In New Zealand: Please write to *Penguin Books (NZ) Ltd, Private Bag 102902, North Shore Mail Centre, Auckland 10.*

In India: Please write to *Penguin Books India Pvt Ltd, 11 Panchsheel Shopping Centre, Panchsheel Park, New Delhi 110 017.*

In the Netherlands: Please write to *Penguin Books Netherlands bv, Postbus 3507, NL-1001 AH Amsterdam.*

In Germany: Please write to *Penguin Books Deutschland GmbH, Metzlerstrasse 26, 60594 Frankfurt am Main.*

In Spain: Please write to *Penguin Books S. A., Bravo Murillo 19, 1° B, 28015 Madrid.*

In Italy: Please write to *Penguin Italia s.r.l., Via Benedetto Croce 2, 20094 Corsico, Milano.*

In France: Please write to *Penguin France, Le Carré Wilson, 62 rue Benjamin Baillaud, 31500 Toulouse.*

In Japan: Please write to *Penguin Books Japan Ltd, Kaneko Building, 2-3-25 Koraku, Bunkyo-Ku, Tokyo 112.*

In South Africa: Please write to *Penguin Books South Africa (Pty) Ltd, Private Bag X14, Parkview, 2122 Johannesburg.*